FOUNDATIONS
OF MENU PLANNING

FOUNDATIONS OF MENU PLANNING

Daniel Traster, CCC, CCE, CCCP

Boston Columbus Indianapolis New York San Francisco Upper Saddle River
Amsterdam Cape Town Dubai London Madrid Milan Munich Paris Montréal Toronto
Delhi Mexico City São Paulo Sydney Hong Kong Seoul Singapore Taipei Tokyo

Editorial Director: Vernon R. Anthony
Senior Acquisitions Editor: William Lawrensen
Project Manager Editorial: Alexis Biasell
Editor, Digital Projects: Nichole Caldwell
Editorial Assistant: Lara Dimmick
Director of Marketing: David Gesell
Senior Marketing Manager: Alicia Wozniak
Production Editor: Kris Roach
Production Manager: Susan Hannahs
Art Director: Jayne Conte
Cover Designer: Suzanne Behnke
Cover Art: barbaradudzinska/Shutterstock
Lead Media Project Manager: Karen Bretz
Full-Service Project Management: Saraswathi Muralidhar, PreMediaGlobal
Composition: PreMediaGlobal
Printer/Bindery: Edwards Brothers Malloy
Cover Printer: Lehigh-Phoenix Color
Text Font: 11/13, Adobe Garamond Pro Regular

Credits and acknowledgments borrowed from other sources and reproduced, with permission, in this textbook appear on the appropriate page within the text.

Library of Congress Cataloging-in-Publication Data

Traster, Daniel.
    Foundations of menu planning/Daniel Traster.
        pages cm
    Includes bibliographical references and index.
    ISBN-13: 978-0-13-802510-6
    ISBN-10: 0-13-802510-X
    1. Menus.   2. Food service—Planning.   I. Title.
    TX911.3.M45T73 2014
    642—dc23

                        2012038110

10 9 8 7 6 5 4 3 2 1

ISBN 10: 0-13-802510-X
ISBN 13: 978-0-13-802510-6

To Rebecca, Elizabeth,
and Benjamin, for continuing to share, celebrate,
and support through all that life has to dish out.

brief contents

contents

Preface

When I was a student in culinary school many years ago, I learned a great deal about a range of culinary subjects, but menu planning was not among them. After some time in the industry and years of creating numerous menus, I found myself working at two different culinary schools. In both cases, the schools subsumed menu planning under the subject of nutrition, as if the only challenge to writing a menu were to accommodate a special diet. This is not to say that nutrition is not a critical subject for a chef to study; however, the act of writing even the most basic menu is not as easy as it might seem.

Thousands of restaurants open up across the country every year only to shut down in their first few years of operation. Plenty of chefs with spectacular culinary talent fail to tailor their menus to the local market. Others simply do not know how to price their menus effectively. Still others start off well only to see their profits erode over time under the yoke of a static menu. In all of these cases, the restaurants might have survived had they managed the menu planning process better from the start.

These challenges afflict not only restaurants but all forms of culinary operations. Caterers, hotels, bars, and noncommercial operations all live or die by the effectiveness of their menus. Menus are marketing mechanisms, cost control tools, and critical communication devices. Without them, revenue and profits wither away. Sadly, anyone looking to study the subject would be hard-pressed to find a comprehensive, easy-to-grasp textbook. I believe culinary and hospitality students deserve better.

Foundations of Menu Planning guides students through the menu planning process in the same order in which the process is typically conducted by a menu planner. The book begins with the resources commonly used to understand and define a target market. The text then progresses to a survey of general nutrition concerns that most menu planners must address in their work. Chapters 3 and 4 focus on menu styles, how they differ, and how different menus organize dishes under various categories and headings to reinforce their company's brand and concept. A chapter focusing specifically on beverage menus follows. The book moves next to recipe costing and menu pricing followed by a chapter on the art of writing menu item descriptions. A chapter on unwritten menus is included to address how to replicate the functions of a menu when the customer is not given a written menu. Next comes a chapter on menu layout and design followed by a study of menu analysis and evaluation. The book closes with a discussion of the pros and cons of a menu-first approach to menu planning. Other textbooks on the market touch on some of these subjects, but not one covers them all.

In addition to addressing the "how" of menu planning from a logical, sequential approach, *Foundations of Menu Planning* delves into the "why," so students understand the purpose behind each step. That the book deals with broad menu planning concepts but also expounds upon variations specific to certain types of food service operations makes the material applicable to undergraduate culinary and hospitality students no matter which career path they choose in the future.

In addition to the primary content of the book, I have included several pedagogical tools to enhance the educational experience of the reader. Because words are no substitute for pictures of real menus, the book contains a great many images of menus from foodservice operations across the country. These menus (and other images) reinforce the book's narrative and illustrate how menu planning principles are applied in the real world. In the math-based chapters, examples permeate the text to illustrate how each equation is executed in practice.

Each chapter concludes with a summary of the chapter's main points, comprehension questions to ensure that students have grasped key concepts from the chapter, and discussion questions to push students to think beyond the chapter and to apply the learning to their own personal experiences. The discussion questions do not necessarily have a single correct answer, but they can spark class discussions to help students probe challenging menu planning concepts.

Readers will notice that the text alternates by chapter between male and female pronouns. While men and women both have much to contribute to and to learn from the culinary industry, the English language makes gender-neutral communication difficult and clumsy. Rather than using "he/she" or similar constructs, I have opted to use male pronouns in the odd chapters and female ones in the even chapters. The use of one set of pronouns in a given subject area is not meant to insinuate anything about the relationship of one sex to that particular material. Rather, the alternation is an attempt to convey the relevance of the book's entirety to both sexes equally.

As a former culinary educator, I have also written the book to accommodate the realities of teaching in a classroom. The opening chapter is shorter than average to allow sufficient time for coverage on the first class day when introductions and syllabus distribution are necessary elements of that first session. Similarly, the final chapter, also brief, gives the instructor time to conduct a course review prior to the final exam. With twelve total chapters, the book is flexible enough to be used effectively in a quarter or a semester system school.

Finally, no textbook is complete without a range of supporting material for students and instructors. Currently in development (with Traster's *Foundations of Cost Control*) is an online educational support system designed to help students practice and refine their learning through online educational experiences. Already available is the teacher's manual to provide recommended in-class educational activities and assessments.

To access supplementary materials online, instructors need to request an instructor access code. Go to www.pearsonhighered.com/irc, where you can register for an instructor access code. Within forty-eight hours after registering, you will receive a confirming email, including your instructor access code. Once you have received your code, go to the site and log on for full instructions on downloading the materials you wish to use.

No book is perfect, but I sincerely hope that students will find *Foundations of Menu Planning* an informative, inspirational, and comprehensive study of the subject matter. Writing an effective menu is no easy task, but with the right book and the right teacher menu writing skills can be learned. Without those skills, culinary and hospitality school graduates have little chance of becoming long-term leaders at foodservice operations. Through this book, I believe readers will gain an understanding of the menu planning process and the ability to create an effective and profitable menu.

Daniel Traster

Acknowledgments

This textbook, my third in five years, would surely have fallen victim to exhaustion and frustration were it not for the incredibly passionate and inspiring team of people who have helped me to create this wonderful book. For my editor Bill Lawrensen, developmental editor Alexis Biasell, and editorial assistant Lara Dimmick I am extremely grateful; it is their continued support and hard work that is most responsible for this book coming out on time and at such a high level of quality. Thanks go as well to my exceptional project manager Saraswathi Muralidhar, who made sure that no typo or punctuation error went uncorrected. I owe a great many thanks to all of the chefs, restaurateurs, hotel managers, catering directors, and other industry professionals who provided the images that greatly enhance the educational value of this book. Their generosity is a testament to their commitment to the industry, their support of education, and their dedication to hospitality and its mission of helping others. I hope all of my readers have a chance to patronize their establishments, credited next to or within each image. Thanks also go to the professors who helped review the manuscript: Charles Becker at Pueblo Community College; Dirk Boon, Oxnard College; Charles King, Amarillo College; Charlie Martin, Spokane Community College; Chay Runnels, Stephen F. Austin State University; and Donald Sprinkle, Maui Community College.

A special thank you goes to graphic designer Linsey Silver, who provided support and guidance on issues of menu design, and to Kent Peterson for his help in securing menus. To all of my past employers who gave me a chance to learn, practice, and teach menu writing of all sorts—thank you. I am truly blessed for my parents, who inspired my career in the culinary arts despite their best efforts to the contrary. Last and most importantly, I owe my entire career as an author to my wife and daughter. Without their love, support, and patience, this book would never have been possible.

About the Author

Author of *Welcome to Culinary School: A Culinary Student Survival Guide* and *Foundations of Cost Control*, Daniel Traster CCC, CCE, CCP has over twenty-five years of experience in the culinary industry, including eight years in culinary arts education, mostly at the program management level. He worked as the dean of Culinary Arts and Hospitality Management at Stratford University in Falls Church, VA, and as the academic director for Culinary Arts at the Art Institute of Washington. Additionally, Traster served two years as the chair of the Cooking Schools and Teachers section of the International Association of Culinary Professionals after already serving two years as the section's vice-chair. Currently the culinary director for the Metropolitan Cooking and Entertaining Show and a freelance writer and consultant, Traster cherishes his experiences in the culinary field. Before teaching, Chef Traster cooked in various types of foodservice operations including "Bagels and . . ." in New Jersey; the Four Seasons Hotel in Philadelphia; Provence Restaurant in Washington, DC; Occasions Caterers in Washington, DC; and a university president's residence as a private chef. Over the past two decades he has served on the boards of the Restaurant Association of Metropolitan Washington and its Education Foundation, the Nation's Capital Chefs Association (a chapter of the American Culinary Federation), the Epicurean Club of Washington, the National Capital chapter of the American Institute of Wine & Food, and the advisory boards for DC Central Kitchen, the Center of Applied Technology North, Stratford University, and Lincoln College of Technology. A strong believer in lifelong education, he holds a B.A. in English and Theater from Yale University, an A.O.S. in Culinary Arts from the Culinary Institute of America, and an M.S. in Adult Learning and Human Resource Development from Virginia Tech. Daniel Traster lives with his wife, Katie, and his daughter, Abigail, in Washington, DC.

As any textbook can be improved through the collective input of culinary school students, teachers, and industry professionals around the country, Daniel Traster welcomes feedback, comments, and suggestions for future editions. He can be reached via email at WelcometoCulinarySchool@gmail.com.

I
Factors That Define a Menu

Perhaps it is best to begin a discussion on menu planning by answering the question: "What is a menu?" In the most basic sense it is a list of products that may be purchased at a foodservice establishment. But a menu can and should be much more than that. A menu is a communication vehicle that describes for the clientele the components of each dish. It is a marketing tool that encourages sales. It is a control mechanism that helps to keep a business efficient, functional, and profitable. The menu can even add to the dining experience by providing history, entertainment, and support of the restaurant's theme. An effective menu meets the needs of both the business and the guests.

Menu planning is the process of creating a menu that achieves all of the aforementioned goals and more. Proper menu planning does not operate in a vacuum but rather begins after a significant amount of research. After all, a menu planner cannot meet the needs of a foodservice establishment and a customer base if he does not first know what those needs are. Analyzing each of the variables that impact a menu is where a menu planner begins; so, too, this text opens with a study of the multiple factors that define a menu.

By the end of this chapter, you will be able to:

- List several factors that impact and define a menu
- Describe how a menu supports a brand
- Define a market using demographic and psychographic studies
- Describe how staff skill levels, equipment and space constraints, and product availability define a menu
- List all of the stakeholders commonly involved in the menu-planning process

1.1 WHICH COMES FIRST, THE MENU OR THE MARKET?

While a menu often determines which individuals from the broader market will choose to patronize an establishment, a business is better served by first analyzing the potential market and then tailoring a menu to meet the needs of one or more segments of that market. Creating the menu first can lead to a business that appeals to a market segment that does not exist in that community. For example, a chef may envision a restaurant that serves the most upscale cuisine in the world, but if his restaurant is located in a blue-collar town with an average household income of $30,000 per year, the locals will likely not dine at that establishment.

With a new business, an owner typically first identifies a target market and then attempts to envision a brand that will appeal to that customer base. A brand is a business's identity, its soul. It is the set of qualities and characteristics that people associate with the business and often the reason that they spend their money there. For a foodservice operation, a brand is defined in part by its mission and vision, its décor and location, its style of service, and yes, its menu. While the items on a menu may change, the "feel" of the menu (price point, cuisine, types of ingredients, caliber of cooking, etc.) usually does not. For example, a restaurant that serves local, organic, from-scratch dishes at a high price point on one menu will not likely change to a low-cost, mass-produced burger and fries menu during the next round of menu revisions. The brand is what appeals to customers, and a properly constructed menu supports the brand. For existing businesses, a menu overhaul continues to support the operation's brand and the needs of the business and the market. A business may choose to modify its brand, but the menu should follow and support a carefully considered brand change, not the other way around.

Businesses that attempt to be all things to all people ultimately end up appealing to no one; their brand is too undefined to meet the needs of any target market. Identifying a target market and determining the type of business that might meet the market's needs is no easy task. Fortunately, there are several tools available to assist a menu planner or business owner in defining the local market segments: demographic studies, psychographic studies, competitive analyses, and feasibility studies.

1.1.1 Demographic Studies

A demographic study compiles certain data for the population in a given area. If a potential business owner knows exactly where he wishes to open his business, the demographic study is best done for a small area around that location—a zip code, for example, rather than a city or a state. The smaller the area studied, the more accurate the depiction of the local market will be. Demographic studies are often easily acquired through the local chamber of commerce, local government, or Census Bureau. (Explore the web page http://quickfacts.census.gov/qfd/index.html to find some brief demographic data for any U.S. state, county, or city.) The factors typically included in a demographic study are as follows:

Age. Listed as both raw numbers and percentages for a series of age ranges, age tells the menu planner if the local customer is more likely to be older or younger. The foodservice needs of teenagers, middle-aged adults, and seniors will vary greatly from each other.

Marital Status. Singles and married couples may visit restaurants during different hours or prefer different types of establishments.

Housing Type and Household Size. Larger households (families) have different dining needs that must be considered in everything from table sizes to menu options. Depending on the area, the ratio of apartments to houses may suggest the level of disposable income locals have to spend in restaurants.

Gender. Owners may choose to adjust their business concept to meet the needs of one sex if the population is significantly tilted toward men or women.

Race and Ethnicity. People from different races and ethnicities may prefer different kinds of cuisines. Individuals from some cultures may have religious dietary restrictions or food taboos as well.

Education. Often, people with higher levels of education seek out healthier foods, display a greater willingness to try unfamiliar foods, and have more disposable income to spend on dining out.

Occupation and Income. The average income and popular occupations alert a business owner to the price point that is most likely to appeal to the local community.

Vehicles. When fewer locals own cars, a business should be located where people can access it easily by foot or public transportation; otherwise, the restaurant may need to appeal to a larger audience beyond the local area.

1.1.2 Psychographic Studies

Psychographic studies provide insight into the values, interests, and habits of the population studied. Such studies provide information on how people get involved in the community, what their hobbies are, where they shop, what sports they support, where they spend their free time, and what their opinions are on a range of subjects from politics to business to education.

While all of the psychographic data contributes to a more complete depiction of the average customer, some of the most important data for a foodservice business owner has to do with where and how people spend their money on food. If most of the population eats at home except on special occasions, a restaurateur may choose to create a destination restaurant. However, all of the psychographic data must be taken in context. If the town has a huge interest in sports but has only recently grown large enough to support any restaurants at all, perhaps the time is right to open a little sports bar.

Income:[1]

2011: Downtown residents reported overall median household income of $86,300, compared to $89,800 for Downtown resident households with at least one employed individual. Median household income was $88,700 for those employed (but not residing) in Downtown.

2008: Downtown residents reported overall median household income of $89,800 compared to $96,200 for Downtown resident households with at least one employed individual and $95,900 for those employed (but not residing) in Downtown.

This income decline is likely due to the impact of the recession on household income due to job losses and work reductions. Additionally, apartment asking rents have not increased since 2008, and residents with a lower income have been able to reside in Downtown.

Ethnicity:

2011: Downtown residents' racial/ethnic composition was relatively consistent to 2008. Caucasian population, the largest group, remained constant at 53%, while the share of Asian-Americans/Pacific Islanders at 22% and Hispanics/Latinos at nearly 18% each rose slightly, while African-Americans' share dropped to 6.5%.

2008: Downtown residents' racial/ethnic composition was 54% Caucasian, the largest group, with Asian-Americans/Pacific Islanders at 21% and Hispanics/Latinos at 17%.

Table 2: Downtown LA Resident Ethnicity 2011 and 2008

	2011	2008
Caucasian	53.3%	53.8%
Asian-American/Pacific Islander	21.6%	20.9%
Hispanic/Latino	17.7%	17.4%
African-American	6.5%	8.3%

Age:

2011: The median respondent age among Downtown residents was 32.5.

2008: The median respondent age among Downtown residents was 32.1.

Gender:

2011: 54% of Downtown resident respondents were female and 46% were male.

2008: 53% of Downtown resident respondents were female and 47% were male.

---

[1]The Los Angeles City median household income was estimated at $48,570 for 2005–2009 (inflation adjusted to 2009 dollars) by the U.S. Census Bureau, the most current available figures.

Figure 1–1

This segment of a larger demographic and psychographic study includes information on market spending patterns, including median guest check and type of restaurant desired. The Downtown Center Business Improvement District, Los Angeles, CA.

Transportation—Commuting Mode:

2011: More than one-half, or 55%, of Downtown residents reported that they commuted alone by car, and another 40% used some type of public transit (e.g., bus, subway, Metrolink). Note that 37% also reported commuting to work via walking or bicycling.

2008: One-third, or 35%, commuted alone by car, another 35% used public transit, and 17% commuted to work via walking or bicycling.

* The large shift to commuting alone by car in 2011 from 2008 may be unexpected, and is attributed to a lower share of Downtown residents reporting working in Downtown in this survey, likely meaning they work outside of Downtown and requiring them to drive to work.

Grocery Spending:

2011: Each residential household spent $102.00 (median—current dollars) per week on groceries.

2008: Each residential household spent $99.00 (median—current dollars) per week on groceries.

Grocery Stores Shop in/Requested:

2011: This year's survey reworded the question asking "in which grocery chain do you usually shop?" Most residents, 76% named Ralphs and 74% named Traders Joe's as the top two mentions.

2008: Most residents, 89% named Traders Joe's and 68% named Whole Foods Market as the most requested grocers to locate in Downtown. A Ralphs Fresh Fare opened in Downtown before the 2008 survey.

Likely to Shop in Trader Joe's:

The 2011 survey specifically asked the likelihood of shopping at Trader Joe's if located in Downtown. Mostly all, or 92%, of Downtown residents said they were extremely or very likely to shop in a Downtown Trader Joe's.

Dining Out—Dinner in Downtown

2011: 92% of residents dined out in Downtown at least once per month. Each resident spent $28.28 (median including tax and tip) when eating dinner out in Downtown.

2008: 96% of residents ate dinner out in Downtown at least once per month. Each resident spent $27.13 (median including tax and tip) when eating dinner out in Downtown.

Dining Out—Dinner in Any Area

2011: 99% of residents ate dinner out in any area at least once per month. Each resident spent $27.93 (median including tax and tip) when eating dinner out (in any area, not just in Downtown).

2008: This question was not asked.

Dining Out—Lunch in Downtown

2011: 89% of Downtown residents reported eating lunch out in Downtown LA at least once per month. Each resident spent $15.56 (including tax and tip) for lunch out.

2008: 95% of Downtown residents reported eating lunch out in Downtown LA at least once per month Each resident spent $14.75 (including tax and tip) for lunch out.

Figure 1–1
(Continued)

Retail/Services Most Wanted in Downtown:

2011: Residents' retail/services most wanted were:

      Mid-level restaurants—72%

      Mid-market department stores—63%

      Book/music/movie stores—61%

2008: Residents' retail/services most wanted were:

      Discount department stores—67%

      Mid-level restaurants—65%

      Movie theaters—59%

In 2011, the most wanted retail types for Downtown shifted to mid-level restaurants and mid-level department stores, away from discount stores, likely due to the announcement of a Target store to open in Downtown. Top retail brands desired included: Nordstrom/Nordstrom Rack, Apple Store, Best Buy, Barnes & Noble Booksellers, Bloomingdale's, and Costco. The lower percentage naming movie theaters was likely due to the opening of the Regal 14 Cinemas at L.A. Live on October 27, 2009.

Pet Ownership:

2011: 43% of residents owned some type of pet; 28% owned a dog and 17% owned a cat.

2008: 40% of residents owned some type of pet; 24% owned a dog and 16% owned a cat.

Figure 1–1
(Continued)

1.1.3 Competitive Analyses

Demographic and psychographic data can be hard to interpret if the business owner or menu planner has no familiarity with the local food scene. A competitive analysis describes the foodservice competition in the area and informs a menu planner of the likely competitors to a given business concept. Such information helps a restaurateur or menu planner theorize whether a restaurant would fulfill a customer need that is currently unmet in the community or if the business concept has been so overdone in the market as to make a similar business unsustainable. Culinary entrepreneurs can investigate other businesses to see if similar concepts might attract more customers by providing better service or cheaper prices. A little historical research may also suggest which business concepts have consistently failed in the area.

1.1.4 Feasibility Studies

A feasibility study combines demographic, psychographic, and competitive analysis data to determine whether a business is likely to succeed. A feasibility study is best performed by professionals who specialize in these types of studies. Not only does their expertise help them to compile the study more efficiently and accurately, but because they have no emotional investment in a given business concept, their analysis is likely to be more objective than a potential business owner's would be.

1.1.5 Generating a Menu from the Data

The various studies provide an overabundance of data, but generating a menu from that data requires some interpretive skill. A menu planner must hypothesize the needs of the various market segments and then see which of those market segments' needs are not being met by the competition. A restaurateur should not be put off by a similar competitor, but he should determine whether there is a large enough market to support both his concept and the competition. If the market is already saturated (unable to sustain another similar business), the newcomer to the market may do better by targeting a different market segment. However, menu planners and entrepreneurs should always confirm that there is a large enough market to sustain a given business concept even if there is no competing business. For example, if a town is primarily a retirement community with almost no one under the age of 55, a hip, loud, experimental restaurant targeted at 20-somethings is unlikely to succeed. Sometimes, there is no competition for a particular market segment for a reason.

Analysis of the various market studies may reveal obvious constraints to a menu. Flexibility with price points, for example, may be limited given the market's average income. If a target market is unlikely to spend more than $30/person for dinner, then the menu's prices should permit a guest to order one or two courses with drinks for that price point. A restaurant that exceeds a market's typical price point may need to strive for special occasion business, as it is unlikely to attract regular customers.

Other menu constraints may only become obvious with personal knowledge of the community. Consider a restaurant targeted toward seniors. While most older patrons cannot endure a dining experience that is too dimly lit to read a menu or too loud to hear a dinner companion, all seniors do not prefer the same limited menu selection. Some mature diners prefer the comfort foods of 1950s America, while others opt for ethnic foods reminiscent of their foreign travels. Softer foods may be a physical necessity for certain seniors, but others may prefer the variety of textures that lend interest to a typical dish. Whether seniors favor cosmopolitan or homey fare may not be obvious from a demographic or psychographic study, but some familiarity or interaction with local senior citizen groups may provide a definitive answer. Making assumptions based on stereotypes alone can lead to an underperforming and ineffective menu, but proven behaviors for a market segment allow a menu planner to design a product for a built-in audience. Fortunately, psychographic studies and competitive analyses describe the proven spending patterns of the community as a whole, if not for each individual market segment.

1.2 LOGISTICAL CONSTRAINTS ON MENUS

Once a business owner and menu planner have selected a business's target market and brand, they should next determine any other factors that would limit a menu's feasibility. There is no point in writing a menu that the staff cannot execute. Listing barbecue on a menu makes no sense if the restaurant cannot fit a grill or smoker into its kitchen. For a menu to be feasible and profitable, it must make efficient use of the employees' skills, the physical space, and purveyors' available products.

In a new restaurant, the menu may determine the caliber of people hired or the equipment purchased for the kitchen. However, menu planners must keep in mind that future menu changes will be impacted by that first menu. Equipment purchases and staff skill levels should be versatile enough to support the business's brand in future menu iterations. For existing operations, the equipment and staff are usually a given constraint that must be accounted for in the menu-planning process.

1.2.1 Employee Skill Level

Complex menus with lots of handmade components per dish typically require highly skilled labor. The same is true for menus that require servers to perform some form of cooking or carving tableside. Since a higher-caliber workforce often necessitates higher wages, a menu's price point is impacted by the skill of the labor required.

If an existing business has a kitchen team that is only capable of reheating and plating prefabricated dishes, then the menu planner must create a menu that does not exceed this skill level. While it is easy to suggest that the employees could be replaced with a more highly trained staff, to do so would increase labor cost and call for significantly higher menu prices. If the business has been successful and a change in prices would undermine the brand, replacing the workers with a higher-caliber team could drive away business and erode profits. Similarly, there is no value to writing a menu that exceeds the staff's abilities. Chances are that the employees would put out substandard food that does not meet the menu planner's or manager's goals. If managers choose to train the employees to increase their skill level, it is best to do so and to confirm that the training has been effective before the new menu is put in place.

Whereas a new restaurant does not have the skill level constraints of an existing operation, it does have some staffing limitations that impact the menu. As mentioned above, a higher-caliber staff requires higher wages. Additionally, some communities may not have the trained workforce envisioned by the menu planner. If none of the restaurants in a given community prepare their food from scratch, the foodservice workers in the area will have had no opportunity to practice and maintain or learn a higher level of culinary skill.

1.2.2 Equipment

Equipment availability places significant constraints on menu planners and what their menus can offer. The most obvious limitation stems from cooking equipment. A kitchen that consists of nothing more than ovens and a deep fryer cannot effectively serve a la carte sautéed or grilled foods. Chefs can create a workaround for certain pieces of equipment—steaming in a pot with a basket rather than in a commercial steamer, for example—but such equipment alternatives should be kept to a minimum. In the steamer example, a pot with a basket could probably handle a single component for one dish, but it would significantly slow production if four entrées required steamed ingredients.

Refrigeration also impacts menu choices. If a kitchen only has a single-door, reach-in freezer, the number of frozen menu components offered on the menu should be limited. Because more extensive menus require larger storage capacity for ingredients, a small kitchen with little refrigeration and dry storage space will perform better with a small menu rather than with a larger set of offerings.

Work flow also comes into play when deciding upon a menu. If a kitchen is laid out with a set number of workstations, the menu should attempt to balance the amount of production coming from each station. For example, if a restaurant kitchen has only a grill station and a sauté station, it would not make sense to write a menu with six grilled items and only one sautéed dish; otherwise, the sauté cook would be fairly idle while the grill cook becomes overwhelmed. It would be better to divide the menu such that half of the dishes come from one station and the other half from the other station.

While a brand-new establishment may design its kitchen around the opening menu, the menu planner should consider whether or not the initial menu inordinately constrains future menus. If the vision for a restaurant is to serve a variety of modern American dishes cooked in a range of ways, it would not make sense to open with an all-barbecue menu that requires a large bank of smokers on the hot line. To do so would effectively force future menus to replicate the barbecue theme. That said, if a restaurant is going for a specific theme (like barbecue or fried seafood), it may make sense to design a menu that begs for a hot line of all one piece of equipment (all smokers or all fryers, for example).

1.2.3 Product Availability

A menu planner must ensure that the ingredients required to execute a given menu are available during the time that the menu will be in place. Some products are available year-round while others are only in season during a short period of time. Ingredients found in one part of the country may be difficult to source elsewhere. For example, walleye, a fish native to the Great Lakes, may be easy to find in Ohio but nearly impossible to source in Louisiana. Similarly, while blood oranges may be a spectacular addition to a winter menu, they are out of season in the United States during the summer and thus would be an inappropriate component to a year-round menu. Including items on a menu that cannot be purchased during the lifetime of the menu only leads to menu shortages, unexpected substitutions, and, ultimately, dissatisfied customers.

1.3 THE STAKEHOLDERS

Nearly everyone involved in a foodservice business has a stake in producing an effective, quality menu. The owners and investors want a menu that will attract business and assist in the operation's profitability. Managers and employees need a menu that can be executed effectively and efficiently given the equipment, product, and employee constraints of the business. Customers want a menu that appeals to their tastes and works within their personal budgets. In short, the menu serves a lot of people, so it is best to involve all of these stakeholders in the menu development process.

When a business is new, owners, managers, and the executive chef usually work together to generate a menu that will meet the needs of the target market. To some degree, this is a guessing game, as the customer preferences are inferred from psychographic data for the area rather than obtained by polling the customers directly. Some restaurants attempt to gather customer input by hosting a series of pre-opening meals from which managers can see which dishes are popular and which are not selling well. The more input the management collects prior to opening its doors officially, the better.

For an existing restaurant, menu changes should incorporate known data on prior sales. Dishes that do not sell well should be adjusted or removed entirely. Popular and profitable ones should be retained. Menu planners should interview employees to see where problems with work flow or product sourcing may exist. Customers should also be consulted to see if certain changes would encourage them to return more or less frequently to the establishment.

Before a foodservice business opens its doors, a poorly researched menu will still define the market, the caliber of the staff, and the design of the kitchen, though not necessarily in the way that the menu planner had hoped. It is often better for all of the stakeholders to define these variables first and then allow them to drive the menu, so it supports the brand. For a foodservice operation that already exists, these factors are already in place and often are quite difficult to change simply to accommodate a new menu.

SUMMARY

The identity of any foodservice operation is its brand. Each brand innately appeals to a specific market, so business owners are wise to research the potential markets in the area to see if they are large enough to support a business and if their needs are currently being met by competing businesses. Data that define a market come from demographic and psychographic studies. Demographic studies describe the population's age, marital status, housing type, household size, gender, race, ethnicity, education, occupations, income, and vehicles, among other information. Psychographic studies describe the values, interests, and habits of the population. A competitive analysis provides a depiction of competing businesses in the area while a feasibility study suggests whether a potential business is likely to make a profit. A foodservice business's brand and its menu must appeal to the target market described in the studies, and they must do so in a way that does not put the business at risk of losing out to the competition. Other variables limit and define a menu as well. Employee skill level, equipment and space constraints, and product availability all impact what a menu planner can include in a menu. As the process of creating a menu is a complex one, it is best to involve as many stakeholders as possible. For new businesses, the stakeholders may be only the owners and managers. For existing operations, guests and frontline employees should be consulted as well.

COMPREHENSION QUESTIONS

1. List four variables that help to define a menu.
2. What role does a menu play in relation to a business's brand?
3. List the two primary tools that help to define a market. What type of information does each one provide?
4. If a chef wants to create a menu that exceeds his staff's ability, why can't he just hire new staff?
5. How does a kitchen's space and work flow impact a menu?
6. Who are the typical stakeholders who contribute to the menu-planning process in a new business? Who is normally added to the process in an existing business?

DISCUSSION QUESTIONS

1. A demographic study shows that the largest percentage of the local population is age 30–50 with a middle-class income and a household size of 3.7. Many of them own their own homes and at least one car. Describe a restaurant concept that would appeal to this target market. (Describe the brand and the menu, but do not write out a menu.)
2. A nearby community has the demographic makeup described in question 1. A psychographic study shows that the community spends the majority of their disposable income on recreational activities for their children (sports, dance, music, movies, travel, etc.), not on food. What kind of foodservice business might you set up in this community to appeal to the local market? Describe the business's brand.
3. Describe the demographic and psychographic qualities that define the target market into which you personally fall. What kinds of foodservice establishments are you and that market segment likely to patronize?
4. Envision a restaurant concept and describe it. Describe the kind of employees, the kitchen layout, and the kitchen equipment you would need to support that concept across several consecutive menus.
5. Imagine that you are the general manager for an existing restaurant. What kind of information would you want to know from the various stakeholders before creating a new menu?

2
Nutrition and Menu Planning

By the end of this chapter, you will be able to:

- Describe why nutrition is a critical component of menu planning
- State how market captivity relates to the healthfulness of menus
- List the major categories of nutrients and broadly describe their functions
- List the principles of a healthy diet
- List the most common food allergens for the population
- Create a healthy menu that addresses the nutritional needs of the majority of the population
- List several common dietary restrictions and create a menu item that accommodates individuals with those restrictions

Accounting for nutrition in the menu planning process should be no minor afterthought. While some special occasion restaurants may expect to see the same customers return only once each year, most foodservice establishments aim to attract repeat business far more frequently. As customers return more regularly, culinary businesses have an increasing ethical obligation to serve the nutritional needs of their clientele appropriately. One unhealthy meal may not harm a diner, but a regular diet of unhealthful meals impacts the consumer's quality of life and life expectancy. While most restaurants need not serve only healthy dishes, they should offer at least some healthy choices to allow customers to patronize the establishment when they crave something more nutritious.

When a customer has no alternative dining choice (think schools, hospitals, prisons, etc.), meeting the consumer's nutritional needs becomes imperative. However, attending to nutrition in menu planning serves two other purposes beyond maintaining a guest's health. First, as Americans continue to focus on nutrition, diet, and weight loss while increasing the number of meals they consume outside the home, they will clamor for healthier meal options. Many national restaurant chains have already adjusted their menus to accommodate dietary needs and, thus, to retain the nutrition-minded market segment. Some of these chains have merely put a nutritional spin on their current menus without actually making their menus healthier, but those that have genuinely adopted a healthier approach to menus will fare better as the population becomes more informed. Second, America is currently battling an obesity epidemic. As the epidemic worsens, there will be governmental pressure on all foodservice establishments to provide healthier menus. It is far more cost-effective for the industry to preempt government by proactively addressing nutrition than it is to have government regulations thrust upon it. The rule that a foodservice operation should appeal to the needs of its target market is still paramount; what is changing is America's increasing awareness of and desire for nutrition on foodservice menus.

This chapter is not intended to be an in-depth study of nutrition, but it will provide some nutrition basics on the more common dietary concerns among Americans. While most foodservice operations do not need to prepare for every conceivable dietary restriction, they should be able to accommodate the most common ones to better serve their clientele. Whether factoring for general health, special diets, or even allergies, the menu planner should always consider nutrition and dietary restrictions when creating a menu.

2.1 WHY IS NUTRITION IMPORTANT TO MENU PLANNING?

While some foodservice businesses rely on constant marketing to attract a new set of clientele each day, the best scenario for a culinary operation is to maintain a core of regular customers who frequent the establishment. Regular customers require less investment in marketing dollars and they ensure a steady flow of revenue for the business, even during slow periods. However, customers with health problems that result from a steady diet of unhealthy food from a given restaurant are likely to return less often, if at all. To attract a regular customer, a restaurant must offer food that that customer can eat frequently without negatively impacting her health. Providing a healthy menu (or at least some healthy options) to customers who have a choice in dining alternatives is a business decision that usually aids in building a steady customer base.

Some diners have no choice in which establishment they patronize. Hospital patients have no alternative but to eat the food provided by the hospital. Schoolchildren who do not bring a lunch with them (and this includes the vast numbers of students who survive on federally subsidized school lunches) must eat the meal provided to them by the school or go hungry. While businesspeople can leave the property to eat at a nearby restaurant, those in a rush often have no choice but to dine in the business's corporate cafeteria. When a foodservice operation has a clientele who must use their services, those customers are called a *captive market*.

Culinary businesses that serve a captive market have an ethical obligation to provide healthy food to their customers. To do otherwise is to force a person to choose between going hungry or eating food that will make her sick. Additionally, in a noncommercial operation—in which supporting a parent organization in its mission takes precedence over generating significant profits—creating a pool of sluggish, unhealthy workers or students may undermine the efforts of the parent company (school, business, or hospital). Businesses with captive markets may not need to attract customers with nutritional offerings, but they still must provide healthy options to their guests.

Addressing nutrition in menu planning also helps the industry as a whole in terms of public perception and government regulation. Several states have enacted or are considering legislation that regulates nutrition in restaurants. The most prominent efforts have centered on nutrition labeling for chain restaurant menus or on the banning of trans fats in food. As the obesity epidemic persists in the country, it is not unlikely that more local and state governments will enact laws regulating nutrition in restaurants.

The *Dietary Guidelines for Americans 2010* is one of the foundational documents that informs American nutrition education programs. In other words, educators turn to this document to learn what they should tell their students about healthy lifestyle habits. In the *Dietary Guidelines*, restaurants are not portrayed as blameless in the obesity crisis. The *Dietary Guidelines*, noting that a person's environment plays a role in how healthily she eats, states that the individual's food "choices are often limited by what is available in a person's environment, including stores, restaurants, schools, and worksites."[1] When restaurants do not offer healthy options, patrons of those restaurants end up making poor choices in regard to their health. According to the *Dietary Guidelines*, "evidence shows that children, adolescents, and adults who eat out, particularly at fast food restaurants, are at increased risk of weight gain, overweight, and obesity."[2] So how does the *Dietary Guidelines* recommend that Americans deal with this problem? The document advises:

Executive Summary

Eating and physical activity patterns that are focused on consuming fewer calories, making informed food choices, and being physically active can help people attain and maintain a healthy weight, reduce their risk of chronic disease, and promote overall health. The *Dietary Guidelines for Americans, 2010* exemplifies these strategies through recommendations that accommodate the food preferences, cultural traditions, and customs of the many and diverse groups who live in the United States.

By law (Public Law 101-445, Title III, 7 U.S.C. 5301 et seq.), *Dietary Guidelines for Americans* is reviewed, updated if necessary, and published every 5 years. The U.S. Department of Agriculture (USDA) and the U.S. Department of Health and Human Services (HHS) jointly create each edition. *Dietary Guidelines for Americans, 2010* is based on the *Report of the Dietary Guidelines Advisory Committee on the Dietary Guidelines for Americans, 2010* and consideration of Federal agency and public comments.

Dietary Guidelines recommendations traditionally have been intended for healthy Americans ages 2 years and older. However, *Dietary Guidelines for Americans, 2010* is being released at a time of rising concern about the health of the American population. Poor diet and physical inactivity are the most important factors contributing to an epidemic of overweight and obesity affecting men, women, and children in all segments of our society. Even in the absence of overweight, poor diet and physical inactivity are associated with major causes of morbidity and mortality in the United States. Therefore, the *Dietary Guidelines for Americans, 2010* is intended for Americans ages 2 years and older, including those at increased risk of chronic disease.

Dietary Guidelines for Americans, 2010 also recognizes that in recent years nearly 15 percent of American households have been unable to acquire adequate food to meet their needs.[1] This dietary guidance can help them maximize the nutritional content of

1. Nord M, Coleman-Jensen A, Andrews M, Carlson S. Household food security in the United States, 2009. Washington (DC): U.S. Department of Agriculture, Economic Research Service. 2010 Nov. Economic Research Report No. ERR-108. Available from http://www.ers.usda.gov/publications/err108.

viii   DIETARY GUIDELINES FOR AMERICANS, 2010

Figure 2–1
The executive summary section of the USDA's *Dietary Guidelines for Americans 2010* shows some of the main nutritional concerns facing Americans today. The complete *Dietary Guidelines* can be found online at http://health.gov/dietaryguidelines/dga2010/DietaryGuidelines2010.pdf.

their meals. Many other Americans consume less than optimal intake of certain nutrients even though they have adequate resources for a healthy diet. This dietary guidance and nutrition information can help them choose a healthy, nutritionally adequate diet.

The intent of the Dietary Guidelines is to summarize and synthesize knowledge about individual nutrients and food components into an interrelated set of recommendations for healthy eating that can be adopted by the public. Taken together, the Dietary Guidelines recommendations encompass two over-arching concepts:

- **Maintain calorie balance over time to achieve and sustain a healthy weight.** People who are most successful at achieving and maintaining a healthy weight do so through continued attention to consuming only enough calories from foods and beverages to meet their needs and by being physically active. To curb the obesity epidemic and improve their health, many Americans must decrease the calories they consume and increase the calories they expend through physical activity.

- **Focus on consuming nutrient-dense foods and beverages.** Americans currently consume too much sodium and too many calories from solid fats, added sugars, and refined grains.[2] These replace nutrient-dense foods and beverages and make it difficult for people to achieve recommended nutrient intake while controlling calorie and sodium intake. A healthy eating pattern limits intake of sodium, solid fats, added sugars, and refined grains and emphasizes nutrient-dense foods and beverages—vegetables, fruits, whole grains, fat-free or low-fat milk and milk products,[3] seafood, lean meats and poultry, eggs, beans and peas, and nuts and seeds.

A basic premise of the Dietary Guidelines is that nutrient needs should be met primarily through consuming foods. In certain cases, fortified foods and dietary supplements may be useful in providing one or more nutrients that otherwise might be consumed in less than recommended amounts. Two eating patterns that embody the Dietary Guidelines are the USDA Food Patterns and their vegetarian adaptations and the DASH (Dietary Approaches to Stop Hypertension) Eating Plan.

A healthy eating pattern needs not only to promote health and help to decrease the risk of chronic diseases, but it also should prevent foodborne illness. Four basic food safety principles (Clean, Separate, Cook, and Chill) work together to reduce the risk of foodborne illnesses. In addition, some foods (such as milks, cheeses, and juices that have not been pasteurized, and undercooked animal foods) pose high risk for foodborne illness and should be avoided.

The information in the *Dietary Guidelines for Americans* is used in developing educational materials and aiding policymakers in designing and carrying out nutrition-related programs, including Federal food, nutrition education, and information programs. In addition, the *Dietary Guidelines for Americans* has the potential to offer authoritative statements as provided for in the Food and Drug Administration Modernization Act (FDAMA).

The following are the *Dietary Guidelines for Americans, 2010* Key Recommendations, listed by the chapter in which they are discussed in detail. These Key Recommendations are the most important in terms of their implications for improving public health.[4] To get the full benefit, individuals should carry out the Dietary Guidelines recommendations in their entirety as part of an overall healthy eating pattern.

---

2. Added sugars: Caloric sweeteners that are added to foods during processing, preparation, or consumed separately. Solid fats: Fats with a high content of saturated and/or *trans* fatty acids, which are usually solid at room temperature. Refined grains: Grains and grain products missing the bran, germ, and/or endosperm; any grain product that is not a whole grain.
3. Milk and milk products also can be referred to as dairy products.
4. Information on the type and strength of evidence supporting the Dietary Guidelines recommendations can be found at http://www.nutritionevidencelibrary.gov.

DIETARY GUIDELINES FOR AMERICANS, 2010   **ix**

Figure 2–1
(Continued)

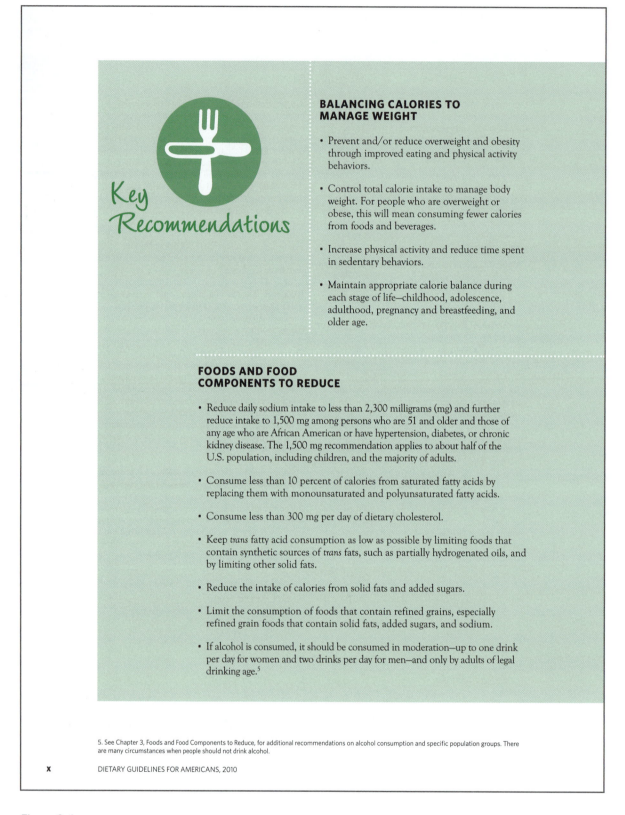

BALANCING CALORIES TO MANAGE WEIGHT

- Prevent and/or reduce overweight and obesity through improved eating and physical activity behaviors.

- Control total calorie intake to manage body weight. For people who are overweight or obese, this will mean consuming fewer calories from foods and beverages.

- Increase physical activity and reduce time spent in sedentary behaviors.

- Maintain appropriate calorie balance during each stage of life—childhood, adolescence, adulthood, pregnancy and breastfeeding, and older age.

FOODS AND FOOD COMPONENTS TO REDUCE

- Reduce daily sodium intake to less than 2,300 milligrams (mg) and further reduce intake to 1,500 mg among persons who are 51 and older and those of any age who are African American or have hypertension, diabetes, or chronic kidney disease. The 1,500 mg recommendation applies to about half of the U.S. population, including children, and the majority of adults.

- Consume less than 10 percent of calories from saturated fatty acids by replacing them with monounsaturated and polyunsaturated fatty acids.

- Consume less than 300 mg per day of dietary cholesterol.

- Keep *trans* fatty acid consumption as low as possible by limiting foods that contain synthetic sources of *trans* fats, such as partially hydrogenated oils, and by limiting other solid fats.

- Reduce the intake of calories from solid fats and added sugars.

- Limit the consumption of foods that contain refined grains, especially refined grain foods that contain solid fats, added sugars, and sodium.

- If alcohol is consumed, it should be consumed in moderation—up to one drink per day for women and two drinks per day for men—and only by adults of legal drinking age.[5]

5. See Chapter 3, Foods and Food Components to Reduce, for additional recommendations on alcohol consumption and specific population groups. There are many circumstances when people should not drink alcohol.

Figure 2–1
(Continued)

FOODS AND NUTRIENTS TO INCREASE

Individuals should meet the following recommendations as part of a healthy eating pattern while staying within their calorie needs.

- Increase vegetable and fruit intake.

- Eat a variety of vegetables, especially dark-green and red and orange vegetables and beans and peas.

- Consume at least half of all grains as whole grains. Increase whole-grain intake by replacing refined grains with whole grains.

- Increase intake of fat-free or low-fat milk and milk products, such as milk, yogurt, cheese, or fortified soy beverages.[6]

- Choose a variety of protein foods, which include seafood, lean meat and poultry, eggs, beans and peas, soy products, and unsalted nuts and seeds.

- Increase the amount and variety of seafood consumed by choosing seafood in place of some meat and poultry.

- Replace protein foods that are higher in solid fats with choices that are lower in solid fats and calories and/or are sources of oils.

- Use oils to replace solid fats where possible.

- Choose foods that provide more potassium, dietary fiber, calcium, and vitamin D, which are nutrients of concern in American diets. These foods include vegetables, fruits, whole grains, and milk and milk products.

Recommendations for specific population groups

Women capable of becoming pregnant[7]

- Choose foods that supply heme iron, which is more readily absorbed by the body, additional iron sources, and enhancers of iron absorption such as vitamin C-rich foods.

- Consume 400 micrograms (mcg) per day of synthetic folic acid (from fortified foods and/or supplements) in addition to food forms of folate from a varied diet.[8]

Women who are pregnant or breastfeeding[7]

- Consume 8 to 12 ounces of seafood per week from a variety of seafood types.

- Due to their high methyl mercury content, limit white (albacore) tuna to 6 ounces per week and do not eat the following four types of fish: tilefish, shark, swordfish, and king mackerel.

- If pregnant, take an iron supplement, as recommended by an obstetrician or other health care provider.

Individuals ages 50 years and older

- Consume foods fortified with vitamin B_{12}, such as fortified cereals, or dietary supplements.

BUILDING HEALTHY EATING PATTERNS

- Select an eating pattern that meets nutrient needs over time at an appropriate calorie level.

- Account for all foods and beverages consumed and assess how they fit within a total healthy eating pattern.

- Follow food safety recommendations when preparing and eating foods to reduce the risk of foodborne illnesses.

6. Fortified soy beverages have been marketed as "soymilk," a product name consumers could see in supermarkets and consumer materials. However, FDA's regulations do not contain provisions for the use of the term soymilk. Therefore, in this document, the term "fortified soy beverage" includes products that may be marketed as soymilk.
7. Includes adolescent girls.
8. "Folic acid" is the synthetic form of the nutrient; whereas, "folate" is the form found naturally in foods.

Figure 2–1
(Continued)

When eating out, choose smaller portions or lower-calorie options. When possible, order a small-sized option, share a meal, or take home part of the meal. Review the calorie content of foods and beverages offered and choose lower-calorie options. Calorie information may be available on menus, in a pamphlet, on food wrappers, or online. Or, instead of eating out, cook and eat more meals at home.[3]

While the *Dietary Guidelines* devotes very little of its space to restaurants, the messaging on restaurants is clear—to avoid weight gain, look for menu options that are healthy or eat at home. Sharing meals or taking home doggie bags helps to reduce the number of dollars a person might otherwise spend in a restaurant. Offering healthy, lower-calorie options on a menu helps a restaurant to retain some of those sales dollars. Additionally, as more restaurants provide healthy menu choices that combat rather than support the obesity epidemic, government is less likely to intervene with menu regulations that require significant documentation and added expense for the restaurant.

As menu planners account for nutritional concerns in the menu planning process, foodservice businesses are more likely to attract and retain nutrition-minded customers, to meet the needs of the parent organizations they support, and to forestall government regulation designed to combat the obesity crisis in America. An entire restaurant menu need not be devoted to health and nutrition, but a menu should include some healthy choices to address those customers for whom nutrition is supreme in their dining selections.

2.2 NUTRITION BASICS

Prior to creating a healthy menu, a menu planner must understand some nutrition basics. Food and drink can be broken down into certain components that the body needs to survive. Carbohydrates, lipids, protein, and water are considered macronutrients as they are required in relatively large quantities—multiple ounces per day. Vitamins and minerals are called micronutrients as they are needed in much smaller quantities, measured in milligrams or micrograms per day. Carbohydrates, lipids, and proteins provide calories while water, vitamins, and minerals do not. A *calorie* (short for kilocalorie) is a measure of energy that the food delivers to the body. When a person consumes more calories than she burns, the excess energy is stored as body fat. Foods that are termed *nutrient-dense* provide a large quantity of nutrients (specifically, vitamins and minerals) per calorie while *calorie-dense* food and drink supplies little more than calories to the body. While this text is not a replacement for a thorough understanding of nutrition, below are some of the most important points to know about nutrition for the purposes of general menu planning:

Carbohydrates Carbohydrates provide 4 calories of energy per gram. While they are an essential component of any diet, they can be found in healthy and less healthy forms. While carbohydrates are present in fruits and vegetables, most Americans consume the majority of their carbohydrates from grains and refined sugars. Whole grains—those that deliver fiber along with calories—generate more gradual increases in blood sugar while refined grains and sugars tend to create sharp spikes in blood sugar. Spikes in blood sugar yield short-term energy "highs" followed by periods of lethargy and hunger. As a result, consumers of large quantities of refined grains and sugars find themselves hungry and craving calories soon after eating. The ongoing cycle of hunger pangs often leads to overeating throughout the day and ultimately to weight gain. Whole grains, on the other hand, provide a longer feeling of satiety or fullness that allows the eater to go without snacking between meals. Additionally, refined grains, unless they are enriched or fortified, lose many of their nutrients and become calorie-dense; whole grains, fruits, and vegetables are nutrient-dense. The *Dietary Guidelines* recommend that 45%–65% of calorie consumption comes from carbohydrates.[4]

Lipids   Lipids are the category comprised of fats, oils, and cholesterol. As the body makes cholesterol in sufficient quantities for survival, there is no need to consume cholesterol in the diet. Fats and oils provide 9 calories per gram—the most of any nutrient. Thus, lipids are calorie-dense and contribute to weight gain when eaten in large quantities. Fats and oils are composed of fatty acids, but not all fatty acids are the same when it comes to physical health. The consumption of fatty acids impacts the levels of high-density lipoprotein (HDL) and low-density lipoprotein (LDL) that the liver produces in the body. (The media often refer to HDL as "good cholesterol" and to LDL as "bad cholesterol.") Higher levels of LDL and total cholesterol typically correlate to heavier deposits of cholesterol and plaque on arterial walls—a risk factor for heart disease. Ultimately, higher levels of HDL and lower levels of LDL and total cholesterol in the bloodstream translate to a lower risk of heart disease. Monounsaturated and polyunsaturated fats maintain a healthy balance between HDL and LDL in the bloodstream while saturated fats and trans fats increase levels of LDL. (Trans fats are unsaturated fats that have been made saturated through a process called hydrogenation.) Distinguishing between the various fats is fairly straightforward. Saturated fats and trans fats are typically solid at room temperature while monounsaturated and polyunsaturated fats are liquid oils at room temperature. Seafood is the rare exception that provides high levels of unsaturated fats that are solid at room temperature. Fats are an essential component of any diet, but most Americans consume far more than they need. The *Dietary Guidelines* recommend that 20%–35% of calories come from fat with no more than 10% coming from saturated fats.[5]

Proteins   Proteins provide 4 calories of energy per gram and are a component of most parts of the body. Proteins are made up of amino acids, and while the body can produce some of the amino acids that it needs, nine of the amino acids are not created by the body in sufficient quantity for survival. These nine are called *essential amino acids*. Foods that provide all nine essential amino acids are termed *complete proteins*; those that are missing at least one of the nine are called *incomplete proteins*. While the body needs all nine essential amino acids, they can be acquired by consuming either complete proteins or several incomplete proteins that supplement each other's missing amino acids. Proteins are found in both plant and animal sources, but animal sources often come with the addition of saturated fat. Lean proteins—those that deliver little fat with the protein—are generally considered the healthiest sources of protein. The *Dietary Guidelines* recommend that 10%–35% of calories come from protein. [6]

Water   Water delivers no calories to the body, but it is an essential nutrient for proper bodily function. While a human being can survive for weeks without food, she will die after just a week or two without water. The average person should consume at least eight 8-ounce glasses of water each day.

Vitamins and Minerals   Vitamins and minerals are critical for a wide range of bodily functions. Some work in tandem with each other while others work independently from the other micronutrients. For basic menu planning purposes, it is more important to understand some general facts about the micronutrients than it is to understand each one's sources and functions. Some vitamins are water-soluble while others are fat-soluble. Thus, cooking liquids can dissolve some of a food's micronutrients and remove them from the meal if the cooking liquid is not served with the rest of the food. Many vitamins are destroyed with heat and time, too, so using fresh ingredients and avoiding overcooking help to preserve these delicate nutrients. While vitamins and minerals are a required part of a healthy diet, they can cause physical harm when consumed in excess. Thus, dietary supplements can aid a person with insufficient nutrient intake, but megadoses of vitamins and minerals may do more harm than good.

Of the dietary vitamin and mineral spectrum, only a few are common sources for dietary concern. Calcium provides strength to bones and teeth; an insufficient quantity of calcium leads to osteoporosis—a weakening of the bones. Vitamin D works with calcium to strengthen bones. Both calcium and vitamin D are prevalent in dairy. Calcium can also be obtained through fish bones (commonly eaten in smaller fishes), certain leafy greens, and calcium-fortified foods. Vitamin D is produced by the body through exposure to sunlight, but some individuals require additional vitamin D through diet. Sodium is often cited for its contribution to high blood pressure. As sodium is plentiful in processed foods, most Americans need to reduce or limit their dietary sodium rather than increase it. Potassium appears to counteract some of sodium's impact on blood pressure, so the *Dietary Guidelines* recommend higher potassium intake for most Americans. Iron deficiency leads to anemia, one of the few nutrient deficiency diseases common in America today. Good sources of iron include lean meats, poultry, seafood, legumes, spinach, and iron-fortified foods. Folate and vitamin B_{12}, which work in tandem with each other, are required for cell generation, so they are critical dietary components for pregnant women and for seniors (who have reduced ability to absorb B_{12}). Folate is found in "foliage"—lettuces and leafy greens. B_{12} is present only in animal products, so vegans must take B_{12} supplements.

Fiber   Though not absorbed by the body as a nutrient, fiber plays a critical role in digestion that impacts health in a positive way. Fiber is indigestible, so it helps to push foods along through the digestive tract and aids in solid waste elimination. Fiber provides a feeling of satiety, which leads to fewer calories consumed each meal. It also helps to regulate blood sugar by slowing the absorption of sugars during digestion and may reduce the risk of certain diseases, including colon cancer and type II diabetes. Fiber is prevalent in fruits, vegetables, whole grains, and legumes.

Alcohol   While alcohol is not a required component of any diet, it is mentioned here because it is consumed by many Americans and does impact health in several ways. Alcohol provides 7 calories of energy per gram, so it is not a calorie-free drink. Some studies have shown positive heart-health benefits stemming from the moderate consumption of wine, especially red wine; however, those benefits disappear with excessive consumption. Moderate consumption is defined as one drink per day for women and two per day for men, but due to the risk of alcoholism, alcohol consumption is not recommended for all individuals.

2.2.1 Principles of a Healthy Diet

With the range of dietary restrictions and allergies across the population there is no single diet that works for everyone; however, there are some universal truths to healthy eating that apply to all Americans. First, any healthy diet should be balanced and varied. As there is no magical food that supplies all of the required nutrients in the right proportions, people must consume a wide range of foods to ensure that they acquire all of the nutrients they need. Balance implies that the foods should come from the several macronutrient categories in appropriate proportions. Variety suggests that the foods within each category should rotate regularly so that all of the micronutrients are ultimately received.

A healthy diet should also be adequate but moderate. A certain percentage of the population does not receive sufficient calories and nutrients due to financial strain or other hardship. Some may have access to food but not necessarily to healthy options. These diets are inadequate to meet the nutritional needs of the individual. However, in America today, the more common dietary challenge is excess consumption. Overeating

Monday:
Macaroni and cheese with whole wheat dinner roll, sunflower seeds and steamed carrots
Or
Dairy free chicken salad sandwich on a fresh baked whole grain roll with green leaf lettuce, sea salt pita chips and sunflower seeds
Tuesday:
Veggie chili with cheese and whole wheat dinner roll
Or
Cheesy chicken quesadilla on a whole grain tortilla with hot sauce and baby carrots
Wednesday:
Cajun pasta Alfredo with fresh butternut squash, whole wheat dinner roll, string cheese and sunflower seeds
Or
Dairy free BBQ chicken sandwich on a fresh baked whole grain roll with baby carrots and sunflower seeds
Thursday:
Chicken mole with Spanish brown rice with steamed corn
Or
Sunbutter and jelly sandwich on a fresh baked whole grain roll with celery sticks, string cheese
Friday:
Chicken chow mein with broccoli stir fry and whole wheat dinner roll
Or
BBQ turkey and cheese wrap on a whole grain tortilla with romaine lettuce and creamy BBQ dressing

Figure 2–2
Addressing nutrition is absolutely essential for a captive audience. This school lunch menu, with a vegetarian option most days, illustrates that nutritious can be delicious and appeal to children. Revolution Foods.

calories leads to weight gain. Overindulgence in sugars, fats, and sodium can lead to cardiovascular disease or diabetes. Imbibing too heavily on alcohol can lead to the various health concerns associated with alcoholism. Thus, maintaining a moderate diet is as important as consuming an adequate one.

While no diet is perfect for everyone, a typical healthy diet is based mainly on fruits, vegetables, legumes, and whole grains with less emphasis on meat, salt, fat, sugar, and alcohol. A menu that approaches food from this philosophy would generally be considered healthier than one that focuses on large portions of fatty meat, rich, sugary desserts, and lots of alcohol.

2.2.2 Allergies and Food Safety Warnings

Allergies are a physical reaction to certain stimuli, and for some people, specific foods can trigger an allergic reaction. Reactions differ from minor swelling or rash to death, so menu planners are wise to account for possible allergic reactions. Chefs must take customer notifications of allergies seriously and make every effort to accommodate the request or to notify the customer of a potential hazard.

While no menu can account for every possible allergy, there are several common food allergens that a menu planner should consider when creating a menu. The most common categories of food allergens are fish, shellfish, dairy, peanuts, tree nuts, eggs, wheat, and soy. It is not necessary to avoid all of these ingredients on a menu, but most menu planners should attempt to have at least one dish on the menu that could accommodate a customer with each of these allergies. Thus, at least one dish should contain no seafood, another should contain no dairy, and so on. There are exceptions, of course—a seafood restaurant can safely assume that someone with a seafood allergy would not likely dine there—but for most general audience menus, all of the allergy categories should be addressed.

Restaurants that do not plan for these allergy categories on their menu should anticipate periodic guest requests for a recipe modification. In most mid-level and high-end establishments, these requests should be accommodated. Consequently, if a steak is served with a lobster sauce, the chef ought to be able to serve it without the sauce to someone who requests it. A dish normally fried in peanut oil should be fried in a different oil upon request. When a chef cannot accommodate a request— for example, for a dish that is made in advance and for which the allergen cannot be removed—the chef and server should be honest with the customer and not attempt to pass off the dish as allergen-free. If a processed component is used and the chef does not know if it contains the allergen in question, she should simply say so to the customer. A guest who must choose from a limited selection of dishes is much happier than a guest who suffers an allergic reaction in a restaurant.

To avoid surprising a guest with an allergic reaction, some establishments state hidden ingredients on the menu when they pose a common allergy risk. For example, a menu should state if it fries its food in peanut oil. It should note if the stir-fry includes shrimp paste. To do otherwise puts at risk a diner who might assume that the dish does not contain a certain allergen.

Another type of safety warning, sometimes mandated by the local municipality, deals with the consumption of undercooked, potentially hazardous food. Most chefs and culinary students are familiar with the minimum internal temperatures required to kill pathogenic bacteria. But how can a restaurant serve a poached egg if the temperature will not reach 165 degrees? Can a chef ever put scallop ceviche or rare hamburgers on a menu? Of course she can, but the menu must alert the restaurant patrons to the potential safety risk. A common way of phrasing this alert is: "Consuming raw or undercooked meats, poultry, seafood, shellfish, or eggs may increase your risk of foodborne illness." Such a warning is typically placed at the bottom of a menu beside an asterisk, and the relevant dishes are starred on the menu as well.

By properly notifying guests of potential allergy or food safety hazards, the menu planner helps to reduce the number of customers who leave the establishment with an unanticipated illness or allergic reaction and helps to mitigate legal liability should an affected customer sue the establishment.

2.3 CREATING A HEALTHY MENU

The first step to creating a healthy menu is to develop nutritious dishes targeted to the general population, not necessarily for any specific diet. Per the *Dietary Guidelines* and mainstream nutrition advice, such dishes should be based primarily on fruits, vegetables, whole grains, and legumes, with smaller quantities of lean meats, poultry, or seafood. For the average adult, 50–70 grams of pure protein is sufficient for the day's intake. As most Americans get at least half of this protein requirement from grains, nuts, legumes, dairy, and/or eggs, 4 ounces of meat, fish, or poultry is enough for the entire day. Thus, a 4-ounce portion of meat, poultry, or fish more than suffices as a portion for one meal. A single serving of cooked grain or vegetable is ½ cup, and one serving of each is typically plenty for a meal that also includes a center-of-the-plate protein. If the restaurant expects guests to also order appetizers and desserts, those should continue the fruit/vegetable/grain focus without overdosing guests on added fats and sugars.

As Americans tend to consume more sodium than necessary in their diets, a healthy menu should also reduce the amount of salt it delivers and focus on alternative flavor enhancers instead. Herbs, spices, and highly acidic ingredients (citrus, wine, or vinegar) provide a flavor boost without the addition of salt and allow the chef to use less sodium in her cooking. When salt is used, it should be added only when each guest's order is placed. That way, if a guest asks for a salt-free or low-sodium version, the chef is able to adjust the recipe accordingly. By presalting a batch recipe, the chef has no such flexibility.

Proper portion sizes are critical on menus in a country that suffers from diseases of overconsumption rather than from insufficient caloric intake. Not only are guests able to eat from such a menu without undermining their health, but a restaurant can sell more courses to customers who don't fill up completely on a single dish. So how should a steakhouse deal with the argument that the proper portion size for a protein is 4 ounces? Is it realistic to expect all restaurants to serve a 4-ounce prime rib or porterhouse steak? Of course not. The best advice for how closely a restaurant should adhere to nutrition guidelines is to factor more for nutrition as customer frequency increases. In other words, a restaurant that sees the same customers return weekly should include a wider range of healthy menu options than a special occasion restaurant that sees the same faces only once or twice a year. When the customer base is a captive market, nutrition should be one of the main concerns of the menu planner, as the consumers have no alternatives. Even in special occasion restaurants diners should be able to find at least some healthy options should they choose to follow a healthy diet. If no restaurants in a community offer healthy choices, then the local market must choose between an unhealthy diet or fewer meals eaten outside the home. When a restaurant delivers a wide range of healthy choices and proper portion sizes, patrons are able to eat there more frequently without detriment to their health.

So how is a menu planner to create dishes that fit the proper portion size mold? The center-of-the-plate concept in which a large piece of meat, fish, or poultry is accompanied by smaller (or nowadays, equally enormous) portions of starch and vegetable is perhaps the most common style of plate presentation and yet one of the most difficult challenges nutritionally. Stir-fries, risottos, curries, salads, pizzas, and pastas are just a few examples of dishes that can include animal proteins in small quantities without fomenting customer dissatisfaction. Slicing and fanning a poultry breast or steak is another approach to providing normal portion sizes that appeal to a customer's desire for visible "bounty." Except for truly captive audiences, such dishes need not be the only options available on the menu, but providing just a few of these healthy selections allows health-conscious customers to enjoy their experience at a restaurant.

With a menu in place that addresses the nutritional needs for the general population, the menu planner should next take into consideration several dietary restrictions common among Americans. While each of these diets represents a small percentage

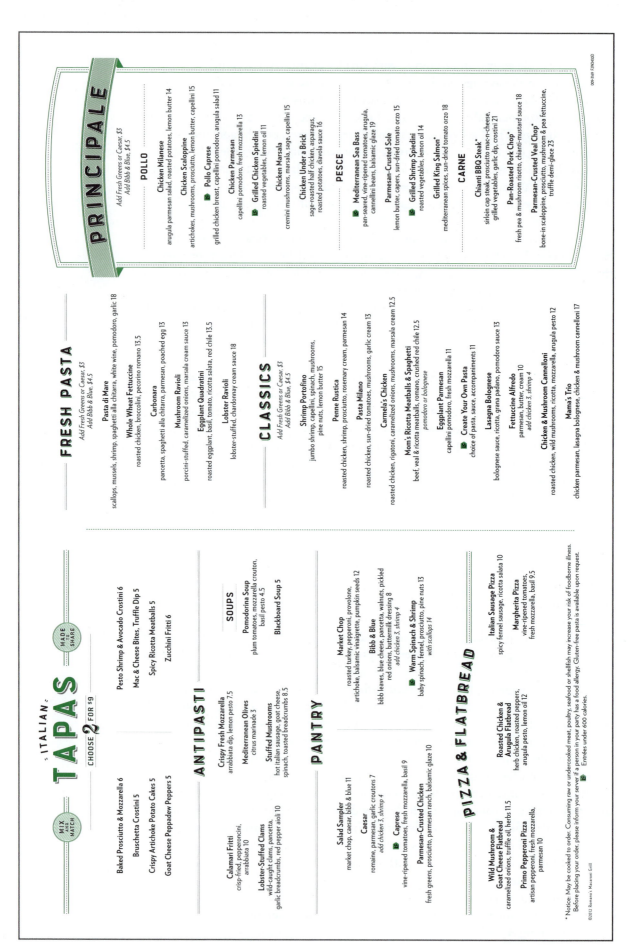

PRINCIPALE

Add Fresh Greens or Caesar, $3
Add Bibb & Blue, $4.5

POLLO

Chicken Milanese
arugula parmesan salad, roasted potatoes, lemon butter 14

Chicken Scaloppine
artichokes, mushrooms, prosciutto, lemon butter, capellini 15

Pollo Caprese
grilled chicken breast, capellini pomodoro, arugula salad 11

Chicken Parmesan
capellini pomodoro, fresh mozzarella 13

Grilled Chicken Spiedini
roasted vegetables, lemon oil 11

Chicken Marsala
cremini mushrooms, marsala, sage, capellini 15

Chicken Under a Brick
sage-roasted half chicken, asparagus,
roasted potatoes, diavola sauce 16

PESCE

Mediterranean Sea Bass
pan-seared, vine-ripened tomatoes, arugula,
cannellini beans, balsamic glaze 19

Parmesan-Crusted Sole
lemon butter, capers, sun-dried tomato orzo 15

Grilled Shrimp Spiedini
roasted vegetables, lemon oil 14

Grilled King Salmon*
mediterranean spices, sun-dried tomato orzo 18

CARNE

Chianti BBQ Steak*
sirloin cap steak, prosciutto mac-n-cheese,
grilled vegetables, garlic dip, crostini 21

Pan-Roasted Pork Chop*
fresh pea & mushroom risotto, chianti-mustard sauce 18

Parmesan-Crusted Veal Chop*
bone-in scaloppine, prosciutto, mushroom & pea fettuccine,
truffle demi-glace 23

FRESH PASTA

Add Fresh Greens or Caesar, $3
Add Bibb & Blue, $4.5

Pasta di Mare
scallops, mussels, shrimp, spaghetti alla chitarra, white wine, pomodoro, garlic 18

Whole Wheat Fettuccine
roasted chicken, broccolini, pecorino romano 13.5

Carbonara
pancetta, spaghetti alla chitarra, parmesan, poached egg 13

Mushroom Ravioli
porcini-stuffed, caramelized onions, marsala cream sauce 13

Eggplant Quadratini
roasted eggplant, basil, tomato, ricotta salata, red chile 13.5

Lobster Ravioli
lobster-stuffed, chardonnay cream sauce 18

CLASSICS

Add Fresh Greens or Caesar, $3
Add Bibb & Blue, $4.5

Shrimp Portofino
jumbo shrimp, capellini, spinach, mushrooms,
pine nuts, lemon butter 15

Penne Rustica
roasted chicken, shrimp, prosciutto, rosemary cream, parmesan 14

Pasta Milano
roasted chicken, sun-dried tomatoes, mushrooms, garlic cream 13

Carmela's Chicken
roasted chicken, rigatoni, caramelized onions, mushrooms, marsala cream 12.5

Mom's Ricotta Meatballs & Spaghetti
beef, veal & ricotta meatballs, romano, crushed red chile 12.5
pomodoro or bolognese

Eggplant Parmesan
capellini pomodoro, fresh mozzarella 11

Create Your Own Pasta
choice of pasta, sauce, accompaniments 11

Lasagna Bolognese
bolognese sauce, ricotta, grana padano, pomodoro sauce 13

Fettuccine Alfredo
parmesan, butter, cream 10
add chicken 3, shrimp 4

Chicken & Mushroom Cannelloni
roasted chicken, wild mushrooms, ricotta, mozzarella, arugula pesto 12

Mama's Trio
chicken parmesan, lasagna bolognese, chicken & mushroom cannelloni 17

ITALIAN TAPAS

MADE TO SHARE

MIX AND MATCH
CHOOSE 2 FOR $9

Baked Prosciutto & Mozzarella 6

Bruschetta Crostini 5

Crispy Artichoke Potato Cakes 5

Goat Cheese Peppadew Peppers 5

Pesto Shrimp & Avocado Crostini 6

Mac & Cheese Bites, Truffle Dip 5

Spicy Ricotta Meatballs 5

Zucchini Fritti 6

ANTIPASTI

Calamari Fritti
crisp-fried, pepperoncini,
arrabbiata 10

Lobster-Stuffed Clams
wild-caught clams, pancetta,
garlic breadcrumbs, red pepper aioli 10

Crispy Fresh Mozzarella
arrabbiata dip, lemon pesto 7.5

Mediterranean Olives
citrus marinade 3

Stuffed Mushrooms
hot italian sausage, goat cheese,
spinach, toasted breadcrumbs 8.5

SOUPS

Pomodorina Soup
plum tomatoes, mozzarella crouton,
basil pesto 4.5

Blackboard Soup 5

PANTRY

Salad Sampler
market chop, caesar, bibb & blue 11

Caesar
romaine, parmesan, garlic croutons 7
add chicken 3, shrimp 4

Caprese
vine-ripened tomatoes, fresh mozzarella, basil 9

Parmesan-Crusted Chicken
fresh greens, prosciutto, parmesan ranch, balsamic glaze 10

Market Chop
roasted turkey, pepperoni, provolone,
artichoke, balsamic vinaigrette, pumpkin seeds 12

Bibb & Blue
bibb leaves, blue cheese, pancetta, walnuts, pickled
red onions, buttermilk dressing 8
add chicken 3, shrimp 4

Warm Spinach & Shrimp
baby spinach, fennel, prosciutto, pine nuts 13
with scallops 14

PIZZA & FLATBREAD

Wild Mushroom &
Goat Cheese Flatbread
caramelized onions, truffle oil, herbs 11.5

Primo Pepperoni Pizza
artisan pepperoni, fresh mozzarella,
parmesan 10

Roasted Chicken &
Arugula Flatbread
herb chicken, roasted peppers,
arugula pesto, lemon oil 12

Italian Sausage Pizza
spicy fennel sausage, ricotta salata 10

Margherita Pizza
vine-ripened tomatoes,
fresh mozzarella, basil 9.5

VINO

BIANCO
Bottle

SPARKLING
Prosecco: La Marca DOC *Italy* 30

SMOOTH, FRUITY WHITE
- White Zinfandel: Woodbridge Robert Mondavi *California* 24
- Moscato: Seven Daughters *Italy* 30
- Riesling: Ste Michelle *Washington* 27
- Riesling: S.A. Prüm Essence QbA *Germany* 32

CRISP, FRESH, DRY WHITE
Pinot Grigio: Banfi Le Rime IGT *Italy* 27
Orvieto Classico: Santa Cristina Campogrande DOC *Italy* 26
- Sauvignon Blanc: Villa Maria Private Bin *New Zealand* 30
- Chardonnay: Emiliana Natura "Unoaked" Organic *Chile* 27
- Chardonnay: Chateau St Jean *California* 36
- Chardonnay: Kendall-Jackson Vintner's Reserve *California* 38

HOUSE WINE
Glass / Bottle

VALOROSO TOSCANO
Toscana IGT

The Edelweiss flower symbolizes the valor, strength and bravery of Count Placido, who brought peace to the Tuscan region where Valoroso Toscano is crafted today exclusively for Romano's Macaroni Grill.

Chardonnay Blend 5.5 / 30

Chianti Blend 5.5 / 30

ROSSO
Bottle

LUSH, FRUITY RED
Pinot Noir: Bridlewood *California* 29
Pinot Noir: La Crema *California* 44
Grenache/Syrah: Almira Los Dos Aragon DO *Spain* 26

MEDIUM-BODIED RED
Chianti: Ruffino Superiore DOCG *Italy* 28
Chianti Classico: Antinori Pèppoli DOCG *Italy* 48
Sangiovese: Cecchi Bonizio *Italy* 26
- Sangiovese/Cabernet Blend: Banfi Col di Sasso IGT *Italy* 27
- Valpolicella: Allegrini DOC *Italy* 34
- Barbera d'Asti: Michele Chiarlo "Le Orme" DOC *Italy* 28
Barbera d'Asti: Vietti "Tre Vigne" DOC *Italy* 38
- Rosso di Montalcino: Castello Banfi DOC *Italy* 45
Tempranillo: Massimo Rioja *Spain* 27
Merlot: 181 *California* 27

RIPE, CONCENTRATED RED
Syrah/Merlot Blend: Tenuta di Biserno Insoglio del Cinghiale IGT *Italy* 46
Nebbiolo d'Alba: Renato Ratti Ochetti DOC *Italy* 40
Aglianico: Feudi di San Gregorio Rubrato Irpinia IGT *Italy* 30
Sangiovese: Luna Vineyards *California* 42
- Merlot: J. Lohr Los Osos *California* 29
- Petite Sirah: Vinum Cellars *California* 27
- Nero d'Avola: MandraRossa IGT *Italy* 27
Malbec: Alamos *Argentina* 27
Barbaresco: Prunotto Classico DOCG *Italy* 67
Cabernet Sauvignon: 14 Hands *Washington* 27
- Cabernet Sauvignon: Paul Dolan Vineyards *California* 40
- Cabernet Sauvignon: Robert Mondavi *California* 52

● Indicates a winery that practices sustainable and/or organic farming.

CRAFTED COCKTAILS

Sorrento Lemonade
absolut vodka, il tramonto limoncello, fresh lemonade 8

Margarita Prima
milagro silver tequila, tuaca, agave nectar, lemon 8.5

Blood Orange Cosmo
ketel one oranje, blood orange 8

Raspberry Smash
1800 reposado tequila, chambord, ginger, agave nectar 8.5

Perfect Martini
tanqueray gin, vermouth, sun-dried tomato olives 8.5

Italian Mojito
bacardi rum, mint, campari, la marca prosecco 8

Bellini Cipriani
la marca prosecco, white peach purée 7

BIRRA
Sam Adams
Peroni
Budweiser
Bud Light

Miller Lite
Coors Light
Corona
Regional Beers

SENZA
Non-alcoholic cocktails

Ginger Root Soda
ginger, lemon, lime, agave nectar, cream 3.5

Fresh Raspberry Lemonade
raspberries, lemonade, san pellegrino limonata 3.5

Limonata Nojito
san pellegrino limonata, agave nectar, lime, mint 3.5

Cranberry Orange Spritz
cranberry, orange, san pellegrino aranciata 3.5

BEVANDE

Italian Soda, Flavored Tea & Lemonade
blackberry, pomegranate, white peach, blood orange or raspberry

Coca-Cola®
Diet Coke®
Sprite®
Dr Pepper®

Minute Maid® Lemonade
San Pellegrino
Acqua Panna
Illy Coffee

QUARTINOS
Half Quartino / Quartino

SPARKLING
Prosecco: La Marca DOC *Italy* glass 8

SMOOTH, FRUITY WHITE
- White Zinfandel: Woodbridge Robert Mondavi *California* 4 / 6.5
Moscato: Seven Daughters *Italy* 7.5 / 10
- Riesling: Ste Michelle *Washington* 6 / 8.5

CRISP, FRESH, DRY WHITE
Pinot Grigio: Banfi Le Rime IGT *Italy* 6.25 / 8.75
Pinot Grigio: Santa Margherita DOC *Italy* 10.5 / 13
- Sauvignon Blanc: Villa Maria Private Bin *New Zealand* 8 / 10.5
- Chardonnay: Emiliana Natura "Unoaked" Organic *Chile* 7 / 9.5
- Chardonnay: Kendall-Jackson Vintner's Reserve *California* 8.5 / 11

LUSH, FRUITY RED
Pinot Noir: Bridlewood *California* 7.5 / 10
Grenache/Syrah: Almira Los Dos Aragon DO *Spain* 5.5 / 8

MEDIUM-BODIED RED
Chianti: Ruffino Superiore DOCG *Italy* 7.25 / 9.75
Sangiovese/Cabernet Blend: Banfi Col di Sasso IGT *Italy* 6.75 / 9.25
Merlot: 181 *California* 7 / 9.5

RIPE, CONCENTRATED RED
- Petite Sirah: Vinum Cellars *California* 7 / 9.5
Nero d'Avola: MandraRossa IGT *Italy* 6 / 8.5
Malbec: Alamos *Argentina* 6.75 / 9.25
Cabernet Sauvignon: 14 Hands *Washington* 6.5 / 9

009-369 97904800

Figure 2–3

For nutrition-minded customers, this menu uses icons to identify those selections that fall under 600 calories per portion.

Printed with the permission of Romano's Macaroni Grill.

23

of the population, combined they can become a significant portion of any restaurant's business. By planning for them, a menu planner expands the potential market for the company. Not every dish need accommodate every diet—to do so would inevitably turn off that percentage of the population without dietary restrictions—but a guest following one of these diets ought to be able to find at least one menu item in each category that meets her needs. Often, a single dish can accommodate the needs of several different diets. Below are seven of the most common specialized diets among Americans.

2.3.1 Vegetarian and Vegan Diets

Vegetarians come in several different forms. Pesco-vegetarians shun meat and poultry but eat seafood. Lacto-ovo vegetarians eat dairy and eggs, but no animal flesh. Vegans eat nothing that comes from an animal—no milk, eggs, or even honey. The rationale behind such diets varies greatly from person to person. People may choose vegetarianism for religious reasons, ethical reasons, financial reasons, health reasons, or environmental reasons. Consequently, some individuals may not be vegetarian all the time but may look for vegetarian options for a significant portion of their weekly meals. (Consider the Meatless Monday movement that has recently gained popularity in some parts of the country.)

Most foodservice establishments—with the possible exception of restaurants with a theme that focuses on animal products, such as a steakhouse, fried chicken joint, or seafood restaurant—should include one or more vegetarian options for each menu category. A vegetarian dish should be more than the operation's standard meat-centered dish with the meat removed. Vegetarians are not usually looking for a side of rice and steamed green beans to make a meal. Instead, a proper vegetarian meal should take into consideration the specific nutritional challenges faced by people who do not eat animal products.

The biggest nutritional challenge for vegetarians is protein. Lacto-ovo vegetarian meals should include dairy and/or eggs to provide some protein as well as vitamin B_{12}. However, vegans must obtain their protein in other ways. Most plant protein sources are incomplete proteins, meaning they do not contain all of the essential amino acids. To provide a complete protein in one meal, the menu planner should combine plant proteins from different sources. The main sources for protein from the plant kingdom are grains, nuts, and legumes. Fortunately, each of these categories is lacking in

---

Example 2.1: Appropriate vs. Inappropriate Vegan Menu Items

Appropriate Vegan Menu—creates a complete protein without using animal products	**Inappropriate Vegan Menu**—first two courses do not constitute a complete protein, and the dessert contains animal products
Mixed Green Salad with Toasted Almonds, Soy Nuts, Dried Cranberries, and Citrus Vinaigrette	Mixed Greens with Cucumbers, Tomato, Bell Pepper, Red Onion, and Balsamic Vinaigrette
Quinoa and Black Bean Chili with Tomatoes, Squash, and Vegetable Broth, served with an Eggless Cornbread	Sautéed Green Beans and Mashed Potatoes
Chocolate Sorbet with Peanut Brittle Crunch	Honey-Corn Bavarian made with Honey, Citrus Juice, Gelatin, and Corn Foam

a different essential amino acid, so combining two of the three categories results in a complete protein. Examples of complete protein combinations include pita and hummus, beans and rice, almond croissants, and falafel sandwiches. Quinoa and soybeans are particularly high in protein, so soy products are commonly found in vegetarian dishes. A properly composed vegetarian dish factors these protein needs heavily into the plate's design. Unlike a meat-heavy dish, which often separates the meat, starch, and vegetables on the plate, a vegetarian dish is perfectly acceptable as a single, integrated set of ingredients on the plate en masse, such as a bowl of pasta, a stir-fry, or a pizza. When the menu planner includes dairy or eggs in the dish, options for a preparation without those ingredients should be noted on the menu for vegans. If the removal of eggs or dairy from a vegetarian dish would result in an incomplete protein, the menu planner should consider a substitution with a nut, grain, or legume as an alternative. Providing bean or nut spreads with bread at the table may eliminate the need to provide complete proteins with each dish. Finally, as the purpose of creating vegetarian and vegan dishes is to accommodate and attract guests with those dietary needs, any dishes that are not obviously vegan should be noted as such on the menu.

2.3.2 Low-Fat Diets

Whether for the purposes of losing weight, recovering from heart disease, or just general health, some Americans seek low-fat options whenever and wherever they eat. Foodservice establishments that can accommodate this dietary request are likely to attract that business. As lower-fat dishes do not fill up the consumer on a single entrée, they also help to drive sales of multicourse meals.

Low-fat should not translate to no flavor. Low-fat dishes generally rely on certain cooking techniques—poaching, steaming, sautéing, grilling, broiling, and roasting. Fried components on a dish do not qualify. If a chef uses processed foods in her recipes, she should confirm that they, too, are low in fat. When meats are used, lean cuts should be employed to avoid adding hidden fat to a dish. Spices, herbs, and strongly flavored ingredients (garlic, chiles, etc.) help to deliver flavor without fat. For dishes in which fat delivers unctuousness, starch thickeners may replicate the thicker viscosity.

Menu planners may wish to highlight their low-fat dishes on a menu. Common symbols include hearts or checkmarks to denote a low-fat selection. The symbols are typically defined at the bottom of the menu. To meet the legal definition of low-fat, a dish must include no more than 3 grams of fat per 100 grams of food, and no more than 30% of the calories may come from fat.[7] Some restaurants prefer to leave nutrient claims off the menu. In such establishments, menu descriptions should make a low-fat dish obvious by stressing low-fat cooking techniques and by highlighting flavors that do not stem from fatty ingredients.

Example 2.2: *Sake-Poached Flounder with Ponzu Sauce, Steamed Bok Choy, and Sesame Sticky Rice* is a menu description that immediately alerts the customer that this dish is low-fat. "Poached" and "steamed" highlight the low-fat cooking techniques while ingredients such as sake and ponzu sauce illustrate a deliberate effort to add flavor without fat. If written as *Flounder with Ponzu Sauce, Bok Choy, and Rice*, the menu description would be less clear in communicating the dish's low-fat qualities.

2.3.3 Low-Sodium Diets

Consumers battling hypertension may look for low-sodium menu choices. While salt is the most prevalent source of sodium in a restaurant, sodium is also hidden in most processed foods, cured meats and fish, and certain other ingredients, such as soy sauce.

Since a person's sensitivity to salt changes as she gets used to a certain consumption level, chefs who normally use salt heavily in their cooking may consider low-sodium dishes bland. Conversely, diners who shun salt would find a "properly seasoned" dish salty. Chefs should keep in mind that it is the diner's taste preference, not the chef's, that matters most.

Chefs can create flavorful, low-sodium dishes by relying on fresh ingredients and by incorporating copious quantities of spices, herbs, and other highly flavorful ingredients. Cooks should not add salt to recipes until an order is placed, so a cook could easily adjust a dish to reduce its sodium content by not adding salt. Chiles, garlic, ginger, and onions provide a salt-free flavor boost. Other ingredients, such as aged cheese, anchovies, and sundried tomatoes, contain some salt, but they also come with high levels of glutamates, which are strong flavor enhancers. Using glutamate-rich ingredients may reduce the need to add straight salt to enhance a dish's flavor. Flavor extracts also help to boost flavor without salt.

Menu planners with a market concerned about sodium should probably denote the low-sodium options on their menus with some sort of symbol. However, unlike low-fat dishes, low-sodium dishes are not usually easy to identify simply by reading a menu description. By law, low-sodium dishes must contain 140 milligrams or less of sodium per 100 grams of food.[8] One approach to addressing guests seeking low-sodium dishes may be to note on the menu that any dish can be made without added salt upon customer request. Chefs may prefer, instead, to create certain dishes with enough alternate flavor sources that added salt is not necessary; servers can recommend those dishes to customers requesting low-sodium options. Either way, having a plan to accommodate the low-salt dieters is imperative for operations with captive audiences and for restaurants and hotels seeking to attract this segment of the market.

Example 2.3: *Sliced Flat-Iron Steak with Chimichurri, Chile-Garlic Roasted Corn, and Grilled Asparagus with Lemon Zest* is a dish that can easily be made low-sodium. The herb-garlic-citrus chimichurri provides strong flavors that come through well even without salt. The chile and lemon zest do the same for the side dishes. By slicing the steak, the chef ensures that the sauce covers a greater surface area of the meat for a more effective flavor hit with each bite.

2.3.4 Low-Carbohydrate Diets

While not recommended by most mainstream nutritionists, the low-carbohydrate diet is popular among some Americans. The diet severely restricts the quantity of carbohydrates consumed per day, which leaves the body to subsist on protein and fat—the reason that most nutritionists do not recommend the diet. A few restaurants have attempted to capitalize on this trend by promoting their already unhealthy foods as appropriate for a low-carbohydrate diet. The merits of the diet may be debatable, but if a restaurant intends to capture this market segment, it ought to at least promote low-carbohydrate dishes honestly and accurately.

Low-carbohydrate dishes are based primarily in meats, proteins, and seafood, but they also consist of a good number of low-starch vegetables as a source of fiber. While mashed potato or bread might not be appropriate for a low-carbohydrate meal, mashed cauliflower or braised greens would be. Sugar is pure carbohydrate, so it has no place in a low-carbohydrate meal. Thus, a rack of ribs with a sugarless spice rub is low-carbohydrate; ribs with a sugary sauce are not. Calorie counts for this diet should not be any greater than they are with other diets, but fats and proteins make up the majority of the macronutrients consumed. With animal protein typically representing the majority of the plate, low-carbohydrate dishes can be expensive to deliver.

The main reason to create low-carbohydrate dishes in a restaurant is to attract a certain segment of the market. Low-carbohydrate dishes should be promoted as such. Some restaurants denote these dishes explicitly in the menu descriptions or with symbols; however, most diners can identify a low-carbohydrate dish if the description references various vegetables but no starches. Similarly, traditional dishes that have had the starch replaced, such as a burger wrapped in lettuce instead of a bun, are understood as low-carbohydrate items by most restaurant patrons.

Example 2.4: *12-oz. Rib-Eye Steak with Herb Butter, Sautéed Spinach, and Celeriac Puree* communicates "low-carb" to the customer by pairing an oversized portion of meat with a butter sauce and two vegetables rather than with a sweet sauce or starch. The large portion of meat is there to make up for the calories lost by eliminating the starch.

2.3.5 Diabetes Diets

People with diabetes either do not produce sufficient insulin to properly process blood sugar or they have developed a resistance to insulin. Either way, diabetics end up with high levels of glucose (a sugar) in their blood, which can cause a range of health problems. While the exact cause of type I diabetes is not known, type II diabetes develops over time from lifestyle choices. Type II diabetes can be triggered by overweight, insufficient exercise, and/or poor diet. While type II diabetes may require insulin injections, it is possible for most people to manage it through diet. Thus, accommodating diabetics in a foodservice operation is critical to those guests' management of their illness.

The diet for diabetics is similar to a diet for good overall health—lots of vegetables and whole grains, lean meats, moderate portions. As type II diabetes often stems from overweight or obesity, diabetics typically need portions with calorie counts that allow them to control their weight. Additionally, spikes in blood sugar are worse for diabetics than are meals that provide a slow, steady supply of glucose across several hours. Unless the foodservice business plans on providing small snacks throughout the day, the best way to prevent blood sugar spikes is through fiber intake and carbohydrate counting. Fiber, present in fruits, vegetables, and whole grains but not in refined sugars, slows the rate at which blood sugar increases. A menu item appropriate for a diabetic should include these sources of fiber while limiting refined sugars or low-fiber carbohydrates. Diabetes-friendly meals should provide only moderate quantities of carbohydrates and calories to prevent spikes in blood sugar. Appropriate meals are also low in fats, refined sugars, and calories to prevent weight gain, which contributes to diabetes.

Because the diet for people with diabetes is similar to that for overall good health, menus do not typically identify diabetes-friendly meals except in captive market environments. That said, a menu planner may consider partnering with a local diabetes association to identify or develop a menu item or two that is highly recommended for diabetics. Such a menu choice might be highlighted or identified as having the recommendation of the local association, assuming the association is willing to give its approval.

Example 2.5: *Grilled Chicken Breast with Sautéed Mushroom and Onion Sauce, Barley-Brown Rice Pilaf, and Wilted Spinach* is potentially a diabetes-friendly dish. With the skin removed, the chicken becomes low-fat. The mushroom and onion sauce must be made without added sugar (think: reduced chicken stock rather than Madeira, which contains sugar). The pilaf and spinach can be made low-fat as well, and both contain significant amounts of fiber to slow sugar increases in the bloodstream. Assuming the portion sizes are moderate, this dish would be appropriate for a person with diabetes.

2.3.6 Gluten Intolerance Diets

A small but significant portion of the population suffers from celiac disease or gluten intolerance. For celiac sufferers, wheat, rye, barley, and possibly oats (the research is ongoing for oats) impact the intestines and cause a range of serious health issues. In short, individuals with gluten intolerance cannot consume any of these ingredients or products made from these ingredients.

While creating a celiac-friendly menu item may seem as simple as avoiding wheat, rye, barley, and oats, there are many processed foods that contain these ingredients. Soy sauce, for example, often contains wheat. Certain alcohols may be made from rye, wheat, or barley. It is critical that chefs using prefabricated products read their labels to ensure that none of the ingredients are wheat, rye, or barley derivatives. Cooks must also take care not to cross-contaminate a celiac-friendly preparation by using dirty utensils or equipment that contain traces of the problematic grains. Even in small amounts they can be harmful to celiac sufferers. Fortunately, other than avoiding the forbidden wheat, rye, barley, and oats, gluten-free dishes may contain anything else. In order to provide proper nutrition, they should include an appropriate balance of protein, fat, and carbohydrate, but the carbohydrates should come from potatoes, rice, corn, or other grains beyond the forbidden four. As many desserts are made from wheat flour, this category of food is often the most challenging, but a gluten-free dessert is likely to be popular among non-celiacs as well.

Restaurants that take the time to create a gluten-free menu item ought to promote that effort to attract customers. A small notation or icon on the menu to identify gluten-free dishes is all that is required. In upscale restaurants, chefs may be asked to modify a dish to make it gluten-free. While customer service is paramount in the hospitality and foodservice industry, a chef should not agree to modify a dish unless she can guarantee that it will be gluten-free. In other words, celiac disease is a serious illness, and attempting to pass off as gluten-free a dish containing wheat, rye, barley, or oats is both dangerous and unethical.

Example 2.6: Appropriate vs. Inappropriate Menu for People with Gluten Intolerance

Appropriate—Avoids wheat, rye, barley, and oats	**Inappropriate**—Croutons, Soy Sauce, and Pie Crust all contain wheat
Mixed Greens Salad with Cucumbers, Tomatoes, Scallions, and a Red Wine Vinaigrette	Classic Caesar Salad
Grilled Tuna with a Ketchup-Cider Vinegar BBQ Sauce, Steamed Rice, and Roasted Carrots	Soy-Glazed Tuna Steak with Steamed Rice and Carrots
Flourless Chocolate Torte with Raspberries	Chocolate Pie with Raspberry Sauce

2.3.7 Lactose Intolerance Diets

Lactose is a sugar found naturally in milk. The body normally digests it with the enzyme lactase, but for people with a lactase deficiency, the lactose is not digested properly and causes gastrointestinal side effects. The best way to manage this condition is either through lactase pills or drops or through dietary changes. From the menu planner's perspective, the restaurant cannot rely on a diner to bring her lactase pills with her, so accommodating menu options are required to attract lactose-intolerant guests. This translates to some menu options that do not include dairy.

The range of sensitivity to lactose varies from person to person. While some lactose-intolerant people can eat low-lactose dairy products like yogurt or hard cheese, others cannot. Thus, it is best to have at least a few menu items that do not contain dairy at all. At a minimum, the chef should be able to modify a dish on the fly to remove any dairy components. For the average menu, this means that not every salad should come with cheese on it, and not every entrée should have a cream or butter sauce. Desserts may be more challenging, as they often contain dairy, but guests will be grateful to have just one nondairy choice for dessert. The biggest obstacle to accommodating lactose-intolerant guests is hidden dairy in processed foods. Ingredient lists may not include a familiar dairy term; lactose, whey, or curds are all dairy byproducts, as are dried milk and milk solids. The chef should know which of her processed ingredients contain dairy and notify any guest with a declared lactose intolerance issue.

Because dairy sources are typically obvious in menu descriptions, most restaurants do not identify a dish specifically as lactose-free. However, menu planners should take care to state any dairy products used in a dish, so a customer can easily navigate around any lactose-containing ingredients.

Example 2.7: Dairy-Based Desserts and Lactose-Free Versions

Includes Lactose	Lactose-Free
Apple Pie with a Butter Crust	Use a shortening crust and do not add butter to the apple filling
Milk Chocolate Soufflé	Use dark chocolate and margarine or oil as the base before adding the whipped egg white
Ice Cream Sundae	Go with a fruit sorbet garnished with nuts and fresh fruit rather than whipped cream

In a hospital, prison, or other environment in which the consumers are captive, it is an ethical necessity for a menu planner or chef to accommodate every dietary restriction and allergy that threatens the health of the diner. However, for most foodservice operations, the decision to accommodate the most popular dietary restrictions is simply smart business: the more diners that the establishment can service, the greater the potential revenue for the company. In restaurants, this translates to return business. For corporate cafeterias, it could mean the difference between renewing versus losing the contract for the cafeteria. Guests with special dietary needs are far more likely to become regular patrons when they have their needs accommodated. And the general population can dine out more often when they can find food that does not impact their health negatively.

SUMMARY

Factoring nutrition into the menu planning process maintains the health of the consumers in a captive market and attracts nutrition-minded individuals with a choice of dining options. All food and drink contain one or more of the major categories of nutrients: carbohydrates, lipids, proteins, water, vitamins, and minerals. Each category promotes good health in a different way. Calories provide energy, but their intake should be controlled, so excess energy is not consumed and stored as body fat. Fiber is not digested, but it does play a role in maintaining health. A proper diet should be balanced, varied, adequate, and moderate. In the United States, overconsumption is as big a problem as inadequate nutrition intake. Allergies impact a person's diet, as someone with an allergy cannot consume certain foods. Menu planners should ensure that someone with one of the more common allergies can find something to eat in their foodservice establishments. When creating or modifying a menu, the menu planner should include some items that adhere to the recommendations of the *Dietary Guidelines for Americans 2010*. These recommendations include focusing on fruits, vegetables, and whole grains; choosing lean meats and dairy; and minimizing refined sugars, fats, and sodium. Menu planners should also consider some menu options for those market segments that follow certain popular diets, such as vegetarian, vegan, low-fat, low-sodium, low-carbohydrate, diabetic, gluten-intolerant, and lactose-intolerant diets. By accommodating a wide range of diets as well as a diet for general good health, a foodservice business can attract a wider audience and for a captive market better serve its clientele.

COMPREHENSION QUESTIONS

1. List one reason why nutrition should be considered in the menu planning process.
2. What is a captive market, and why is nutrition an important consideration for a captive market?
3. How many calories per gram are provided by carbohydrates, lipids, proteins, and alcohol?
4. What is the difference between HDL and LDL? How does consumption of each type of fat impact the levels of HDL and LDL?
5. What is a complete protein, and how does one eat complete protein?
6. Name three vitamins and minerals that are concerns for modern American diets.
7. What does fiber do, and what foods are significant sources of fiber?
8. List the common categories of food allergies.
9. Write a common menu phrasing for a warning about eating undercooked, potentially hazardous food.
10. List three guidelines for creating a healthy menu option for the general public.
11. Create a three-course menu (one option for each course) that qualifies as healthy and nutritious for the general public.
12. Select one of the specialized diets common among Americans. Describe the principles of that diet and create a three-course menu that meets the needs of those dieters.

DISCUSSION QUESTIONS

1. Think of a restaurant you have visited that markets its healthy menu options. How were the menu items identified? What type of diet was addressed in those options?
2. When you go out to eat, how big a factor is a dish's nutritional value in your decision making? Can you think of anyone you know for whom nutrition or diet plays a bigger role in their menu selection?
3. Some restaurateurs have argued that the obesity crisis in America is not due to restaurant food but rather to Americans' lack of physical activity. Why do you think restaurateurs might make this argument? Is there any problem that stems from the fact that restaurateurs are making this case?
4. What nutrition or diet issues have you heard in the news in the past three months? How could a menu planner address this issue? Should a menu planner or restaurant bother addressing this issue? Why?
5. Of the several specialized diets described in the chapter, which is the most common among your friends and family? How easily are those people able to find food that meets their dietary needs?

ENDNOTES

1. http://health.gov/dietaryguidelines/dga2010/DietaryGuidelines2010.pdf, accessed 12/13/11, p. 11.
2. Ibid.
3. Ibid., p. 19.
4. Ibid., p. 15.
5. Ibid.
6. Ibid.
7. http://www.fda.gov/Food/GuidanceCompliance RegulatoryInformation/GuidanceDocuments/Food LabelingNutrition/FoodLabelingGuide/ucm064911. htm, accessed 12/19/11. Definitions of Nutrient Content Claims.
8. Ibid.

3

Menu Styles and Categories I— Traditional Basics

By the end of this chapter, you will be able to:

- Describe the menu pricing approaches of a la carte, semi a la carte, table d'hôte, and prix fixe menus
- List the most common menu categories found on traditional breakfast, lunch, and dinner menus
- Describe the types of items typically listed under each menu category
- Create a menu of food options that incorporates balance and variety
- Create a menu of food items that satisfies management concerns for work flow and product utilization

As a menu reflects the theme of its corresponding foodservice establishment and target market, it is difficult to provide a universal set of guidelines for menu categories. A casual Italian restaurant might have a menu heading just for pizzas, but other types of restaurants may not even offer pizza on their menus. How the menu planner addresses this challenge is part understanding of the restaurant's marketing goals and part adherence to customer familiarity with menu conventions. While Chapter 4 deals with a wide variety of possible menus, this chapter focuses on the most traditional formats and category headings for restaurant breakfast, lunch, and dinner menus.

After determining the menu categories, the menu planner is finally ready to begin creating specific menu items. However, a listing of random dishes, no matter how delicious, is not automatically appropriate for a menu. The menu planner must take into consideration how the menu listings will impact kitchen work flow, food cost, customer dining speed, and guest satisfaction with the variety of choices. When done properly, a one-page menu allows every guest to find something he wants to eat; done poorly, a ten-page menu still leaves some customers feeling that there's nothing listed that they'd like to order. Understanding the basics of menu item selection and categorization helps a menu planner to create a menu that meets the needs of the consumers and the employees.

3.1 MENU PRICING STYLES

While a single item's price would not normally impact the selection of menu categories, how the entire menu is priced does influence the category headings appropriate for that menu. Menus are typically divided into four pricing types: a la carte, semi a la carte, table d'hôte, and prix fixe.

In an a la carte menu, each menu item is priced separately and nothing is bundled together. For example, in an a la carte steakhouse, a guest who orders a grilled porterhouse steak will receive only the steak and nothing else. Any vegetable or starch accompaniments must be ordered separately for an additional cost. Some foodservice operations provide a la carte pricing for some or all of their menu items in addition to another pricing approach; this is particularly common on breakfast menus and in fast food establishments. A la carte menus allow for the most extensive set of menu categories and must include at least one subheading for the side dishes/accompaniments (vegetables, starches, etc.).

A semi a la carte menu packages all of the components of the entrée into a single price but charges separately for all other courses. This is the type of menu most common in American restaurants. For example, a semi a la carte menu might offer a main protein, vegetable, starch, and sauce

THE PRIME RIB®
The Civilized Steakhouse

WASHINGTON, D.C.   PHILADELPHIA   BALTIMORE

Soups

Roasted Tomato   9   **Maine Lobster Bisque**   11

Appetizers

Cold

Jumbo Shrimp Cocktail	18
Oysters on the Half Shell	18
Jumbo Lump Crab Cocktail	18
Sliced Norwegian Smoked Salmon	18
Cherrystone Clams	15
Petrossian Caviar	M.P.
Cold Seafood Tower	49
Shrimp, Oysters, Smoked Salmon	

Hot

Sesame Seared Tuna	16
Jumbo Lump Crab Cake	18
Imperial Crab	18
Clams Casino	17
Oysters Chesapeake (2)	17
Oysters Rockefeller (4)	17
Escargots	15
Soft Shell Crab *(in season)*	M.P.
Hot Seafood Tower	49
Crab Cake, Oysters Chesapeake, Clams Casino	

Our Famous Potato Skin Basket   9
Originated by us in 1965, served with horseradish sauce

Salads

House
Our famous house dressing

Caesar
*Romaine Hearts,
Egg-free dressing*

Buzz's
*Romaine, tomato, avocado,
chopped egg with white
balsamic vinaigrette*

Hearts of Lettuce
Blue Cheese dressing

Vine Ripe Tomatoes
Vidalia Onions and Grated Feta Cheese

Hearts of Palm
*Brazilian Palm Hearts
with Deviled Eggs*

ALL SALADS
12

A 20% pre-tax gratuity will be added to parties of six or more.

Figure 3–1
In an a la carte menu, the entrée accompaniments are purchased separately from the main item. The Prime Rib, Inc.

Entrees

*We will __not__ be responsible for meat ordered medium well or well done.
To insure that the steak has been cooked as ordered, please cut it through the center.*

ROAST PRIME RIB	*signature entree*	49
	our split cut	36
USDA PRIME FILET MIGNON	8-oz.	45
USDA PRIME FILET OSCAR *with Jumbo Lump Crab, Asparagus and Béarnaise Sauce*		57
DRY AGED USDA PRIME NY STRIP	12-oz.	45
	16-oz.	55
STEAK AU POIVRE	12-oz.	48
ROQUEFORT STEAK	12-oz.	48
CHOPPED STEAK *with all-natural angus beef*	*with sautéed onions*	23
	with melted Blue Cheese	26
CENTER CUT VEAL CHOP		37
RACK OF LAMB		40
CHICKEN PICCATA		26
VEGETARIAN PLATE		26

Vegetables

Grilled Artichoke Hearts 10   Spinach - *creamed or sautéed* 9
Sautéed Mushroom Trio - *shitake, oyster and button* 12   Grilled Asparagus 10
Fresh Corn off the Cob 9   Broccoli Rabe 10

Potatoes

Classic Mashed 9   Baked Idaho 9   Our Famous Potato Skins 9
Au Gratin 10   French Fries 8   Steak Fries 10

Bearnaise, Hollandaise *or* Crumbled Blue Cheese 4

2011 Zagat #1 Steakhouse – Washington, Baltimore and Philadelphia.

Figure 3–1
(Continued)

Seafood Entrees

ASK YOUR SERVER ABOUT TODAY'S FRESH FISH

JUMBO LUMP CRAB CAKES
Our award-winning recipe. The finest all Jumbo Lump Crabmeat   35

IMPERIAL CRAB
The finest jumbo lump, lightly seasoned and baked in a shell   35

CHILEAN SEA BASS   33

FILLET OF WILD SALMON *(in season)*   33

YELLOWFIN "AHI" TUNA
Sesame seared   35

FILLET OF FLOUNDER   29
Stuffed with Imperial Crab   38

SOFT SHELL CRABS
A delicious regional favorite. Served only in season   M.P.

LIVE MAINE LOBSTER
2 or 3 lbs.
Also available stuffed with our famous Imperial Crab   M.P.

> *"Dressing well is a way of showing respect for other people."*
> Warren Christopher

GIFT CARDS AVAILABLE

Consuming raw or undercooked meats, poultry, seafood, shellfish or eggs may increase your risk of food-borne illness, especially if you have certain medical conditions.

2/12

Figure 3–1
(Continued)

for one price. If a guest wishes to purchase an appetizer or dessert, those items must be ordered separately and will cost extra. As with an a la carte menu, this style of menu pricing allows for a large number of menu categories, but "side dishes" may or may not be among them.

Table d'hôte and prix fixe menus offer a complete set of courses for one set price. The appetizers, soups, salads, and desserts are included with the price of the entrée. The difference between the two styles is that a table d'hôte menu will list different prices next to each entrée, and the price that the customer pays depends on his choice of entrée. For a prix fixe menu, all of the entrées are the same price. These types of menus greatly impact the names and number of menu headings used. Customers who pay a set price for a set of courses often want to experience something from each menu category; otherwise, they feel cheated. If the price includes four courses, then the menu will typically list only four categories. If the guest gets to select a soup, a salad, an entrée, and a dessert, then those may be the headings for the categories. Alternatively, the menu might simply list "First Course," "Second Course," etc. If the diner must choose between a salad, soup, or appetizer for the first course, then all of those options should be listed under a single heading, usually "First Course" or "Appetizers." Some menu planners may skip the naming convention entirely for a prix fixe or table d'hôte menu and simply place lines, asterisks, or some other visual separator between the categories. Because of the nature of the table d'hôte and prix fixe menus, it is also acceptable to list a category that includes only one option— "Intermezzo" with a grapefruit sorbet being the only selection, for example. A la carte and semi a la carte menus would not normally list a menu category with only one option beneath it.

Which pricing approach to take depends on the business's theme and its target market. If a restaurant wants to appeal to special occasion diners who spend several hours at dinner, it may adopt a prix fixe or table d'hôte style. That way, once guests have decided to patronize the establishment and pay the hefty per person cost to eat there, they can focus solely on their food choices rather than on how much each additional course will add to the bill. A la carte and semi a la carte menus appeal to guests who prefer flexibility in how many courses they order. These types of menus appeal to customers who are more price sensitive, have less time available to linger over a meal, or who simply do not want a multicourse dining experience. Semi a la carte menus provide a sense of value over a la carte menus because the components of the entrée are packaged and priced together. A la carte menus really work well only when the portions are significant enough that customers would be satisfied with the purchase of a single item and one (or fewer) accompaniments; the sharing of side dishes at a table is common in an a la carte setting. A table d'hôte approach is usually chosen over a prix fixe pricing strategy when the food cost for each entrée varies significantly.

3.2 PRINCIPLES OF MENU ITEM SELECTION

The material from the earlier chapters is the foundation upon which menu items and categories are built. The menu must make sense with the business concept, appeal to the target market, and take into account any nutritional or dietary concerns as well as the menu's anticipated pricing style. Keeping those variables in mind, the menu planner considers the names and number of menu categories to include on the menu. Greater numbers of categories can increase the number of courses that people order. For example, a menu that lumps all first courses (soups, salads, and appetizers) into a single category suggests that only one course should be selected prior to the entrée while a menu that separates those categories may encourage some

THE RESTAURANT AT PATOWMACK FARM

WELCOMES YOU

May 26, 2012

Amuse Bouche
ensadilla rusa

Strawberry Salad
arugula, pecorino, puffed rice, green tea froth, aged balsamico
Amalie Robert 2010 Pinot Meunier, Oregon

Anson Mills White Flint Corn Grits
our own asparagus, chesapeake bay jumbo lump crab, mustard vinaigrette
A Paola 2009 Chardonnay, Italy

Intermezzo
chamomile sorbet and candied lime

Fields of Athenry Spring Lamb
hoppin' john, BBQ hash, garlic mustard tempura
Luigi Bosca 2008 Malbec Reserva, Argentina

Mulberry Pie
panna cotta, mulberry mash, port wine reduction, chocolate ganache
Broadbent, Auction Reserve Porto, Portugal

Friandise
a sweet surprise

Executive Chef, Christopher Edwards

Prix Fixe $85.00 – Wine Pairing $45.00

Consuming raw or undercooked food may increase your risk of foodborne illness
20% gratuity on parties of 6 or more
Owner: Beverly Morton Billand

**The Restaurant at Patowmack
Farm | 540 822-9017 | www.patowmackfarm.com**

Figure 3–2
On this prix fixe menu, each guest receives the entire menu for a single set price. A prix fixe menu may allow guests to choose from a limited selection for each course and still pay the same set price. Printed with the permission of The Restaurant at Patowmack Farm and Executive Chef Christopher Edwards.

Pagano's Pasta & Specialty Dishes

	à la Carte	Full
Lasagna	11.95	13.95
Made from our family's recipe-a favorite		
Fettuccine Alfredo	13.75	15.75
Pasta Sicilian ☆	11.95	14.95
Our manager's delight-pasta imported from Italy solely for us, topped with our Sicilian Sauce for your dining pleasure		
Pasta a Forno ☆	11.75	13.95
Lee's favorite; layered pasta filled with ham, peas, salami, beef, Romano then topped with sauce & mozzarella cheese		
Gnocchi	11.50	13.50
A soft potato dumpling		
Manicotti	12.95	14.95
Pasta tubes filled with ricotta cheese & topped with sauce & mozzarella cheese		
Pasta con Broccoli ☆	11.95	13.95
Short pasta, cooked with fresh broccoli florets, served with olive oil; also great with Sicilian sauce		
Pasta con Zucchini ☆	12.95	14.45
A delicious Sicilian dish - Rina's favorite - short pasta with either Sicilian sauce or olive oil & fresh pan-fried zucchini slices topped with Romano cheese		
Tortellini alla Panna	11.95	13.95
Small pasta cheese filled pies served in a thick white cream sauce - totally delicious		
Linguine alla Pagano	11.75	13.75
Served with a Bolognese sauce		
Mama Anne's Homemede Ravioli ☆	12.95	14.95
Carole's favorite; made from Mama's recipe, filled with ricotta cheese or a mixture of ricotta & beef		
Spaghetti alla Casa Pagano	10.50	12.50
Large dish of pasta with tomato sauce		

*Change of sauce or pasta type, additional $1.00 each

	à la Carte	Full
Spaghetti & Mushrooms	11.95	13.95
A hearty dish of pasta cooked "al dente" and topped with sauteed mushrooms		
Spaghetti Aglio e Olio	10.95	12.85
Garlic sauteed in olive oil over pasta		
Excellent when you add sauteed mushrooms	11.75	13.95

Figure 3–3

This menu offers both table d'hôte (labeled as "full") and semi a la carte (labeled as "a la carte") options. For the table d'hôte option, the guest pays a different price depending on the choice of entrée, but receives soup, salad, and breadsticks with dipping sauce for the same price. For the semi a la carte option, the entrée comes with all of its sides but soup and salad are not included. Printed with the permission of Rhonda Davis and Pagano's Restaurant.

	à la Carte	Full
Chicken Fettuccine Primavera	14.95	16.85

Grilled chicken breast with spring veggies in a white sauce

	à la Carte	Full
Seafood Pasta	16.50	18.50

Angel hair pasta topped with lump crab, shrimp, clams, & sauteed mushrooms in a light creamy red sauce

Veal Marsala .... 15.95 .... 17.95

Veal medallions with a seasoned breading, sauteed with garlic and mushrooms, & finished with Marsala wine

Scampi Linguine .... 17.95 .... 19.95

Bite size shrimp in a garlic butter atop imported pasta

Veal Scaloppini .... 15.95 .... 17.95

Tender veal pieces, sauteed with Marsala wine, mushrooms, apple juice, & spices

Chicken Romano .... 13.95 .... 15.95

Chicken breast fillets, coated with a seasoned batter, pan fried in olive oil & steamed in a chicken broth

Chicken Marsala .... 12.95 .... 14.95

Chicken fillets with seasoned breading, sauteed with the right amount of garlic & mushrooms. Marsala wine finishes it!

☆ **Denotes a Pagano's Restaurant specialty.**

Parmigiana Delights

(Side dish with à la carte entree)

	à la Carte	Full
Eggplant	11.95	13.95
Chicken Breast Fillets	14.95	16.95
Veal Cutlet	16.95	18.95
Zucchini	11.75	13.95

All **Full course entrees** in the Pasta & Specialty Dishes and Parmigiana Delights sections include a cup of our homemade soup, a dinner salad, breadsticks, a side of Sicilian sauce. **À la carte** includes the entree item with breadsticks & a side of Sicilian sauce.

For Your Pasta

Sauces: Pasta & Specialty Dishes, include any of the following at **NO** additional charge.
Aglio & Olio - Alfredo - Meat - Pesto - Sicilian - Tomato - Bolognese

Pagano Sides: For your Pasta & Specialty Dishes or Parmigiana meals
the following toppers are available:

Sauteed Mushrooms	3.50	Fried Zucchini	4.25
Meatballs (2)	2.55	Italian Hot Sausage	4.75
Char-Grilled Chicken Fillet	3.95	Pasta or Potatoes	2.25

Figure 3–3
(Continued)

Pagano's

Entrees from the Sea

House Breaded Cod Fillet (½ #, baked or fried) 14.75
Baked Stuffed Flounder 16.95
Shrimp Scampi 18.95

Entrees from the Land

Stuffed Chicken Breast 15.75
Char-grilled Pork Chops 14.50
Char-grilled New York Strip Steak 16.95
Baby Beef Liver & Onions 11.95
Stuffed Pork Chops 16.50
Chicken Breast-Char-Grilled . . . . King .15.25 . . . . Queen .. 11.75
Chicken Breast-Barbecued . . . . King .15.25 . . . . Queen .. 11.95
Veal Milanese (breaded cutlet, served with a lemon wedge) 18.50
Sirloin Steak, 6 oz. - Certified Angus Beef 14.95
Cowboy Steak, 16 oz. - Certified Angus Beef 22.95

The above entree items include: cup of our house soup, house salad & breadsticks
and the choice of two sides (potato, veggie, and/or pasta).

Hot & Cold Beverages

Bottomless: Regular or Decaffeinated Coffee 2.25
Fountain Beverages 2.25
House Brewed Iced Tea 2.25
Lemonade 2.25

Espresso . . . . 3.95   Hot Cocoa 2.50
Cappuccino . . . . 4.25   Chocolate Milk 2.25
Milk . . . . 1.95   Hot Tea 2.25
Juice 2.50

Dessert alla Pagano

Carrot Cake . . . . 4.50   Ice Cream 2.50
Sherbet . . . . 2.50   Spumoni 3.25
N.Y. Cheesecake . . . . plain . 4.25   Torta Italian 5.25
. . . . fruit . 4.95   Sweet Street Cakes & Pies .. 4.50

Pagano's

Figure 3–3
(Continued)

customers to order multiple courses before the entrée. The names of the categories help to attract customers as well who are looking for a certain experience. For example, a menu that lists a pizza category separately from an entrée category suggests to customers that whether they prefer a fancy meal or simply an evening of pizza, this establishment can accommodate them.

Larger numbers of categories are not always a good thing, however. Although some operations only include just a couple of choices per menu category, most a la carte and semi a la carte businesses offer five or more choices per category. Some restaurants have over a dozen choices per category. With more to read, diners in a restaurant with an extensive menu require more time to peruse the menu before placing their orders. The extra reading time leads to a longer dining experience overall, so the rate at which tables are turned over to new customers is lower. Extensive menus cost more than limited menus not only in fewer table turns but also in the number of dollars tied up in inventory, the amount of space needed for inventory, and the cost of printing menus with multiple pages. However, if the restaurant's dining room is large and the broader menu attracts a significantly larger market, these extra costs may be justified.

3.2.1 Balance and Variety

Two of the most important considerations when settling on menu listings are balance and variety. The menu should offer a wide range of options (variety) without focusing too heavily on any one product, cooking technique, or other menu item characteristic. Of course, as with any rule there are always exceptions. A business with a narrowly focused concept—a BBQ shack, a pizza place, a fried chicken joint, a seafood restaurant, a salad or sandwich shop, etc.—must be true to its concept. In these examples, variety and balance are constrained within the vision of the business. For example, a burger establishment may approach variety and balance by offering a range of burger patties and toppings; that the menu is skewed heavily or exclusively to burgers is treated not as a variety and balance issue but rather as fidelity to the business concept.

The variables for which variety and balance are most relevant are as follows:

Ingredient and Flavor Generally speaking, a menu should not rely too heavily on any single ingredient in the menu unless such uniformity is key to the business's concept. Thus, an entrée category might include a lamb option, but not all of the entrée choices should include lamb. In fact, repetition of any main ingredient (protein, starch, vegetable, or sauce) is generally not a sound approach to menu planning. Imagine that a customer is repulsed by parsnips. If every entrée includes parsnips, then that customer would have difficulty finding a dish to enjoy. The concept of flavor operates similarly. If every dish on a menu is somewhat sweet, then a person for whom sweetness is not a preferred flavor will not enjoy the dining experience. The same is true for spicy, sour, or salty dishes that dominate a menu category. Subdivided even further, dishes can be thought of as heavy or light, simple or complex, fresh or caramelized, etc.; if a menu relies too heavily on one flavor profile, it will appeal to a smaller audience than it would with greater balance and variety.

There is one more exception to rule of variety in ingredients. A menu planner may consider product utilization when creating menu items. Product utilization, incorporating the byproducts of a single ingredient into more than one dish, helps to keep a business's operating costs and menu prices low. To support the principles of variety and balance, the same ingredient may be used only in separate categories, during different meal periods, or in a very different form. Examples of appropriate product utilization abound. A chef might serve prime rib at dinner and utilize the leftovers in a sandwich at lunch. The potato "scraps" generated from making Parisian potatoes (balls) may be turned into mashed potatoes for another dish. While the nice cuts of cod may be seared for an entrée, the tail end pieces may be tossed into a seafood stew. When a chef can convert ingredient byproducts into something edible rather than throwing those items into the trash, he saves both the business and the customer money.

Cooking Technique   A quality menu usually varies the cooking techniques used within a single menu category. Moist-heat cooking techniques (steaming, simmering, and poaching) yield delicate flavors and lower-fat dishes. The dry-heat cooking techniques of grilling, broiling, roasting, and sautéing generate low-fat dishes with more assertive, caramelized flavors, while frying creates heavier, richer dishes. The combination methods of braising and stewing create extremely rich and tender meals. As some guests prefer certain cooking techniques, a wider range of cooking techniques will appeal to a broader audience. Variety and balance apply equally to the components within a dish as well. It is far more interesting to offer a dish that includes steamed, grilled, fried, and braised components than it is to serve a dish in which all of the ingredients are fried.

Cooking technique impacts not only customer satisfaction but also kitchen work flow. A menu planner is limited to the equipment present (or purchasable) in the kitchen. For example, grilling is not an option if the kitchen does not contain a grill, and the menu planner must take this into account. There is no point in creating a menu item for which the kitchen lacks the proper cooking equipment. Additionally, balance in cooking techniques keeps a single line cook from becoming overloaded with orders. For example, if a six-option menu category has four of the options coming from the sauté station, then the sauté cook will be extremely busy while the other stations remain relatively idle. Alternatively, a menu planner that divides the dishes evenly across the various kitchen workstations will create a better balance and work flow within the kitchen. If separate components of a single dish come from different stations, the menu planner must consider whether the dish can be efficiently executed with the given kitchen layout and work flow. Otherwise, the dish may cause production problems for the entire kitchen.

Temperature and Texture   The mouth feel of a dish is as important to the dining experience as its flavor is. Menu items with a single texture are less interesting to eat than ones with multiple textures. Soft, chewy, crunchy, and crisp components make for an interesting salad or dessert, while a one-dimensional plate of salmon terrine, mashed potato, and butternut squash custard turns diversely textured ingredients into a uniform mouth feel of mush.

Variety in texture and temperature apply equally across menu items and categories. Offering an ice cream sandwich, a room temperature cake, and a warm peach cobbler helps the guest who is sensitive to certain temperature zones. Similarly, a selection of appetizers that are all crisp and crunchy will frustrate a diner who has trouble chewing, while an entrée category saturated with soft, stewed dishes will come across as boring. Variation in cooking technique and ingredients helps to provide variety in texture as well.

Color, Shape, and Size   Repetition of colors, shapes, or sizes across several dishes is less of an issue than it is within a single plate. A plate of all off-white components, such as poached chicken with cauliflower and rice, is unattractive and less appetizing than a dish with a variety of colors. Ingredient shapes and sizes operate similarly. It is far more interesting to eat a creation with different knife cuts than it is to have everything the same shape and size. Not only do different shapes and sizes provide different feels within the mouth, but the visual impact is far more impressive. Since guests eat with their eyes before they consume with their mouths, providing variety and balance in color, shape, and size creates a more enjoyable dining experience for the customer.

Composition and Plate Presentation   Composition and plate presentation are the final variables for which variety and balance enhance the dining experience for the guest. A dish that is impossibly tall may seem spectacular to the guest, but it is less impressive if every dish is presented that way. Having some dishes presented in cast iron skillets, some on colored, rectangular china, and some on traditional round white plates lends interest to the dining experience as guests peer across the table at what others have ordered. Tableside preparations are exciting, but when every dish is assembled tableside, the service becomes tiresome. The best approach to plating is to offer variety in presentation and plate composition. Some plates may be tall and static; others may have a low, circular flow. Some may be intricately composed with each element in its place while others may be simply ladled into a large bowl or crock. The greater the variety, the more interesting the menu is for the guest.

3.3 TRADITIONAL MENU CATEGORIES

While there are no hard and fast rules for naming menu categories, there are some traditional conventions that are commonly used throughout the industry. It is important to note that these naming conventions do not apply for all foodservice business concepts, and the most important drivers for creating category names are the business's theme and the market's needs. A Chinese restaurant may prefer to categorize its entrées under the headings of "Beef," "Chicken," "Pork," and "Seafood." A tapas restaurant, on the other hand, may simply use "Hot Tapas" and "Cold Tapas." What follows are not the only or even the best options, just the most common ones.

3.3.1 Breakfast Menus

Because breakfast is typically a quick meal (except for destination restaurants), breakfast menus tend not to divide their foods based on a sequence of courses. Most breakfast businesses assume that their customers will only order one course. Consequently, breakfast menus are usually divided by the type of food rather than the order in which it is eaten, to help guests find what they are looking for quickly.

Most breakfast menus include an a la carte section for guests who wish to have a lighter breakfast or snack. Not all breakfast customers are hungry in the morning, so they may prefer a simple piece of toast or a cup of yogurt. An a la carte section does not preclude the menu planner from offering a semi a la carte section as well. Semi a la carte options increase sales by packaging multiple items together for one price. The price is lower than it would be if the customer ordered all of the items a la carte, but the package deal usually encourages people to buy more than they would if they only had the a la carte option. Additionally, by putting multiple items together as a single order, the order-taking process is expedited and the seat turnover rate is improved.

Because many customers eat breakfast before heading off to work, it is important that most or all breakfast menu choices are quick to prepare. Foodservice businesses may wish to consider portable menu options that can be eaten on the go. Everything from pastries to hot breakfast sandwiches are easy to sell without tying up table space, and guests can enjoy a meal out without significantly delaying their commute to work. For the sake of speed, the popularity of certain breakfast foods, and their generally lower cost, some operations offer breakfast all day. In such instances, the breakfast items are listed on the menu on their own page, separate from the lunch and dinner

Figure 3–4
An example of an extensive breakfast menu. Printed with the permission of Nick Fifis and Ponzio's Diner.

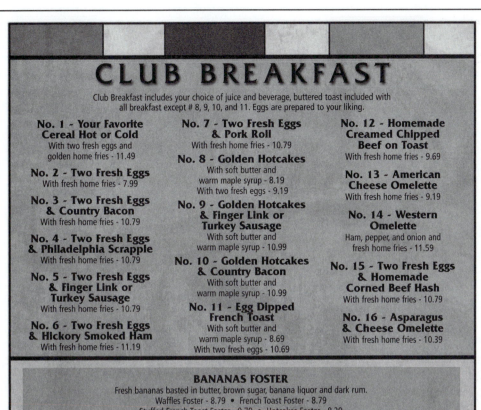

CLUB BREAKFAST

Club Breakfast includes your choice of juice and beverage, buttered toast included with all breakfast except # 8, 9, 10, and 11. Eggs are prepared to your liking.

No. 1 - Your Favorite Cereal Hot or Cold
With two fresh eggs and golden home fries - 11.49

No. 2 - Two Fresh Eggs
With fresh home fries - 7.99

No. 3 - Two Fresh Eggs & Country Bacon
With fresh home fries - 10.79

No. 4 - Two Fresh Eggs & Philadelphia Scrapple
With fresh home fries - 10.79

No. 5 - Two Fresh Eggs & Finger Link or Turkey Sausage
With fresh home fries - 10.79

No. 6 - Two Fresh Eggs & Hickory Smoked Ham
With fresh home fries - 11.19

No. 7 - Two Fresh Eggs & Pork Roll
With fresh home fries - 10.79

No. 8 - Golden Hotcakes
With soft butter and warm maple syrup - 8.19
With two fresh eggs - 9.19

No. 9 - Golden Hotcakes & Finger Link or Turkey Sausage
With soft butter and warm maple syrup - 10.99

No. 10 - Golden Hotcakes & Country Bacon
With soft butter and warm maple syrup - 10.99

No. 11 - Egg Dipped French Toast
With soft butter and warm maple syrup - 8.69
With two fresh eggs - 10.69

No. 12 - Homemade Creamed Chipped Beef on Toast
With fresh home fries - 9.69

No. 13 - American Cheese Omelette
With fresh home fries - 9.19

No. 14 - Western Omelette
Ham, pepper, and onion and fresh home fries - 11.59

No. 15 - Two Fresh Eggs & Homemade Corned Beef Hash
With fresh home fries - 10.79

No. 16 - Asparagus & Cheese Omelette
With fresh home fries - 10.39

BANANAS FOSTER
Fresh bananas basted in butter, brown sugar, banana liquor and dark rum.
Waffles Foster - 8.79 • French Toast Foster - 8.79
Stuffed French Toast Foster - 9.79 • Hotcakes Foster - 8.29

Available on weekends and holidays only.

FRENCH TOAST

Egg Dipped French Toast
Served with powdered sugar, soft butter and warm maple syrup - 5.99

Include any of the following:
Philadelphia Scrapple - 8.79 • Finger Link Sausage - 8.79
Turkey Sausage - 8.79 • Hickory Smoked Ham - 9.19 • Pork Roll - 8.79
Canadian Bacon - 9.19 • Country Bacon - 8.79
Ponzio's Hot Italian Sausage - 9.39
Ponzio's Corned Beef Hash - 8.79 • Two Eggs - 7.99

Stuffed French Toast
Homemade cinnamon bread filled with Philadelphia cream cheese. Dipped in egg and grilled to perfection, topped with cinnamon and powdered sugar. Served with soft butter and warm maple syrup - 6.99

WAFFLES

Served with powdered sugar, soft butter and warm maple syrup - 5.99

Include any of the following:
Philadelphia Scrapple - 8.79 • Finger Link Sausage - 8.79
Turkey Sausage - 8.79 • Hickory Smoked Ham - 9.19
Canadian Bacon - 9.19
Country Bacon - 8.79 • Pork Roll - 8.79
Ponzio's Hot Italian Sausage - 9.39
Ponzio's Corned Beef Hash - 8.79 • Two Eggs - 7.99

EGGS

All egg orders are served with fresh home fries or potato pancakes and choice of toast.

Two Country Eggs (Any Style) - 5.29
Philadelphia Scrapple - 8.09
Finger Link Sausage - 8.09
Turkey Sausage - 8.09
Hickory Smoked Ham - 8.49
Pork Roll - 8.09
Canadian Bacon - 8.49
Country Bacon - 8.09
Ponzio's Hot Italian Sausage - 8.69
Ponzio's Corned Beef Hash - 8.09

GOLDEN HOTCAKES

Five fluffy hotcakes - 5.49
Served with soft butter and warm maple syrup.

Blueberry Hotcakes - 8.29
Include any of the following:
Philadelphia Scrapple - 8.29 • Finger Link Sausage - 8.29
Turkey Sausage - 8.29 • Hickory Smoked Ham - 8.69
Pork Roll - 8.29 • Canadian Bacon - 8.69 • Country Bacon - 8.29
Ponzio's Hot Italian Sausage - 8.89
Ponzio's Corned Beef Hash - 8.29
Two Eggs - 7.49 • Short Stack (3 hotcakes) - 4.49

HOTCAKE, WAFFLE & FRENCH TOAST ADD-ONS

Add Fresh Strawberries and Whipped Cream - 3.50
Add Fresh Bananas and Whipped Cream - 2.50
Add Fresh Blueberries and Whipped Cream - 3.50

Figure 3–4
(Continued)

SMOKED FISH PLATTERS

Smoked White Fish Salad
Served with lettuce, tomato, Kalamata olives, red onions, toasted bagel and cream cheese - 9.99

Smoked Nova Salmon
Served with lettuce, tomato, Kalamata olives, red onions, capers, toasted bagel and cream cheese - 11.99

OMELETTES

Served with fresh home fries or potato pancakes and choice of toast.

Cheese
American, Swiss, provolone, mozzarella, cheddar or imported feta - 6.49

Spanish
Pepper, onion, celery, mushrooms sautéed with tomatoes - 6.79

Western
With ham, pepper, and onion - 8.89

Asparagus & Cheese - 7.69

TRY SOMETHING **NEW!** **Fajita**
Two eggs folded with roasted onions and sweet peppers then topped with cheddar cheese and sour cream - 7.99

TRY SOMETHING **NEW!** **Loaded Potato**
Home fried potatoes folded into two eggs with crispy bacon, chives and cheddar cheese, then topped with sour cream - 9.99

Ham & Cheese - 9.29

Bacon & Cheese
Country bacon and American cheese - 9.29

Spinach & Feta Cheese
Imported feta cheese and spinach - 7.69

Smoked Nova Salmon & Onion
Smoked salmon and sautéed onion - 10.29

Eggs Benedict
Five Variations of our Signature Breakfast
Two poached eggs complemented with our Classic "made from scratch" hollandaise sauce. Served with home fries, coffee and choice of juice.
With
TRY SOMETHING **NEW!** English Muffin & **A Blend of Sautéed Spinach, Onions & Imported Feta Cheese** - 10.59
or
English Muffin & **Canadian Bacon** - 10.29
or
English Muffin & **Smoked Nova Salmon** - 13.29
or
Two **Jumbo Lump Crab Cakes** - 13.29
English Muffin & **Spinach** - 10.29

Available on weekends and holidays only.

REFRESHING FRUITS

Yogurt Parfait
Parfait glass filled with yogurt, granola and berries - 4.29

Half Grapefruit In season - 2.79
Fresh Cut Fruit Bowl - 3.99
Refreshing Melon In season - 2.99

FROM OUR BAKERY

Fresh Danish - 2.49
Fresh Cinnamon Bun
We recommend this heated on the grill with butter - 2.49
Muffin Blueberry, Bran, Corn or Sunrise - 2.49

Scrambled Eggs with Smoked Nova Salmon & Onions - 10.29

NY Strip (8 oz.) & Two Eggs (Any Style) - 16.49

Creamed Chipped Beef
Thin slices of dried beef mixed in a homemade creamy béchamel sauce and smothered on white toast. Served with home fries or potato pancakes - 6.99

CEREALS

Cereal - 3.49
Corn Flakes, Rice Krispies, Raisin Bran, Special K, Froot Loops, Frosted Flakes, or Cheerios
Topped with any of the following:
Bananas - 4.99   Strawberries - 5.99
Blueberries (In Season) - 5.99

Granola with Raisins & Almonds - 3.49
Bananas - 4.99   Strawberries - 5.99
Blueberries - 5.99

Old Fashion Oatmeal
With choice of Raisins, Cinnamon or Brown Sugar - 3.99

Cream of Wheat (Seasonal)
Choice of Raisins, Cinnamon or Brown Sugar - 3.99

SIDE ORDERS

Philadelphia Scrapple - 2.80

Finger Link Sausage - 2.80

Hickory Smoked Ham - 3.20

Turkey Sausage - 2.80

Canadian Bacon - 3.20

Country Bacon - 2.80

Pork Roll - 2.80

Ponzio's Hot Italian Sausage - 3.40

Potato Pancakes - 2.80

Ponzio's Corned Beef Hash - 2.80

Toast with Butter - 1.79
White, Wheat, 6-Grain, Rye, Bagel, English Muffin, Homemade Cinnamon or Homemade Raisin

Toast with Philadelphia Cream Cheese - 2.69

18% gratuity added to all parties of seven or more. • No Personal Checks. • Major Credit Cards Accepted.

Figure 3–4
(Continued)

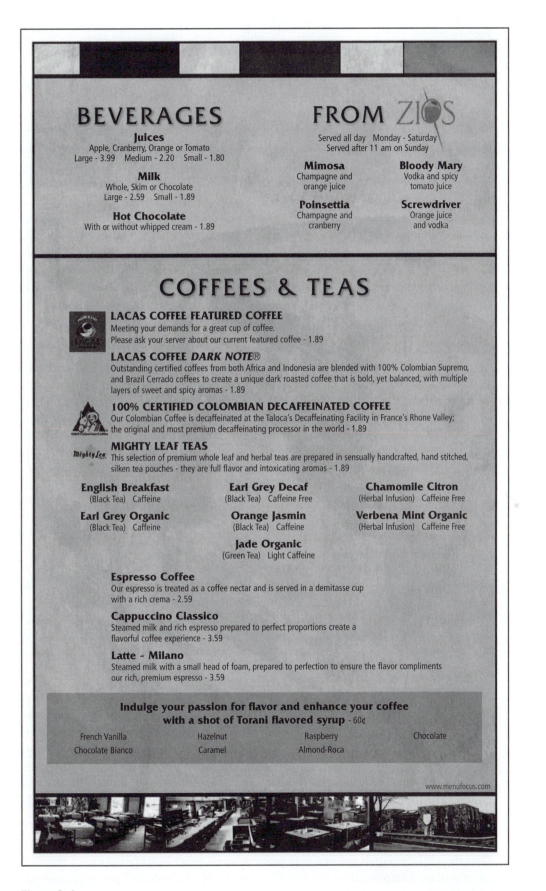

BEVERAGES

Juices
Apple, Cranberry, Orange or Tomato
Large - 3.99   Medium - 2.20   Small - 1.80

Milk
Whole, Skim or Chocolate
Large - 2.59   Small - 1.89

Hot Chocolate
With or without whipped cream - 1.89

FROM ZIOS

Served all day   Monday - Saturday
Served after 11 am on Sunday

Mimosa
Champagne and
orange juice

Bloody Mary
Vodka and spicy
tomato juice

Poinsettia
Champagne and
cranberry

Screwdriver
Orange juice
and vodka

COFFEES & TEAS

LACAS COFFEE FEATURED COFFEE
Meeting your demands for a great cup of coffee.
Please ask your server about our current featured coffee - 1.89

LACAS COFFEE *DARK NOTE*®
Outstanding certified coffees from both Africa and Indonesia are blended with 100% Colombian Supremo,
and Brazil Cerrado coffees to create a unique dark roasted coffee that is bold, yet balanced, with multiple
layers of sweet and spicy aromas - 1.89

100% CERTIFIED COLOMBIAN DECAFFEINATED COFFEE
Our Colombian Coffee is decaffeinated at the Taloca's Decaffeinating Facility in France's Rhone Valley;
the original and most premium decaffeinating processor in the world - 1.89

MIGHTY LEAF TEAS
This selection of premium whole leaf and herbal teas are prepared in sensually handcrafted, hand stitched,
silken tea pouches - they are full flavor and intoxicating aromas - 1.89

English Breakfast
(Black Tea) Caffeine

Earl Grey Decaf
(Black Tea) Caffeine Free

Chamomile Citron
(Herbal Infusion) Caffeine Free

Earl Grey Organic
(Black Tea) Caffeine

Orange Jasmin
(Black Tea) Caffeine

Verbena Mint Organic
(Herbal Infusion) Caffeine Free

Jade Organic
(Green Tea) Light Caffeine

Espresso Coffee
Our espresso is treated as a coffee nectar and is served in a demitasse cup
with a rich crema - 2.59

Cappuccino Classico
Steamed milk and rich espresso prepared to perfect proportions create a
flavorful coffee experience - 3.59

Latte - Milano
Steamed milk with a small head of foam, prepared to perfection to ensure the flavor compliments
our rich, premium espresso - 3.59

**Indulge your passion for flavor and enhance your coffee
with a shot of Torani flavored syrup** - 60¢

French Vanilla	Hazelnut	Raspberry	Chocolate
Chocolate Bianco	Caramel	Almond-Roca	

www.menufocus.com

Figure 3–4
(Continued)

menu options. The same menu with the same category headings can be presented no matter what meal is being served at the time; the menu simply lists the times during which each part of the menu is available.

Some of the most common category headings for a breakfast menu are as follows:

Beverages   Beverages are an important part of the breakfast experience for most customers. Unlike lunch, brunch, and dinner, which may use a separate beverage menu for alcoholic options, breakfast beverages are almost always listed on the same menu as the food. Caffeinated drinks, such as coffee and tea, are a must. Casual operations may offer very few hot drinks, while fancier establishments may include espresso drinks and hot chocolate, too. Juice is an essential inclusion for the beverage section. Orange juice is the most popular juice option, but grapefruit, pineapple, apple, tomato, and others may be offered as well. Milk should also be listed; the number of milk options (whole, skim, 2%, soy, etc.) to offer depends on the local market's taste preferences. The number and type of options listed under the beverage heading immediately conveys the style and theme of the establishment. Restaurants serving only coffee, decaf coffee, and tea suggest a small-town, homey feel, while those offering a range of espresso drinks and tea options imply a more cosmopolitan (and pricy) dining experience.

Entrées   Because of the nature of breakfast, some operations opt to list all of their multicomponent menu items under the single heading "Entrées." For a shorter menu with less than a dozen choices, this makes a lot of sense. It makes the number of choices appear bountiful and allows the menu planner to organize the options in any order. (The value of menu item placement will be discussed in Chapter 10.) Other breakfast places choose to categorize their menu items by main ingredient type.

Eggs and Omelets   Eggs are an extremely common offering at breakfast, and many establishments prefer to list them as their own category. An option of eggs cooked to order (customer choice) is popular in most operations, typically served with meat, toast, and/or potatoes. However, offering a variety of egg dishes lends interest to the menu and may help to increase sales revenue. Poached egg dishes (e.g., Benedict or Florentine), frittatas, and omelets are high-value items for which a restaurant can charge more. Omelets, in particular, allow a menu planner to show off a wide range of classic and local flavor combinations that may include meat, vegetables, cheese, and/or seafood. Egg sandwiches also allow a restaurant to offer hot to-go options to its patrons. When the number of omelet and egg offerings is significant, the menu planner may choose to separate "Eggs" and "Omelets" into two different categories.

Griddle Items   Another popular hot breakfast category is "Griddle Cakes" or items "From the Griddle." These include pancakes, French toast, waffles, and, in some cases, crepes and blintzes. Because of the high carbohydrate content of these items, they may be served with meat, eggs, or fruit, but not usually with toast or potatoes. The possibilities for flavor variation within this category abound. Pancakes may include a range of ingredients or toppings beyond the classic maple syrup. French toast and waffles may be stuffed or garnished with various sweet or savory toppings as well. Crepes and blintzes provide a similar canvas for culinary creativity. If the menu focuses exclusively on one type of griddle quick bread, the category heading may simply list that item by name, such as "Pancakes," or "Hot Cakes."

Cereals   While cereals are not as popular as some other breakfast options, they are an important component of any breakfast menu. Hot cereals and porridges provide high-fiber, low-fat nutrition for guests with dietary concerns. In some operations, they are incorporated creatively rather than relegated to "old standby" status. For example, grits might be served plain or with fish, cheese, and/or chiles. Oatmeal might be served simply with brown sugar and milk or more innovatively with other grains, dried fruit, and nut milk. Cold cereals, too, are important for guests, especially children, who prefer not to waiver from their morning routine. Cold cereals may be purchased ready-to-eat in individual boxes/bowls, or in bulk. If the operation serves a captive audience, the options should not all be sugary cereals but rather should include a range of flavor profiles. An upscale restaurant may choose to prepare certain cold cereals, such as granola or Birchermüesli, from scratch. When offering cereals, it is important to provide milk options—whole and reduced fat at a minimum.

Other Breakfast Entrées   Depending on the business, some foodservice establishments choose to offer specialty items that do not fit easily under any of the other category headings. Examples include steak and eggs, bagels and lox, corned beef hash, or Greek yogurt with fruit and honey. If these items are not simply placed under a general "Entrées" heading, they may be grouped under a category entitled "House Specialties" or something similar. Such specialty items may be an attraction for customers as they are not readily available at all breakfast operations.

A La Carte or Sides   As stated earlier, most breakfast menus include an a la carte section, often entitled "A la Carte" or "Sides," depending on what options are included under the heading. Side dishes for a breakfast menu usually include breakfast meats, individual eggs, potatoes, breads, and one or more fruit options. A more complete a la carte section will also include pastries, muffins, bagels, doughnuts, and yogurt. A la carte sections, from which some entrée accompaniments are pulled, are an opportunity to show off regional products and to lend interest to a menu. In addition to bacon and sausage, meat options might include country ham or scrapple. Muffins and pastries may be made from scratch in a variety of flavors. Potatoes can be prepared in a wide range of styles beyond basic hash browns. In short, while some menu planners treat the a la carte section as an afterthought, it should serve the customer's needs, add some uniqueness to the menu, and work symbiotically with the entrée listings. Some of the a la carte choices will naturally be components intended as add-ons to entrées, but the section should also satisfy the needs of those guests who wish to patronize the establishment without indulging in a large meal.

3.3.2 Lunch and Dinner Menus

Lunch and dinner menus are generally more comparable to each other than they are to breakfast menus. In fact, some foodservice businesses use the same menu for lunch and for dinner. While there are similarities to the way that lunch and dinner menus are categorized, there are a few differences between the two meals that are important to address. First, Americans typically eat less food over a shorter period of time at lunch than they do at dinner (special occasion lunches excepted). Consequently, lunch options should be quick to prepare, and they should be served in smaller portions at lower prices than their dinner counterparts. It is possible to offer the same menu at lunch and dinner but with smaller prices and portion sizes at the earlier meal. Second, sandwiches, soups, and salads are more popular as entrées at lunch than they are at dinner, where soups and salads are often treated as preludes or accompaniments to a more substantial entrée. Thus, lunch menus tend to rely more heavily on these menu options than dinner menus do. Otherwise, the categories for lunch and dinner menus tend to be the same. If the local market includes large numbers of individuals with significant amounts of leisure time (stay-at-home parents or retirees, for example), lunch business may include guests willing to linger over several courses of food, just as they do at dinner. Other operations may only service guests with time for a single quick-service course. Tailoring the menu categories and offerings to the target market's eating habits is always the best approach.

The most commonly used menu categories for lunch and dinner are as follows:

Appetizers   The purpose of an appetizer is both to awaken the taste buds and to lengthen the dining experience. Appetizers should be flavorful but small in portion. Acidic or spicy ingredients work well as they foment salivation. Too often, restaurants serve rich, heavy appetizers that cause the consumer to fill up just as the meal is beginning. Portions that are too large or appetizers that are too filling can undermine the business goal of increasing revenue. With some exceptions, large numbers of guests opting for appetizers instead of entrées suggests that the appetizers are not properly serving their function. Bar and lounge environments in which many customers opt for drinks and appetizers rather than for full meals are the obvious exception to this rule.

As with other menu categories, appetizers should provide variety and balance across the category. Appetizers should include cold and hot options as well as meat, seafood, poultry, and vegetarian options. Cooking technique should vary as well. Appetizers are also excellent opportunities to utilize byproducts from ingredients used in the entrée section. No matter what ingredients and cooking techniques are used, foodservice businesses should be able to prepare appetizers quickly. As these are the first courses guests will consume, an extended cooking time for a single appetizer will leave guests without food for an uncomfortably long period of time after being seated.

In operations with shorter menus, the appetizer heading may include soups and salads; in other establishments, soups and salads may have their own category listing. In upscale restaurants, separate listings for appetizers versus soups and salads may encourage sales of multiple pre-entrée courses in ways that a single category label will not.

Soups   Soup on a menu plays an important role both for the guest and for the establishment. Customers enjoy the homey, familiar feel of this nutrient-dense concoction. Hearty soups, sometimes paired with a salad, may be a complete meal for those on a tight budget or low-calorie diet. Soups serve as a welcoming introduction or liquid respite when part of a multicourse meal. From the chef's perspective, soups are the ultimate opportunity for product utilization. Scraps of vegetables, bits of meat or fish, leftover rice can all become part of an elegant soup even if they are inappropriately shaped for use in another dish.

When planning soup options for a menu, variety of type is critical. Soups come in many forms including cream, broth, puree, and specialty. (Specialty encompasses many classic national and international soups that do not fall into the other categories.) Menu planners are wise to select soups of different types for their menus. For example, cream of broccoli, chicken noodle, lentil puree, and gazpacho soup would all appeal to different audiences, but a series of "cream of" soups would only attract guests who prefer that particular style. In warmer months, offering a cold soup helps to increase menu variety and soup sales.

Some operations offer soup in two sizes—a cup or a bowl. The bowl is always the bigger portion. Having two sizes allows for guests to enjoy a small cup of soup as an appetizer or a bowl as a main course. Restaurants that wish to encourage multicourse sales often offer only a single small size.

Salads   Salad, like soup, can be an accompaniment to a larger meal or a standalone entrée. The most basic of salads consists of simple mixed greens, but the garnish possibilities are endless. Vegetables, fruits (fresh or dried), nuts, seeds, cheeses, croutons, olives, legumes, eggs, seafood, meat, and poultry are all appropriate additions to a salad. Side salads usually rely on simplicity so as not to overshadow an entrée. Entrée salads typically include a hearty portion of protein, such as chicken, shrimp, steak, cheese, or beans. Sometimes, a restaurant allows the guest to choose whether to add animal protein to a salad for an additional cost, as is common with chicken Caesar salad. In some operations, entrée salads are listed under "Entrées," particularly on a lunch menu.

No matter its size or function, there are certain qualities that guests expect from a salad. Variety of texture, color, and flavor is critical in almost every salad. While the texture and color differences are obvious in a mixed green salad with dried cranberries, orange sections, chevre, red onion, and sunflower seeds, the variation is less conspicuous in a traditional Caesar salad. However, the crunch of the croutons, the crisp bite of the lettuce, and the creaminess of the dressing all lend a textural interest to the classic Caesar that is not present in a salad composed only of romaine lettuce, oil, and vinegar. A salad that includes only lettuce and dressing should use several lettuces to provide a variety of flavors and shapes. While some chefs prefer to pair a specific dressing with each salad, other operations offer guests their choice of dressing. When guests choose their own salad dressing, four to five dressing options are typically considered a minimum for the menu.

High-quality, fresh ingredients are essential for raw salads. Wilted, browned, or sandy lettuce is unappealing to eat, and it is impossible to hide in a salad. If certain fresh ingredients cannot be reliably sourced, then they should not be included among the salad options. Cooked or processed ingredients make perfectly acceptable salads and are often easier to obtain during certain times of the year. Cabbage slaws, pickled vegetables, or cooked beans provide a nice contrast to the more common lettuce salad. And while many salads are served cold, they need not all be so; for example, a warm bacon dressing over spinach gives some temperature variation to this popular category of food. Finally, although salads are typically served prior to the entrée in the United States, there is no reason that a salad could not be offered after the entrée as is done in parts of Europe.

Sandwiches Sandwiches come in almost limitless varieties. The outer wrappers may be tortillas, bread slices, biscuits, buns, or lettuce, just to name a few. They may be served hot or cold, closed or open faced. Typically, a sandwich includes one or more main items, a spread, and some garnish within the wrapper. The main items may be fresh or cured meat or fish, bound salads, cheeses, or vegan selections such as mushrooms or falafel. The spreads may be common condiments, like mustard or mayonnaise, or they may be house-made concoctions like herb oil or cranberry butter. Garnishes, too, span a range from the traditional lettuce, tomato, and onion found on hamburgers to anything that adds flavor and textural interest to the complete dish.

Sandwiches are often served with a side of fries, chips, or salad to add another element to the dish. Because they do not always require utensils, sandwiches make excellent options for meals made to go. Unlike the aforementioned menu categories, sandwiches may be a standalone category for any meal of the day, including breakfast, but if they are few in number, they may be subsumed under the "Entrées" category.

Entrées The "Entrées" category on a menu is usually the longest and most important part of the menu for most foodservice concepts. This section contains the items that most guests order if they are only going to order one thing, and its contents are often the most expensive on the menu. Depending on the business's brand, the entrées may be portioned quite large to satisfy guests who do not order anything else, or they

ZEST
★ AMERICAN BISTRO ★

starters

Seasonal Soup 4.95   **Tomato Soup** 4.95

Mixed Greens 4.50
chopped tomatoes, preserved lemon chive vinaigrette

Beet Carpaccio Salad 6.50
arugula, goat cheese, candied pecans, sherry vinaigrette

Caesar Salad 6.25
romaine, garlic croutons, anchovy, parmigiano reggiano,
caesar dressing

Spicy Ahi Tartare* 9.50
avocado & mango salsa, fried ginger, wonton chips

Fried Ginger Calamari 9.50
ginger glaze, wasabi, jalapenos, chili peppers

Sauteed Garlic Shrimp 9.50
olive oil, garlic, arbol chili pepper, brandy

Artichoke & Cheese Dip 7.95
artichoke hearts, asiago, parmesan, pita chips

entrées & specialty sandwiches

Southwest Chicken Risotto 12.95
roasted tomato salsa, corn & black bean relish, pico de gallo,
avocado, queso fresco, fried corn tortilla strips

Mediterranean Penne Pasta 11.95
kalamata olives, preserved lemon, artichoke hearts,
roasted garlic, kale, fennel, marinara sauce
chicken 13.95   shrimp 15.95

Blackened Salmon with Crab Bearnaise* 14.95
lump crab, garlic mashed potatoes, sauteed kale

Shrimp Risotto 13.95
asparagus, mushrooms, white wine, garlic

Grilled Tuna Club* 12.50
curried slaw, pancetta, arugula, tomato, garlic aioli, grilled
sourdough, served with mixed greens or fries

Roasted Leg of Lamb 12.95
caramelized onions, feta, pomegranate bbq, grilled flatbread,
served with mixed greens or fries

Fried Oyster Po' Boy 12.50
arugula, tomato, spicy remoulade, french roll, served with
mixed greens or fries

entrée salads

Chicken Milanese 11.95
arugula, capers, pine nuts, tomatoes, parmesan,
tomato vinaigrette

Bistro Steak Salad* 13.95
romaine, tomato, blue cheese, fried pickled onions,
red wine vinaigrette

Soy Ginger Salmon* 14.95
arugula, carrots, purple cabbage, sesame noodles, peanuts,
tomato ginger vinaigrette
tuna 16.95

Spinach Cobb 10.95
egg, granny smith apple, manchego cheese, bacon, avocado,
pickled onions, sherry vinaigrette
chicken 12.95   steak 13.95   shrimp 15.95

$12 Bistro Lunch Special *

Monday thru Friday 11am-3pm

Choice of Tomato Soup or Mixed Green salad AND any Bistro
Sandwich served with mixed greens or fries.

*excludes specialty sandwiches

bistro sandwiches choice of mixed greens or fries

Grilled Asiago, Pancetta and Tomato on sourdough 8.95

Muffaletta with Smoked Turkey 9.50
provolone, kalamata olives, arugula, basil oil, toasted ciabatta

Grilled Breast of Chicken 9.50
roasted peppers, pickled onions, citrus mayo, toasted ciabatta

Char Grilled Cheddar Burger* 9.50
lettuce, tomato, onion, brioche bun

Grilled Portabello 9.95
roasted tomato, arugula, feta, pesto, toasted ciabatta

Falafel 9.50
lettuce, tomato, pickled onions, garlic tahini, grilled flatbread

sides

Parmesan Polenta 4.25   Sauteed Kale 4.25
Garlic Mashed Potatoes 4.25 24 Hour Tomatoes 4.25
Herb Fries 3.50   Grilled Asparagus 4.25
Sweet Potato Mash 4.25

~ lunch ~

* This item may be served undercooked. Consuming raw or undercooked products may increase your risk of foodborne illness.   Executive Chef Dot Steck

Figure 3–5
This lunch menu includes multiple entrée salad and sandwich options. Courtesy of Amanda Briggs and Zest American Bistro.

may be somewhat smaller in size with the expectation that customers always order multiple courses.

The term "Entrées" may not actually appear on the menu. Some operations use the term "Main Courses" while others divide the entrée options among several categories based on the main ingredients or on the cooking technique used. For example, a restaurant that focuses on just a few cooking techniques might use headings like "From the Hearth" or "From the Grill." Others may use the labels "Chicken," "Pork," "Beef," etc., as they do in many Chinese restaurants, or "Pasta," "Meat," "Seafood," as is done in some Italian restaurants. As always, the terminology used should mesh seamlessly with the business's concept and theme.

Unless the menu is strictly a la carte, the entrées include all sides and accompaniments that are part of the main course. Depending on the concept, these sides may be listed as part of the entrée description or in a separate section that allows guests to choose their own sides. When the sides are predetermined by the menu planner, the entirety of the plate should be considered for variety and balance in shape, color, flavor, texture, and cooking technique. Variety and balance are important for the category as a whole, too. Assuming the business concept permits it, the entrée section should include meat, poultry, seafood, and vegetarian options. In some operations, pizza, pasta, and casseroles may represent a significant portion of the entrée offerings and may even merit their own subheading.

Sides or Accompaniments Some menus include a section entitled "Sides" or "Accompaniments" from which guests choose the starches and vegetables to pair with their entrée. Even businesses that predetermine the entrée accompaniments may include a list of sides for guests who wish to order additional portions or for eaters who prefer to make a meal out of side dishes. As with the other categories, this section should provide variety and balance. The vegetable choices should include lighter options, such as steamed with herbs, and heavier choices, such as fried or buttered. The vegetables should come from a range of colors (not all green, for example) and families (as in not all from the cabbage family). Several sides should be vegetarian for those who do not eat meat. In some operations, fruits like applesauce or peaches may be included among the choices, too. Starches follow a similar set of guidelines, though it is not uncommon to see potatoes listed several times with different preparations, as in fried, baked, or mashed. Still, potatoes should not be the only choice for a starch. Rice, beans, corn, quinoa, couscous, and pasta are only some of the possible options for starchy sides. Because nutrition-minded guests often select one starch and one vegetable (or two vegetables), it is important not to overload the "Sides" category with starches. For example, if only five sides are listed, potatoes, rice, beans, and couscous should not represent four of them. Vegetables provide a greater range of colors and flavors than starches do anyway.

Desserts Some restaurants locate desserts on their own menu, while others include them on the main menu. Generally speaking, the more upscale the dining experience, the more appropriate it is to give desserts their own menu. Desserts, like the other categories, offer a huge opportunity for variety and balance. Selections may include cakes, custards, fruit, nuts, chocolate, frozen treats, and other types of desserts. A dessert menu that offers six different pies is not as interesting as one that lists six vastly different desserts. Besides, a guest who does not care for pie would never order dessert if pie were the only option. Menu planners can account for variety within a dessert, too. A single dessert may combine hot and cold temperatures, soft and crunchy textures, and sweet and tart flavors. As a dessert exhibits greater variety, not only does it become more interesting, but it also commands a higher sales price.

Starters

Goat Cheese Fritters
Crispy Panko Crusted with Aged Balsamic Dressing and Grilled Brioche $8

Chesapeake Bay Oysters on a Half Shell
$9 for 1/2 Dozen / $15 for 1 Dozen / $26 for 2 Dozen

Brewer's Famous Buffalo Oysters
Six Lightly Fried Bay Oysters, Blue Cheese Dressing, Buffalo Sauce and Lemon Wedge $12

Eastern Shore Classic Style Calamari
*Fried House-Breaded Old Bay Seasoned Calamari Rings with Cocktail Sauce,
Lemon and Smoked Tomato Aioli $10*

Korean Style BBQ Pork Belly
Grilled Kurobuta Pork Belly with Sesame Hoisin Sauce and Kimchi $12

Chili Cheese Nachos
*Baked Corn Tortilla Chips Topped with Beef and Black Bean Chili, Melted Jack and
Cheddar Cheese, Banana Peppers, Pico De Gallo and Sour Cream $11*

Fried Pickles
Cajun Battered Pickle Spears with Ranch and Smoked Tomato Aioli $5

Crispy Fried Chicken Fingers
*Lightly Fried Chicken Tenders with Shoestring Fries
Choice of: Honey Mustard, BBQ or Buffalo Sauce $8*

Screamin' Alley Wings
*Tossed in Buttery Hot Sauce with Blue Cheese Dressing and Crisp Celery Sticks
$8 for 1/2 dozen / $14 for 1 dozen*

Maryland Crab and Poblano-Chili Cheese Dip
Piping Hot and Served with Corn Tortillas and Spicy Tomato Salsa $11

Jalapeño Cheese-Stuffed Soft Pretzel
Served with Herbed Buttermilk Ranch Dip and Dijon Mustard $6

Chef's Housemade Soup Selections

Brewer's Clam Chowder
Little Neck Clams, Old Bay Cream, Potatoes, Celery and Onion $5 cup/ $7 Bowl

Bowl of Chili
*Beef and Black Bean Chili Topped with Red Onion, Jack and Cheddar Cheese
Served with a side of Tortilla Chips $7*

Bistro-Style French Onion Soup
Caramelized Onions, Rich Beef Broth, Garlic Croutons and Melted Provolone Cheese $6

Our Soup of the Day
Changes Daily with Chef's Mood.....

April 11, 2012

Figure 3–6
This dinner menu provides a good example of various ways to categorize menu items.
Printed with the permission of Brewer's Alley.

Specialty Sandwiches

All Sandwiches Come with a Kosher Pickle Spear and Your Choice of French Fries, Cole Slaw or a Cup of Our Soup of the Day

Pete's Smoked Pulled Pork Barbeque
House-Smoked with Aged Hickory for Fourteen Hours! Piled High on a Toasted Kaiser Roll with Creamy Cole Slaw and Brewer's Barbeque Sauce $9

Italian Hoagie
Capicolla, Salami, Mortadella, Provolone, Lettuce, Tomato, Onion and Oregano Aioli Served on Toasted Amoroso Roll $11

PBLT
Grilled Pork Belly with Lettuce, Tomato and Honey Mayo on Grilled Brioche Bread $12

BBQ Chicken Wrap
Grilled Red Onion, Bacon, Barbeque Sauce, Jack Cheddar Cheese, Lettuce and Tomato Wrapped in a Flour Tortilla $10

Nezih's Grilled Chicken Sandwich
Grilled Chicken Breast, Pepper Jack, Turkish Chili, Feta Aioli, Lettuce, Fresh Sliced Jalapenos and Avocado on a Kaiser Roll $12

Roasted Jumbo Lump Crabcake
Fresh Crabmeat Seasoned with Old Bay and Served with Smoked Tomato Aioli, Lettuce and Tomato on Toasted Kaiser Roll $18

Portabella Mushroom Panini
Brewer's Hand Made Mozzarella, Roasted Red Pepper, Arugula and Basil Aioli on Panini Pressed Ciabatta Bread $12

Crispy Fried Cod Sandwich
Lightly Battered Cod Fillet, House Made Tarter Sauce, Lettuce and Tomato on a Kaiser Roll $12

Black Bean Burger
Black Beans, Cilantro, Cumin, Red and Green Peppers with Pico de Gallo and Housemade Guacamole on Toasted Kaiser Roll $8

Add Your Choice of White Cheddar, Swiss, Pepper-Jack, American, Provolone, or Blue Cheese for $1.00

Salads

Organic Mixed Greens Salad
Earth Bound Farms Certified Organic Spring Mix tossed in House Champagne Vinaigrette with European Cucumbers, Baby Tomatoes and Sliced Red Onions .... $5 Half/$8 Entree

Classic Caesar Salad
Crisp Romaine Hearts tossed in Creamy Caesar Dressing with Garlic Croutons and Parmesan Cheese .... $5 Half/$8 Entree

Bacon Spinach Salad
Baby Spinach, Hickory Bacon, Shallots, Hard Boiled Egg and Warm Dijon Bacon Vinaigrette $10

Looking For A Little More on Your Salad Then Add to Any of the Above:
Chicken $3, Flank Steak $5, Grilled Shrimp $5, Goat Cheese Fritters $5 or Grilled Salmon $8

Grilled Steak and Iceberg Salad
Marinated Grilled Flank Steak with Crispy Iceberg Lettuce, Creamy Blue Cheese Dressing, Crispy Onion Straws and Firecracker Oil $13

Beef Taco Salad
Marinated Grilled Flank Steak, Crisp Romaine, Field Greens. Jicama, Green Peppers, Tomatoes, Bermuda Onions. Tortilla Chips and Jalapeno-Cilantro Lime Vinaigrette $14

Figure 3–6
(Continued)

Half Pound Corn-Fed Beef Burgers

All Burgers Come with a Kosher Pickle Spear and Your Choice of French Fries, Cole Slaw or a Cup of Our Soup of the Day

Alley Burger
One-Half Pound of Lean Hereford Beef with Crispy Tobacco Onions, Leaf Lettuce and Vine-Ripe Tomato. Served Plain on a Toasted Kaiser Roll $9

Add Your Choice of White Cheddar, Swiss, Pepper-Jack, American, Provolone, or Blue Cheese for $1.00

Mushroom Burger
One-Half Pound of Lean Hereford Beef with Sautéed Mushrooms, Grilled Onions, Lettuce, Tomato and Swiss Cheese on a Kaiser Roll $13

Buffalo Burger
One-Half Pound of Lean Hereford Beef with Blue Cheese, Buffalo Aioli, Lettuce and Tomato on a Kaiser Roll $11

Blackened Burger
One-Half Pound of Lean Hereford Beef with Blackened Seasoning, Pepper Jack Cheese, Lettuce, Tomato, Red Onion and Horseradish Cream on a Kaiser Roll $12

Dijon Burger
One-Half Pound of Lean Hereford Beef with Double Cheddar Cheese, Grilled Red Onion, Dijon Horseradish Cream, Lettuce and Tomato on a Kaiser Roll $11

Ludicrous Burger
One-Half Pound of Lean Hereford Beef Stuffed between Two Grilled Cheese Sandwiches with Bacon, Smoked Tomato Aioli and Barbeque Sauce $14

The Grill

(Land items come with Au Jus and Sea items come with Garlic Butter)

LAND:	SEA:
TENDERLOIN STEAK 10 oz....$28	**RAINBOW TROUT 9 oz....$16**
RIBEYE STEAK 12 oz $22	**MAHI-MAHI 8 oz....$19**
NEW YORK STRIP 12 oz...$23	**SHRIMP 10 oz....$18**
VEAL RIB CHOP 14 oz....$32	**CHEF'S FRESH FISH OF THE DAY....MP**

ADD ANY OF THESE SIDES TO YOUR GRILL ITEM:
Sweet Potato Fries, Individual Mac & Cheese $5 each
House Cut Fries, Vegetable Fried Rice or Twice Baked Potato $4 each
Shoestring Fries, Sauteed Asparagus, Broccoli Crowns, Creamy Mashers or Vegetable Melange $3 each

"Warning - The consumption of raw or undercooked eggs, meat, poultry, seafood or shellfish may increase your risk of food borne illness."

Check Out Our Beautiful 2nd Floor Banquet Spaces Overlooking Historic Downtown Frederick. They are Perfect for Rehearsal Dinners, Wedding Receptions, Birthday or Retirement Parties or any Other Special Occasions

Figure 3–6
(Continued)

Big Plates

Wood-Fired Smokehouse "Macaroni and Cheese"
Our Comforting Favorite From the Wood-Oven with Three Melted Cheeses, Ripe Tomato and Ziti Noodles -- Served with Roasted Garlic Ciabatta Bread $11
Topped with Smoked Country-Cured Ham For $2 More
 # India Pale Ale (2009 Bronze GABF English Style IPA Winner & 2010 Silver World Cup Winner)

Granny Smith's Salmon
Grilled Atlantic Salmon, Sautéed Tart Apples, Olive Oil-Scallion Mashed Potatoes and Apple-Soy Reduction $18
 # 1634 Ale

Ancho-Chili Steak
Spice Rubbed Grilled 10 oz Skirt Steak with Ancho Chili Meat Sauce and Avocado Butter $21
 # Nut Brown Ale

Jumbo Lump Crabcake
Oven-Roasted and Served with Creamy Potato Puree, Corn Relish, Sautéed Asparagus and Old Bay Butter .... $19 Single / $34 Double
 # Kölsch (1998 Bronze GABF Winner)

Chesapeake Surf and Turf
Old Bay Seasoned 5 oz Filet Mignon and 4 oz Jumbo Lump Crab Cake with Creamy Mashers, Sautéed Asparagus, Red Wine Jus and Old Bay Butter $31
 # Nut Brown Ale

Blackened Tilapia
Cajun Seared Tilapia Fillet, Andouille Sausage and Yellow Corn Fried Rice, Old Bay Butter and Horseradish Cream $17
 # India Pale Ale (2009 Bronze GABF English Style IPA Winner & 2010 Silver World Cup Winner)

Cheese Tortellini
Ricotta and Parmesan Stuffed Pasta with Alfredo Sauce, Roasted Red Peppers and Spinach $15
 # India Pale Ale (2009 Bronze GABF English Style IPA Winner & 2010 Silver World Cup Winner)

Fish and Chips
Old Bay Battered North Atlantic Cod with Crispy Shoestring Fries, Creamy Coleslaw and Our Housemade Tartar Sauce $15
 # Kölsch (1998 Bronze GABF Winner)

Crispy Spare Ribs
Braised and Fried Pork Spare Ribs with Hickory Barbeque Sauce, Twice Baked Potato and Coleslaw $16
 # 1634 Ale

Chesapeake Chicken
Panko Crusted Chicken Breast, Jumbo Lump Crab Butter, Fried Oysters, Tartar Sauce, Asparagus and Creamy Mashers $22
 # India Pale Ale (2009 Bronze GABF English Style IPA Winner & 2010 Silver World Cup Winner)

Our Brewmaster's Suggested Pairing

Figure 3–6
(Continued)

Wood-Fired Pizza

Classic Pepperoni
Slices of Pavone Pepperoni with Marinara Sauce and Shredded Mozzarella Cheese
$10 Small/$16 Large

Barbeque Chicken Pizza
Roasted Chicken Breast, Hickory Smoked Barbeque Sauce, Red Onions, Cilantro, Mozzarella, Jack and Cheddar Cheese .... *$11 Small/$17 Large*

Meat Monster
Italian Sausage, Hereford Ground Beef, Bacon, Pepperoni, Marinara and Mozzarella Cheese
$12 Small/$18 Large

Margherita Pizza
Brewer's Hand Made Mozzarella, Sliced Tomato, Fresh Basil, Roasted Garlic and Marinara Sauce .... *$10 Small/$16 Large*

Chipotle Pork Pizza
House Smoked and Hand Pulled Pork, Spicy Barbeque Sauce, Black Beans, Pico De Gallo and Jack-Cheddar Cheese .... *$12 Small/$18 Large*

Country Ham Pizza
Diced Country Ham, Caramelized Onions, Spinach, Garlic Oil and Mozzarella Cheese
$12 Small/$18 Large

Chicken Fajita Pizza
Roasted Chicken Breast, Red Onions, Red and Green Peppers, Creamy Salsa, Cilantro and Jack-Cheddar Cheese .... *$11 Small/$17 Large*

California Dreamin' XVI
Brewer's Hand Made Mozzarella, Garlic Roasted Eggplant, Marinara, Kalamata Olives, Capers and Oregano .... *$12 Small/$18 Large*

Wood-Fired Pizza of the Day
Please Check with Your Server

Substitutions and additional toppings are subject to extra charges

> **Every Thursday Night**
> **1¼ lb Whole Maine Lobster or**
> **Grilled 10 oz Choice New York Strip Steak Dinner**
> **$14.95**
> **Get Both for $25.95**

Figure 3–6
(Continued)

Sides

Individual Mac & Cheese
Creamy and Cheesy!!! $6

Sweet Potato Fries
Served with a side of Ranch Dressing $6

Twice Baked Potato
Bacon, Cheddar and Jack Cheese $5

Broccoli Crowns
Steamed with Butter $4

Vegetable Melange
*Zucchini, Squash, Carrots and Cherry
Tomatoes* $4

French Fries
Crunchy and Hot!!! $4

House Cut Fries
Cut, Cooked and Seasoned in House $5

Sautéed Asparagus
Jumbo Crispy Stalks $4

Vegetable Fried Rice
Stir Fried Rice with Carrots and Corn $5

Creamy Mashers
Creamy and Buttery $4

For the Kids

Pepperoni Pita Pizza
Traditional Cheese Pita Pizza
Peanut Butter and Jelly Sandwich with French Fries
Grilled Cheese with French Fries
Chicken Dinosaurs and French Fries
All kids meal $6 including soft drink (Root Beer refills .50 cents)

Final Temptations

Warm Double Chocolate Brownie Sundae
*Topped with Brewer's Housemade Vanilla Ice Cream, Chocolate and Caramel Syrups,
Crushed Pecans and Whipped Cream* $6

Blueberry Cobbler
*Blueberries Topped with Cinnamon Crumble Served Warm with Brewer's Housemade Vanilla
Ice Cream* $6

Chocolate Crème Brulee
Fresh Strawberry and Whipped Cream $5

Nutella Cheesecake
Nutella Ganache, Whipped Cream and Fresh Mint $5

The "Elvis"
Peanut Butter Mousse Tart with Banana and Chocolate Ganache on Cookie Dough $6

Lemon Meringue Tart
Raspberry Coulis, Whipped Cream and Fresh Mint $6

Chocolate Hazelnut Terrine
Layers of Flourless Chocolate Cake and Hazelnut Ganache with Caramel and Chocolate Sauce
$6

Brewmaster's Draft Root Beer Float
*A Classic Combination of Brewer's Housemade Vanilla Ice Cream and
Old Dominion's Draft Root Beer Served in Our Pint Glass with Hershey's Chocolate Syrup
and a Candied Cherry* $5

Figure 3–6
(Continued)

There are pros and cons to listing desserts on the main menu. As guests make their entrée selections, they may see a dessert and begin craving it early. Even if they are stuffed at the end of the main course, they may still order dessert just to satisfy the craving. Table tents, which market desserts throughout the meal, have a similar effect. On the other hand, a customer who sees interesting dessert options too early may avoid ordering appetizers in order to save room for dessert. The process of bringing an entire menu to a table just for a guest to read the tiny dessert section at the bottom of the page is also less elegant. It leaves less space for the marketing of dessert, and it reminds customers of everything they have already eaten. Simple, straightforward desserts in a casual restaurant do just fine in their own section of the main menu; more complex desserts in need of description do not.

Cheese and Charcuterie   While a separate cheese section on a menu is not extremely common, it is slowly seeing a resurgence in upscale restaurants in certain parts of the country. Cheese may serve as an appetizer, as the course between the entrée and dessert, or as a dessert alternative. Because it goes well with wine, guests may order cheese as they finish off their wine from the main course. Some menu planners choose to list the cheese course on both the main menu and on a separate dessert menu to appeal to customers who prefer cheese at different points in the meal. Restaurants in cheese-making regions of the country often do well selling a local cheese course to tourists.

Variety in a cheese course comes from the milk source (cow, goat, sheep), the texture (soft, firm, hard), the origin (local or international), and the kind of processing (blue, smoked, aged). The menu planner may choose to offer a single plate that includes a predetermined set of cheeses or to list a range of cheeses from which the customer may choose. Either way, variety is key. With the cheese course, the menu planner may choose to offer fruit or other sweet condiments, such as jams, honey, or fig paste, to balance the saltiness of the cheese. An accompaniment of crackers, toast, or some other neutral base on which to spread the softer cheeses is essential.

One recent trend is to pair charcuterie and cheese as an appetizer or even as an entire menu category. As some operations focus on artisanal products, a few chefs have taken to creating and curing their own hams, fish, sausages, and deli meats. Some even make and/or age their own cheeses. These charcuterie boards, which sometimes allow customers to choose the specific components from a larger selection of meats and cheeses, work well in certain operations, like wine bars or microbreweries. Whether this movement evolves into a broader trend or stays boutique remains to be seen; however, it is not inappropriate to list cheese and/or charcuterie as its own category on a menu.

Beverages   Establishments with numerous beverage offerings often locate their alcoholic drinks on a separate menu. However, those with few or no alcoholic options tend to list their beverages as a section on the main menu. The category may be entitled "Beverages" or "Drinks." Even those restaurants with extensive lists may opt to include their wines by the glass on the menu or to pair certain drink choices with each entrée. Pairing a beverage with each dish encourages those who may be intimidated by wine or beer to order an alcoholic beverage. By-the-glass listings also encourage sales to those parties who cannot consume a full bottle of wine in a single sitting. If an operation specializes in cocktails, those should be included on the menu (or at least on a table tent) to help increase that revenue. A menu is only effective as a marketing tool if it lists the products management wishes to sell.

For those operations that do not serve alcohol, a beverage section on the main menu is essential. It should include a selection of cold and hot beverages, including juices, coffee, hot tea, iced tea, sodas, still and sparkling waters, milk, and any specialty drink creations. Just because a restaurant does not serve alcohol does not mean that its beverage selection must be boring. A nonalcoholic spritzer made from cranberry juice and sparkling water, mango lassi, watermelon agua fresca, or even a simple raspberry iced tea can convert a basic beverage list to one that seems special. In the case of homemade purees or fruit juices, a house beverage can even be an outlet for product utilization purposes.

While all of these menu categories are popular, it is important to emphasize that the category names and menu items listed must support and make sense with the company's brand. A restaurant catering to a clientele that is unlikely to linger may list only "Appetizers," "Entrées," and "Desserts," while an upscale, leisurely paced restaurant might have a far more expansive number of categories. A prix fixe or table d'hôte menu might ignore all of the traditional headings and instead write "First Course," "Second Course," etc., or dispense with the labels entirely and simply separate the courses with asterisks or other visual dividers.

SUMMARY

The category names and menu items appropriate for a menu depend both on the business's concept and on the style of pricing. A menu may use a la carte, semi a la carte, table d'hôte, or prix fixe pricing. Numbers of categories and items listed impact both the quantity of courses most guests will order as well as the length of time it takes for customers to read through the menu. Balance and variety, both on the plate and across the menu, are critical elements to creating an interesting menu that will attract and retain customers. Variety and balance are applicable to ingredients, flavor, cooking technique, temperature, texture, color, shape, size, composition, and plate presentation, though certain variables may be limited by the available kitchen equipment and desired work flow. While there are no absolutes when it comes to naming menu categories, there are certain labels that are more commonly used in the industry. Breakfast menus often include beverages, a la carte items or sides, and entrées, which may be subdivided into eggs, omelets, griddle items, cereals, and house specialties. Lunch and dinner menus may use similar terminology, though soups, salads, and sandwiches are often bigger sellers at lunch than they are at dinner. These menus often include appetizers, soups, salads, sandwiches, entrées, and sides or accompaniments. Desserts, cheeses, and beverages may appear on the main menu, on a separate menu, or, in the case of cheeses, not at all. Depending on the business concept, the entrée categories may be subdivided by cooking technique or by main ingredient. Alternatively, a menu planner may choose to simply list the categories numerically as in "First Course," "Second Course," etc. Whatever terminology is used, it must support the business's brand and concept.

COMPREHENSION QUESTIONS

1. What are the four approaches to menu pricing described in this chapter?
2. For what variables are variety and balance most relevant?
3. Under what circumstances might a business use the same ingredient (other than basic pantry staples) in multiple dishes? (List two possibilities.)
4. List three categories into which breakfast entrées might be subdivided.
5. List five common category headings used for a lunch or dinner menu.
6. How do menu category headings differ from a breakfast menu to a lunch menu?
7. How does a menu impact work flow in the kitchen? What can a menu planner do to prevent kitchen bottlenecks?
8. List two examples of ways in which a menu planner can control food cost through product utilization (i.e., use of scraps other than throwing them in the trash).

DISCUSSION QUESTIONS

1. List some menu category headings you have seen in a restaurant that are not among the traditional headings listed in the chapter.

2. Describe a restaurant (or other foodservice business) experience you have had in which the menu was not effective in your opinion. What aspect of the menu made it an unpleasant experience for you?

3. When dining out in a casual restaurant, how many menu items do you consider ideal to see under each category heading? How would the number differ if you were dining at an upscale restaurant?

4. If you were to open your own restaurant, what pricing style would you prefer to utilize? Why?

5. Name three entrées that might generate scraps or leftovers through their production. Name the ingredients that would be left over and create a menu item (not an entrée) that could utilize those leftovers.

6. Describe in detail an original entrée of your creation. Make sure that it incorporates the concepts of variety and balance on the plate. Describe all of the ways in which the dish exhibits variety and balance.

4

Menu Styles
and Categories II—
Beyond the Basics

While restaurant breakfast, lunch, and dinner menus may be what most people think of when they hear the term "menu," menus span a much broader range of styles. All menus provide a listing of food available for service, but menus differ based on the market they serve and the type of dining experience they describe. Some menus, such as brunch or high tea menus, are designed for specific meal periods beyond the traditional three. Some cater to a narrowly focused market, such as children's menus or room service menus. A special occasion banquet menu may be used only for a single event and provide limited choices, if any. Ethnic or tasting menus are utilized by certain restaurants, but they do not necessarily follow the conventions of traditional restaurant menus. In short, the range of menus goes way beyond the traditional breakfast, lunch, and dinner types.

It is important for a menu planner to understand the differences and nuances of each kind of menu. Although the menu planner for a business is often the chef or manager of that one business, a single company is sometimes called upon to create specialized menus for specific occasions. For example, a chef in a restaurant might create the main lunch and dinner menu, but if the restaurant owner wants to periodically do catering or special events in the restaurant for large groups, the chef must design menus for those purposes as well. Simply providing the standard dinner menu for a group of one hundred that has bought out the restaurant is a recipe for disaster. Hotels are classic examples of businesses that must offer various types of menus. A single hotel kitchen might service an upscale restaurant for three meals a day with brunch on Sundays, the hotel banquet halls, room service, afternoon tea, and a late-night lounge. The better a menu planner understands how these types of menus differ, the better shot she has of meeting the needs of both the guests and the business.

By the end of this chapter, you will be able to:

- Describe the characteristics of various menu types, including take-out, room service, cycle, noncommercial, banquet or special occasion, catering, brunch, ethnic, tasting, children's, lounge, high tea, and dessert menus

- Create a set of food items and categories for any of the aforementioned menu types that addresses the needs of both the customer and the business

4.1 SIMILARITIES TO TRADITIONAL MENUS

The complete range of menu types varies greatly, but there are some commonalities between all of them. All menus must cater to the needs and eating habits of the market or client. Sometimes the client is an individual who determines the menu for a larger crowd, as for a wedding or business meeting, but even then the menu planner should guide the client to select foods likely to appeal to the audience.

The rules of variety and balance play a role in all forms of menus, not just restaurant menus. For example, a banquet menu should vary the ingredients and cooking technique used for each course (unless, of course, the meal is sponsored by a food-related association like a beef council or a grill company). Nutrition plays a role as well, though it may be less of a focus for a single, special occasion event.

When choices are offered within a menu category, the naming conventions may or may not resemble those of a traditional restaurant menu. For example, a catering menu may list options for appetizers and entrées, but it may also include categories such as hors d'oeuvres or business meeting refreshments, as these types of services are common in a catering environment.

A discussion of a number of menu types and their unique concerns and characteristics follows.

4.1.1 Take-Out Menus

A take-out menu is a list of food products that may be ordered from a foodservice establishment, often a restaurant, for consumption off the premises. Some types of businesses, such as Chinese restaurants or pizza places, offer all of their food to go. Others do not offer take-out at all. The biggest concern with take-out foods is that there is no telling how long it will be before the customer consumes the food. Thus, anything offered on a take-out menu should hold up well over long periods of time with minimal quality loss. As many consumers will store the leftovers and reheat hot foods later, take-out menus should include foods that store and reheat well, too. Pulled pork barbecue on a biscuit might be a good choice for take-out; poached eggs with hollandaise sauce would not.

Portability is another concern. Because customers carry their food from the restaurant to another location, the food could be easily destroyed when jostled in a bag. A delicate plate presentation that collapses with the slightest movement is a poor choice for a take-out menu. Sandwiches work well as they can be eaten on the run, but plated foods are perfectly acceptable as long as they will remain attractive with some minor movement. Packaging helps to keep the food looking edible. Covered containers, sometimes with raised dividers for different components of the plate, can keep a dish from turning into a single, amorphous blob. Even better are dishes that are designed to be a uniform mixture, such as stir-fries or tossed salads.

While some restaurants simply use their full restaurant menu as their take-out menu, there is no requirement to do so. It is best to include on the menu only those choices that will represent the business well. A disappointed customer is less likely to return, even if the flaws in the food result from the purchaser's treatment of it. Take-out menus should be available both on paper and online, so customers can take the menus with them or look the menu up on a business's web page. Many take-out operations today allow for customers to place orders not only by phone or in person but also electronically through a web page or smart phone application. Take-out menus are typically found in casual and fast-food restaurants, carryout-only businesses, and certain corporate foodservice operations.

4.1.2 Room Service Menus

The issues with a room service menu are similar to those for take-out menus. While a room service menu need not account for guests reheating the food, the food does need to be transportable and must hold its quality for at least twenty minutes. In a large hotel, the walk alone from the kitchen to a distant room could easily take ten minutes. The plate presentations cannot be too high, as most hotels use plate covers to help protect the food in transport. The presentations should not be too delicate, either, as even a highly trained waiter may bump into a careless hotel guest en route. The food should be palatable even if it is not piping hot or ice cold as room service food slowly inches toward room temperature on the walk from the kitchen. A beautiful risotto might gel

IN-ROOM DINING

We are pleased to offer our In-Room Dining and Hospitality Catering Menu.
Sunday through Thursday from 6:00am–1:00am and
Friday and Saturday from 6:00am–2:00am
Extension 4621
Listed within the menu are individual service times for each meal period.

The pride of Chicago, The Drake Hotel has been the choice of celebrities and heads of state since its opening in 1920. The Drake has combined tradition with elegance and style to amaze our guests and accommodate all of your needs, whether you are in Chicago for business or pleasure.

Our casual restaurant is located in the upper lobby and features The Hilton Breakfast Buffet.
Breakfast is served daily
Lunch is served Monday - Saturday
Extension 4626

An elegant setting adjacent to the lobby, providing daily afternoon tea service, scheduled live entertainment and live harp music.
Also located in The Palm Court is the Lobby Bar
Extension 4615

The Coq d'Or opened its doors the day after Prohibition was repealed and has been packing in crowds ever since. Local residents delight in our specialty, Executive Cocktails.
Located on the Arcade Level
Open daily
Scheduled Live Entertainment
Extension 4623

"The Best Seafood Restaurant in Town" ~
Inducted into the Fine Dining Hall of Fame by Nations Restaurant News ~
Located on the Arcade Level
Dinner is served daily
Extension 4625

Figure 4–1
This room service menu includes a wide range of offerings that transport well to a hotel room. Shaun Rajah, Palm Court and Chef Baasim Zafar, Drake Hotel.

BREAKFAST

Served from 6:00am to 11:30am

FULL BREAKFAST

THE AMERICAN 27
  Florida Orange or Grapefruit Juice
  Two Farm Fresh Eggs Any Style
  Choice of Ham, Bacon or Sausage
  Served with Breakfast Potatoes, Toast and Preserves
  Lavazza Coffee, Decaffeinated Coffee or Hot Tea

THE DRAKE 27
  Two Organic Eggs Cooked Your Way, Choice of Double Smoked Applewood Thick Cut Bacon, Dry aged Pork Loin or Turkey
  Sausage, Breakfast Potatoes, Toast, Orange or Grapefruit Juice and Lavazza Coffee

CONTINENTAL BREAKFAST 23
  Selection of Freshly Baked Pastries or Toast, Seasonal Fruit Plate, Lavazza Coffee, Orange or Grapefruit Juice

THE ULTIMATE BIRCHERMUESLI 21
  Florida Orange or Grapefruit Juice
  Whole Wheat Toast or Raisin Bran Muffin
  Bowl of Birchermuesli
  Lavazza Coffee, Decaffeinated Coffee or Hot Tea

THE PERFECT BREAKFAST 20
  House Parfait, Seasonal Berry Martini, Selection of Juices, Lavazza Coffee, or
  Green Tea

THE WALTON 26
  Six ounce Angus New York Steak, Two Organic Eggs Cooked Your Way, Crispy Hash Browns, Toast, Selection of Juice, Lavazza Coffee

HEALTHY START

Ruby Red Grapefruit Brûlée 8
  Half a Red Grapefruit Topped with Caramelized Sugar

Seasonal Fresh Fruit Plate 16
  Sliced Fresh Seasonal Fruit, Local Honey Infused Labna

Fresh Seasonal Melon 11
  Half a Seasonal Melon with Cottage Cheese

Mixed Berry Mélange 11
  Mint and Crimé Fraîche

Morning Banana Split 16
  Banana, Candied Pecans, Fresh Berries, Crunchy Granola, Crime Anglaise, Caramel Sauce

Birchermuesli 11
  A Traditional Swiss Favorite Combining Oats, Yogurt, Raisins and Fresh Fruits

Oatmeal 11
  Served with Raisins and Brown Sugar, Milk or Cream

Assorted Cold Cereals 8
  All Bran, Branflakes, Cornflakes, Granola, Product 19, Raisin Bran, Rice Krispies,
  Shredded Wheat, Special K or Wheaties
  ~ With Sliced Strawberries or Bananas 10

* Consumption of raw or undercooked foods may increase risk of food borne illness.
Individuals with certain health conditions may be at a higher risk.

All Food and Beverage prices are subject to 17% Gratuity,
an In-Room Dining Charge of $6.00 per delivery
Appplicable State and Local Taxes

Figure 4–1
(Continued)

BREAKFAST

HEALTHY START
(continued)

Smoked Salmon **21**
> Fennel Cucumber Salad, Sliced Tomatoes, Shaved Red Onions, Capers, Sliced All
> Butter Brioche, Salmon Caviar, and Horseradish Sauce
> **~ Add a Fresh Bagel and Cream Cheese**.. **6**

Layered Granola Parfait **14**
> Seasonal Berries or Fruits, Tahitian Vanilla Yogurt, Turkish Dried Apricots

Brioche French Toast
> Whipped Butter and Syrup.. 17
> Grilled Peaches and Candied Pecans... 18

Buttermilk Pancakes
> Maple Syrup.. 17
> Blueberries... 18
> M&M's.. 18

Belgian Waffle
> Maple Syrup.. 16
> Strawberries, Whipped Cream and Chocolate Syrup.. 17

EGGS

Chorizo and Egg Burrito... **17**

> Spanish Chorizo, Tri-Color Peppers, Pepper Jack Cheese, Two Organic Eggs, Whole Wheat Tortilla, Crispy Hash Browns, and
> Fire Roasted Salsa

Two Eggs.. **17**

> Two Eggs Cooked Your Way, Choice of Sausage, Applewood Smoked Bacon, Dry Aged Pork Loin or Turkey Sausage, Crispy Hash Browns

Create or Select an Omelet... **17**

> **All omelets are available with Egg Whites or Egg Beaters. They are made with three whole eggs and are served with signature breakfast potatoes;**
> Your Choice of Three Ingredients: Smoked Aged Pork Loin, Crisp Bacon, Spanish Chorizo, Turkey Sausage, Swiss, Cheddar, Buffalo Mozzarella, Tri-Color Peppers, Wild Mushrooms, Onions, Tomatoes, Asparagus, Fresh Herbs (Add $1 for Each Additional Item)
>> **Margherita,** Vine Ripened Tomatoes, Buffalo Mozzarella, Fresh Basil.............................. 17
>> **Cape Cod Omelet,** Shrimp, Asparagus, Dill.. 18
>> **South of the Border,** Spanish Chorizo, Tri-Color Peppers, Pepper Jack Cheese, Fire Roasted Salsa.......................... 18
>> **Smoked Ham and Cheese,** Aged Pork Loin, Wisconsin Cheddar... 18
>> Smoked Salmon, Mushroom, Spinach, with Egg Whites... 20

Eggs Benedict
> Traditional, Two Poached Eggs, Dry Aged Pork Loin, Hollandaise...................................... 18
> Smoked Salmon, Two Poached Eggs, Mandarin Orange Hollandaise.................................. 20
> Cape Cod Crab Cake, Two Poached Eggs, Grain Mustard Hollandaise............................... 20

Spanish Style Fried Eggs... **18**
> Olive Oil Fried Organic Eggs, Sliced Iberian Style Ham, Romensco Sauce, Grilled Sourdough Bread, and Manchego Cheese

** Consumption of raw or undercooked foods may increase risk of food borne illness.
Individuals with certain health conditions may be at a higher risk.*

All Food and Beverage prices are subject to 17% Gratuity,
an In-"Room Dining Charge of $6.00 per delivery"
and applicable State and Local Taxes

Figure 4–1
(Continued)

BREAKFAST

Served from 6:00am to 11:30am

SIDES

One Egg Any Style.. 8

Bacon, Ham or Link Sausage.. 8

Side of Breakfast Potatoes.. 8

Plain or Fruit Yogurt... 8

English Muffin, White, Whole Wheat, Rye or Raisin Toast..................... 7

Croissant, Danish, Bran or Blueberry Muffin... 7

Toasted Bagel with Cream Cheese... 7

BEVERAGES

Freshly Brewed Lavazza Coffee.............3-4 Cups...9   6-8 Cups........ 13
Decaffeinated Available

Hot Tea.. 5
Earl Grey, English Breakfast, Herbal, Orange Pekoe or Decaffeinated

Hot Chocolate... 6

Whole, 2%, Skim or Chocolate Milk... 5

Florida Orange or Grapefruit Juice... 6

Other Juices.. 6
Tomato, Apple, Cranberry, Prune, Pineapple or V8

Mimosa.. 14
Mini Carafe of Orange Juice with a Split of Sparkling Wine

Figure 4–1
(Continued)

into a single, solid mass by the time it reaches the guest. A warm apple pie a la mode might become pie with cream sauce after a ten-minute walk. There are ways to address these concerns, such as delivering apple pie and ice cream separately, but the transportation issues must be considered as part of the menu development process.

When a hotel operates a full-service restaurant, the room service menu is typically not a duplication of the restaurant menu. It tends to be limited to just a few popular items in each category that change with the time of day. That said, a room service menu should include beverages, appetizers, salads, entrées, and desserts, except for the breakfast menu, which follows a traditional breakfast format. Room service menus should plan for guests of all ages, especially children, who may not want the normal adult fare. Hotel guests sometimes want food late at night, long after the restaurant has closed. Menu planners may wish to adjust the menu to offer only a few late-night snacks (wings, burgers, salads—lounge food) after a certain hour to eliminate the need for a large overnight kitchen staff. Other hotels simply cut off room service after a certain hour.

Room service for breakfast is common in many hotels. When breakfast room service is offered, guests should have the ability to place the order the night before for a given arrival time in the morning. While evening room service customers are more likely to be guests who arrived late or just want privacy over a meal, users of room service for breakfast may be in a hurry in the morning. Placing the order the night before allows the guest to focus on getting ready for her day instead of wondering how long it will take for the kitchen to complete her order. Advance ordering also allows the kitchen to be more efficient in its planning. Breakfast room service menus should offer a range of juices and cold items (pastries, breads, cereals, etc.) with a few quick-service hot options, so delays due to cooking time are minimal.

4.1.3 Cycle Menus and Noncommercial Businesses

A cycle menu is one that rotates a set of menu options over a period of time. It could be as simple as serving spaghetti every Monday and meatloaf every Tuesday or as complex as creating a thirty-day cycle that repeats the more popular dishes within the same month but leaves others to return only once the cycle repeats. Cycle menus are common for captive audiences in such places as schools, corporate cafeterias, and hospitals, but they can also be used to rotate the specials in a restaurant. For example, a restaurant might decide to cycle its soup du jour, so that every Friday is clam chowder, every Saturday is beef barley, and so on.

Cycle menus help to balance the business's need for efficiency with the customer's need for variety. The most efficient foodservice operation would offer the same one dish every day. That way, the business could minimize inventory, staff, equipment, and training. But no one would come to such a restaurant, and for a captive audience, the monotony would be unappetizing and unhealthy. A captive market, such as college students, might want a new dish every day of the semester, but that would require a huge investment in inventory, training, and recipe development. A cycle allows for some balance between these two opposing needs.

How frequently the cycle repeats depends on the level of audience captivity and their length of stay. For example, a hospital has a highly captive audience but few of its patients may stay for more than a week. Such a hospital could easily operate a one-week cycle menu for its patients. A corporate cafeteria, on the other hand, will likely need a longer cycle with more frequent repetition of the most popular items. The businesspeople whom the cafeteria serves have some ability to leave the office to eat elsewhere if they get bored by the menu, but if served well by the cafeteria, many of them will remain frequent cafeteria customers for the length of their employment.

DATE	Sunday, September 09, 2012	Monday, September 10, 2012	Tuesday, September 11, 2012	Wednesday, September 12, 2012	Thursday, September 13, 2012	Friday, September 14, 2012	Saturday, September 15, 2012
Notes		*Mediterranean*	*Latin*	*Asian*	*Traditional American*	*Traditional American*	
Special	Steelcut Oats Steelcut Oatmeal Bar						Steelcut Oats Steelcut Oatmeal Bar
Soups Broth Cream/Puree		Tuscan Bean Soup Beef & Barley Soup	Cold Yucatan Gazpacho Pozole	Rice Soup with Chicken & Ginger Sweet & Sour Shrimp Soup with Herbs	Cremini Mushroom & Potato Soup Roasted Corn & Tomato Soup	Manhattan Clam Chowder	
Entrée(s)	Breakfast Sausage Quiche Lorraine Quiche Spinach YC	Chicken and Sausage Contadina	Chili-Cumin Shredded Beef Tacos	Miso Glazed Coho Salmon	Buffalo Chicken Pizza	Chicken Breast Parmigiana Brd	Bacon Slices Cajun Fritatta
Vegetarian Entrée	Scrambled Eggs Scrambled Egg Whites	Farro with Vegetable Ragout and Parsley-Toasted Almond Salsa	Enchiladas Verdes		Eli Pizza with Mushrooms & Thyme		Scrambled Eggs Scrambled Egg Whites Waffle Batter
Vegan Entrée	Vegan Waffles		Swiss Chard with Tomatoes & Potatoes	Seasonal Squash Curry with Tofu	Vegetable Orzo	Cannellini Beans with Spinach & Cavatelli	Vegan Waffle Batter
Grill Place	Banana Pecan Pancakes	Roasted Vegetable & Provolone Panini	Tex-Mex Chicken Breast	Thai Turkey Burgers	Grilled Ham, Brie & Apple Sandwich	Grilled Olive Flatbread	Eli Breakfast Sandwich
Starch	Potato Scallion Hash	Pasta with Fresh Herbs & Extra Virgin Olive Oil	Steamed Rice with Herbs & Peas	Cilantro Rice		Quinoa Black Bean & Corn Pilaf	Sweet Potato Home Fries
Vegetable	Fresh Market Vegetable	Fresh Market Vegetable Fresh Market Vegetable	Fresh Market Vegetable Fresh Market Vegetable	Fresh Market Vegetable Fresh Market Vegetable	Fresh Market Vegetable Fresh Market Vegetable	Fresh Market Vegetable Fresh Market Vegetable	Fresh Market Vegetable
Deli	Tuna Club Wrap Fresh Cut Fruit	Red Pepper Hummus and Baba Ghanouj with Lavash	Mexico City Chicken & Chipotle Sandwich	Marinated Tofu Sandwich with Greens	Argentinean Sierra Beef Sandwich	Classic Tuna Salad Sandwich	Baja Chicken Rollup Fresh Cut Fruit
Salads	Salad Bar #2	Salad Bar #3	Salad Bar #3	Salad Bar #3	Salad Bar #3	Salad Bar #3	Salad Bar #3
Dessert							
Misc							

LUNCH

DINNER

DATE	Sunday, September 09, 2012	Monday, September 10, 2012	Tuesday, September 11, 2012	Wednesday, September 12, 2012	Thursday, September 13, 2012	Friday, September 14, 2012	Saturday, September 15, 2012
Notes	*American Comfort*						
Special							
Soup	Classic Tomato Soup						Curry Ginger Carrot Soup
Entrée(s)	Southern Fried Chicken	Chermoula Stuffed Chicken Breast	Haitian Style Salmon	Asian Style Sweet & Spicy Spareribs	Porketta Old Country	Turkey Tenderloin Roasted with Herbs	Buffalo Chicken Wings YC
	Chicken Gravy	Pork Souvlaki	Adobo Pork Loin with Avocado Salsa		Brown Gravy	Roasted Corn Salsa	
Vegetarian Entrée	Mushroom Frittata	Spinach & Feta Quiche	Mexican Grilled Vegetable Flatbread	Asian Sesame Peanut Pasta	Sweet Potato & Quinoa Burger	Vegetable Casoulette with	Stuffed Shells
					with Caramelized Onion Relish	Quinoa Basmati Herb Crust	
Vegan Entrée	Spaghetti with Marinara Sauce	Roman Orechiette w/ Swiss Chard		General Tso's Tofu	Quinoa Almond Pilaf	Portabella Tetrazzini	Tofu Provencal
		& Tofu					
Grill Place	Pulled Pork Quesadilla	Pandorato	Mushroom Fajita	Szechuan Beef Stir-fry	Sauteed Fresh Catch with Tapenade	Bratwurst Grilled	Griddled Gruyere & Mustard Sandwich
						Knockwurst Grilled	
						Pennsylvania Dutch Sauerkraut	
Starch	Corn Casserole	Cherry Tomato Risotto	Haitian Red Beans & Rice	Basmati Rice	Barley Mushroom Pilaf	Roasted Yams & Bliss Potatoes	Polenta with Marinated Tomatoes
Vegetable	Fresh Market Vegetable	Fresh Market Vegetable	Fresh Market Vegetable	Fresh Market Vegetable	Fresh Market Vegetable	Fresh Market Vegetable	Fresh Market Vegetable
		Fresh Market Vegetable	Fresh Market Vegetable	Fresh Market Vegetable	Fresh Market Vegetable	Fresh Market Vegetable	
Salads	Salad Bar #2	Salad Bar #3	Salad Bar #3	Salad Bar #3	Salad Bar #3	Salad Bar #3	Salad Bar #3
Dessert							
Misc							

Figure 4–2 This is a one-week segment of a larger cycle menu that was created to exhibit or generate "diversity, bold tastes, fresh each day, sustainable foods, fun, excitement, and happy students"—Ron DeSantis, Director of Culinary Excellence & Quality Assurance at Yale University. Yale University and Chef Ronald DeSantis.

In creating a cycle menu, the menu planner must account for all portions of the meal—the appetizers, entrées, sides, beverages, and desserts. In some cases, like a college cafeteria, all of the courses may be offered with multiple choices; in others, like an elementary school cafeteria, only a few courses may be offered with no choice for any of the courses. Either way, nutrition and general popularity are critical. When a captive audience usually or always eats from a single food provider, their physical health depends heavily on the foodservice company. The food should provide a balance of nutrients both within a meal and across the entire cycle. However, the consumer gains no nutrition if she does not eat the food. Thus, the food must appeal greatly to the audience. Offering options may satisfy the customers' taste buds, but if only one selection is nutritious, the menu planner fails in her responsibility to the customers' nutritional needs.

A cycle menu should also account for product utilization. In fact, a rotating soup, omelet, quiche, or stir-fry of the day may allow the chef an outlet to use up leftovers on a schedule. If she knows that there is a set of ingredients or byproducts that build up over the week (bell pepper tops or turkey scraps, for example), the chef can plan to use them up via the cycle menu (possibly through a once-a-week bell pepper soup or turkey hash).

Cycle menus may or may not be printed for the guests to see. In a cafeteria setting, the customers may only learn the menu when they see the food on display, even though the kitchen staff surely has a copy of the menu behind the scenes for their own planning needs. Promoting the cycle is a much better option that keeps the customer base happy. If a planned meal is unappealing to a regular customer, it is better for that patron to know in advance and to plan an alternative than to have to settle for an undesirable meal. If the choices in the cycle are all fairly popular, the printed menu can be a draw to attract business. For noncommercial operations, the cycle menu may be posted in print or listed electronically on a web page. For commercial restaurants, the cycle rotation may be printed on the restaurant menu itself. For example, a restaurant that advertises Wednesdays as prime rib night may attract a bigger crowd than it would by having servers notify guests of a prime rib special at the table. The cycle menu is not only a control and planning tool for the business but also a marketing tool to attract and keep loyal customers.

It should be noted that while cycle menus are quite popular in noncommercial operations, a noncommercial kitchen need not always resort to a cycle menu system. (A *noncommercial* foodservice business is one that services another organization whose mission is not food, such as a hospital, school, or museum.) The chef could vary the menu daily to take advantage of seasonal ingredients. Alternatively, the menu might be expansive but never change. For example, if a corporate cafeteria contains several stations including a large salad bar, a pizza station, a barbecue and grill station, and a sandwich station, there may be enough variety in the one menu that customers can order something different each day for a month without repeating. Such an approach works well for a large operation that services hundreds of guests daily, like a museum. When such a comprehensive menu is not feasible, the cycle menu is usually the best option.

4.1.4 Banquet and Special Occasion Menus

Normally defined simply as a "feast," a banquet is a culinary event that provides a sequence of courses, usually with little to no choice for the individual diner, though the courses could be served buffet style. The menu itself is typically determined by just one or two people—the actual client—in conjunction with the chef or a salesperson from the foodservice business. Banquets are often performed only for special, one-time events, such as a wedding or a business meeting, though the same menu could be repeated for a completely different audience. Consequently, nutrition is less of a concern unless it is expressed as a consideration for the group by the client.

Banquets follow a classic meal sequence, dependent somewhat on the number of courses being planned. A three-course banquet would usually offer an appetizer, entrée, and dessert, but the appetizer could be a soup, salad, or some more complex creation. The entrée could highlight any number of ingredients. A lengthier banquet menu might instead begin with a soup, progress to an appetizer, then a salad, then an intermezzo before finally arriving at the entrée. In this longer version, the appetizer is traditionally a seafood course while the entrée is meat-based. Of course, there are many variations to this traditional pattern. Europeans may prefer the salad after the main course. Vegetarians, obviously, would not require that meat or seafood be a part of any of these courses. A cheese course may follow the entrée, but cheese might have been part of a stand-up cocktail hour that preceded the sit-down meal. The only universal is that dessert usually concludes the meal, possibly with a second treat of mignardise (small bite-size sweets, such as chocolates, petit fours, or cookies) following a plated dessert.

A banquet of many courses can become tiresome to the palate and the stomach if the menu planner does not plan appropriately. The best approach to avoid palate fatigue is to alternate light and heavy courses with an overall trend toward richer courses through the entrée. The lighter courses—broth soups, simple salads, sorbet intermezzos—work both as a palate cleanser to give the taste buds a rest and as a calorie break on the stomach. Portion sizes should remain small throughout the banquet so the guests do not "run out of room" before reaching dessert.

The number of guests at a banquet and the style of service greatly impact what the menu planner can suggest to the client. Other than the first course, which can be set down at the table before the guests arrive, the courses must be quick to plate and serve when a large crowd is planned. For this reason, some companies recommend Russian service for a banquet. In Russian service, the food for an entire table is placed on a single platter, and the server transfers it to the guests' plates at the table. This style of service reduces the amount of table space needed in the kitchen for plating and divides the plate-up work among the servers. Russian service provides the best shot at serving all of the tables at the same time. If the menu planner chooses to go with American service (plated in the kitchen), the chef may need several teams of people to plate the same dish simultaneously, which requires significant table space, or the use of a conveyor belt.

When a banquet menu offers guests a choice within a course, the number of options should be limited to three or fewer. Too many choices slow service and require a larger inventory of ingredients. With fewer dishes to prepare, the kitchen can cook the food in bulk and speed the meal along, a critical element in a banquet during which no table progresses to the next course until every table has been served the previous course. Some operations expedite the process by requiring guests to pre-order their entrée choices, usually as part of their RSVP to the client. This way, the kitchen can better prepare its mise en place and have the food ready on time in the proper quantities. Coded place cards on the table make the process even faster, as servers deliver the correct meal to each guest without having to ask what each one ordered.

A special occasion menu need not be served banquet style. It is possible for a restaurant to create a special menu just for a holiday and to serve its guests American style. However, many of the rules of banquet menu creation still apply. The menu should adhere to an overarching theme and should follow a traditional course sequence. The number of choices between courses should still be limited to reduce the amount of inventory that will be left over when the restaurant returns to its regular menu the following day. Finally, because the meal is a one-time event, nutrition is less of a factor than is adhering to the theme of the day—a holiday, a cultural event, a winery providing the drinks, or a single ingredient theme, such as pork. A special occasion menu can be served buffet style; buffets and their unique concerns are described in Chapter 9.

It should be noted that hotels, country clubs, and other operations that do a lot of special events often refer to their catering menus as "banquet" menus. To avoid confusion, this text will reserve the term "banquet menu" for the final menu experienced by the guests at a special event. "Catering menu" is the term that will be used to reference the extensive list of options (food, beverage, and more) from which a client selects the ultimate banquet menu. Catering menus are covered in section 4.1.6.

Figure 4–3
A sample banquet menu
from a wedding.
Linsey Silver, Element 47 Design.

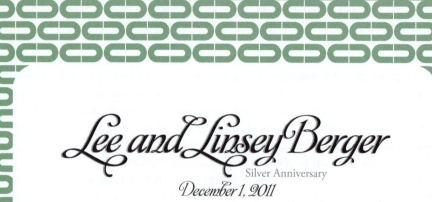

Lee and Linsey Berger
Silver Anniversary
December 1, 2011

Chicken Consommé, Shiitake Mushrooms, Purple Carrots
Nicolas Feuilatte, Brut Blanc de Blancs, Champagne, 2004

....

Poached Salmon with Tarragon Beurre Blanc, Celery Root,
Fennel, Belgian Endive
Veuve Clicquot, Brut, Champagne, 1998

....

Intermezzo of Grapefruit Sorbet

....

Beef Tenderloin with Fig Demiglace, Garlic Mashed Potatoes,
Bacon Brussels Sprouts
Billecart-Salmon, Brut Rose, Champagne, NV

....

Pear-Frangipane Tart, Raspberry Coulis
Moet & Chandon, "Nectar Imperial," Demi Sec, Champagne, NV

4.1.5 Tasting Menus

A tasting menu is usually an extremely lengthy gustatory experience in which the guest submits to the chef's recommendations for course selection and sequence. Tasting menus may be as small as five courses or may run over twenty courses. Regardless of the number of courses, the total quantity of food can only go so high before guests become uncomfortably full. Larger numbers of courses require smaller portion sizes, possibly of just one or two bites.

Tasting menus are most commonly found in restaurants with extremely talented chefs. They may follow a classic banquet course sequence, but because of the small portion sizes, a tasting menu may appear to be an ongoing series of appetizers. As with banquet menus, the best tasting menus provide a periodic palate cleanser, which may be a salad or sorbet or may instead be a light, acidic course not all that different in appearance from the other courses. Short tasting menus and banquet menus may appear to be quite similar, but the client heavily influences a banquet menu while the chef completely controls a tasting menu and rarely offers guests choices other than to accommodate dietary restrictions. Banquets typically support a larger event, like a wedding or conference; tasting menus are 100% about the food and dining experience.

Because tasting menus are rare indulgences for most diners, guests often wish to take a copy of the printed menu with them to remember the experience. Thus, tasting menus should be printed on durable paper but without permanent covers that the restaurant would reuse for other guests. Chefs may wish to personalize the menus by signing them or by listing the date and name of the party. In some restaurants, a tasting menu is only offered to a small subset of the evening's patrons, usually to a small party that reserves a special room or a table in the kitchen. Tasting menus are generally expensive to produce, so they command high prices. To justify the price, a tasting menu should show off the best talents and innovations of the chef. Because guests want to feel that they've had a series of original dishes and not the same course over and over, ingredients should never be repeated across courses in a tasting menu.

4.1.6 Catering Menus

Caterers, which include standalone catering companies, hotel and country club catering departments, special event sites, and sometimes even personal chefs, accommodate the needs of a client to service a larger group. Caterers may supply a banquet, a buffet, a cocktail reception, or simply a bunch of sandwiches dropped off on disposable platters. Caterers range from inexpensive to extremely pricy, and their job is to meet the needs, no matter how unusual, of a guest whose needs are not met simply by going to a restaurant. At the higher end of the spectrum, caterers make dreams come true.

Catering can be done on-premise or off-premise, meaning respectively that the guests may come to a catering hall next to the caterer's kitchen or to a location to which the caterer must transport the food. Hotels and country clubs are examples of on-premise caterers. Many of the companies advertised explicitly as caterers are often off-premise caterers. Because caterers must adapt to a wide range of clients with vastly different needs, a catering menu is an enormous menu from which the client picks to create the event or banquet menu. The client may choose from dozens or hundreds of choices to create the shorter menu that the event attendees see.

Because a catering menu is never executed in its entirety at one event, variety is critical, but balance is not. It is perfectly acceptable for a caterer to list

Figure 4–4
This tasting menu highlights the talent of TV celebrity chef Bryan Voltaggio and showcases his support of agriculture local to his restaurant in Frederick, MD.
Chef Bryan Voltaggio, VOLT Restaurant.

KITCHEN MENU

jonah crab cucumber, green mango, coriander

ravioli black trumpet mushrooms, ash, celery root

wahoo asparagus, hen yolk, fines herbs, caper

pork belly red cape beans, chimichurri, cocoa

sweetbreads sunchoke, black kale, bacon

beef english pea, kennebeck potatoes, rutabaga, green garlic

chocolate marshmallow, caramel, peanut

VEGETABLE MENU

beets walnuts, blue cheese, watercress, sherry vinegar

ravioli black trumpet mushrooms, ash, celery root

cauliflower golden raisin, chickpea, piquillo pepper, eggplant

hen egg rye, english pea, morel mushroom

jerusalem artichoke maroon carrot, fennel, chickweed

maitake steel cut oats, sea greens, yeast

parsnip walnut, cream cheese, caramel

seven course menu | 95 cheese course | 12 beverage pairings | mkt twenty chicken entrées on a catering menu, from which the client will pick one. That said, chicken should not be the only option for an entrée or the client is likely to seek out another caterer. A catering menu often includes menu categories not seen on other menus. Caterers often offer hors d'oeuvres as part of a reception prior to a main meal. Thus, "hors d'oeuvres" is usually its own section on a catering menu. *Hors d'oeuvres* are simply one- or two-bite items that guests can navigate easily while holding a drink in one hand. They should rarely require utensils other than a toothpick or perhaps a spoon on which a single bite rests. They should also not be messy to consume, or guests will end up with food all over their clothes.

Full-service caterers—as opposed to caterers who only do drop-off, disposable trays of food—should have the ability to provide buffet, American (plated), or Russian (platter) service. The buffet might include carving stations, too. Consequently, the prices on a catering menu differ from the way prices are written on other menus. Prices may be listed by the piece (for hors d'oeuvres), by weight or volume (for buffet salads or soups), or per person (which lets the caterer determine how much food to supply). When a catering menu sells its food per person for a buffet, the portion sizes should be planned such that the food does not run out. After all, if the client paid for twenty people to eat, the buffet cannot run out of food before all twenty have had their fill. Services such as having a bartender, carver, or server(s) are often charged separately.

Because the client ultimately selects the event menu from the catering menu, it is up to the chef or salesperson to guide the client to make good choices. This is very much a give-and-take exchange. If a client wishes to offer three entrées, all beef, at her party, the chef or salesperson should encourage her to pursue greater variety. However, if the client describes the attendees as cattle ranchers in town for a conference, the plethora of beef may be appropriate. The chef could recommend a set banquet menu in which each course contains some beef instead of congregating all of the beef into a single course. In the end, if the chef or salesperson and the client understand the attendees' needs and the caterer's capabilities, the menu is easier to determine. The client will almost always request a written (in print or online) catering menu from which to choose, but a caterer should also anticipate requests for items that are not listed on the catering menu. Once the caterer executes a new dish effectively for one event, the menu planner may add it to the comprehensive catering menu. Ultimately, the catering menu should include everything that the company is capable of providing and that it wishes to sell again.

Catering menus, unlike most other menus, go beyond the straightforward listing of food and drink options. Clients pursue caterers rather than restaurants because they want specific services (not just food) that a typical restaurant cannot provide. Thus, a catering package (sometimes called a banquet package) includes options for tables, chairs, cloths, decorations, number of servers, floral arrangements, photography, room rentals—in short, anything that the customer might need for the event—for a fee. For example, rather than ordering one hundred cocktails for a party, a client might order a full bar for which she pays for the bartender, the physical bar setup, and the amount of alcohol consumed at the event. Some services are provided by caterers through their in-house staff; others are contracted out for a percentage. For example, a caterer might agree to manage all of the details surrounding purchases from a florist, and a percentage of the florist's fee gets added to the client's bill to cover the caterer's time. While most people think of a menu as dealing only with food and drink, a full-service catering menu includes a much broader range of services from which a client selects to create her personalized event.

On Display

CLASSIQUE CATERING

Poached Prawns   4.25 Piece
Lemon Wedges & Cocktail Sauce
  (100-Piece Minimum)

Baked Brie En Croûte
Imported Brie Wrapped In Puff Pastry,   150.00 Small *(Serves 35 People)*
With Choice Of Fillings, Select From: 275.00 Large *(Serves 75 People)*
  o Apples, Walnuts & Brown Sugar
  o Pesto
  o Blackberry Preserves
  o Sun-Dried Tomatoes
Gourmet Crackers & Sliced Baguettes

Cocktail Sandwich Platter   6.50 Person
Assorted Cocktail Rolls, Honey Glazed Ham, Smoked Turkey,
Roast Beef, Gourmet Cheeses

Market Fresh Vegetable Display   3.75 Person
Seasonally Inspired Vegetables, Three Dipping Sauces

Gourmet International Cheese Platter   6.25 Person
Selection Of The Finest Imported & Domestic Cheeses
Assorted Crackers & Baguettes

Fruit Display   6.00 Person
Lavish Array Of The Season's Best Local & Imported Fruits

Smoked Salmon Display   6.75 Person
Cream Cheese, Capers, Chopped Eggs, Red Onions
& Fresh Dill, Mini Bagels

Antipasto Display   6.75 Person
Olives, Peppers, Salami, Mortadella, Cheeses, Artichokes,
Grilled, Roasted Vegetables, Breadsticks

Vegetarian Antipasto Display   5.50 Person
Grilled & Roasted Vegetables, Olives, Artichokes, Peppers,
Cheeses, Breadsticks

Assorted Gourmet Pinwheel Wraps   6.00 Person
Assorted Fillings Wrapped With Lavosh & Tortillas

May Include:
  o Chicken Caesar
  o Black Forest Ham & Asparagus
  o Grilled Mediterranean Vegetable

All Items Subject To 20% Service Charge & 8.75% Sales Tax

Figure 4–5
This hors d'oeuvre section of a larger catering menu illustrates the format typical of a catering menu. Classique Catering.

CLASSIQUE CATERING

The Cutting Board

An additional $150.00 will be charged for each Uniformed Attendant necessary

Steamship — 875.00
Dijon Mustard & Herb Crusted Certified Angus Beef
Served With Fresh Deli Rolls, Mustard, Mayonnaise,
And Creamed Horseradish (Serves 200 People)

Prime Rib — 475.00
Pepper Crusted & Roasted Prime Rib
Served With Deli Rolls & Condiments (Serves 50 People)

Turkey Breast — 350.00
Boneless Turkey, Oven Roasted
Served With Assorted Deli Rolls & Condiments
(Serves 50 People)

Clove Studded Ham — 350.00
Honey Glazed Ham
Served With Assorted Mustards & Deli Rolls
(Serves 50 People)

Leg Of Lamb — 475.00
Leg Of Lamb Rubbed With Rosemary, Garlic, & Dijon
Mustard, Roasted, Served With Deli Rolls & Condiments
(Serves 50 People)

Lime Marinated Pork Loin — 350.00
Boneless Pork Loin Marinated With Lime
Served With Chile Pasilla & Roasted Corn Relish
(Serves 50 People)

Planning For A Successful Reception

We Would Like To Suggest The Following Guidelines For Estimating Consumption Of Hors d'Oeuvres & Alcoholic Beverages

Hors d'Oeuvres

For A Reception Preceding Dinner
    30 — 60 Minutes   3 To 5 Pieces Per Guest

For A Reception Without Dinner
    30 — 60 Minutes   5 To 8 Pieces Per Guest
    60 — 90 Minutes   8 To 13 Pieces Per Guest

Alcoholic Beverages

    First Hour   2 Drinks Per Guest
    Each Hour Thereafter   1 Drink Per Guest

All Items Subject To 20% Service Charge & 8.75% Sales Tax

Figure 4–5
(Continued)

CLASSIQUE CATERING

Themed Hors d'Oeuvre Stations

These Stations are intended as a complement or addition to other hors d'oeuvres and are equivalant to approximately three hors d'oeuvre sized portions per person.

All Theme Stations require a fifty person minimum order.

An additional $150.00 will be charged for each Uniformed Attendant necessary.

Shrimp Puttanesca
Fusilli Pasta, Roma Tomatoes, Capers, Olives, Fresh Garlic, Rock Shrimp

12.50 Person

Grilled Fajita Bar
Chicken & Beef, Grilled Peppers & Onions, Sour Cream, Guacamole, Shredded Cheeses, Lettuce, Jalapeños, Red & Green Salsa, Flour Tortillas

14.50 Person

Southwest Station
Chicken Chingalingas, Avocado Relish, Roasted Chilies Cilantro Cheese Quesadillas, Blue, Yellow Corn Chips, Assorted Salsas

9.50 Person

Supreme Nacho Bar
Freshly Fried Corn Tortilla Chips, House-Made Salsa, Fresh Guacamole, Chopped Tomatoes, Onions, Picadillo, Refried Beans, Black Olives, Cheese, Jalapeños, Sour Cream

9.50 Person

French Station
Sautéed Chicken, Shallots, Tomatoes, Fresh Tarragon, Baby Greens, Crumbled Goat Cheese, Toasted Hazelnut Vinaigrette

11.50 Person

Italian Station
Cheese Tortellini, Basil Cream Sauce
Beef Ravioli, Fire Roasted Tomato Sauce
Fresh Grated Parmesan Cheese, Fresh Baked Breadsticks

10.50 Person

Asian Noodle Bar
Udon Noodles, Seafood Curry, Beef & Broccoli Stir Fry, Vegetable Stir Fry

10.50 Person

Sushi and Sushi Bar
Selection of Assorted Nigiri Maguro (red tuna), Shiro Maguro (white tuna), Sake (fresh salmon), Ebi (steamed shrimp)and Selection of Rolls including California

18.00 Person

Mushroom Bar
Sautéed Fresh Seasonal Mushrooms, Brandied Garlic Sauce, Sherry Cream, Balsamic Soy Sauce, Toasted Baguettes, Herbs

11.50 Person

Carved Porterhouse
Giant Steaks Carved, Gorgonzola Mashed Red Skin Potatoes, Balsamic Reduction

17.25 Person

Carved Salmon En Croute
Puff Pastry Fresh Salmon Fillet, Wild Rice, Herbs, Creamy Herb Sauce

15.00 Person

Classique Portabella
Beer Battered Jumbo Portabella Mushrooms, Black Forest Ham, Fontina Cheese, Dijon Mustard

10.25 Person

Mini Reuben Station
Petite Grilled Reuben Sandwiches, Swiss Cheese, Corned Beef, Sour Kraut, Dijon Mustard

8.25 Person

All Items Subject To 20% Service Charge & 8.75% Sales Tax

Figure 4–5
(Continued)

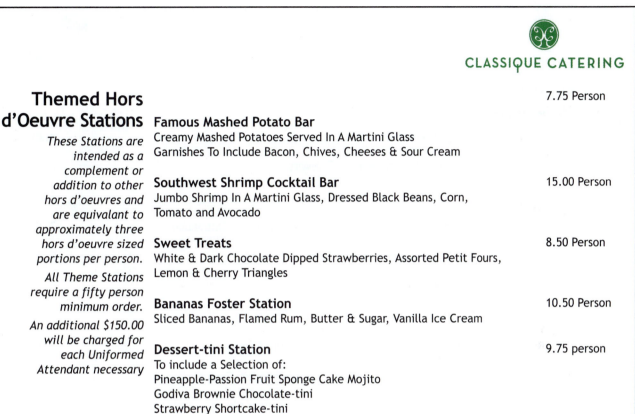

CLASSIQUE CATERING

Themed Hors d'Oeuvre Stations

These Stations are intended as a complement or addition to other hors d'oeuvres and are equivalant to approximately three hors d'oeuvre sized portions per person.

All Theme Stations require a fifty person minimum order.

An additional $150.00 will be charged for each Uniformed Attendant necessary

7.75 Person

Famous Mashed Potato Bar
Creamy Mashed Potatoes Served In A Martini Glass
Garnishes To Include Bacon, Chives, Cheeses & Sour Cream

Southwest Shrimp Cocktail Bar   15.00 Person
Jumbo Shrimp In A Martini Glass, Dressed Black Beans, Corn,
Tomato and Avocado

Sweet Treats   8.50 Person
White & Dark Chocolate Dipped Strawberries, Assorted Petit Fours,
Lemon & Cherry Triangles

Bananas Foster Station   10.50 Person
Sliced Bananas, Flamed Rum, Butter & Sugar, Vanilla Ice Cream

Dessert-tini Station   9.75 person
To include a Selection of:
Pineapple-Passion Fruit Sponge Cake Mojito
Godiva Brownie Chocolate-tini
Strawberry Shortcake-tini
Banana Nut Bread Pudding-tini

All Items Subject To 20% Service Charge & 8.75% Sales Tax

Figure 4–5
(Continued)

CLASSIQUE CATERING

Chilled Hors d'Oeuvres

75 Piece Minimum

Roasted Garlic Prawns	4.25 Piece
Grilled Chile Lime Shrimp Skewers	4.25 Piece
Crab Artichoke Crowns	3.95 Piece
Artichoke Bottoms, Bay Shrimp Salad, Lemon Dill Sauce	3.25 Piece
Red Grapes, Bleu Cheese, Toasted Pistachios	2.95 Piece
Fresh Fruit Skewers	3.25 Piece
Tarragon Chicken Salad Endive	2.95 Piece
Endive, Oranges, Walnuts, Blue Cream Cheese	2.95 Piece
Roasted Baby Red Potatoes, Crème Fraîche, Caviar	2.95 Piece
Roasted Baby Red Potatoes Herbed Cream Cheese	2.95 Piece
Mediterranean Salsa Crostini	2.50 Piece
Bruschetta, Red & Yellow Tomatoes, Basil, Olive Oil	2.50 Piece
Red Bosc Pears, Gorgonzola Cheese	2.50 Piece
Cherry Tomatoes Stuffed with Dilled Bay Shrimp	2.50 Piece
Strawberry Halves, Cracked Black Pepper Cream Cheese	2.50 Piece
Mint Grapefruit Spring Rolls	3.25 Piece
Grilled Asparagus, Blackforest Ham	3.50 Piece
Hoison BBQ Duck Scallion Pancakes	3.95 Piece
Skewered Snow Pea Asian Meatballs	3.25 Piece
Gorgonzola Polenta Crouton, Beef Tenderloin, Pine Nuts, Port Reduction	3.95 Piece
Grilled Asparagus, Roasted Red Pepper Sauce	3.25 Piece
Shrimp Gazpacho	3.95 Each
White and Dark Chocolate Dipped Strawberries	3.50 Piece
White and Dark Chocolate Dipped Biscotti & Fortune Cookies	3.75 Piece

All Items Subject To 20% Service Charge & 8.75% Sales Tax

Figure 4–5
(Continued)

CLASSIQUE CATERING

Hot Hors d'Oeuvres

75 Piece Minimum

Baby Lamb Chops, Cherry Chutney	5.50 Piece
Coconut Prawn Skewers, Ginger Apricot Chutney	4.25 Piece
Petite Beef Wellington	4.25 Piece
Lime Tarragon Crab Cakes	3.95 Piece
Bleu Cheese Artichoke Fritters	3.95 Piece
Vegetarian Samosas, Cilantro Chutney, Mango Chutney	3.25 Piece
Teriyaki Chicken Skewers	2.95 Piece
Javanese Curried Chicken, Cucumber Raita Dipping Sauce	2.95 Piece
Parmesan Chicken Wings, Galliano Sauce	2.95 Piece
Thai Chicken Wings	2.95 Piece
Spanakopita Triangles	2.95 Piece
Tiropita Triangles	2.95 Piece
Italian Sausage Quattro Formaggio Mushrooms	2.95 Piece
Asian Vegetarian Spring Rolls, Hot Mustard	3.75 Piece
Pot Stickers, Dipping Sauce	2.95 Piece
Southwestern Chicken Chingalingas, Guacamole	3.25 Piece
Carnitas Masa Cakes, Avocado Salsa	2.95 Piece
Chevre Apple Cinnamon Beggars Purse	3.25 Piece
Sausage Puff Pastry Rolls	2.95 Piece
Swedish Meatballs	2.95 Piece
Asian Orange Glazed Dumpling	3.25 Piece
Tomato Crème Brulee	3.25 Piece
Pork Empanadas, Pumpkin Seed Salsa	3.75 Piece
Beef Empanadas, Mole Sauce	3.75 Piece
Bacon wrapped Crab Cake Puff	3.75 Piece
Avocado Egg Roll	3.50 Piece

All Items Subject To 20% Service Charge & 8.75% Sales Tax

Figure 4–5
(Continued)

4.1.7 Ethnic Menus

Ethnic menus are similar to their traditional counterparts except that they tend to follow the trends and traditions of the culture they represent. Course category names and sequences, menu items, styles of presentation and service, and even levels of variety and balance all adhere to the norms of the presented culture. For example, a Tuscan restaurant might opt to use only four menu categories—antipasta, pasta, main course, and dessert—as this provides the traditional meal sequence of Tuscany. Chinese restaurants divide their menus by each dish's main ingredients—chicken, beef, pork, seafood, vegetable, etc.—so the guests may order a variety of dishes that are traditionally served family style at the same time for all of the diners to share. Tapas (Spanish) and mezze (Middle Eastern) restaurants, in which guests choose a variety of small plates to create a full meal, are gaining in popularity as both allow for a wide sampling of foreign flavors. Dim sum (Chinese) is similar in that it allows for lots of small tastes, but with dim sum, the food is brought around on carts and customers get to see the food before deciding to order it from the cart. All of these examples of ethnic menus illustrate how ethnic restaurants impact not only the food selections but also the sequence of courses and approach to ordering and eating.

Ethnic restaurants offer guests a chance to experience another culture's dining experience, not just its food and drink. The food, the décor, the employee uniforms, and the style of service all work to enhance this experience. The menu itself may include descriptions of the cultural and culinary traditions of the country. Such text can increase sales and facilitate a dining experience that the guests cannot find at another nearby restaurant. An Ethiopian restaurant, for example, can explain on its menu the traditional use of injera—a flat, spongy bread—for picking up small pieces of stewed food as an alternative to the fork. This menu might also describe an Ethiopian coffee ceremony and thus drive coffee sales either at the end of the meal or in the afternoon between traditional meal periods. Guests unfamiliar with Ethiopian cuisine will find themselves both educated and reassured as they experiment with the dining style of another culture. Perhaps most important from a business perspective, the more authentic the dining experience, the higher prices the restaurant can command on its menu.

4.1.8 Brunch Menus

A brunch menu is typically utilized only for weekend meals. Brunch is a meal served across the late-breakfast and lunchtime period, and as such it usually offers foods traditionally associated with both meals. A brunch menu often offers heavier breakfast foods alongside lunch salads, sandwiches, and entrées. Because people usually treat brunch as a substitute for two meals, the menu offerings may be richer and more substantial than one usually sees on a basic breakfast menu.

A simple brunch menu often includes omelets, poached egg dishes, fancy versions of pancakes, waffles, and French toast. It may also include heartier breakfast meat dishes, such as steak and eggs or corned beef hash. Lunch options can range from entrée salads to hot sandwiches to simple entrées. Desserts are typically offered, too, and should be listed under their own heading or on a separate menu. A fancier brunch may be served buffet style to allow guests to sample a wider range of foods in a single sitting. A buffet brunch may include displays of breakfast breads, fruits, salads, egg dishes, potatoes, and cured pork alongside grand presentations of chilled shellfish and cured or smoked seafood, chafing dishes full of hot entrée components (meats, starches, and vegetables), carving stations with multiple large roasts, and tables groaning with desserts.

SPRING MENU
LATASCAUSA.COM

THE STORY OF TAPAS: THE SPIRIT OF SHARING

Tapa means "lid" in Spanish. It is widely believed that centuries ago farmers and laborers would visit local "tascas" for a well-earned drink, on top of which they would place a slice of bread to protect it from pesky flies. Over time, the innkeepers gradually began placing snacks, such as cured meats and sausages, on top of the bread slices. The "edible lids" slowly evolved into the exciting tapas experience we are familiar with today.

At La Tasca, our tapas dishes are designed to provide guests with an assortment of both traditional and more contemporary dishes, showcasing the best of this unique and exciting style of eating. Buen provecho!

BREADS AND STARTERS

Degustación de Aceites A trio of flavor-infused extra virgin olive oils: fresh herb, olive tapenade and spicy mushroom -- served with rustic bread 6

Pan de Ajo con Queso Slices of grilled rustic bread brushed with garlic and topped with melted mozzarella cheese 4

Pan a la Catalana Slices of toasted garlic bread served with our classic grated vine-ripened tomato spread along with fresh garlic 4

Dátiles con TocinoGF Skewered and grilled bacon-wrapped dates stuffed with blue cheese 6.50

Aceitunas MixtasGF Spanish Black, Gordal, Manzanilla and Arbequina olives lightly marinated in olive oil, herbs and spices 4.75

Patatas de Churrería Finely sliced potato deep fried to a golden crisp and served with a Cabrales cheese sauce and our spicy paprika aioli 5.50

Coca Mallorquina Spanish rustic bread "pizza" prepared with Manchego cheese and samfaina red sauce -- served with or without anchovies 6

Berenjenas Fritas Our signature platter of fried eggplant slices served with a warm Cabrales cheese dip 6.50

Croquetas de Pollo Pulled chicken béchamel, lightly breaded and battered and then deep fried to a golden brown 6.75

Croquetas de Espinacas Croquettes prepared with chopped spinach and pine nuts, lightly battered and deep fried 6.75

Montaditos de Jamón y Queso* Slices of our pan a la catalana bread: two topped with Manchego cheese and two topped with jamón Serrano 6.50

CURED MEATS AND CHEESES

Enjoy any combination of imported Spanish cured meats and cheeses -- feel free to mix and match to create your own meat and cheese board

Select One 5   Three 14   Five 22

Cured Meat Selections* Served with toasted bread
Salchichón Spicy pork sausage with fatty white chunks
Caña de Lomo Lean pork tenderloin cured with garlic
Fuet Young, lightly cured Catalan dry pork sausage
Chorizo Castilian aged sausage with paprika
Jamón Serrano Famously nutty flavored "mountain ham"

Cheese SelectionsGF Served with fig jam and bread
Tetilla Mild cow's milk cheese, aged only one week
Delicia de Cabra Creamy, elastic, white goat's cheese
Serena Soft, spreadable, buttery sheep's milk cheese
Cabrales Blue cheese cured in mountainous caves
Manchego Spain's most famous cheese -- salty sheep's milk cheese with a grainy texture

TASTING MENUS

A perfect choice for both newcomers to tapas and aficionados alike. The tasting menus are designed as a dinner for two, but any sized group may enjoy one or more of the chef-selected menus.

Meat Tapas Tasting Menu
Tasting menu centered on signature meat tapas 50
Buey al Jerez* Grilled angus steak with mushroom sauce
Pollo Frito Fried chicken tossed in a roasted garlic sauce
Dátiles Bacon-wrapped dates stuffed with blue cheese
Chorizo a la Parrilla Grilled spicy Spanish sausage links
Solomillo de Cerdo* Grilled bacon-wrapped tenderloin
Berenjenas Fritas Fried eggplant with Cabrales sauce
Espinacas Sautéed spinach with pine nuts and raisins
Ensalada de Manzana Sliced apple with Tetilla and quince

La Tasca Tasting Menu
Sampling of our most loved and popular tapas 65
Solomillo de Buey* Beef tenderloin with blue cheese
Chuletitas de Cordero* Grilled lamb chops
Brocheta de Pollo Grilled chicken and pepper skewers
Langostinos Jumbo shrimp sautéed in Grand Marnier
Calamares Quick fried, battered calamari rings
Brocheta de Gambas Bacon-wrapped scallops and shrimp
Espárragos Grilled fresh asparagus with sea salt
Patatas Bravas Fried potatoes with a spicy tomato sauce
Ensalada de Tomates Tomatoes, goat cheese, vinaigrette

Seafood Tapas Tasting Menu
Menu designed around specialty seafood tapas 55
Vieiras Escabeche Grilled scallops and artichoke hearts
Calamares Quick fried, battered calamari rings
Salmón Grilled salmon and spinach, fried mussels
Gambas al Ajillo Shrimp sautéed in olive oil and garlic
Atún a la Plancha* Herb-crusted grilled tuna with berries
Canelones Tomato and goat cheese stuffed eggplant rolls
Setas al Ajillo Mushrooms sautéed in garlic and olive oil
Ensalada de Espinacas Spinach, Cabrales cheese salad

PAELLAS

The word "paella" comes from the name of the pan in which it is made -- it is a rice dish originating in eastern Spain, but today it is served worldwide using any ingredient that goes well with rice.
Serves 2-3 People
Please allow 30-40 minutes to prepare. 38 Dollars

Arroz a Banda Seafood paella with shrimp and scallops -- with (upon request) or without squid ink

Paella Valenciana Traditional paella with grilled chicken, shrimp, scallops, mussels and calamari

Paella de Carne Paella with chicken and sausage

Paella Castellana Specialty paella made with lamb, duck and beef tenderloin

Arroz de Temporada Paella with zucchini, leeks and swiss chard; Serrano ham is optional

Arroz de Mejillones y Chorizo Paella with mussels and Spanish chorizo

Old Town Alexandria   Arlington   Baltimore Inner Harbor   Washington, DC   Rockville Town Square

Figure 4–6

This tapas menu illustrates the use of cuisine-specific menu category headings, authentic foreign terminology, and historical/cultural descriptions of the cuisine typical of an ethnic menu.

Printed with the permission of La Tasca USA.

SALAD TAPAS

Ensalada MixtaGF* Mixed green salad with cherry tomatoes, cucumber and an olive vinaigrette 6

Ensalada de Espinacas con Peras Spinach salad with slices of fresh pear, dates and walnuts, topped with crumbled Cabrales cheese 7.50

Ensalada de TomatesGF Colored tomato medley with mild goat cheese and an herb dressing 7

Crudo de Atún con ArugulaGF* Arugula topped with yellowfin tuna carpaccio, dressed with a porcini mushroom emulsion and balsamic glaze 8

Ensalada de ManzanaGF Thinly sliced, crisp green apples tossed with slivered almonds, soft Tetilla cheese and a lemon quince vinaigrette 7

Ensalada de Rábanos y Solomillo* Mixed greens with radishes, thinly sliced beef tenderloin and a horseradish vinaigrette 8

MEAT TAPAS

Chuletitas de Cordero* Grilled lamb chops served with garlic mashed potatoes and a green peppercorn sauce 14

Botifarra amb MongetesGF Grilled Catalan pork sausage over a bed of sautéed white beans with mint, red peppers and caramelized onions 7.50

Buey al Jerez* Grilled angus beef steak in a sherry mushroom sauce served with roasted potatoes 8.75

Pollo Frito al Ajo Fried, bone-in chicken tossed with a roasted garlic sauce 7

Solomillo de Buey* Grilled beef tenderloin, served with red-skinned garlic mashed potatoes and crumbled Cabrales cheese 12

Paella Valenciana Miniature paella with chicken, calamari, mussels and shrimp 7

Brocheta de CorderoGF* Grilled lamb marinated in cinnamon, skewered with dried apricots and served with a blackened carrot reduction 8

Brocheta de PolloGF Skewers of grilled chicken breast marinated in Andalusian spices with roasted red peppers 6.75

Chorizo a la Parrilla Grilled, imported Spanish sausage 7

Albóndigas a la Jardinera Beef meatballs served in a vegetable and herb marinara 6.50

Empanadas de Carne o Pollo Your choice of either two beef and cheese empanadas or two chicken and wild mushroom empanadas 7

Solomillo de Cerdo Ibérico* Grilled pork tenderloin medallions wrapped in bacon and served with our famous Cabrales cheese sauce 7.50

Paella de Chorizo Miniature paella with diced chorizo sausage and sliced mushrooms 7

Pato ConfitadoGF Duck leg confit baked with nutmeg and orange peel, served with caramelized figs 8.50

Mar y Tierra Beef tenderloin, shrimp, calamari rings and wild mushrooms tossed with a sweet sherry sauce 9

SEAFOOD TAPAS

Rollitos de Txangurro Crab meat, onions and a touch of roasted tomato spread onto a pastry shell and rolled into cigars 7.50

Gambas al AjilloGF Shrimp sautéed in olive oil with garlic and hot peppers 8

Calamares a la Andaluza Quick-fried, battered calamari rings 7.50

Gambas Gabardina Skewered shrimp, dipped in beer batter and deep fried 7.25

SalmónGF Grilled salmon topped with sautéed spinach and lightly fried mussels, served over a creamy spinach sauce 7.75

Langostinos al Licor de NaranjaGF** Jumbo shrimp sautéed with mandarin oranges and Grand Marnier 12

Vieiras en EscabecheGF Grilled scallops and artichoke hearts in a Spanish vinaigrette 9

Atún a la Plancha* Herb-crusted and blackened ahi tuna, served rare, and topped with berries 8

Brocheta de Gambas y VieirasGF Skewer prepared with grilled shrimp and bacon-wrapped scallops 7.75

Mejillones a la Marinera Mussels sautéed with a pepper and tomato marinara 7.50

Lubina a la PlanchaGF Grilled wild rockfish over sautéed cherry tomatoes with basil 8

Pulpo con Arroz de Negro Grilled octopus skewers served on a bed of squid ink rice 7.50

VEGETABLE TAPAS

Patatas Bravas Fried potatoes with a spicy tomato sauce and garlic aioli 5.25 / 7.50 grande

Canelones de BerenjenasGF Eggplant rolls stuffed with herb-roasted roma tomatoes, grilled sweet piquillo peppers and a mild goat cheese 7

Paella de Verduras Miniature paella with assorted garden vegetables 6.50

Verduritas a la BarbacoaGF Barbecue-grilled vegetables topped with a fried egg 7

Setas al AjilloGF Wild mushrooms sautéed in garlic and extra virgin olive oil 6.50

Vainas de Arveja SalteadasGF Snow peas sautéed in olive oil and garlic (our traditional recipe includes Serrano ham -- optional) 6

Tortilla Española Spain's traditional potato and onion omelet 6

Espinacas SalteadasGF Freshly sautéed spinach with garlic, pine nuts and raisins 6.50

Espárragos Verdes a la PlanchaGF Grilled asparagus drizzled with olive oil and sea salt 6.50

Coles de BruselasGF Brussel sprouts sautéed with garlic and onions, tossed with Cabrales and Manchego cheeses and sliced almonds 7

Piquillos RellenosGF Grilled piquillo peppers stuffed with white mushrooms and Manchego cheese, drizzled with olive oil and and a touch of honey 7.50

PREPARATION NOTES

*May contain cured, raw or undercooked ingredients. Consuming raw or undercooked meats, poultry, seafood, shellfish or eggs may increase your risk of food-borne illness, especially if you have certain medical conditions. **These items have some alcohol content. GF - These items are gluten-free. We cannot guarantee that our dishes are free from traces of gluten. Dishes may contain ingredients not mentioned in our menu descriptions, so please notify your server if you have a particular allergy or requirement.

Old Town Alexandria   Arlington   Baltimore Inner Harbor   Washington, DC   Rockville Town Square

Figure 4–6
(Continued)

brunch

burrata cheese   focaccia toast and extra virgin olive oil, pink peppercorns 12

housemade sticky buns 4

seasonal fruit plate 12

clay oven bread with cinnamon sugar 4

steel cut oatmeal   bruleed bananas, toasted almonds and whipped cinnamon cream 8

seasonal soup 6

almond stuffed french toast   local strawberries, toasted almonds and local maple syrup 13

lemon souffle pancakes   blueberry compote 13

house cured salmon plate   bialy's bagel, egg salad, shaved onion and capers 14

chopped cobb salad   chicken, egg, bleu, bacon, tomato, cucumber, grilled onion, avocado, croutons and mustard vinaigrette 12

tossed karen's caesar salad   cured salmon, grilled red onion, capers, sieved egg, bacon, croutons and reggiano parmesan 12

vegetable frittata 12

scrambled eggs   yukon gold home fries 10

breakfast pizza 13

mushroom pizza   gruyere cheese and caramelized onions 14

egg sandwich   clay bread, local fried eggs, bacon, lettuce, tomato and homefries 12

bbq beef crepes   housemade crepes, cilantro crema, local egg and black beans stew 13

crispy chicken livers   frisee and watercress salad, poached egg, house made bacon and dried fruit compote 13

fire benedict   housemade english muffin, housemade ham, poached eggs and hollandaise 14

house made corned beef hash   local egg, home fries, mustard aioli, caramelized onions and apples 16

pesto pasta   tomatoes, burrata cheese, pinenuts, parmesan and basil 11

local grass fed beef burger   local cheddar, tomato relish, mustard aioli and garlic herb fries 18   jj style add 3

fish fry sandwich   herb focaccia, tartar sauce, pepper and olive relish, arugula, and yukon gold potato chips 13

shrimp fried rice   shiitakes, leeks, scallions, bacon, spinach and scrambled egg with chile aioli 16

sides

mixed greens with sherry vinaigrette 6

traditional caesar salad 6

seasonal fruit 5

yukon gold home fries 4

housemade bacon 5

housemade breakfast sausage 5

multigrain, pave or brioche toast 2

bialy's bagel plain or onion 2.75

beverages and specialty drinks

seasonal fruit smoothie 5

fresh squeezed orange juice 4

coffee 3

hot chocolate 4

espresso 4

macchiato 4

cappuccino 4

latte 4

mocha 4

loose teas 3.5

bloody mary with dr katz's pickle 8

bellini 8

mimosa 8

brunch served every saturday and sunday from 10am - 2pm
we use locally grown produce, meats and environmentally sound seafood whenever possible
consuming raw or undercooked meats, poultry, seafood, shellfish or eggs may increase your risk of foodborne illness
many ingredients are not listed on the menu; please let us know if you have any dietary restrictions

---

Figure 4–7   This brunch menu shows how heartier breakfast and lunch items are combined on the same menu with classic brunch beverages. Douglas Katz and Fire Food and Drink.

Unlike on a basic breakfast menu, alcoholic drinks are traditional components of brunch menus. Champagne, mimosas, and Bloody Marys are common, but opportunities for creativity abound in this area. All beverages, alcoholic and nonalcoholic, should be marketed heavily on the main menu. Because of the propensity for people to wake up late on weekend mornings (after late Friday and Saturday nights out), to dine late after church services, or to lounge around a bar all day watching sports, restaurants may offer brunch on weekends starting as early as 9:00 a.m. and continuing until the restaurant converts over to its dinner menu. Brunch, especially Sunday brunch, is quite common in fancier establishments, including hotels and country clubs.

4.1.9 Afternoon Tea Menus

Like brunch, tea (the meal, not the beverage) is reserved for a time between traditional meal periods. Tea is normally served mid-to-late afternoon and can function as either a snack or a light meal. Often thought of as an English tradition, tea may celebrate the foods of England or the foods of Asia, where tea is also a popular beverage. The traditional English afternoon tea includes a range of sweet pastries, scones, and tea sandwiches, which are simple sandwiches that usually have a main item on crust-free bread or biscuit but without the addition of lettuce, tomato, or other garnishes common on large sandwiches. Tea sandwiches and pastries are usually no more than two bites in size. Scones may be larger and served with jam, lemon curd, and/or clotted cream. The popular way to present these delights is on a multi-tiered tray from which the entire table dines, though some establishments provide each guest her own tiered tray.

During afternoon tea, both hot tea and alcoholic beverages are traditionally offered. Multiple tea choices should be highlighted on the main menu or on a separate menu. They are typically served in pots rather than by the cup; in fancier establishments looseleaf teas are used. Sherry, wine, and champagne are common alcoholic offerings for a tea. Some guests may treat afternoon tea as their evening meal, but most tea patrons use it as a bridge to stave off hunger between a light lunch and a late dinner.

Some foodservice operations serve tea only on weekends and holidays while others, especially high-end hotels, provide the service daily.

4.1.10 Lounge Menus

Some people consider a lounge menu to equate to bar food. A lounge is an environment in which people can relax before, during, or after dinner, usually for drinks and accompanying snacks. Most lounges offer full menus following the pattern of appetizers, entrées, and desserts, but the purpose of the food is generally to accompany the alcoholic drinks, not the other way around. Consequently, lounge menus tend to offer larger numbers of appetizers and more casual entrées than the average restaurant might provide. Desserts are usually limited in number unless the business focuses on liqueurs and other after-dinner drinks.

The items on a lounge menu are typically high in protein, fat, and salt. These nutrients serve a purpose beyond flavor in a bar or lounge. Salt makes people thirsty, so menu planners include salty foods to encourage the sales of beverages. However, alcohol, consumed too quickly, causes customers to go from comfortable to inebriated rather quickly. Protein and fat slow the rate at which the stomach empties and thus the speed at which alcohol is absorbed into the body. They give a person a chance to process some of the alcohol in her system before getting walloped with the full impact of her total alcohol consumption. Fried appetizers, nachos and other cheese-heavy snacks, burgers, and chicken all make excellent lounge menu options. Fancier operations may list steaks and seafood as well. This is not to say that a lounge cannot offer a salad or a light entrée, but the vast majority of the listings on a lounge menu should be protein- and calorie-rich.

A Tradition Begins

Afternoon Tea is a tradition that began in 1840 by the Seventh Duchess of Bedford. Due to a long period between the meals, the Duchess experienced a sinking feeling that afflicted her between 3 and 4 o'clock. One afternoon she requested a tray of tea, bread, butter, and cake to be brought to her room.

Gradually, she became accustomed to this habit and invited her friends to partake in her daily ritual. Within a short period of time, this affair, known as Afternoon Tea, became an elaborate social event. During this time, the Earl of Sandwich invented the sandwich, enhancing the overall experience of Afternoon Tea.

Afternoon Tea remains to this day a graceful affair to enjoy in the company of friends and associates. Afternoon Tea takes place daily in our traditional Tea Lobby featuring live harp music performed 365 days a year.

Hours

Daily from 1:00PM to 5:00PM

Each seating lasts approximately one and a half hours

Harpist performs daily from

1:00PM to 5:00PM, Weekends

2:00PM to 4:30PM, Weekdays

Dress Code

Smart Casual

Dress code allows for dressy jeans but no baseball cap, shorts, sportswear, ripped jeans or beach sandals

Reservations

(312) 787-2200 or e-mail Shaun.Rajah@hilton.com. Punctuality is recommended as reservations are held for ten minutes.

Traditional Afternoon Tea
$36 per person

Assortment of:

Sandwiches

Four selections of Sandwiches prepared on House made Breads: Roasted Beef on a mini black Asiago pepper roll, Tomato and Cucumber on White Bread, Avocado and Bacon on multigrain Egg Salad on Brioche

Pastries

2 selections per person designed by our Pastry Chef

Fruit Bread & Scones

Accompanied by Preserves, Lemon Curd & English Double Devon Cream

Little Prince & Princess Tea
$18.00 per person

For our junior guests (4years to 12 years)

Assortment of:

Sandwiches

Three selection of Sandwiches prepared on House made Breads: Tomato and Cucumber on White Bread, Egg Salad on Brioche Little Miss Sandwiches of Peanut Butter & Jelly

Pastries

1 selection per person designed by our Pastry Chef

Fruit Bread & Scones

Accompanied by Preserves, Lemon Curd, & English Double Devon Cream All Servings include Tea or Coffee

Why not add a touch of sparkle to your Afternoon Tea with a glass of Champagne for $11, Mimosa $13, & Bellini's $13

An 18% gratuity charge will be added to parties of 6 or larger

Figure 4–8
This afternoon tea menu boasts the kind of food and beverage offerings expected at a quality afternoon tea.
Shaun Rajah, Palm Court and Chef Baasim Zafar, Drake Hotel.

The finest, freshest & fragrant teas

Black Tea – Most Caffeine

Palm Court
Now served with distinction at the Drake Hotel, Chicago, the rich blend of four teas made its premier 25 years ago from US Master Blender , Harney & Sons Fine Teas. A timeless collection of Indian Assam with soft chocolate notes of Chinese Keemun, along with the smoothest Ceylon and a toasty Formosa Oolong makes this fine enough to be sipped by Royalty.

Bombay Chai
Cinnamon chips, ginger, cloves, nutmeg make this exquisite, intensely flavored black tea.

Darjeeling
Tea leaves yield a fruity and floral flavor resulting in an aromatic cup – it's best without milk.

Earl Grey
With organic cold pressed Italian Bergamot Oil, a rare variety of Citrus

English Breakfast
Stays true to the exacting standards of the popular original – works well with milk and sugar.

Irish Breakfast
It smoothly blends the high notes of a high-grown Ceylon with the underscore of a hearty Assam. Did you know the Irish drink more tea than anyone else in the world?

Lapsang Souchong
A rich Chinese black tea made in the age-old tradition of slowly smoking leaves over natural pine tree roots. Lapsang Souchong produces an intensely smoky brew that is considered to be a unique treat – a good tea for stimulating digestion.

Orange Dulce
Brew teeming with notes of bergamot, orange, vanilla and jasmine blossoms. Reminiscent of an aged Port, the flavor is sure to please – a self drinker.

Pear Caramel
Washington state pears blended with Ceylon and China black teas & a touch of sweet caramel makes it the perfect after dinner dessert tea or afternoon treat

Wild Blackberries
Made of exquisite China black tea blended with wild blackberries – a self drinks

Oolong Tea – Medium Caffeine

Blue Peacock
Subtle and sweet spices, inspired tranquility as notes of citrus tease the palate. A new addition to our exclusive teas. Try it. Tell us how you feel.

Green Tea – Less Caffeine

Gunpowder
A premium green tea known for its distinctly penetrating flavor – a self drinker.

Tropical Green
The most exciting tropical green leaf tea in the world. Fresh pineapple, orange peel and fruit extracts – a self drinker.

White Tea –Least Caffeine

White Jasmine
Tossed with superior jasmine flowers, this rare tea boasts a smooth and naturally sweet flavor. This tea is known to prolong life expectancy and lower cholesterol levels.

Tisanes / Herbal Infusions
Caffeine Free

Wild Blossom & Berries
Blackberry and black currant, infused with lemongrass, hibiscus, chamomile, mint, licorice root and spices – its best without milk.

Chamomile Citrus
Made with Soothing Egyptian Chamomile flowers and subtle slices of citrus fruit, this vibrant blend will rejuvenate the spirit

Chocolate Mint Truffle
A blend of chocolate cacao nibs, mint and rooibos leaves

Tea-Tini $12

Mint Tea-Tini
Mint leaves, sweetened ice tea, splash of Roses lime juice, Ketel One Vodka. Lime wheel, for garnish

Lemon Tea-Tini
Ketel One Citroen vodka, unsweetened ice tea, super fine sugar, splash of Lemon-Lime soda. Lemon slices of garnish

Chai Tea-Tini
Baileys Coffee liquor, Vanilla Vodka, Chai-Tea concentrate, milk shaved chocolate, freshly grated nutmeg and fresh mint sprig for garnish

Bombay Tea Punch $15
Hum liquor, strongly brewed Bombay Chai, honey syrup, lemon juice, lemon wheel and mint sprig, served in red wine glass

Tea Cocktail $15
Hum liquor, served in a brandy snifter with a sprig rosemary, garnish with a slice of apple, pear or ginger and a pot of earl grey tea on side.

Figure 4–8
(Continued)

MIST
Restaurant • Lounge

MIST LOUNGE MENU

SLIDERS - $8
Your Choice of 3 Sliders Below served with house cut fries.
Each Additional Slider $2

Angus Cheeseburger Slider- With cheddar, lettuce, pickle & garlic mayo

Crab Cake Slider- House made crab cake with lettuce and spicy aioli

Cod Fish Slider- Beer battered and topped with tarter and lettuce

Fried Chicken Slider-Garlic mayo & pickle

Philly Slider- Roasted Beef with onions, peppers and melted cheese

---

Basket of Fries- House cut & fried to golden brown and served with ketchup. $4

Basket of Onion Rings Beer battered onion rings fried to golden brown and served with a smoky barbeque sauce. $5

Tillamook Cheddar Potato Skins - Wedges of potatoes topped with Tillamook cheddar cheese and bacon, garnished with green onions and sour cream. $6

Spinach and Artichoke Dip- our house blend of fresh spinach, artichoke hearts and roasted red peppers in a rich cream sauce. $5   ***add crab $6

Fried Calamari- Flour dusted and fried to a golden brown. Served with marinara. $8

3 Fish Taco's - grilled cod served in warm corn tortillas with shredded cabbage, Pico de Gallo, and chipotle aioli. $9

Fish and Chips- beer battered fish and chips fried to golden brown and served with house cut fries.   ***Cod $11   ***Halibut $16

The Mist Burger- ½ lb burger patty, ground in house, char broiled and topped with lettuce, tomato, onion, pickles and mayonnaise served with house cut fries. $9
***add Cheese $1   ***add Bacon $1

MIST RESTAURANT

SURFTIDES LINCOLN CITY | 2945 NW JETTY AVENUE | LINCOLN CITY, OR 97367

ALL PARTIES OF SIX OR MORE ARE SUBJECT TO AN 18% GRATUITY

Figure 4–9 This lounge menu illustrates the kinds of food typical for a well-done lounge menu.
Printed with the permission of Nathan Carlson and Surftides Resort.

4.1.11 Dessert Menus

A dessert menu is a separate document from the dessert offerings listed on the main menu in certain establishments. Many mid-range to high-end dining establishments opt to place their dessert listings on their own menu. While such an approach does not assist with the marketing of dessert early, it has many advantages.

A dessert menu provides plenty of space for a menu planner to describe delectable creations for the diner. The extra space also allows for the marketing of dessert beverages, from coffees to dessert wines to after-dinner cordials. Psychologically, having a separate menu to introduce a course suggests to the guest that this is an essential component to the meal, not simply another menu category relegated to the corner of the main menu. With a dessert menu, the guest is handed a list from which to choose, but the only options are dessert, or after-dinner beverages, or both. The guest may still decline to order anything, but the psychological pressure is to select something from the menu. (After all, the server's job is to deliver the menu, and the customer's job is to place an order, right?) When desserts are listed on the main menu, the guest can rest easy knowing that she has already done her job and purchased something (a main course); with a dessert menu the guest has yet to order something from the menu and thus feels some small pressure to do so.

The sole food category on a dessert menu is typically listed as "Desserts" or with no category heading at all. As with other menus, the dessert menu should include variety and balance. Also, to merit its own menu, a dessert menu should offer at least six choices and may list many more. If a restaurant provides cheese as a dessert alternative, it is listed among the dessert options. Dessert beverages, on the other hand, may require several categories on the menu. Possible categories include ports, dessert wines, bourbons, scotches, brandies, liqueurs, and tea, coffee, and espresso drinks (with or without alcohol).

Some menu planners, upon discovering that desserts are not popular sellers in their restaurants, have begun experimenting with portion sizes. Rather than serve a full portion of dessert, a pastry chef can prepare mini-desserts of just one or two bites for a low price. These mini-desserts help to encourage dessert sales to guests who arrive at dessert already stuffed. The concept can be expanded to allow for dessert samplers for those guests who wish to have a couple of bites of every dessert on the menu. With creative strategies, a menu planner can make dessert an essential component of the dining experience for nearly every guest. Creating an effective dessert menu is the first step of that marketing strategy.

4.1.12 Children's Menus

A children's menu is a must for those businesses that cater to families with small children. Many parents are tight on money and prefer not to spring for a full meal portion from which their kids will eat only three bites. When a restaurant chooses not to offer a separate kids' menu, it communicates to parents that children are not common patrons and are not easily accommodated. (This is not to say that such a restaurant would turn away a child, but rather that the child is expected to behave like an adult and to order off the adult menu.) Children who get their own "special" menu tend to feel more welcome in a restaurant than they do if they are forced to act like adults.

A children's menu may include many courses, but it definitely should list three—entrées, beverages, and desserts. The kind of food offered on a kids' menu should be simple and child-friendly. This does not necessarily mean that it must resort to chicken fingers, pizza, and pasta. Ethnic restaurants may offer less spicy, simplistic versions of their culture's dishes. Because their taste buds are extremely sensitive, children often prefer foods that are blander and milder than their parents' preferences—thus the

g r i l l

****

Tahitian Vanilla Bean Creme Brulee 7

  Rum Marinated Berries

Chocolate Chi-Chi 7

Dark Chocolate Shell, White & Dark Chocolate
Mousses, Raspberry Sauce

Mile High Coconut Lemon Cake 7

  Madagascar Vanilla Bean Ice Cream

Flourless Chocolate Cake 7

Black Peppercorn Ice Cream, Red Wine Caramel Drizzle

Strawberry Rhubarb Crisp 7

  Madagascar Vanilla Bean Ice Cream

Banana Cream Pie 7

  Salty Bourbon Caramel, Almond Crispies

House Made Ice Creams & Sorbets- two scoops 6

Ice Cream: Pear Balsamic, Bourbon Butter Pecan,
Girl Scout Cookie, Chocolate Ginger,
Salted Caramel

Sorbets: Strawberry, Grapefruit-Prosecco,
Limoncello, Coconut-Lime

Pastry Chef Anne Mason

****

d e s s e r t s

Figure 4–10 This dessert menu provides variety and balance in its offerings while also marketing dessert beverages effectively.
Pastry Chef Anne Mason.

g r i l l

* *

Dessert Wines and Port

Michele Chiarlo "Nivole" Moscato (375) 2009 $25 Glass $5
Frogmore Creek Iced Riesling (375) 2006 $28 Glass $7
Dolce/Far Niente (375) 2005 $120. Glass $18
Moscato d' Asti "Saracco" Italia 2010 $25. bottle

Kopke 10 year Tawny Glass $8.
Warre's Ruby LBV 1999 Glass $8.
Warre's "Otima" 10 year Tawny Glass $9.

Coffee, Espresso

Coffee 1.25
Espresso 2.00
Cappuccino, Latte 3.25

Steven Smith Teamaker 2.50
Small Batch Organic Teas from Portland, Oregon

Herbal: Hibiscus Red, Chamomile, Peppermint, Lemongrass

Caffeinated: Brahmin Black (English Breakfast), Lord Bergamot (Earl
Grey), Jasmine Silver Tip, Fez Mint

* *

d e s s e r t s

Figure 4–10
(Continued)

reason for the popularity of chicken fingers, cheese pizza, and plain pasta. However, mild does not mean boring. Kids do quite well with quesadillas, beans and rice, carrots and other mildly sweet vegetables, and fruit. Mild meats, like chicken, are good protein sources, but so are cheese and seafood. Whatever the ingredient, the portion size should be small. Kids eat less food than their parents, and their parents do not want to pay for excessive portions.

The ingredients on a kids' menu should be served as separate components where feasible, so children can identify each of the ingredients easily. If a child with an aversion to peas finds one pea in a stew, she may dismiss the entire dish. However, given a plate of stewed meat, sliced carrots, and buttered peas, the same child could enjoy the meat and carrots and simply skip the peas. The separation of ingredients also helps parents to spot potential allergens. Because of the danger of allergic reactions, common food allergens should be listed clearly in any dish in which they appear.

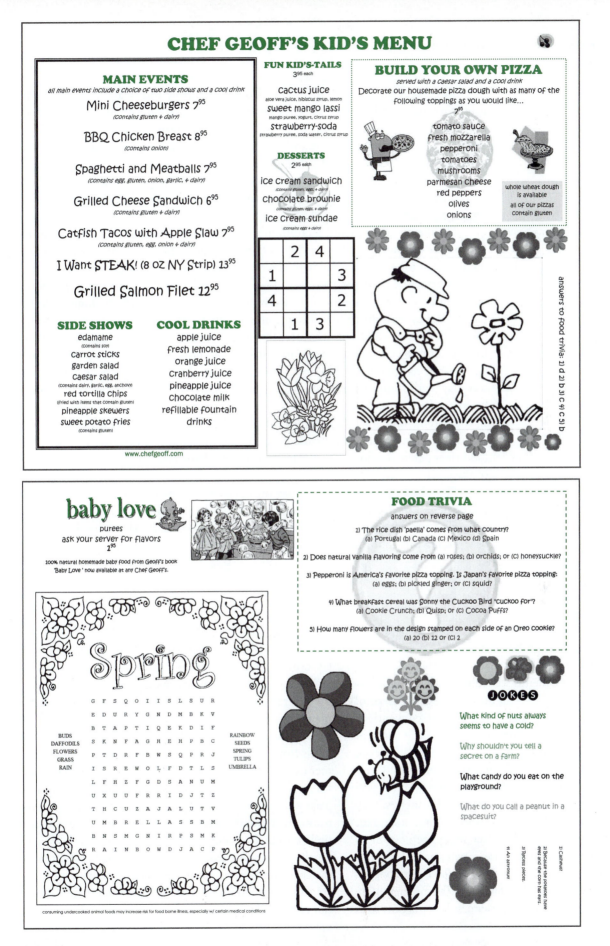

Figure 4–11

This highly effective kids' menu shows how child-friendly food and drink can be creative and how a children's menu provides entertainment as well as food and beverage options. Chef Geoff's.

Beverages on a children's menu should be simple but healthy. While soda might excite a child, most parents wish to see a selection of juices and milks instead. Fun, creative drinks are not the sole domain of adults, either. Hot chocolate with whipped cream and crushed peppermint candy can make a child's eyes sparkle at breakfast, and a virgin strawberry daiquiri may have greater appeal than a basic soda. When feasible, beverages for the youngest children should be served in a cup with a lid and a straw to avoid spills unless the parent or child requests otherwise.

Unlike an adult menu, a children's menu may double as an activity sheet to occupy the kids until the food arrives. Often, they are paper printouts with games or pictures that the kids can color with crayons supplied by the restaurant. If the kids are happy during the meal, the parents will be happy (and very likely to return). The food on a children's menu should all be relatively quick to prepare. Servers should ask the parents if they wish the child's dish to come out right away, which also helps to occupy the child. When a child eats her entrée during the parents' appetizer course, she is then in a position to color more, engage in conversation, or possibly taste her parents' food without the nagging pain of hunger to disgruntle her. For a more energetic child, dessert may be the only civilized option. Offering dessert, usually just a couple of choices listed on the main kids' menu, gives parents the chance to distract a child with sweets, so the parents can enjoy their main course (or their own dessert). As with the entrée, a child's dessert should be a smaller portion than the adult-size desserts. To keep kids (and their parents) as loyal customers, some menu planners include dessert in the price of the meal.

Pint-sized customers may not pay the bill or determine the tip, but they are often instrumental in deciding which restaurant a family patronizes on any given night. Providing a menu that meets their needs is a surefire way to develop a loyal customer base among this youthful market.

SUMMARY

Specialty menus that go beyond the traditional breakfast, lunch, and dinner menus abound in the foodservice world. Most of these menus still adhere to the rules of variety and balance, and they all must address the needs of the intended market or client. The naming conventions may vary, but the menus continue to serve the needs of both the customer and the business. Take-out and room service menus focus on foods that transport well. Cycle menus repeat their options on a schedule. While cycle menus are used often in noncommercial businesses, they are sometimes utilized for certain specials on a restaurant menu. Banquet menus offer a set sequence of courses with few choices; the options are constrained by the target audience or client and the need to serve everyone efficiently and at roughly the same time. Tasting menus are often elaborate gustatory experiences, but portion sizes must allow guests to make it through the entire meal. Catering menus list a plethora of options from which a client selects; the ultimate menu that the guests see at the catered event is a subset of the catering menu. Ethnic menus highlight the foods and cultural traditions of the represented culture. Brunch menus boast traditional foods from both breakfast and lunch while afternoon tea menus offer tea sandwiches and pastries along with hot tea or alcohol. A lounge menu should provide food that pairs well with the consumption of alcohol in a bar environment. Dessert menus focus the guest's attention entirely on the dessert course's food and beverage offerings. Finally, children's menus attend to the food and often to the entertainment needs of a business's youngest customers to keep them happy and occupied, so their parents can enjoy their own meals.

COMPREHENSION QUESTIONS

1. List two commonalities between traditional menus and other menus.
2. What characteristics should food on a take-out menu have?
3. When do many restaurants begin taking orders for room service breakfast?
4. What is a cycle menu?
5. What two factors impact how often a cycle menu repeats?
6. List an example of a type of food in a restaurant that might be offered on a cycle.
7. How might a menu planner help guests avoid palate fatigue during a lengthy banquet?
8. As guests at a banquet must all be served the same course before any table moves to the next course, what style of service other than American service is often used at banquets?
9. How do catering menus differ from other types of menus?
10. What "course" is often listed on a catering menu but not on most other menus?
11. List five beverages commonly offered on a brunch menu.
12. List three kinds of foods typically served at afternoon tea.
13. What qualities should food on a lounge menu possess?
14. What function does a children's menu often serve other than providing a list of food and beverage choices?

DISCUSSION QUESTIONS

1. Select a specific ethnic restaurant in your area. How does its menu differ from a traditional menu format?
2. Think of a time that you ordered take-out or room service. How well did the food meet your expectations? Was it an appropriate choice for take-out or room service? Why?
3. Think of two restaurants you have patronized—one that offers dessert on the main menu and one that presents a separate dessert menu. Which set of dessert options sounded better to you? Was one more effective than the other at encouraging you to buy dessert? Why?
4. Describe a favorite children's menu from your childhood. What made it your favorite? How often did you go to that restaurant as compared with others that your parents chose?
5. Select one of the types of menus (other than catering) listed in the chapter. Create a menu (names of dishes only) appropriate for the menu type you selected. Explain why it works well as a model for that particular menu type.

5
Beverage Menus

The categories, menu content, and descriptions for a beverage menu are vastly different from those on a food menu but no less deserving of attention. Beverage menus are excellent opportunities for revenue and profit generation. Beverages usually require less labor to prepare and serve than food, and they command huge profit margins. However, while beverages are considered essential components of a meal for most diners, a poorly written beverage menu can intimidate a guest and discourage beverage sales. A well-written beverage menu encourages guests to enjoy multiple or higher-priced beverages as part of the dining experience.

Not too long ago, "beverage menu" was synonymous with "wine list." Many of today's restaurants recognize that not all patrons are wine drinkers and that beverages of all types represent an opportunity to meet a guest's needs while increasing revenue. Depending on the business's concept and the target market's demographics and psychographic preferences, a beverage menu may highlight cocktails, liquor, wine, beer, or nonalcoholic drinks such as tea, coffee, juice, or water. When an establishment becomes known for an excellent beverage program, drinks can become as much a draw for business as the food and service are. Learning how to create a quality beverage menu that meets the needs of the business and the clientele is a necessity for any menu planner.

5.1 WINE MENUS

While modern beverage menus often include a range of alcoholic beverages, wine menus were for years the default option for any upscale restaurant. Because wine pairs well with food, wine lists continue to be popular in high-end establishments, even if no other type of alcohol is served. Wine menus range from a single page of fewer than twenty options to bound books with several hundred listings.

As with every other type of menu, a wine menu must support the company's concept and appeal to the target audience. For example, a casual lounge that focuses on inexpensive bar food and beer and liquor sales may have a short wine list with inexpensive options for those consumers who only drink wine. An expensive French restaurant may opt to focus mainly on pricy French wines with only a few cheaper options. A wine list that includes only expensive options is likely to sell less wine overall, but the problem is magnified when the food and wine are at very different price points. Generally speaking, less expensive restaurants should offer less expensive wine choices, but even extremely expensive operations should have available at least a couple of more affordable wine selections. No matter what the price point, guests should always be able to find wine by the glass that costs less than the cost of an entrée.

Wine menus should provide variety across several variables including grape type, region, color, body, and vintage. The New World wines of North and South America, Australia, and Africa are typically labeled by

By the end of this chapter, you will be able to:

- List several approaches to writing a beverage description on a menu
- List several approaches to categorizing beverages on a menu
- List several beverage types and describe the breadth of options available for each type
- Create a beverage menu that follows a common approach to beverage categorizing and naming and supports a given restaurant concept

grape type; European wines are usually identified by region. Finally, any producer can create a wine and give it a proprietary name based on neither grape type nor region. While a wine menu can list wines from any number of regions, at a minimum it should include local wines (in the United States that means from nearby states or at least from somewhere in America) and wines from the same country as the cuisine being served. For example, an Italian restaurant in New York should include Italian, American, and, ideally, New York State wine options. A Greek restaurant in Texas may include Greek and American wines. Restaurants serving American fare may opt just for a selection of American wines. The logic behind these rules of variety is that Americans will want either the beverage traditionally served with that food or the local wines with which they are most familiar. These rules are only minimum guidelines for variety; a restaurant is always free to include wines from all over the world.

When determining which wines to include on the wine list, a menu planner should ensure that several whites and reds are included. Sparkling and rosé wines offer even greater variety but should not be considered a substitute for a healthy listing of reds and whites. The selection should include light, medium, and heavy wines to pair well with the range of light to heavy foods. Most of the wines should be dry with at least one semi-dry option to drink with the entrée. Sweet wines may be included to pair with dessert. Finally, because wine qualities depend in part on the weather during the grapes' growing season, the wines served should not all come from the same vintage or year.

5.1.1 Naming and Categorizing Wines

Because of the many variables that identify a wine, a listing on a wine menu should include the wine's producer, grape type, appellation (region), and vintage (or at least as much of that information as is available). Old World wines may not state a grape type, but connoisseurs of those wines are familiar with the grapes used in certain regions. Nonvintage wines will not provide a year. If the wine producer has given its wine a proprietary name, that name should be listed with other basic information available about the wine. Figure 5–1 illustrates the several naming conventions.

The order in which the components of a wine's name are listed depends upon how the menu planner chooses to organize the wine list and to name the wine categories. There is no universal standard, but generally speaking, if a category states the commonality among the wines under that heading, the commonality should not be the first thing mentioned for each listing. In fact, that variable may be eliminated entirely. The variable that most distinguishes each wine from the others under the same subheading should be listed first. For example, if a wine list has a category entitled "Cabernet Sauvignon," a wine under that heading might be written as "Cakebread Cellars, Cabernet Sauvignon, Napa Valley, 2008" or simply as "Cakebread Cellars, Napa Valley, 2008." If the same wine were listed under the heading of "California" or "Red," then the grape type would lead the listing as "Cabernet Sauvignon, Cakebread Cellars, Napa Valley, 2008." In essence, wines named by grape type should list the

Cabernet Sauvignon, Cakebread Cellars, Napa Valley, 2008	Named by grape type (cabernet sauvignon). Lists in order: grape, producer, region, and vintage.
Chateauneuf-du-Pape, Chateau de Beaucastel, 2008	Named by region (Chateauneuf-du-Pape). Lists in order: region, producer, and vintage.
Caymus Vineyards, Conundrum, California, 2010	Named by proprietary name (Conundrum). Lists in order: producer, proprietary name, region, and vintage.

Figure 5–1

Examples of wine-naming conventions

grape type first, unless the grape type is stated in the category heading. Similarly, wines named by region should list the region first unless the category name does that already. Proprietary names are rarely used as a heading, so they are often listed with the producer first, followed by the proprietary name. Vintage is usually listed at the end of the wine's name, although some menu planners choose to list the vintage first because the layout creates a natural column with each wine beginning with a four-digit year in its name.

No matter how a menu planner chooses to sequence a wine's name, if the wine list includes more than a dozen or so wines, it should provide a bin number for each wine. A bin number is simply a number given to a wine that corresponds to the number on the bin or container in which the wine is stored at the restaurant. Listing a bin number allows for the guest to order by number instead of by wine name. The use of a bin number helps to avoid communication errors, as some wines have similar names. Additionally, guests who are uncomfortable pronouncing the foreign words in a wine's name can simply provide the bin number without embarrassing themselves in front of their tablemates. When listed, bin numbers are usually placed in a separate column to the left of the wine names.

Just as there is no standard format for naming a wine, there is no universal approach to naming the categories on a menu. Some menu planners use grape types as headings; others use countries or regions. Still others divide the menu simply into sparkling, white, rosé, red, and dessert. Of course, these are not the only approaches. Wine menus can be intimidating to some customers, so some menu planners have taken the approach of categorizing wines by their body and flavor. In these cases a category heading might be "Light and Fruity" or "Crisp, Mineral-y Whites." Extensive wine lists at upscale restaurants often assume that guests know something about wine, so they tend to sort wines by country and then by grape type or region. One- or two-page wine lists in a casual, kitschy, or trendy restaurant are better suited to employ more innovative, user-friendly naming conventions.

5.1.2 Pairing Wine and Food

Upscale restaurants often have a sommelier to guide and advise diners in their wine purchases; at a minimum, the servers are trained to play this role. More casual restaurants may rely on the menu to do the job of pairing wines with food. Short wine lists can include brief tasting notes for each wine. An example of a brief tasting note might be "A crisp, dry, light-bodied white wine with hints of grapefruit and hay." Other menu planners take the liberty of listing a recommended wine for each entrée. For example, directly underneath a seafood stew, the menu might state, "Recommended pairing: Estancia Chardonnay" or simply "Pairs well with an American Chardonnay." There are conflicting theories as to the value of specifying a wine to pair with each dish. On the one hand, guests who are intimidated by wine may be relieved to see a suggested pairing and may order wine that they otherwise might have shunned. On the other hand, a guest who does not care for the recommended wine type may choose to skip wine entirely for fear that his preferred wine would not go with his chosen meal. The only way to know which theory makes sense for a given restaurant's audience is to test it. A menu planner might list recommended wine pairings for a month or two to see if wine sales go up or down. The lessons learned from that data let the menu planner know whether to maintain menu pairings or to remove them in the next iteration of the food menu.

To determine which wines go perfectly with which foods can require years of study. Fortunately, the best wine choice for a guest is partly based on his menu choice and partly based on his taste preferences. The best match for a dish might be

Wine Director: Caterina Mirabelli

Reserve List Available

district

SPARKLING / WHITES
6 oz glass / bottle

Bubbles Around the World

Ca' Vittoria Brut Rose, *Raboso Blend*, Veneto, Italy NV — 12 / 48
Full bodied with notes of lemon zest, kafir lime and rose petals on both the nose and palate. Crisp and refreshing with a dry finish.

Lenoble Brut, Champagne, France NV — 20 / 80
Full bodied with notes of warm brioche and lemon zest and green apple. Elegant bubbles and a long, fresh finish.

Ca' Del Roro, *Prosecco*, Veneto, Italy NV — 9 / 36
Fresh and clean, showing notes of green apple, lemon zest and marzipan.

Musva, *Muscat*, Valencia, Spain NV — 10 / 40
Notes of white flower, pear, marzipan and white peach. Crisp and fruity with elegant bubbles.

Gruet, *Blanc du Noirs*, New Mexico NV — 10 / 40
100% Pinot Noir. Fresh and fruity, showing notes of apple, brioche and lime.

Aromatic Whites
Taste how these varietals differ between warm and cool climates

Schwarzbock, *Gruner Veltliner*, Austria 2010 *1L bottle* — 10 / 50
Spicy nose of white pepper with notes of lemon, key lime and grapefruit citrus on the palate. The body is crisp and refreshing with a bright acidity.

Juliusspital, *Scheurebe*, Franken, Germany 2010 — 12 / 48
Notes of white peach and tangerine on the nose and palate. A fresh and crisp body with a hint of sweetness and a sparkling minerality.

Dr. Heyden, *Riesling Auslese*, Rheinhessen, Germany 1989 — 12 / 48
Notes of clementine, orange blossom and honey on the nose and palate. The body is sweet and rich with a refreshing, crisp acidity on the finish.

Tasting flight of above 17

Exotic Whites
Similar to a Chardonnay, but with a more distinct finish

Vevi, *Verdejo*, Rueda, Spain 2010 — 9 / 36
Notes of papaya, peach, tangerine and key lime on both the nose and palate. Crisp and clean with a mild acidity and a juicy finish.

Durin, *Pigato*, Liguria, Italy 2010 — 12 / 48
Nose and palate of meyer lemon, white peach, nectarine and grapefruit. Crisp acidity and a fine minerality with a long, savory finish.

La Yunta, *Torrontes*, La Rioja, Argentina 2011 — 9 / 36
Aromatic with notes of honeysuckle and gardenia. White peach and honeydew on the palate with a crisp acidity and juicy finish.

Tasting flight of above 15

Chardonnaysiens
Old and New World versions of the classic Bourgogne white

Domaine Fichet, *Macon-Villages*, Burgundy, France 2009 — 10 / 40
Aromas and palate of green apple, lime and exotic fruit. Crisp and fresh on the finish.

Mount Eden, *Chardonnay*, Santa Cruz Mountains, CA 2008 — 11 / 44
A rich nose and palate with notes of ripe apple, pear and buttered popcorn. The body is full and creamy with a slight acidity on the finish.

Baileyana, *Chardonnay*, Edna Valley, CA 2009 — 11 / 44
Tropical flavors of pineapple, coconut and crisp lemon zest. The palate shows great acidity with a firm minerality throughout.

Tasting flight of above 16

Oak vs. Stainless
Taste how aging styles can make a difference with these dry whites

Le Petite Chambord, *Sauvignon Blend*, Loire Valley, FR 2010 — 11 / 44
Blended with Chardonnay. Nose and palate of tangerine, ruby red grapefruit and stone fruit. Crisp and clean with a refreshing acidic finish.

Les Trois Chenes, *Sauvignon Blanc*, Touraine, France 2009 — 12 / 48
Full and fresh displaying notes of pineapple, ruby red grapefruit and lime on the nose and palate. Full bodied with a crisp, refreshing finish.

Robinia, *Sauvignon Blanc*, Russian River, CA 2009 — 12 / 48
Palate of tangerine, lemon/lime and red peach. The mouth is rich, but tangy with bright acidity, mineral tones and a crisp lingering finish.

Tasting flight of above 18

REDS
6 oz glass / bottle

Pinot Lovers Unite
From Oregon to Germany...taste the difference

Nelles, Ruber, *Pinot Noir*, Ahr, Germany 2008 — 16 / 64
Nose and palate of dark black cherry and tart cranberry. The palate is light and fresh with a bright acidity and long finish.

Joseph Drouhin, *Pinot Noir*, Chorey-Les-Beaune, FR 2009 — 15 / 60
Bright black cherry, tart raspberry and strawberry on the nose and palate. Light and fresh with hints of lavender and a dry, smooth finish.

Stoller, *Pinot Noir*, Dundee Hills, Oregon 2009 — 13 / 52
Bright red cherry, strawberry and tart raspberry on the nose and palate. The body is light and fruity with refreshing acidity and a long finish.

Tasting flight of above 22

Mountains to the Sea
Cruise the high elevations of Northern Italy and end on the shores of the South

Angiolino Maule Rosso Masieri, *Lagrein*, Veneto, Italy 2010 — 13 / 52
Blended with Merlot and 100% biodynamic. Nose and palate of cherry, blueberry and earth. Medium bodied with fresh acidity and a long tannic finish.

Sottimano, *Dolcetto D'Alba*, Piemonte, Italy 2010 — 13 / 52
Bright notes of red cherry, raspberry and blueberry on the nose and palate. Medium bodied with a long, dry finish and a refreshing acidity.

Montesecondo, *Rosso Toscana*, Tuscany, Italy 2010 — 12 / 48
Nose and palate of ripe cherry and cranberry with hints of earth. Medium body with a firm acidity and smooth tannins.

Tasting flight of above 19

Spices and Berries
Spice up your palate or give it a kick of fruit

Tami, *Frappato*, Sicily, Italy 2010 — 12 / 48
Nose and palate of bright red cherry and a hint of fig. Medium bodied with elegant tannins and an earthy finish.

Cucao, *Carmenere*, Rapel Valley, Chile 2009 — 9 / 36
Notes of jalapeno, dark chocolate, blackberry, pepper and coffee on the nose and palate. Full bodied with mild tannins and a long finish.

Unti, *Zinfandel*, Dry Creek Valley, Sonoma, CA 2008 — 14 / 56
Blended with Petite Syrah. A nose and palate of black berry, boysenberry, cherry cobbler and licorice. A full body with mild tannins and a long, dry finish.

Tasting flight of above 18

Bordeaux Blends
Traditional French varietals from around the world

Durigutti, *Malbec*, Mendoza, Argentina 2009 — 13 / 52
Nose and palate of dark chocolate, leather, blackberry and currant. Full bodied with smooth tannins and a long, lingering finish.

Today's Featured Reserve, *Cabernet Sauvignon*, Napa, CA MV — 16 / 64
Reserve Cabs from our private collection. Typical Napa flavors: bold, full-bodied wines with elegant and silky tannins on the finish. Rare by the glass.

Château Guibeau, *Merlot Blend*, Saint Emillon, Bordeaux, FR 2009 — 12 / 48
Notes of black plum, tobacco and red currant on the nose and palate. Full bodied and dry with firm tannins and long, elegant finish.

Tasting flight of above 21

Big Earthy Reds (Syrah, Grenache & More)
Big, full bodied, earthy and spicy

Zuazo Gaston, *Tempranillo*, Rioja, Spain 2008 — 10 / 40
Nose and palate of tobacco, cranberry, rhubarb and red cherry. Full bodied and rustic with elegant tannin and a long, fresh finish.

Dom. Alain Voge "Les Peyrouses", Cote du Rhone, France 2008 — 13 / 52
Notes of ripe cherry, black berry, anise and pepper on the nose and palate. The body is full with firm tannins, mild acidity and a lingering finish.

Monje Hollera, *Listan Negro*, Canary Islands, Spain 2010 — 13 / 52
Dark notes of black cherry, tobacco and earth on the nose. Full-bodied peppery palate with firm tannins and a long, dry finish.

Tasting flight of above 18

Figure 5–2

This wine menu, with its many wines by the glass and available tasting flights, incorporates playful category headings and user-friendly beverage descriptions. Printed with the permission of District San Francisco.

a chardonnay, but if the guest only likes red wines, a lighter red wine would be the appropriate recommendation. The old mnemonic of red wines with red meat and white wines with white meat is far too simplistic, and it does not take into account guest flavor preferences. The better rule of thumb is to pair light-bodied wines with lighter foods and full-bodied wines with heavier foods. (Body is simply the weight or viscosity felt in the mouth. Just like the difference between skim milk and heavy cream, body can vary greatly even with wines of similar flavor profiles.) Body is important because a mismatch causes the wine to overpower the food or vice versa. When the food and wine align in body, the aftertaste of each remains perceptible while the other is consumed, and both interact to create pleasant new flavors. Only once the body of the wine is determined appropriately should the menu planner or server worry about pairing wine aromas or overtones to the food. Sweetness in wine does not always pair well with savory dishes, but semi-dry (slightly sweet) wine is an excellent choice for the strong flavors of smoke, piquant, or salt in food. Very sweet wines should be reserved for dessert.

While a wine menu should provide variety and balance in its listings, all of the wines should match appropriately with the food. An Indian restaurant that serves a lot of spicy food should devote some percentage of its list to semi-dry wines that pair well with heat. A restaurant that only serves seafood should focus almost exclusively on light and medium-bodied wines. When a restaurant menu runs the gamut from light to heavy dishes, the wine list should follow suit. However, even when a wine list is limited by the food choices, it should still offer variety. For example, a seafood restaurant's wine menu could include Sauvignon blanc, Chardonnay, Riesling, Gewürztraminer, and Pinot blanc as well as lighter reds, such as French Beaujolais or Italian Dolcetto. Similarly, the wine list might include wines from Australia, France, Italy, Germany, and several U.S. states. Simply because a wine list must match with a narrowly focused food menu does not mean that it cannot provide variety.

5.1.3 Portion Sizes

The most common format for a bottle of wine is a 750-mL bottle, which provides approximately five 5-ounce servings. Almost every wine list devotes a significant portion of its selections to this format. However, not every table will want a bottle of that size. Some guests want only a glass of wine, while others want something in between. Operations that can support a large wine inventory should include several bottle sizes on their wine menu. A half bottle allows a table of two to share a bottle of wine without overindulging. It also gives guests a chance to order a small bottle for each course rather than selecting a single bottle to pair with multiple courses. Large-format bottles, like a magnum (1.5 L), allow large parties to share from a single bottle, which can make a special occasion feel even more special. When possible, an extensive wine list should include a few half-size and a few large-format bottles among the menu choices.

No matter how big or small the wine menu is, it should always include some wines by the glass. Some guests dine alone and only want a glass or two to drink. Some individuals in a party will prefer to select different types of wine (or other alcoholic beverages). Whatever the reason, wines by the glass sell very well and help to encourage wine sales. At a minimum, a restaurant should offer at least two whites and two reds by the glass—one light-bodied and one full-bodied of each color. Wine-centered establishments may list over a dozen different options by the glass.

The portion size for wine served by the glass is up to the establishment, but a 5-ounce portion of wine is considered standard. (Wine glasses are not intended to be filled to the top.) It contains approximately the same quantity of alcohol as a 12-ounce beer, which makes counting drinks for the purposes of safe alcohol service easier. Wine bars may give guests a choice among several smaller pour sizes to encourage the purchase of multiple tastings or flights. Given the choice between a set of three 2-ounce pours or a single 5-ounce glass, some customers will opt for the extra quantity and cost of the three-wine flight just to experience the variety. That said, the more common approach to wine service in the average restaurant is to offer only one size—usually a 5-ounce glass for table wines (though less for dessert or fortified wines, like port or sherry).

5.2 BEER MENUS

Not all that long ago, a restaurant's beer menu would have been a short list of mass-produced beers divided between those on tap and those in a bottle. While this type of beer list still exists in many places, it is not the only approach to beer. Boutique, regional American beers abound and come in a range of styles. Beer consumers no longer think of beer as a product but rather as a category of products that includes lagers, ales, stouts, porters, and even more subsets of those types. In a world that produces Belgian tripels, German hefeweizens, and American pumpkin ales, it is too simplistic to assume that the only choice Americans want is between regular and light beer.

Like a wine menu, a well-done beer menu should display variety in type and location. Beer is made around the world, and an extensive beer list should include beers from a wide range of countries. At a minimum, the menu should include some local microbrews (or other American beers) and beers from the same country as the style of cuisine being served. In other words, a Belgian restaurant should list Belgian beers, a German restaurant should have German beers, and so on. Similarly, a beer list should include at least a few types of beer styles. Beer can be brewed from different grains including barley, wheat, and oats. Beers also vary in the level of bitterness and hops. A menu planner should research the kinds of beer popular in the local area, but recognize that there may be variation within a style. For example, if ales are popular in a given community, the beer list might include pale ale, India pale ale, blond ale, red ale, brown ale, golden ale, cream ale, and/or amber ale. The greater the number of choices, the more a restaurant becomes a destination for beer connoisseurs. Except for the most minimalist of beer menus, a menu planner should offer some bottled beer and some beer on tap.

Beer comes in a wide range of price points, too. As with wine, the price point for beer should align with the price point of the food on the menu. An upscale restaurant can offer high-end beers in 750-mL bottles, but an inexpensive bar should stick with cheaper beers on tap or in 12-ounce bottles.

The category names used for beers on a menu depend greatly on the length of the beverage menu and the business's approach to beer. The menu might list all of its offerings under the single heading of "Beer" with an alphabetical listing of choices by producer or by country. Alternatively, the menu might divide the categories by style or by country of origin. As with wine, there is no universally accepted format, but a consumer should be able to find his preferred beer easily on the list. If the list includes a significant number of boutique beers that are not well known in the community, brief tasting notes for each beer may increase sales and help assuage guests' insecurity in ordering.

When serving beer from a tap (portioning glasses from a larger keg), a restaurant has the flexibility of determining a desired portion size. A 12-ounce portion is considered a standard size for tracking alcohol consumed, though some places prefer to serve a pint. The type of glassware should support the brand of the business. German beer halls might use beer steins while upscale Belgian restaurants might have a different glass (supplied by the beer producer) for each beer they serve. Oversized portions (like a yard) should be reserved for specialty bars or drinking halls.

Figure 5-3

This beer placemat menu illustrates great variety in beer style and origin.

Jim, John, Fred, and the many staff and fans of the Winking Lizard.

It is not inappropriate to list recommended pairings for beer and food on a menu, but this approach is less commonly done with beer than it is with wine. Microbreweries that also operate a restaurant should provide such pairings, as their menus ought to provide an opportunity to show off each beer with at least one food item. However, in the average restaurant most customers will order the beer they like based on personal taste preferences rather than on the food they have ordered.

5.3 LIQUOR AND COCKTAIL MENUS

Cocktails and other liquor-based drinks have become trendier in recent years. Some upscale restaurants give their mixologists (bartenders) equal billing with the chef. The arena of mixology provides a huge opportunity for creativity. Unlike beer and wine, which are created in their entirety by another company (except at winery and brewery restaurants), a cocktail is designed and prepared by the restaurant's employees. Some of the best mixologists even create their own mixers from scratch, making house infusions and bitters.

A cocktail and liquor menu should include beverages based on a range of different liquor types. For example, unless a business promotes itself as a vodka bar, all of the cocktails should not be based on vodka. Typically, the menu should offer at least one mixed drink based on each of vodka, gin, rum, tequila, and whiskey. A more varied menu might have drinks from an even broader range of sources. A well-done cocktail menu also incorporates multiple flavor profiles (sweet, sour, and bitter drinks) and utilizes a range of glassware.

How a menu planner describes a drink on a cocktail menu depends greatly on how innovative the drinks are. If the menu includes only classic drinks, it is perfectly acceptable to list only the drink names. However, once a mixologist strays from the classics, the menu must include the list of ingredients. Even with complex cocktails, the ingredient list is still pretty short. If premium liquors are used, those brand names should be highlighted. Cocktail descriptions work quite well as minimalist ingredient lists; there is no need to insert flowery additions such as "shaken with ice and strained into a chilled cocktail glass for your drinking pleasure."

There are several ways to present a cocktail menu. It may be placed on the inside cover of the food menu, the first pages of a comprehensive beverage menu, or a table tent. Signature cocktails should be heavily marketed wherever they are listed. Guests know that they can order common classic drinks when a full-service bar is on display, but the only way they'll know about a business's unique creations is if they see them in print or hear about them from a server.

Cocktails are not the only use for liquor. A restaurant can highlight a wide range of liquors of a given type. Usually, the type selected supports the business's brand and the cuisine. For example, a Mexican restaurant might stock a dozen different tequilas; an Irish pub might list a dozen or more whiskeys. Even lounges or bars with nondescript food choices can make themselves known for a broad selection of bourbons, scotches, or vodkas. The best way to promote these beverage options is through a menu listing each brand name, any special qualities such as age or flavoring, and the price for a shot. Bars that rely on guests to find the brand name on display behind the bar will lose sales from those guests who cannot see the bar clearly from their seats.

When writing the menu, a menu planner can list the cocktails under a single heading of "cocktails" or create innovative category names. Extensive lists might simply state "gin drinks," "rum drinks," and the like in a serious establishment. More playful operations might incorporate headings like "sweet and fruity" or "manly drinks." When a menu highlights liquor by the shot, those are almost always categorized by the type of liquor ("scotches," "brandies," etc.). Liquor that is appropriate for after

COCKTAILS

BLUE NOTE *(Kirk Estopinal & Neil Roche)* 10
BLUEBERRY & CUCUMBER SHRUB . SPARKLING WINE . MINT

A THOUSAND BLUE EYES *(Nick Detrich)* 9
NOILLY PRATT DRY VERMOUTH . TANQUERAY GIN . ORANGE FLOWER
WATER . BITTERMEN'S BOSTON BITTAHS . LEMON

FLORIDIAN VOID *(Nick Detrich)* 10
FERREIRA WHITE PORT . YELLOW CHARTREUSE . TRADER NICK'S
FRERET FALERNUM . LIME . HONEY . ANGOSTURA BITTERS

HARDEST WALK *(Turk Dietrich)* 9
CARPANO PUNT E MES VERMOUTH . PLANTATION OVERPROOF RUM .
GRAN CLASSICO BITTER . ORANGE BITTERS

LAVENDER AFFAIR *(Turk Dietrich)* 9
BOOMSMA JONGE GENEVER . DOLIN BLANC VERMOUTH . LEMON .
LAVENDER . PEYCHAUD'S BITTERS

ARROW IN THE GALE *(James Ives)* 9
BUFFALO TRACE BOURBON . NARDINI MANDORLA ALMOND GRAPPA .
LEMON . GINGER . STRAWBERRY . BLACK PEPPER

BANDITO *(Neal Bodenheimer)* 9
EL CHARRO BLANCO TEQUILA . SOMBRA MEZCAL . LIME . GRAPEFRUIT PEEL
D'ARISTI XTABENTUN LIQUEUR . STRAWBERRY . ABSINTHE

NERVOUS BRIDE *(James Ives)* 9
BARSOL PRIMERO PISCO . PAGES VERVEINE DU VELAY EXTRA LIQUEUR .
HOUSE-MADE GRENADINE . GRAPEFRUIT PEEL . SPRING ELIXIR

IT WAS NOTHING *(Kirk Estopinal)* 11
CAMPO DE ENCANTO PISCO . BITTERMAN'S CITRON SAUVAGE .
LEMON . GRAPEFRUIT . EGG WHITE

EXPENSE ACCOUNT *(Rhiannon Enlil)* 12
PLYMOUTH GIN . BECHEROVKA . LIME . HONEY . PERNOD ANISE .
ORANGE BLOSSOM WATER

FIRE WITHIN *(James Ives)* 10
HIGH WEST DOUBLE RYE . CHINACO BLANCO TEQUILLA .
CARPANO ANTICA . KÜMMEL . MARIE BRIZARD CRÈME DE CACAO .
ORANGE

ART OF DISCUSSION *(Rhiannon Enlil)* 12
EL TESORO BLANCO TEQUILA . DOLIN BLANC VERMOUTH .
DIMMI LIQUORE DI MILANO . ARBOL CHILI PEYCHAUD'S BITTERS .
HONEY . ORANGE PEEL

CURE PUNCH · CHANGES DAILY 6

HAPPY HOUR 5-7PM
CURE CLASSIC COCKTAILS · 5

PIMM'S CUP
SAZERAC
RUM OLD FASHIONED
LA PALOMA
CHAMPAGNE COCKTAIL
HOUSE WHITE WINE
HOUSE RED WINE
HOUSE SPARKLING WINE

....

RESERVE CLASSICS

A'BUNADH ROB ROY 16
ABERLOUR "A'BUNADH" CASK STRENGTH SPEYSIDE SINGLE MALT
SCOTCH . CARPANO ANTICA VERMOUTH . ANGOSTURA BITTERS .
LEMON PEEL

21 YR. DAIQUIRI 17
EL DORADO 21 YR. RUM . FRESH LIME JUICE . SUGAR

HANDY SAZERAC 17
THOMAS H. HANDY CASK STRENGTH RYE WHISKEY . VIEUX
PONTARLIER ABSINTHE . DEMERARA SUGAR . LEMON PEEL

V.E.P. LAST WORD 17
OXLEY GIN . CHARTREUSE V.E.P. LUXARDO MARASCHINO LIQUEUR .
LIME JUICE

W.L. WELLER MANHATTAN 17
W.L. WELLER CASK STRENGTH BOURBON . CARPANO PUNT E MES
VERMOUTH . ANGOSTURA BITTERS . ORANGE PEEL

DARROZE SIDECAR 18
FRANCIS DARROZE BAS ARMAGNAC RESERVE SPECIAL . COMBIER
ORANGE LIQUEUR . FRESH LEMON JUICE

HUDSON FOUR GRAIN WHISKEY BITTERED SLING 19
HUDSON FOUR GRAIN WHISKEY . DEMERARA SUGAR . ANGOSTURA
BITTERS . ORANGE BITTERS . ORANGE PEEL

MENUS AVAILABLE FOR PURCHASE UPON REQUEST.

Figure 5–4
This cocktail menu boasts both classic and house-invented cocktails. Printed with the permission of Neal Bodenheimer and Cure New Orleans.

dinner should be highlighted on a dessert menu to encourage sales of liquor alongside or instead of dessert. After-dinner beverages that combine liquor with other ingredients, such as coffee, should also appear on a dessert menu to drive those sales as well.

5.4 NONALCOHOLIC BEVERAGE MENUS

Alcoholic beverages get a lot of attention from menu planners because of the opportunity for significant revenue and profit margins. However, nonalcoholic drinks are extremely popular and most guests order at least one, even when they order alcohol as well. Most casual restaurants prefer to list their nonalcoholic options on the main food menu. Some may leave them off the menu entirely and simply allow the server to address requests for soda or juice. Most customers assume that sodas and juices are available even if they are not listed on the menu. Menu planners for businesses with significant alcohol programs may take this approach in order to drive sales of alcohol. However, nonalcoholic drink sales should not be taken for granted. They are fabulous opportunities for increased revenue and profit. Not all nonalcoholic beverage programs merit their own menus, but depending on the approach the restaurant takes, they may deserve their own page on a comprehensive beverage or dessert menu. Unless the menu planner wishes to highlight a particularly boutique set of beverages, the nonalcoholic drinks are usually listed under the single heading of "beverages," but any single beverage type could merit its own category heading if there are a large number of drinks from which to choose.

5.4.1 Cold Beverages

The push toward environmentalism and sustainability has taken some of the momentum out of sales of bottled water. A few trendy restaurants filter their own water (and charge for it), while others only offer tap water. However, boutique bottled waters still allow foodservice operations a chance to sell a product that would otherwise be given away for free as tap water. Some guests maintain a preference for certain brands of bottled water and automatically choose that brand over tap water when it is available. Similarly, certain customers prefer sparkling water over still, so they opt for bottled sparkling water when it is offered. A restaurant with an extensive water menu should highlight it on a beverage list or on the main food menu. One that only stocks one brand of still and sparking water is better served by having the server push the sales orally upon greeting the table.

Most businesses that do not serve breakfast still stock orange and cranberry juice for the bar. Restaurants that accommodate children often serve pineapple and/or apple juice as well. When a foodservice establishment caters to young families, it should list its juice offerings on the main menu and/or on a children's menu. A restaurant that goes beyond this basic set of juice offerings should definitely showcase its selection on the main menu. Apricot, sour cherry, mango, and peach are but a few of the many juices that a restaurant could provide. In ethnic restaurants, these selections give the establishment a sense of authenticity. A Turkish restaurant with apricot nectar or an Indian restaurant with mango lassi (a yogurt and mango drink) on the menu differentiates itself from other restaurants that focus on food rather than on a complete dining experience. Finally, a juice menu does not require that each juice be served on its own. Mixed juice drinks with other ingredients such as spices, herbs, coconut milk, yogurt, or other garnishes make for interesting choices for those who do not or cannot drink alcohol.

Milk is a simple offering that is usually listed only in family-friendly restaurants. However, it is a common request from children. Options include not only whole, reduced-fat, low-fat, and skim milk but also chocolate and other flavored milks.

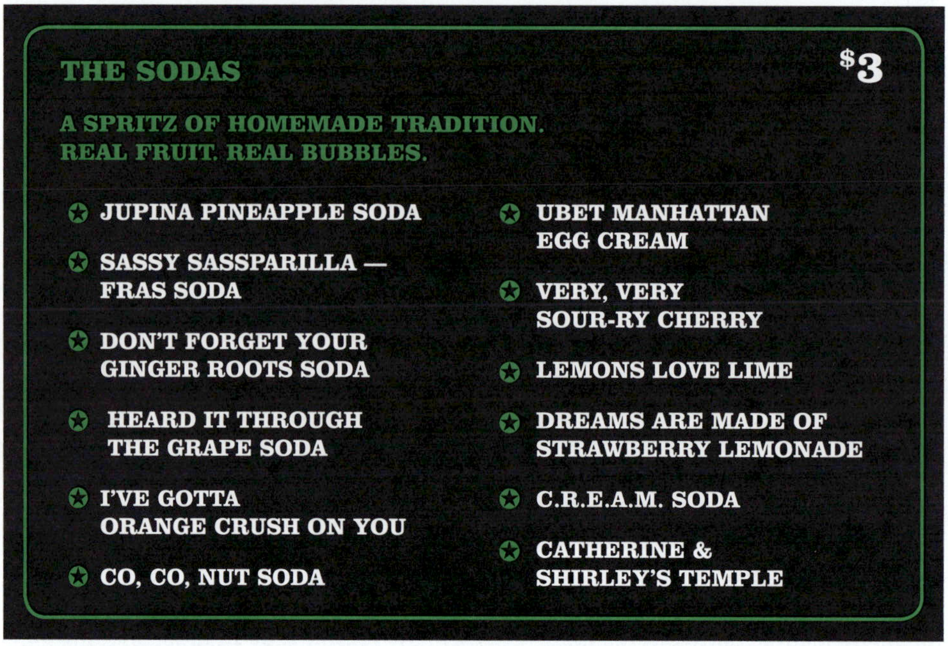

Figure 5–5
This operation creates
its own boutique sodas
to order. Spike and Cathy
Mendelsohn.

THE SODAS   **$3**

A SPRITZ OF HOMEMADE TRADITION.
REAL FRUIT. REAL BUBBLES.

- **JUPINA PINEAPPLE SODA**
- **SASSY SASSPARILLA — FRAS SODA**
- **DON'T FORGET YOUR GINGER ROOTS SODA**
- **HEARD IT THROUGH THE GRAPE SODA**
- **I'VE GOTTA ORANGE CRUSH ON YOU**
- **CO, CO, NUT SODA**
- **UBET MANHATTAN EGG CREAM**
- **VERY, VERY SOUR-RY CHERRY**
- **LEMONS LOVE LIME**
- **DREAMS ARE MADE OF STRAWBERRY LEMONADE**
- **C.R.E.A.M. SODA**
- **CATHERINE & SHIRLEY'S TEMPLE**

Sodas are one of the most popular cold beverages among nonalcoholic options. Usually, restaurants go with a single brand name and stock only that brand's line of products. In fact, Coke or Pepsi will often provide a free fountain dispenser in exchange for an exclusivity agreement. However, big brand names are not a requirement for soft drink options. Old-fashioned flavors and brands are seeing a small but steady resurgence. Cream, orange, cherry, or grape soda distinguishes a beverage menu from the competition, as does small-batch root beer and ginger ale. A few properties have taken to creating their own soft drinks using carbonated water and house-made syrups. These old-fashioned fountain drinks command high prices and convert an ordinary soda into something extraordinary.

Iced tea, iced coffee, lemonade, and other cold beverage creations allow for simplistic or creative menu listings depending upon what the market will sustain. Iced teas come in a range of flavors and house-made versions can originate from black, green, or herbal tea infusions; fruit- or herb-flavored teas can be made from scratch or purchased. Iced coffee can also be offered as an alternative to iced tea. Additions of milk or flavored syrups can generate a wide range of cold coffee and espresso beverages. Lemonade is rarely served in more than one version, but it, too, can be made from scratch to create a house specialty. Besides, lemonade infused with mint and lemon verbena can sell for a much higher price than a menu listing of "lemonade."

All of these cold nonalcoholic beverages may appear in their own section on the main menu. However, if a business's beverage program is significant, they may merit a separate beverage page or even their own menu. Listing a separate category for iced tea (or any other type of beverage) would not make sense for just one or two offerings, but with a dozen or so possible choices, a menu planner might opt to separate out some beverage categories and highlight those choices, particularly if the products are home-made and unique to the business.

5.4.2 Hot Beverages

While most guests will not order an alcoholic drink to accompany dessert, many will purchase tea or coffee. Not long ago, even the most upscale restaurants listed only a choice between regular and decaf coffee; several tea bags may have been presented in a tea box or other container. Today, some foodservice establishments treat these beverages as categories rather than as a single drink.

Coffee shops sometimes provide coffees of different origins and roasting levels. A dark roast Ethiopian Yirgacheffe tastes vastly different from a medium roast Guatemalan Antigua. When a restaurant provides several types of coffees from various regions, a separate beverage menu or a page on the dessert menu is deserved. As most guests are not experts in coffee, tasting notes are highly appropriate for such a coffee menu. Usually, these tasting notes refer to the acidity levels and other flavor overtones. Sometimes a restaurant will vary coffees with different flavor additions, such as hazelnut or vanilla. Flavored coffees do not require the separate menu page that regional coffees do, as their tasting notes are incorporated into their names. Offering multiple coffees on a menu does not necessitate a bank of brewing machines. Individual ceramic filters or French presses allow a server to brew any type of coffee to order in individual portions, while insulated thermoses allow servers to brew coffee in batches and to hold each variety warm until needed.

Espresso drinks continue to gain popularity in restaurants as well. Lattes, cappuccinos, mochas, and espressos all command higher prices than brewed coffee and make an evening a little more special for the guests. Espresso drinks also allow for flavored syrups, but they are a common canvas for creating alcoholic after-dinner drinks, too. A cappuccino with sambuca or frangelico makes for an alcoholic drink that goes well with dessert yet does not seem out of place among guests choosing plain coffee for dessert. Alcohol and coffee combinations also allow for tableside presentations, which can drive up sales quickly for guests who crave the spectacle.

Tea, like coffee, comes in a wide range of styles. Types include white, green, oolong, black, and herbal, although any of these varieties can be expanded with the addition of other herbs, spices, or flavoring agents. Within each category exists great variation as well. Sencha, dragonwell, and hojicha taste vastly different from one another even though all are green teas. Upscale businesses that cater to tea drinkers may stock teapots and strainers and serve loose tea, while others simply allow guests to choose a single tea bag from a selection for steeping in the guest's cup. The more interesting the choices are, the more likely guests are to order tea as a beverage. For those businesses that serve afternoon tea (the meal), a wide selection of teas is a must.

Hot chocolate is less common than tea or coffee as an after-dinner drink because its sweetness may seem like a sugar overdose alongside a dessert. However, hot chocolate can be a popular breakfast option, especially among children. Served with whipped cream or marshmallows, hot chocolate provides a sweet caffeine rush for those who do not care for the bitterness of coffee or the tannins of tea. Hot chocolate also makes a fun addition to brunch, where it may include additions of alcohol to flavor it. While hot chocolate rarely commands its own category on a beverage menu, it can come in white, milk, and dark chocolate varieties. As with the other hot beverage choices, a unique product in a given community is a draw for customers who wish to partake of that indulgence.

While coffee, tea, chocolate, and espresso drinks would normally be listed together or among other beverages, they may merit separate categories if the business offers enough variations of each. That said, alcoholic versions of any of these drinks should be listed separately and should state the alcohol that has been added. To do otherwise runs the risk that a child or teetotaler will order an alcoholic drink. Whether listed on the main food menu, a dessert menu, a comprehensive beverage menu, or their own menu page, hot beverages belong on the menus in most foodservice operations.

Figure 5–6
This menu showcases teas among other cold beverage options. Teaism: A Tea House.

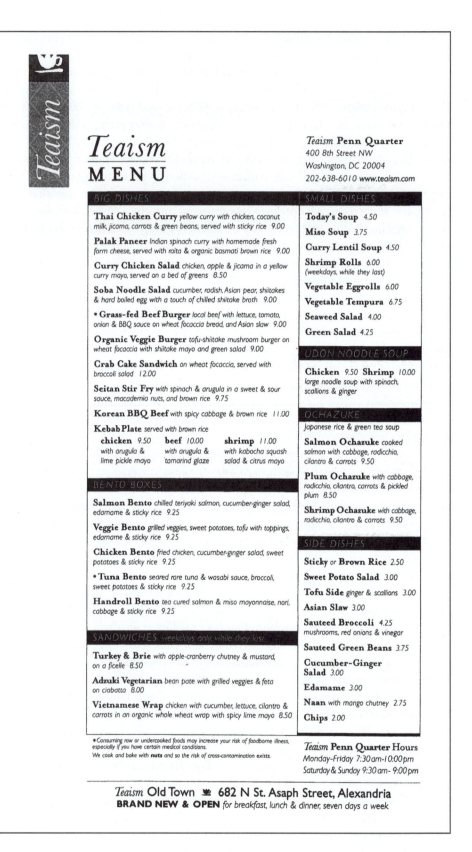

Teaism
MENU

Teaism **Penn Quarter**
400 8th Street NW
Washington, DC 20004
202-638-6010 www.teaism.com

BIG DISHES

Thai Chicken Curry *yellow curry with chicken, coconut milk, jicama, carrots & green beans, served with sticky rice* 9.00

Palak Paneer *Indian spinach curry with homemade fresh farm cheese, served with raita & organic basmati brown rice* 9.00

Curry Chicken Salad *chicken, apple & jicama in a yellow curry mayo, served on a bed of greens* 8.50

Soba Noodle Salad *cucumber, radish, Asian pear, shiitakes & hard boiled egg with a touch of chilled shiitake broth* 9.00

• Grass-fed Beef Burger *local beef with lettuce, tomato, onion & BBQ sauce on wheat focaccia bread, and Asian slaw* 9.00

Organic Veggie Burger *tofu-shiitake mushroom burger on wheat focaccia with shiitake mayo and green salad* 9.00

Crab Cake Sandwich *on wheat focaccia, served with broccoli salad* 12.00

Seitan Stir Fry *with spinach & arugula in a sweet & sour sauce, macadamia nuts, and brown rice* 9.75

Korean BBQ Beef *with spicy cabbage & brown rice* 11.00

Kebab Plate *served with brown rice*

chicken 9.50	**beef** 10.00	**shrimp** 11.00
with arugula &	*with arugula &*	*with kabocha squash*
lime pickle mayo	*tamarind glaze*	*salad & citrus mayo*

BENTO BOXES

Salmon Bento *chilled teriyaki salmon, cucumber-ginger salad, edamame & sticky rice* 9.25

Veggie Bento *grilled veggies, sweet potatoes, tofu with toppings, edamame & sticky rice* 9.25

Chicken Bento *fried chicken, cucumber-ginger salad, sweet potatoes & sticky rice* 9.25

• Tuna Bento *seared rare tuna & wasabi sauce, broccoli, sweet potatoes & sticky rice* 9.25

Handroll Bento *tea cured salmon & miso mayonnaise, nori, cabbage & sticky rice* 9.25

SANDWICHES *weekdays only, while they last*

Turkey & Brie *with apple-cranberry chutney & mustard, on a ficelle* 8.50

Adzuki Vegetarian *bean pate with grilled veggies & feta on ciabatta* 8.00

Vietnamese Wrap *chicken with cucumber, lettuce, cilantro & carrots in an organic whole wheat wrap with spicy lime mayo* 8.50

SMALL DISHES

Today's Soup 4.50

Miso Soup 3.75

Curry Lentil Soup 4.50

Shrimp Rolls 6.00
(weekdays, while they last)

Vegetable Eggrolls 6.00

Vegetable Tempura 6.75

Seaweed Salad 4.00

Green Salad 4.25

UDON NOODLE SOUP

Chicken 9.50 **Shrimp** 10.00
large noodle soup with spinach, scallions & ginger

OCHAZUKE
Japanese rice & green tea soup

Salmon Ochazuke *cooked salmon with cabbage, radicchio, cilantro & carrots* 9.50

Plum Ochazuke *with cabbage, radicchio, cilantro, carrots & pickled plum* 8.50

Shrimp Ochazuke *with cabbage, radicchio, cilantro & carrots* 9.50

SIDE DISHES

Sticky *or* **Brown Rice** 2.50

Sweet Potato Salad 3.00

Tofu Side *ginger & scallions* 3.00

Asian Slaw 3.00

Sauteed Broccoli 4.25
mushrooms, red onions & vinegar

Sauteed Green Beans 3.75

Cucumber-Ginger Salad 3.00

Edamame 3.00

Naan *with mango chutney* 2.75

Chips 2.00

• Consuming raw or undercooked foods may increase your risk of foodborne illness, especially if you have certain medical conditions.
*We cook and bake with **nuts** and so the risk of cross-contamination exists.*

Teaism **Penn Quarter** Hours
Monday-Friday 7:30 am-10:00 pm
Saturday & Sunday 9:30 am- 9:00 pm

Teaism Old Town ✿ 682 N St. Asaph Street, Alexandria
BRAND NEW & OPEN *for breakfast, lunch & dinner, seven days a week*

Figure 5–6
(continued)

5.5 SPECIAL CONCERNS OVER ALCOHOL

Beverages, including alcoholic ones, can be a valuable addition to a meal, but a guest's overconsumption of alcohol can be a serious threat to a business's survival. One intoxicated guest who gets into a physical fight at the property or kills someone in a car accident on the way home can bring down the company through third-party lawsuits. Alcohol may be fun, but it has its limitations and its dangers. There are in-depth programs, such as the ServSafe Alcohol training program, to provide managers and servers a thorough approach to serving alcohol safely; however, as safe alcohol service relates to the menu planner's role, the basics follow in this section.

To address the risks of alcohol overconsumption by guests, a menu planner should ensure that special pricing and drink creations do not encourage excessive drinking. Selling alcohol is fine, but allowing customers to drink and drink for little to no money is a bad idea. Alcohol should not be used as a loss leader (sold below cost to attract business in food or entertainment sales). When alcohol is sold cheaply, servers must take extra care to count drinks and to cut off any customers who have had too much. Menu promotions that advertise free drinks, bottomless pitchers, or contests for quantity drinking are a recipe for disaster.

The drinks that are served on the menu should be moderate in size and should not hide huge quantities of alcohol inconspicuously. A 12-ounce beer, 5-ounce glass of wine, and 1½-ounce shot of 80 proof liquor all deliver roughly equal amounts of pure alcohol. In industry terms, they are all thought of as equivalent to one drink. When a recipe calls for 2¼ ounces of 80 proof liquor, that beverage is equivalent to one and a half drinks. A customer or server who attempts to count drinks will have difficulty if 7 ounces of wine are poured into a huge glass that hides the quantity. A guest might think of that as one glass of wine when it is closer to one and a half drinks. Cocktails may equate to one or two drinks, but more than that becomes excessive. An oversized cocktail, if equal to three drinks, would put a customer over the legal blood alcohol limit with a single beverage order. The best approach to controlling alcohol consumption is through proper portioning and moderate drink sizes.

However, foodservice operations that serve alcohol usually hope to generate a profit. The menu planner plays a critical role in facilitating that goal. A simple alcoholic drink may not cost much, but one that uses high-end or premium liquor, wine, or beer commands a much higher sales price. By making sure that a wine and beer list includes some premium choices, the menu planner helps to increase revenue and profits from those customers willing to purchase a higher-quality product at a higher price point. Cocktails work similarly. A drink listed as a "margarita" will not sell for as much money as one that lists by name a high-priced brand of tequila. Alternatively, when a guest places an order for a classic drink, the server can attempt to upsell the customer on the spot. *Upselling* alcohol means simply inviting the customer to select a premium liquor for use in the drink. For example, if the guest orders a gin and tonic, the server might respond, "Would you like that made with Tanqueray?" If a drink made with Tanqueray sells for more money than one made with the well brand, the server makes additional revenue for the business every time a customer says yes. Of course, the number of upscale products that the operation is able to store depends on the amount of inventory space available and the expected rate at which these premium products will sell. Still, having just a few for sale can increase overall beverage revenue tremendously. Total alcohol consumption is inherently limited by the amount guests can consume before becoming intoxicated. Increasing alcohol revenue is best done by encouraging the sales of premium products, not by persuading guests to consume more alcohol.

5.6 NON-RESTAURANT MENUS

While most of this chapter has focused on beverage menus for restaurants, beverages are a critical component of nearly every dining experience and thus deserve a spot on other types of menus as well. Children's menus should include juices and milk. Lounge menus follow the guidelines of restaurant menus, with particular attention paid to providing an interesting alcoholic beverage selection appropriate for the market. Brunch and afternoon tea menus should offer traditional beverages classically paired with those meals. Dessert menus, too, should display both alcoholic and nonalcoholic beverage options on their pages.

Room service beverage menus should offer most or all of the nonalcoholic beverages available in the hotel's full-service restaurant (with the possible exception of drinks like cappuccino, which may not transport well). Room service drinks are usually delivered in sealed containers or carafes to keep the liquid from spilling. A hotel that normally serves soda from a dispenser may need to stock bottled sodas for room service use. Otherwise, the bubbles will escape en route to the room. Hot beverages should be transported in insulated carafes to help them maintain their temperature. The alcoholic beverage room service menu may be more limited, but it should include several wines, beers, and liquors popular among guests. The beer and wine choices should span the range of styles and flavors. The liquor choices should include one popular brand of each major category of liquor (tequila, rum, whisky, scotch, brandy, etc.). Room service menus need not list cocktails and mixed drinks, only the liquors themselves. Guests who wish to have a specific cocktail may order the components separately and mix the drink to their personal taste in the room or purchase the cocktail in the hotel lounge. If prepared in a bar for room service delivery, a mixed drink served on ice will be diluted by the time it reaches the guest, and a chilled but strained drink will no longer be cold. Providing the liquor and mixers in bottles and allowing guests to mix the drinks in their rooms with ice provided by the hotel yields a better result for the guest (though some boutique hotels are now offering services in which a bartender comes to the room with mixers and ice and mixes the drinks for the guests). Many hotels offer a few alcoholic beverage options through minibars in each guest room, listed on a separate minibar menu; the guest is charged based on what bottles are removed from the minibar. Minibars typically stock only individual portion sizes of each beverage. For 750-mL bottles of alcohol or a broader set of alcoholic options, guests must usually order through the room service menu.

Take-out beverage menus follow similar rules to room service menus, but local laws may prevent restaurants from selling alcohol to go. As a rule, all take-out beverages should be sold in sealed containers, so they do not spill in transport. Unlike most other menus, a take-out menu may list large quantity (party-size) beverages. For example, a pizza place may sell soda in 20-ounce, 1-liter, or 2-liter bottles on a take-out menu. For a room service menu, a 20-ounce bottle might be the largest size available. If a beverage is sold by the cup, it should come with a tight-fitting lid.

Banquet menus should provide a very limited set of beverage options for guests. As banquets offer only one or two options per course, the beverages (often wine) can be paired with each course or one red and one white wine selected for the entire meal. Obviously, if the banquet is designed to highlight a particular beverage, that beverage should be served with each course. Nonalcoholic beverages should always be available for a banquet, even if an alcoholic drink is being highlighted. Water should be poured for every participant. Soda, tea, coffee, and juice should be available upon request. If the banquet provider is a hotel or other operation with full bar capability, the menu planner should work with the client in advance to determine whether to accommodate guests who want an alcoholic beverage not listed on the menu and what the additional

Figure 5–7
This room service beverage menu offers a range of alcoholic and nonalcoholic beverages.
Shaun Rajah, Palm Court, and Chef Baasim Zafar, Drake Hotel.

BEVERAGE LIST

Liquor Prices Include Service of Ice, Glasses and
Two 1L Bottles of Mixers

LIQUOR

SCOTCH

Dewar's White Label	130
Chivas Regal	140
Johnny Walker Black	150

BOURBON

Jack Daniels	130
Maker's Mark	140

VODKA

Skyy	120
Absolut	130
Ketel One	140
Belvedere	150
Grey Goose	180

GIN

Beefeater	130
Tanqueray	140
Bombay Sapphire	150

RUM

Bacardi Light	130
Myer's Dark	140
Captain Morgan Spiced Rum	150

BLENDED WHISKY

Canadian Club	130
Crown Royal	140

BEER

Bud, Bud Light, Miller Lite, Coors Light	6
Heineken, Heineken Light, Corona, Sam Adams Boston Lager	7

MINERAL WATER

Evian (500mL)	6
Evian (liter)	10
Badoit (330mL)	4
Badoit (750mL)	7.50

MIXERS & SOFT DRINKS

Coca-Cola, Diet Coke, Sprite, Ginger Ale, Club Soda, Tonic Water (10oz bottles)	4
Ginger Ale, Club Soda, Tonic Water (One-Liter Bottles)	12
Red Bull Energy Drink (can)	8

JUICE

Florida Orange Juice, Grapefruit Juice	6
Tomato, V8, Apple, Cranberry, Prune, Pineapple Juice	5

HOSPITALITY

Bucket of Ice	10
Large Tub of Ice	15
Bar Refresh (ice, glasses and fruit	25

It is the Hotel's policy that alcoholic beverages
may not be brought into the Hotel from outside sources

* Consumption of raw or undercooked foods may increase risk of food borne illness.
Individuals with certain health conditions may be at a higher risk.

All Food and Beverage prices are subject to 17% Gratuity,
an In-Room Dining Charge of $6.00 per delivery
and applicable State and Local Taxes

Figure 5–7
(continued)

WINE LIST

RED WINE

CABERNET SAUVIGNON

Bin #		Glass	Bottle
2000	Canyon Road, California	9	40
2001	BV Coastal Estates, Sonoma	10	42
2002	William Hill, Central Coast	11	46
2003	Silver Palm, North Coast		65
2004	Tangley Oaks, Napa Valley		95

MERLOT

2020	Canyon Road, California	9	40
2021	14 Hands, Washington	10	42
2022	Sterling Vintner's Collection, Central Coast	14	62
2023	Frei Bros., California		70

PINOT NOIR

2030	Jargon, California	9	40
2031	Firesteed, Oregon	11	46
2032	Brancott, New Zealand	14	62
2033	Ponzi, Willamette Valley		75
2034	Belle Glos "Meiomi", Sonoma		90

SHIRAZ

2051	McWilliams Hanwood Estate, SE Australia	12	52
2052	Cline "Cool Climate", Sonoma		65

ZINFANDEL

2070	Dancing Bull, California	9	40
2071	Murphy-Goode "Liar's Dice", Sonoma	14	62
2072	Sebastiani, Sonoma		65

ALTERNATE RED

2080	Apothic Red, California	12	52
2081	Renacer "Punto Final" Malbec Clasico, Argentina	10	42
2082	Ferrari-Carano "Siena", Sonoma		75

It is the Hotel's policy that alcoholic beverages
may not be brought into the Hotel from outside sources

* Consumption of raw or undercooked foods may increase risk of food borne illness.
Individuals with certain health conditions may be at a higher risk.

All Food and Beverage prices are subject to 17% Gratuity,
an In-Room Dining Charge of $6.00 per delivery
and applicable State and Local Taxes

Figure 5–7
(continued)

WINE LIST

WHITE WINE

CHARDONNAY

Bin #		Glass	Bottle
1000	Canyon Road, California	9	40
1001	William Hill, Central Coast	11	46
1002	Sonoma-Cutrer, Russian River Valley	16	72
1003	Joel Gott, Monterey		50
1004	Chateau St Jean, Sonoma		55

SAUVIGNON BLANC

1041	Night Harvest, California	9	40
1042	Napa Cellars, Napa Valley	11	46
1043	Girard, Napa Valley	12	52
1044	Cakebread Cellars, Napa Valley		74

PINOT GRIGIO/GRIS

1020	Loredona, Monterey	9	40
1021	Willakenzie, Willamette Valley	14	62
1022	Kim Crawford, New Zealand	16	72
1023	Columbia Winery, Washington		53
1024	Santa Margherita, Alto Adige, Italy		68

ALTERNATE WHITE

1070	Next Riesling, Washington	10	42
1071	Chateau d'Aqueria Tavel Rose, Rhone	14	62
1072	Pacific Rim Organic Riesling, Washington		60
1073	Conundrum White Blend "California"		60

SPARKLING

1502	LaMarca Prosecco, Italy	11	46
1503	Domaine Chandon Brut, California	14	62
1504	Korbel Brut Split (187ml), California		15
1505	Domaine Ste. Michelle Brut, Washington		50
1506	Veuve Clicquot "Yellow Label" Brut, France		120
1507	Perrier-Jouet "Fleur", France		205
1508	Moet & Chandon "Dom Perignon", France		330

It is the Hotel's policy that alcoholic beverages
may not be brought into the Hotel from outside sources

* Consumption of raw or undercooked foods may increase risk of food borne illness.
Individuals with certain health conditions may be at a higher risk.

All Food and Beverage prices are subject to 17% Gratuity,
an In-Room Dining Charge of $6.00 per delivery
and applicable State and Local Taxes

cost would be. Fees for alcoholic drinks may be charged to the guest based on his consumption or to the event host based either on an upfront per person cost or total usage at the event.

Cycle menus require beverage options that, like the food, address the nutritional needs of the audience. Sodas may be listed, but healthier alternatives of juice, milk, and water should also be included. Coffee and tea are common inclusions for adult markets as well. Alcoholic beverages are rarely appropriate for a captive audience but may make sense for a cycle menu that operates as part of a cafeteria or restaurant. Except for specialty drinks, such as an ethnic beverage designed to pair specifically with one ethnic recipe in the cycle rotation, the beverage component of a cycle menu does not usually rotate. It makes more sense to offer fewer juice, milk, and water options every day than to offer only pineapple juice one day, only grape juice another, etc. When people prefer a specific beverage for a given meal, they want it most days.

Catering menus should include an extensive set of options for customers. The caterer can purchase approximately what he needs for the event, and sealed bottles can be stored for a long time assuming the caterer has the storage space available. Usually, caterers only sell full bottles, meaning that once the caterer opens a bottle, the client has purchased the entire bottle, even if only one drink is poured from it. Sometimes, the caterer gives the partial bottles to the customer; sometimes, the caterer keeps the excess. When the caterer is a hotel or restaurant that sells that bottle on its regular menu, it may charge the client per drink instead. If a client wants a beverage that is not on the catering menu, the caterer may agree to purchase it for the client under the condition that the client pays for the purchase. Because catering clients are a much broader market than the guests who visit a particular restaurant, the beverage offerings should be extensive. That said, the client should be guided to choose a fairly narrow selection of beverages to serve at the event.

The attendees at a single catered event are usually a very clearly defined market and their beverage preferences are known. If the client wishes to provide a cocktail hour, it is often sufficient to offer just one or two wines of each color, a couple of beers, and four or five different liquors with a few basic mixers and garnishes. Clients may want a full bar available, but they often reconsider once they are advised that they pay for six bottles if six guests each want a different brand of bourbon for their one drink. Under that scenario, all of the guests are usually perfectly happy just to have any whiskey available. The brands selected for a catered event should accommodate the client's budget and be popular choices for the market. For example, a super-premium vodka that none of the guests have heard of is less likely to satisfy the attendees than a cheaper one that they drink regularly. During the main meal, beer and wine are usually the alcoholic beverages served alongside nonalcoholic drinks. For adult-only events, soda and water may be the only nonalcoholic choices available, though mixers from the bar could also be served alone. If the caterer offered liquor during the cocktail hour, the client may want it available upon request through the meal or may insist that the bar close once the guests are seated. The ways that caterers charge for beverages mirror banquet beverage charging options.

As with traditional restaurant menus, the rules of safe alcohol service apply to all types of menus. Guests should be cut off once they have reached their alcohol limit; excessive consumption should not be promoted. Guests should never be allowed to self-serve alcoholic drinks. Nonalcoholic beverages should always be available, and water automatically provided to seated guests. Finally, as with all food and beverage menus, the most important factor from the menu planner's perspective is to ensure that the offerings meet the needs of the target market and the business.

SUMMARY

Beverage menus include a wide range of both alcoholic and nonalcoholic offerings appropriate for the target market, the business's brand, and the meal period. Variety and balance make for a proper wine menu, which often lists wine by producer name, grape type, region, and/or vintage. Wines may be categorized by color, grape type, region, or flavor profile. Some menu planners may include recommended wine and food pairings on the menu. Beer menus, like wine menus, should offer variety of region and style. The price points for the beer and wine listed should align appropriately with the business's food menu prices (cheap, midrange, or pricy). Liquor and cocktail menus are printed in the food menu, on table tents, on a dessert menu, or as part of a larger beverage menu. While beer and wine listings may provide tasting notes, cocktails usually list only ingredients. Nonalcoholic beverage menus are just as important as alcoholic ones. Water, juice, milk, soda, iced tea, lemonade, coffee, tea, and other beverages are extremely popular and represent opportunities for additional sales. When these categories include creative or boutique products, nonalcoholic beverages can be as much of a customer draw as the alcoholic drinks. Because alcohol cannot be consumed safely in unlimited quantities, alcohol revenue should be driven through sales of some premium products, not by persuading increased consumption. Portion sizes of alcohol should be moderate as well. Finally, room service, takeout, banquet, cycle, and catering menus all require some special consideration when planning for their beverage offerings.

COMPREHENSION QUESTIONS

1. List four variables that may provide variety and balance to a wine list.
2. List four bits of information that are normally included in the name of a New World wine.
3. What is a bin number, and why is it used?
4. What is the standard portion size for one drink of each for wine, beer, and 80 proof liquor?
5. List four different categories of beer styles.
6. In an ethnic restaurant that serves beer, list the two countries from which at a minimum the beer options should be sourced.
7. How do cocktail menu descriptions differ from descriptions of other menu items?
8. If a menu planner does not list liquor drinks under a single heading of "Cocktails" or "Liquor," how might these drinks be categorized? List five possible subheadings.
9. List five categories of nonalcoholic beverages that might be found on a restaurant menu.
10. List one way that a menu planner or server can safely increase beverage revenue.

DISCUSSION QUESTIONS

1. Consider two different beverage menus. One has eight pages of wine listings, two pages of beer listings, and two pages of cocktails. The other fits all of its alcoholic and nonalcoholic beverage offerings on a single page. Describe the restaurant for which each of these menus would make sense.
2. Do an Internet search to find a fairly extensive beer menu for a restaurant. What categories does the menu use to subdivide its beer offerings?
3. Imagine that you are a mixologist in an upscale restaurant. Think of three mixers (syrups, infusions, flavorings, etc.) that you could create in-house for use in your scratch-made cocktails.
4. Imagine that you are a menu planner for a boutique restaurant that makes all of its beverages from scratch. Create one soda, one flavored iced tea, one flavored lemonade, one juice beverage, and one espresso drink that you could prepare in-house but that cannot be purchased commercially as a ready-made product.
5. Create a beverage menu (item listings only) for a residential college dining hall.
6. Imagine that you are an off-premise caterer with a client who wishes to offer a cocktail hour before a sit-down meal at his private event. What advice would you give him for selecting beverages to serve at the cocktail hour and during the meal? If the event is a private party on the client's estate, how would you handle an attendee who has become intoxicated and wants to have another alcoholic drink?

6

Standardized Recipes and Recipe Costing

After determining the list of foods and beverages to include on a menu, the menu planner next turns to the calculation of menu prices. The prices that the customer sees on a menu are not picked willy-nilly from thin air but rather arise from a careful analysis of the operation's costs. The biggest cost component to consider is the cost of each item sold—its food cost or beverage cost.

Many menu planners calculate each item's selling price directly from its food (or beverage) cost per portion. It is important to recognize that the true cost per portion for an item includes the costs for all of the consumables provided to the customer, even if some of those products are included "for free." While this chapter focuses exclusively on how to calculate a product's true cost per portion, it is merely a prelude to the ultimate goal of determining a sales price for each listing on the menu. For ease of reading, this chapter explains costing concepts through food recipes, but the concepts apply equally to beverages. Both utilize recipes, and the cost per portion for each derives directly from the cost of the ingredients used in each recipe. When there is a difference between food and beverage costing, the chapter points it out.

6.1 STANDARD RECIPES AND PORTION CONTROL

In order for a recipe costing exercise to be valid, a foodservice operation must utilize standard (or standardized) recipes. A standard recipe is one that is written in sufficient detail that each and every employee who uses it creates an identical product. Standard recipes account for the equipment, employee skills, purveyor products, and quality and quantity standards at the business where they are used. They are always followed exactly by all employees and not thought of simply as guidelines. Finally, they deal with all aspects of food production, from ingredient preparation to portioning and presentation to storage of leftovers.

Standard recipes may be written down or communicated verbally through training. Specificity is critical. A recipe that gives the cook too much leeway is likely to waver greatly in production costs from day to day. For example, if a portion size for a swordfish entrée is listed as "one steak," the cook might serve one guest a 5-ounce steak and another one a 7-ounce steak. The costs for these two dishes differ significantly and make calculating a fair selling price nearly impossible.

Portions may be measured by volume, by weight, or by count, but they should always be measured somehow. A kitchen may employ measuring cups, ladles, scales, or even certain presentation dishes to

By the end of this chapter, you will be able to:

- State the importance of using standard recipes and portion control
- Define the concepts of as-purchased, edible portion, and yield percentage
- Calculate a product's as-purchased quantity, edible portion quantity, or yield percentage given the other two variables
- Calculate a product's as-purchased cost, edible portion cost, or yield percentage given the other two variables
- Use a costing sheet to calculate a recipe's total cost
- Calculate an item's true cost per portion including a spice factor and Q factor

control portion sizes. For example, a 6-ounce gratin dish cannot hold more than 6 ounces of product as long as the dish is only filled level and not mounded above the rim. When an operation does not use standard recipes and portion control methods consistently, calculating a cost per portion becomes a fruitless activity that yields irrelevant information.

6.2 AP, EP, AND YIELD PERCENTAGE

To calculate a recipe's cost accurately, it is important to understand the concepts of as-purchased (AP), edible portion (EP), and yield percentage (Y%). As-purchased refers to an ingredient in the form in which it arrives at the business from the purveyor. For example, if a restaurant purchases its potatoes unprocessed, then the raw, unpeeled potatoes are the as-purchased form. If the chef purchases potatoes raw but peeled, then the peeled potatoes are the as-purchased form. The key to understanding as-purchased is that the kitchen has not processed the product from the form in which it arrived at the operation's door.

Edible portion is the form each product takes after it has been processed by the kitchen. For produce, edible portion refers to the trimmed and cut but not cooked product. For example, peeled and diced carrots for a glazed carrot recipe or trimmed green beans are in their edible portion form. For meat (or poultry or seafood), edible portion may refer to the ingredient after it has been cooked. Whether edible portion meat is based on a raw or a cooked weight depends on how the product is advertised. A menu that states that its 6-ounce burgers are measured by their "precooked weight" employs an edible portion based on raw ground beef. However, a restaurant that advertises a sandwich with "4 ounces of sliced corned beef" refers to a cooked edible portion weight; the meat is sliced and measured after the corned beef has been cooked.

Yield percentage is the tool for comparing the relative sizes between a product's as-purchased and edible portion forms. An as-purchased ingredient represents 100% of the weight of that ingredient. During processing, some of that ingredient's weight may be lost through peeling, trimming, or in the case of certain meats, cooking. The percentage of product that remains is the ingredient's yield. When the same ingredient is processed the same way by individuals with similar skills, the percentage of product yielded remains fairly consistent over time. This allows a manager to utilize a yield percentage to calculate how much of a given ingredient will remain after it has been processed.

To calculate a yield percentage, a cook must weigh (or measure) an ingredient both before processing (as-purchased weight) and after processing (edible portion weight). Using this information, the yield percentage is calculated as follows:

$$\text{Yield \%} = \frac{\text{Edible Portion (EP) Weight}}{\text{As-Purchased (AP) Weight}}$$

Example 6.1: A cook takes a 23-ounce rutabaga and trims and dices it down to 15 ounces. What is the yield percentage for rutabaga processed this way?

$$\text{Yield \%} = \frac{\text{EP}}{\text{AP}} = \frac{15 \text{ oz}}{23 \text{ oz}} = 0.652 \text{ or } 65.2\%$$

It is important to note that for this formula to work both EP and AP must be expressed in the same units—all ounces or all pounds or all cups. Also, the result will be the yield percentage in its decimal form. To convert it to its percentage form, simply move the decimal point two spaces to the right and add the percentage sign.

Given this equation, a manager can solve for any of the three variables (yield %, EP weight, or AP weight) given the other two. The equation can be expressed as a graphic formula as follows:

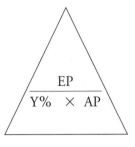

In this graphic formula, EP represents edible portion quantity, AP represents as-purchased quantity, and Y% is the yield percentage in decimal form. To solve for any of the variables, simply cover up the unknown one and follow the calculation depicted with the other two variables.

Example 6.2: Sliced, peeled cucumbers have a yield percentage of 84%. If a cook has to prepare 2½ pounds of peeled, sliced cucumbers for lunch, how many pounds of as-purchased cucumbers should she start with?

In this example, we know Y% (84% or 0.84) and EP weight (2.5 lbs). We need to solve for AP. By covering up AP, we are left with EP ÷ Y%.

$$AP = \frac{EP}{Y\%} = \frac{2.5\ lbs}{0.84} = 2.98\ lbs$$

The cook should begin with roughly 3 pounds of cucumbers to yield 2.5 pounds of sliced, peeled cucumbers. It should be emphasized that in this formula Y% is always entered in its decimal form.

The concepts of EP, AP, and Y% apply equally to food and to beverage; however, in the case of beverages, the loss that creates a yield percentage of less than 100% stems from evaporation and spillage rather than from intentional trimming and peeling. To determine an accurate yield percentage for a beverage, a manager must closely track purchases and sold beverage quantities to determine what quantity, if any, is lost in the process of pouring drinks. Using the AP quantity purchased and the EP quantity sold, the manager can easily calculate the yield percentage from the aforementioned graphic formula.

The graphic formula applies to any product for which the loss or waste either has no value or has the same value as the rest of the product. For example, potato peel may be thought of as having no value (if it is thrown in the trash) or as having the same value as the rest of the potato if the peel is cut thick and used in a potato skin appetizer. However, the components of large cuts of meat, poultry, and seafood do not often work that way. A whole chicken, for example, costs one price per pound, but when broken into smaller cuts, the breasts, wings, thighs, and bones all have different values per pound because they would each cost a different price per pound if purchased separately. Determining an accurate cost per pound for a product in this situation requires a butcher's yield test. A butcher's yield test can be somewhat complicated to explain, but most cost control books provide thorough explanations of the process. Traster's *Foundations of Cost Control* (Pearson Education) provides an excellent description of the butcher's yield test and cooking loss calculations. When a product does not require a butcher's yield test or cooking loss test, its edible portion cost can be derived quite simply from its as-purchased cost and yield percentage as described in the next section.

6.2.1 AP and EP Costs

When a product is processed from an AP to an EP form, its effective cost per weight or volume changes as well. For example, onions might cost $1.00/lb, but if sliced, peeled onions have a 70% yield, then a chef needs to buy 1.4 pounds to get a 1 pound yield. The cost for 1.4 pounds = $1.00/lb × 1.4 lbs. = $1.40. Thus, the cost for sliced, peeled onions is actually $1.40/lb, not $1.00/lb. This logic illustrates the difference between edible portion cost and as-purchased cost. In this particular case, $1.00/lb is the AP cost and $1.40/lb is the EP cost.

Fortunately, calculating an EP cost is quite simple given an AP cost and a yield percentage for a given product. The equation to do so is as follows:

$$EP\$ = \frac{AP\$}{Y\%}$$

where EP$ represents edible portion cost, AP$ represents as-purchased cost, and Y% is the yield percentage in its decimal form. Both EP$ and AP$ are per-unit costs, meaning that they are written in terms of dollars per pound, ounce, cup, piece, etc. If the AP cost for a product is $30.00 for a 50-pound bag, the cost should first be divided to a cost per single unit (per pound, in this case). Thus, $30/50 lbs is effectively $30 ÷ 50 lbs = $0.60/lb. To enter $30 into the above equation without converting it to $0.60/lb first would not provide valuable information. Any cost per unit can be calculated by dividing the total cost by the total weight or volume. Mathematically, this is written as follows:

$$Cost\ per\ unit = \frac{Total\ cost}{Total\ weight\ or\ volume}$$

Example 6.3: What is the edible portion cost per pound for diced potatoes if the as-purchased potatoes cost $37.60 for a 40-pound box and the yield percentage for diced potatoes is 66%?

First, calculate the AP cost per pound.

$$Cost\ per\ pound = \frac{Total\ Cost}{Total\ Weight} = \frac{\$37.60}{40\ lbs} = \$0.94/lb$$

Now it is possible to calculate EP$. Remember that the Y% of 66% is written as 0.66 in decimal form.

$$EP\$ = \frac{AP\$}{Y\%} = \frac{\$0.94/lb}{0.66} = \$1.42/lb$$

The edible portion cost for diced potatoes is $1.42/lb.

As with AP and EP quantity, the relationship between AP$, EP$, and Y% can be written in a single graphic formula as follows:

As with the earlier graphic equation, simply cover up the variable you wish to determine and follow the mathematical instructions depicted with the remaining two variables.

Example 6.4: A chef has planned for an EP cost of $0.77/lb for her collard greens. The new purveyor supplies collards that are more closely trimmed of stem, so the yield percentage has changed to 91%. What price should the chef expect to pay (AP) for her EP cost to be accurate?

$$AP\$ = EP\$ \times Y\% = \$0.77/lb \times 0.91 = \$0.70/lb$$

In this example, if the chef pays $0.70/lb or less AP, then her expense on collard greens should remain within budget. If they cost more, she will be over budget on collard green costs.

While chefs use the AP, EP, Y% and AP$, EP$, Y% formulas for a variety of reasons ranging from calculating order quantities to determining target AP prices, the menu planner primarily needs them to calculate the EP$ for each ingredient. Using the EP$ = AP$ ÷ Y% formula, a menu planner can quickly determine the total cost for a given standard recipe in a foodservice operation.

6.3 RECIPE COSTING

In most foodservice businesses, recipes are costed using the aid of a costing sheet (either on paper or set up in a computer). Costing a recipe is the next step in determining the cost per portion for a dish on a menu. To begin the calculations on a recipe costing sheet, a menu planner must first know each ingredient's name and quantity, yield percentage, and AP cost. The names and quantities (number and unit) for each ingredient are transferred to the costing spreadsheet directly from the standard recipe. For most professional kitchens, ingredients are written in EP amounts. The yield percentage comes from prior kitchen tests. While books are available to provide average yield percentages across the industry for various products, the more accurate information comes from a test of the product as it is prepared in the restaurant's kitchen. For example, if a book states that carrots have a yield percentage of 87%, but the cook who prepares the carrots consistently averages an 85% yield, then the 85% figure is the one to use. It is more accurate for this particular operation. Finally, the AP cost comes directly from the purveyor invoices. This data is typically entered into the spreadsheet in its raw format as a total cost per case or weight. The cost per unit for each ingredient is derived from this information.

Chefs can purchase recipe costing software or utilize that function within their company's point of sales system; however, the costing process is not so difficult that it cannot be performed by hand or by creating one's own recipe costing program in an Excel worksheet. Either way, the chef or menu planner must enter the same starting information into the program for the computer to perform the calculations.

Figure 6–1a depicts a sample recipe costing sheet with the known information entered. The information in the heading will be explained later in the chapter, as will the spice factor entries listed for salt and pepper.

The next step to costing a recipe is to convert the AP cost to units that match the EP quantity units listed in the recipe. For example, if a recipe requires 18 ounces of flour and flour is purchased by the pound, the AP cost must be converted from cost per pound to cost per ounce. If the units do not match, multiplying the two figures together provides completely useless information. Only an AP cost with a per dollar unit that matches the recipe EP unit is a useful figure.

Figure 6–1a
Recipe costing sheet—EP quantity, Y%, and AP$ entered.

Recipe: Chicken Chasseur					Spice Factor:	
No. of portions: 12					Q Factor:	
Cost per portion:			FC%:		Selling Price:	
Ingredient	Recipe (EP) Quantity (from recipe)	Yield Percent (from kitchen tests)	AP Cost (from invoice)	Converted AP Cost	EP Cost	Extended Cost
Chicken Breast, 5 oz, airline, prefab, frozen, indiv. pack	12 ea (60 oz)	100%	$31.45/24 ea			
Butter, unsalted	6 oz	100%	$64.40/36 lb			
Shallot, minced	2 oz	77%	$4.68/5 lb			
Mushrooms, button, trimmed, sliced	4 oz	94%	$8.25/3 lb			
White wine, dry	3 oz	100%	$5.50/750 mL			
Demi-glace	9 oz	100%	$0.18/oz (made in-house)			
Tomato, plum, concassé	8 oz	58%	$34.00/40 lb			
Tarragon, chopped	3 Tbsp	64%	$2.77/2 oz			
Salt	To taste	100%	Spice Factor			
Pepper	To taste	100%	Spice Factor			
Total						

Example 6.5: A recipe calls for 27 ounces of diced tomato. Tomatoes are purchased at $61.45/40-lb case. Convert the AP cost to useful units.

Since the EP ingredient is listed in ounces, the AP cost must be converted to dollars per ounce.

$61.45 ÷ 40 lbs = $1.54/lb

$1.54/lb ÷ 16 oz/lb = $0.10/oz

The useful AP cost is $0.10/oz.

Many culinary school textbooks explain the process of converting units, so an in-depth discussion of how to convert units is not described here. For a more thorough description of the unit conversion process, reference Traster's *Foundations of Cost Control* (Pearson Education).

Using the costing sheet, the menu planner or other manager changes each entered AP cost to a useful AP cost by converting the AP cost so that its units match the EP units from the recipe. Figure 6–1b illustrates this step in the process.

The next column in the costing sheet is "EP Cost." The EP cost is performed with the equation EP$ = AP$ ÷ Y%. Recall that the Y% is always written in its decimal form in the equation. This computation is done for each ingredient using the converted AP cost (useful units). When an ingredient has a yield percentage of 100%, the EP cost will match the converted AP cost.

There are a couple of exceptions to this process that should be noted. First, when an ingredient is measured per "each," yield percentage is not a factor. For example, if a recipe asks for "4 large onions, diced," it does not matter how much of the onion

Recipe: Chicken Chasseur					Spice Factor:		
No. of portions: 12					Q Factor:		
Cost per portion:			FC%:		Selling Price:		
Ingredient	Recipe (EP) Quantity (from recipe)	Yield Percent (from kitchen tests)	AP Cost (from invoice)	Converted AP Cost (AP units converted to match EP units)	EP Cost	Extended Cost
Chicken Breast, 5 oz, airline, prefab, frozen, indiv. pack	12 ea (60 oz)	100%	$31.45/24 ea	$1.310 ea		
Butter, unsalted	6 oz	100%	$64.40/36 lbs	$0.111/oz		
Shallot, minced	2 oz	77%	$4.68/5 lbs	$0.059/oz		
Mushrooms, button, trimmed, sliced	4 oz	94%	$8.25/3 lbs	$0.172/oz		
White wine, dry	3 oz	100%	$5.50/750 mL	$0.217/oz		
Demi-glace	9 oz	100%	$0.18/oz (made in-house)	$0.18/oz		
Tomato, plum, concassé	8 oz	58%	$34.00/40 lbs	$0.053/oz		
Tarragon, chopped	3 Tbsp	64%	$2.77/2 oz (1 oz yields ¼ c chopped)	$0.346/ Tbsp (Y% already accounted for in 1 oz = ¼ c)		
Salt	To taste	100%	Spice Factor	N/A		
Pepper	To taste	100%	Spice Factor	N/A		
Total						

Figure 6–1b
Recipe costing sheet—AP cost converted to useable units.

is lost in processing. In the end, the cook is still left with four large onions worth of product. This logic is even more obvious with the example of shrimp cocktail. Assume a recipe for shrimp cocktail requires that a cook serve five large shrimp per customer. If the cook loses 20% of the weight through peeling and deveining five shrimp, it is irrelevant. She still has five shrimp left to serve to the customer. (If the shrimp were measured by the ounce for a recipe, the situation would be different. She would need to start with a larger weight of shrimp to pare down to the right number of ounces.) Another exception to the rule is for products that have undergone a butcher's yield test or cooking loss test already. These tests calculate an effective EP cost for the product (usually per ounce and per pound). In such an instance, the menu planner should simply utilize the EP cost from these tests and enter it directly into the EP cost column, adjusting it only so the units match the ingredient EP units. Finally, if a kitchen test conversion already factors in yield, then the EP cost should not account for yield a second time. This occurs typically when a chef must convert from weight to volume or vice versa for ingredients that are not mostly water. For example, if a chef determines that 2 ounces of fresh rosemary usually yields 6 tablespoons of chopped rosemary after stemming and chopping, then she can convert an AP cost in dollars per ounce to a useful AP cost in dollars per tablespoon using the formula 2 oz = 6 Tbsp. This formula has already accounted for the loss of the rosemary stems, so the yield percentage for

Figure 6–1c
Recipe costing sheet—EP cost calculated.

Recipe: Chicken Chasseur				Spice Factor:		
No. of portions: 12				Q Factor:		
Cost per portion:			FC%:	Selling Price:		
Ingredient	Recipe (EP) Quantity	Yield Percent	AP Cost	Converted AP Cost	EP Cost (converted AP$ ÷ Y%)	Extended Cost
Chicken Breast, 5 oz, airline, prefab, frozen, indiv. pack	12 each (60 oz)	100%	$31.45/24 ea	$1.310 ea	$1.31 ea	
Butter, unsalted	6 oz	100%	$64.40/36 lbs	$0.111/oz	$0.111/oz	
Shallot, minced	2 oz	77%	$4.68/5 lbs	$0.059/oz	$0.077/oz	
Mushrooms, button, trimmed, sliced	4 oz	94%	$8.25/3 lbs	$0.172/oz	$0.183/oz	
White wine, dry	3 oz	100%	$5.50/750 mL	$0.217/oz	$0.217/oz	
Demi-glace	9 oz	100%	$0.18/oz (made in-house)	$0.18/oz	$0.18/oz	
Tomato, plum, concassé	8 oz	58%	$34.00/40 lbs	$0.053/oz	$0.091/oz	
Tarragon, chopped	3 Tbsp	64%	$2.77/2 oz (1 oz = ¼ c chopped)	$0.346/Tbsp	$0.346/Tbsp (Y% already factored into 1 oz = ¼ c)	
Salt	To taste	100%	Spice Factor	N/A	N/A	
Pepper	To taste	100%	Spice Factor	N/A	N/A	
Total						

rosemary should not be factored for a second time to calculate EP cost. In such a situation, the EP cost is the converted AP cost.

Figure 6–1c illustrates the step of calculating EP cost from the converted AP cost in the sample recipe.

Example 6.6: Calculate the EP cost for the shallots from Figure 6–1c.

The shallots are listed in ounces, but sell for $4.68/5 lbs. They have a yield percentage of 77%.

First, convert the AP cost to useful units.

$4.68 ÷ 5 lbs = $0.936/lb

$0.936/lb ÷ 16 oz/lb = $0.059/oz

Next, use the EP$ = AP$ ÷ Y% formula

EP$ = $0.059/oz ÷ 0.77 = $0.077/oz

Example 6.7: Calculate the EP Cost for the tarragon from Figure 6–1c.

The recipe calls for chopped tarragon measured in tablespoons, but the tarragon costs $2.77/2 oz. The yield percentage is 64%, and the kitchen test reveals that 1 ounce of tarragon = ¼ cup chopped tarragon.

First, convert the AP cost to useful units.

$2.77 ÷ 2 oz = $1.385/oz

Since 1 oz = ¼ c, and ¼ c = 4 Tbsp, $1.385/oz is the same as $1.385/4 Tbsp.
Thus, the cost per tablespoon is:

$$\$1.385 \div 4\ Tbsp = \$0.346/Tbsp$$

To get the conversion 1 ounce = ¼ cup, the chef would have already stemmed the tarragon and kept only the chopped leaves. The loss (stem) has already been removed and thus the yield percentage has already been accounted for. Consequently, the EP cost is the same as the converted AP cost. EP$ = $0.346/Tbsp.

With the EP costs determined, it is quite simple to calculate the extended cost or extension for each ingredient in the recipe. The extended cost is the cost that a single ingredient contributes to a recipe. When all of the extended costs for a recipe are added together, they represent a preliminary total recipe cost, pending any adjustments for spices or other add-ons.

To calculate an ingredient's extended cost, multiply the EP quantity by the EP cost. Mathematically,

$$\text{Extended Cost} = \text{EP Quantity} \times \text{EP\$}$$

Since the units in the extended cost formula match, the result is simply a dollar figure (not dollars per unit).

Example 6.8: A chicken chasseur recipe calls for twelve (each) chicken breasts. The breasts have an EP cost of $1.31 each. What is the extended cost for the chicken in this recipe?

$$\text{Extended Cost} = \text{EP Quantity} \times \text{EP\$} = 12\ ea \times \$1.31/ea = \$15.72$$

To calculate a preliminary total recipe cost, just sum all of the extended costs in the recipe. Figure 6–1d shows the sample recipe from the Figure 6–1 series with the extended costs and preliminary total recipe cost calculated.

6.3.1 Cost per Portion

The preliminary cost per portion is simply the total recipe cost divided by the number of portions that the recipe yields. The formula is written as follows:

Preliminary Cost per Portion = Preliminary Total Recipe Cost ÷ Number of Portions in Recipe

Example 6.9: A recipe has a preliminary total recipe cost of $21.309 and yields 12 servings. What is the preliminary cost per portion for this dish?

Preliminary Cost per Portion = Preliminary Total Recipe Cost ÷ Number of Portions

$$= \$21.309 \div 12 = \$1.776$$

It is important to note that this is strictly a preliminary cost per portion. The true cost per portion must first factor in any spice factor adjustment. For entrées in certain establishments, the Q factor must be taken into account as well.

6.3.2 Spice Factor

Spice factor and Q factor are simply short cuts for calculating a recipe's true cost per portion when not every single ingredient or item provided to a customer is figured in the recipe cost calculation. Imagine trying to account for the cost of a small amount of salt and pepper used in a recipe. What if these seasonings are added "to taste"? How would a chef calculate the extended cost for these spices then? The simplest way to

Figure 6–1d
Recipe costing sheet—
extended costs and total
recipe cost.

Recipe: Chicken Chasseur					Spice Factor:	
No. of portions: 12					Q Factor:	
Cost per portion:			FC%:		Selling Price:	
Ingredient	Recipe (EP) Quantity	Yield Percent	AP Cost	Converted AP Cost	EP Cost	Extended Cost (EP Quantity × EP$)
Chicken Breast, 5 oz, airline, prefab, frozen, indiv. pack	12 ea (60 oz)	100%	$31.45/24 ea	$1.310 ea	$1.31 ea	$15.72
Butter, unsalted	6 oz	100%	$64.40/36 lbs	$0.111/oz	$0.111/oz	$0.666
Shallot, minced	2 oz	77%	$4.68/5 lbs	$0.059/oz	$0.077/oz	$0.154
Mushrooms, button, trimmed, sliced	4 oz	94%	$8.25/3 lbs	$0.172/oz	$0.183/oz	$0.732
White wine, dry	3 oz	100%	$5.50/750 mL	$0.217/oz	$0.217/oz	$0.651
Demi-glace	9 oz	100%	$0.18/oz	$0.18/oz	$0.18/oz	$1.62
Tomato, plum, concassé	8 oz	58%	$34.00/40 lbs	$0.053/oz	$0.091/oz	$0.728
Tarragon, chopped	3 Tbsp	64%	$2.77/2 oz	$0.346/Tbsp	$0.346/Tbsp (Y% already factored into 1 oz = ¼ c)	$1.038
Salt	To taste	100%	Spice Factor	N/A	N/A	S.F.
Pepper	To taste	100%	Spice Factor	N/A	N/A	S.F.
Total (sum of extended costs)						$21.309

account for items added "to taste" or for ingredients like herbs and spices, which are measured "by eye," is to utilize a spice factor.

A spice factor is a figure that represents the additional cost to a recipe for any ingredients not specifically listed with an amount in the recipe. Some chefs may choose to include a wide range of ingredients in the spice factor, while others will limit it solely to salt and pepper. The spice factor may include garnishes, herbs, spices, table seasonings, and even bread and butter that are provided to the customer "for free." These ingredients represent real costs to the business. Even though the customer does not pay for them directly, these costs should be included in the menu prices of all sold products.

The spice factor is always written as a percentage and it is applied equally to all menu items regardless of their level of seasoning. A chef may choose to use the spice factor for all herbs and spices, rather than calculating each one individually (like the tarragon in the sample chicken chasseur recipe). The same spice factor percentage would be used for both heavily and lightly spiced dishes. This approach spreads the cost of herbs and spices across all menu items rather than making the heavily spiced dishes more expensive. While this may seem unfair, most guests assume that the menu price reflects the main ingredients, not the spices. Many customers would have trouble paying as much for a saffron and cardamom chicken dish as they do for a simply grilled steak. Although saffron and cardamom are both very expensive spices, most customers would view these menu choices as the difference between chicken and steak, not between expensive spices and cheap seasonings. The spice factor applies the spice cost to all of the dishes, making the chicken a less expensive option than the steak.

To determine the spice factor for a foodservice operation, the chef or manager must first determine which ingredients will be included in the spice factor. Next, the chef must track the cost of all spice factor ingredients and all other ingredients over a period of time, usually one to six months. If one ingredient is sometimes considered a spice factor and sometimes considered a standard ingredient, the chef must determine how much of the cost goes toward the spice factor. For example, if a chef includes a fresh raspberry garnish in the spice factor but also prepares a raspberry tart, she must determine the amount of raspberry expense that went toward spice factor versus tart. Finally, the chef totals the cost of all of the spice factor items over the period and compares them to the total cost of the food purchases for the same period. The spice factor is calculated using the following formula:

$$\text{Spice Factor} = \frac{\text{Value of Spice Factor Items (over a period of time)}}{\text{Value of Total Food Purchases (over the same period)}}$$

The spice factor will always be a decimal and may be converted to a percentage by moving the decimal point two spaces to the right.

Example 6.10: In a restaurant, the spice factor items cost $3,150 over three months. During the same three months, all food purchases were $174,890. What is the spice factor for this restaurant?

$$\text{Spice Factor} = \frac{\text{Value of Spice Factor Items}}{\text{Value of Total Food Purchases}} = \frac{\$3,150}{\$174,890} = 0.018 \text{ or } 1.8\%$$

To adjust a recipe's preliminary cost per portion to account for the spice factor, simply multiply the preliminary cost per portion by (1 + spice factor in decimal form). Thus, if a company's spice factor is 1.8%, each preliminary cost per portion would be multiplied by (1 + 0.018) or 1.018 to get a spice factor adjusted cost per portion. For many restaurants, this is the true cost per portion for a dish.

Example 6.11: A restaurant has a spice factor of 2.3%. The chicken chasseur recipe has a preliminary cost per portion of $1.776. What is the cost per portion after adjusting for the spice factor?

Spice Factor Adjusted Cost = Preliminary Cost × (1 + Spice Factor)
= $1.776 × (1 + 0.023)
= $1.776 × 1.023 = $1.82

The spice factor may be multiplied by a cost per portion or by a total recipe cost. Whether the cost per portion is calculated before or after the spice factor adjustment is irrelevant. The result will be the same.

6.3.3 Q Factor

While most restaurants use a spice factor, only some use a Q factor. In a la carte and semi a la carte restaurants, a customer must purchase each menu category separately. For those restaurants, each starch, vegetable, and other accompaniment is costed separately. When starches and vegetables are paired with a specific dish, their costs per portion are added to the cost per portion of the main item to yield a total cost for the dish. However, in some restaurants, the guest, not the chef, chooses the sides to pair with the entrée selection. In others, the purchase of an entrée includes a guest's choice of salad, soup, and/or dessert (or more). Q factor becomes a highly useful tool when the customer gets a choice of "free" add-ons.

The Q factor accounts for the cost of the add-ons that a customer may select. To determine the Q factor value for a restaurant, the chef or manager first calculates the cost for one serving of each of the possible add-ons on the menu. Next, the chef determines which are the most expensive choices the customer could choose. This determination depends upon which categories the customer can choose from. For example, if a guest has a choice of salad, choice of soup, and choice of dessert, then the chef will note the most expensive salad, soup, and dessert. However, if the guest must choose between salads and soups for a first course, then only the most expensive of the soup and salad selection is relevant. The Q factor value is the sum of the costs of the most expensive add-on choices.

Example 6.12: Using the data in the chart below, determine the Q factor for this restaurant. With the purchase of an entrée, the guest may choose a salad, a soup, and a dessert. Bread and butter are automatic add-ons for entrées as well.

Add-on	Cost per Portion
House Salad	$0.78
Caesar Salad	$1.02
Chicken Noodle Soup	$0.49
Beef Barley Soup	$0.54
Ice Cream Sundae	$1.14
Molten Chocolate Cake	$0.99
Pecan Pie	$1.46
Bread	$0.15
Butter	$0.09

In this operation, the most expensive options that the guest may choose are Caesar salad, beef barley soup, pecan pie, bread, and butter. Note that the bread and butter are the only options in their category, so they are selected by default. The Q factor is the sum of the most expensive choices that the guest may select, so Q factor is calculated as follows:

Q Factor = $1.02 (salad) + $0.54 (soup) + $1.46 (dessert) + $0.15 (bread) + $0.09 (butter) = $3.26

With a Q factor determined, the menu planner can simply add the Q factor to each of the entrée costs per portion (spice factor adjusted) to determine the true cost per portion. After all, if a steak entrée is calculated to cost $4.22 per portion, but the guest has the ability to add on another $3.00 worth of sides for no additional cost, then the real cost to the restaurant when a guest orders steak is $7.22 ($4.22 + $3.00).

Note that unlike spice factor, which is *multiplied* times a cost per portion, Q factor is *added* to the cost per portion.

Example 6.13: What is the true cost per portion for an entrée that costs $1.79 per portion in a restaurant that uses a Q factor of $2.11?

True Cost per Portion = Cost per Portion + Q Factor
= $1.79 + $2.11 = $3.90

Through the use of a Q factor, a restaurant accounts for the expense that a guest will generate if she orders the most expensive menu choices. If the guest picks less expensive options, the restaurant simply makes a greater profit off of that customer.

It is important to stress that Q factor only deals with items that are added on to a meal "for free" *by customer choice*. Starches, vegetables, sauces, and garnishes that are predetermined by the chef to accompany an entrée are part of the entrée's preliminary cost per portion. If the menu planner costs this entrée and its partner components separately rather than in one costing sheet, then the per portion cost of the components must all be added together to get a base cost per portion for that entrée. For example, if a lamb chop with mint sauce costing $1.88 per portion comes with potatoes ($0.23 per portion) and asparagus ($0.37 per portion), then the preliminary cost for the lamb entrée is $1.88 + $0.23 + $0.37 = $2.48. The spice factor and Q factor adjustments (for additional "free" courses) would be based on this price.

In summary, after a menu planner calculates a recipe's total cost, she must still complete three more steps to determine the dish's cost per portion. Those steps are as follows:

1. Calculate preliminary cost per portion as total recipe cost ÷ number of portions

2. Adjust for spice factor by multiplying preliminary cost per portion by (1 + spice factor as a decimal). In restaurants that do not use a Q factor or for non-entrées, this is the true cost per portion.

3. Adjust for Q factor by adding the Q factor to the spice factor adjusted cost per portion for entrées only.

Figure 6–1e shows the completed costing sheet for the chicken chasseur sample recipe. In this particular example, the Q factor covers the side dishes of which the

Recipe: Chicken Chasseur No. of portions: 12 Cost per portion: $2.86			FC%:		Spice Factor: 2.3% Q Factor: $1.04 Selling Price:		
Ingredient	Recipe (EP) Quantity	Yield Percent	AP Cost	Converted AP Cost	EP Cost	Extended Cost
Chicken Breast, 5 oz, airline, prefab, frozen, indiv. pack	12 ea (60 oz)	100%	$31.45/24 ea	$1.310 ea	$1.31 ea	$15.72
Butter, unsalted	6 oz	100%	$64.40/36 lbs	$0.111/oz	$0.111/oz	$0.666
Shallot, minced	2 oz	77%	$4.68/5 lbs	$0.059/oz	$0.077/oz	$0.154
Mushrooms, button, trimmed, sliced	4 oz	94%	$8.25/3 lbs	$0.172/oz	$0.183/oz	$0.732
White wine, dry	3 oz	100%	$5.50/750 mL	$0.217/oz	$0.217/oz	$0.651
Demi-glace	9 oz	100%	$0.18/oz	$0.18/oz	$0.18/oz	$1.62
Tomato, plum, concassé	8 oz	58%	$34.00/40 lbs	$0.053/oz	$0.091/oz	$0.728
Tarragon, chopped	3 Tbsp	64%	$2.77/2 oz	$0.346/Tbsp	$0.346/Tbsp	$1.038
Salt	To taste	100%	Spice Factor	N/A	N/A	S.F.
Pepper	To taste	100%	Spice Factor	N/A	N/A	S.F.
Total						$21.309
Preliminary Cost per Portion (total recipe cost ÷ number of portions in recipe) = $21.309 ÷ 12						$1.776
Spice Factor Adjusted Cost per Portion ((1+SF) × cost per portion) or (1.023 × $1.776)						$1.82
True Cost per Portion, Q Factor Adjusted (SF adjusted cost per portion + Q Factor) = $1.82 + $1.04						$2.86

Figure 6–1e
Recipe costing sheet—spice factor, Q factor, and cost per portion included.

customer gets a choice. If a vegetable and starch were specifically paired with this dish, those per portion costs would be added to the preliminary cost per portion for the chicken to get a preliminary cost per portion for the entrée. Spice factor and Q factor for the business are listed in the recipe heading, so the menu planner knows how to adjust the preliminary cost per portion. Once the true cost per portion is calculated, it is entered into the costing sheet's heading as well.

SUMMARY

A menu planner must consider pricing as part of the menu creation process. Costing a recipe is the first step to calculating an appropriate menu price. Standard recipes allow the menu planner to assume that the recipe she costs is the recipe that is executed in the operation. Portion control is essential to keeping the costs accurate as well. Food is purchased in a form known as "as-purchased" or "AP." After it is peeled, trimmed, or otherwise processed prior to cooking, it is referred to as "edible portion" or "EP." The yield percentage represents the portion of food left as edible portion after processing from the original as-purchased product. The AP and EP costs of a product can also be calculated using the yield percentage. With the standard recipe, yield percentage, and AP cost known, a menu planner

can calculate the total cost of a recipe by converting the AP cost to useable units, calculating EP cost using yield percentage, determining the extended cost for each ingredient, and finally summing the extended costs. The menu planner uses the recipe cost and the number of portions the recipe makes to determine the preliminary cost per portion. The cost per portion must be adjusted using a spice factor to account for any spices or herbs that are not calculated directly in the cost of the recipe. If the dish being costed is an entrée that comes with "free" add-ons, a Q factor must be added to determine the true cost per portion for the dish. Only once the true cost per portion has been calculated for a dish can the menu planner determine its appropriate menu sales price.

COMPREHENSION QUESTIONS

1. What is a standard recipe, and why is it important for a foodservice operation to use standard recipes?
2. List three ways that a cook might measure serving portions to ensure proper portion control.
3. A bunch of carrots weighing 18 ounces is peeled, trimmed, and sliced prior to cooking. The prepped weight of the carrots is only 15 ounces. What is the yield percentage for this carrot preparation?
4. Diced turnip in a particular restaurant has a yield percentage of 88%. If a cook begins with 38 ounces of turnips, how many ounces of diced turnips should she expect to yield after processing?
5. A head of lettuce is prepped for use in a salad. The lettuce has a yield percentage of 79% and an AP cost of $0.84/lb. What is the EP cost per pound for this lettuce?
6. What is the EP cost for cherry tomatoes that have a yield percentage of 100% and cost $2.50/lb?
7. Complete the recipe costing sheet below and calculate the true cost per portion. The restaurant's spice factor and Q factor are listed in the heading. This dish is an appetizer and no add-ons come automatically with the dish.

Recipe: Calamari with Mango Salsa					Spice Factor: 2.1%		
No. of portions: 8					Q Factor: $1.64		
Cost per portion:			FC%: X		Selling Price: X		
Ingredient	Recipe (EP) Quantity	Yield Percentage	AP Cost	Converted AP Cost	EP Cost	Extended Cost	
Calamari, cleaned, sliced	4 lbs	91%	$12.81/5 lbs				
Rice Flour	8 oz	100%	$4.22/5 lbs				
Mango, peeled, diced	14 oz	54%	$8.45/10 lbs				
Red onion, peeled, diced	3 oz	88%	$23.97/50 lbs				
Jalapeno, seeded, diced	1 oz	84%	$2.38/lb				
Cilantro, chopped	½ bunch	100%	$0.59/bunch				
Salt	To taste	S.F.	S.F.	S.F.	S.F.	S.F.	
Pepper	To taste	S.F.	S.F.	S.F.	S.F.	S.F.	
Total							

8. An entrée has a preliminary cost per portion of $3.12. It comes with a choice of soup or salad, bread, and dessert. If the restaurant uses a spice factor of 3.4% and a Q factor of $2.25, what is the true cost per portion for this dish?

DISCUSSION QUESTIONS

1. If a restaurant does not use written recipes, how might it still employ standard recipes?
2. No cook measures products perfectly. For a steak that is supposed to be 10 ounces, what is an acceptable variance (weight plus or minus 10 ounces) that you would consider appropriate for portion control purposes?
3. The chapter mentioned that products portioned by count (by "each") have a 100% yield percentage even if they lose weight in trimming. List three products that might be portioned by count and describe the dish in which they would appear that way.

4. If you were in charge of costing recipes for a business, would you use a spice factor or cost every ingredient separately? Why?
5. Imagine that a restaurant serves bread to every table, whether they order entrées or only appetizers. If the restaurant does not charge for the bread directly, how should it be accounted for—spice factor or Q factor? Why?
6. Describe a restaurant with which you are familiar that likely uses a Q factor. What items would the Q factor probably cover?

7
Menu Pricing

By the end of this chapter, you will be able to:

- Calculate a preliminary sales price for a menu item using one of several pricing strategies
- List several factors that impact the final price written on a menu
- Describe the role that customer psychology plays in menu pricing
- Determine an appropriate sales price for buffet, prix fixe, table d'hôte, and noncommercial offerings

The ultimate goal of costing recipes is to determine an appropriate sales price for the items listed on the menu. If the sales price is too high, the business will lose customers to other restaurants. If the sales price is too low, the establishment may not bring in enough money to cover its costs, and it certainly won't maximize its profits. While the cost of the food or drink sold is only one of the expenses that must be covered through sales revenue, it is almost always the starting factor used to determine an item's sales price.

A menu planner generally uses one of several methods to calculate a tentative menu price from a given cost per portion for that menu item. The price is then modified even further to account for customer psychology, product differentiation, and other variables. When the product being sold is an all-you-can-eat buffet, a prix fixe or table d'hôte menu, or noncommercial operation, other factors further impact the ultimate price listed on the menu. Through a thorough approach to menu pricing, the menu planner can create a menu that sells well, appeals to the target market's price sensibilities, and maximizes profits for the business.

7.1 MENU PRICING STRATEGIES

There is no single best approach to determining a menu price for a given operation. Some businesses do well focusing on food cost percentage while others begin with a menu item's prime cost. Many of the menu pricing strategies discussed in this section are appropriate for a la carte or semi a la carte menus. (Other types of menus are examined later in the chapter.) Which method to utilize depends on the business's brand, the menu's food and beverage options, and the management's philosophy toward cost control.

That this chapter follows one on costing recipes suggests that menu pricing is a strictly linear process moving from recipe costing to price determination. In truth, the menu planner may jump back and forth between costing, pricing, and recipe modification to generate an effective menu. Typically, menu prices for a given menu category should vary within a fairly narrow range. For example, if entrée prices range from $16 to $20, guests will focus on the menu items rather than on the prices, but if the prices instead range from $6 to $35, customers are more likely to choose their entrées based on price. Thus, a menu planner who finds that his preliminary prices span too wide a range may go back and modify the recipes to adjust their costs per portion. Some menu planners may opt to leave the recipe costs alone and simply modify the preliminary menu prices to shrink their range. Either way, the final menu prices must fall within an appropriate zone to appeal to the target market. For instance, if the business concept is to appeal to budget-conscious customers in search of high-value, low-cost items, the final menu prices should all support that vision. Any menu prices that do not appeal to the target audience are likely to undermine sales of those menu items and possibly to reduce revenue overall.

7.1.1 Food Cost Percentage Pricing Methods

Perhaps the most popular approach to determining a preliminary menu price is the *food cost percentage method*. With the cost per portion for a recipe and a given food cost percentage, the menu planner simply employs the formula:

$$\text{Sales Price} = \frac{\text{Food Cost}}{\text{Food Cost \%}}$$

In the formula, Food Cost is the cost per portion for the menu item, and Food Cost % is a predetermined percentage written in its decimal form. The word "Food" may be substituted with "Beverage" to calculate preliminary sales prices for drinks.

Example 7.1: What is the preliminary sales price for a dish that costs $3.22/portion if the restaurant uses a food cost percentage of 31%?

$$\text{Sales Price} = \text{Food Cost} \div \text{Food Cost \%}$$
$$= \$3.22 \div 0.31 = \$10.39$$

Example 7.2: Given a beverage cost percentage of 18.5% and a cost per portion for a bottle of beer of $0.89, what should the bar charge for the beer using the food cost percentage method?

$$\text{Sales Price} = \text{Beverage Cost} \div \text{Beverage Cost \%}$$
$$= \$0.89 \div 0.185 = \$4.81$$

The food cost percentage formula is quite simple. The real-world challenge is determining an appropriate food cost percentage. Average food cost percentages vary widely in the industry. High-end restaurants may use a 20% food cost percentage while fast-food establishments may go as high as 40%. Most often, a business experiments with a food cost percentage around 30% and then adjusts the percentage after a few months—once some historical, financial data has been collected—to improve the business's profitability.

When a foodservice business already has some historical data and a budget in place, it may use the *overhead-contribution method* to determine an appropriate food cost percentage. The amount of money collected from a menu item's sale pays for the cost of the item itself and a portion of the additional overhead required to run the business—salaries and wages, rent, utilities, etc. Viewed collectively across a month or year, revenue collected from food and beverage sales covers the cost of the food and beverage sold and the overhead expenses; any remaining money goes toward profit. Mathematically, food and beverage costs + overhead costs + profit = 100% of the sales revenue.

If a manager is working from a fairly accurate budget or from historical data, he can calculate the percentage of sales that goes toward profit and overhead expenses. Since all that remains from sales is food and beverage cost, the remaining percentage is the food cost percentage that should be used in the sales price = food cost ÷ food cost % formula. This is how the process looks mathematically:

1. $\text{Contribution Margin \%} = \dfrac{(\text{Overhead Costs} + \text{Profit})}{\text{Sales}}$

2. Food Cost % = 100% – Contribution Margin %

   (Note: Convert contribution margin from its decimal to its percent form first.)

3. $\text{Sales Price} = \dfrac{\text{Food Cost}}{\text{Food Cost \% (in decimal form)}}$

Example 7.3: A restaurant uses the overhead-contribution method to determine its menu prices. If the budget plans for $850,000 in overhead expenses, $1,400,000 in sales, and a profit of $50,000, what should the menu charge for an entrée with a cost per portion of $2.88?

1. $\text{Contribution Margin \%} = \dfrac{(\text{Overhead} + \text{Profit})}{\text{Sales}}$

$$= \dfrac{(\$850{,}000 + \$50{,}000)}{\$1{,}400{,}000} = 0.643 \text{ or } 64.3\%$$

2. Food Cost % = 100% − Contribution Margin %
   = 100% − 64.3% = 35.7% or 0.357

3. $\text{Sales Price} = \dfrac{\text{Food Cost}}{\text{Food Cost \%}} = \dfrac{\$2.88}{0.357} = \$8.07$

The restaurant should use a food cost percentage of 35.7%, and the menu should charge $8.07 for the entrée.

Because the overhead-contribution method references the budget as a whole, the food cost percentage that it calculates must be applied equally to all food (and beverages) in the business. However, this is not always the best approach to maximizing a company's profits. Most price-sensitive customers assess a restaurant's affordability based on the entrée prices. After all, entrées are what most people order in the average restaurant, if they only order one thing. Appetizers, alcoholic drinks, and desserts, on the other hand, are considered add-ons that the budget-conscious customer may not choose to purchase. A savvy menu planner might prefer to keep the entrée prices low to attract customers while inflating the prices of other menu items to increase profit.

The *Texas Restaurant Association (TRA) Method* uses food cost percentages to calculate menu prices, but unlike the overhead-contribution method, it allows for different food cost percentages for each menu category. The menu planner still calculates the total percentage of sales that overhead expenses (but not profit) represent, but he also decides for each category how much of the menu price should go toward profit. For example, assume that a budget shows that 65% of all sales go toward the coverage of overhead expenses. If the menu planner decides that entrées should only make a profit of 5%, then using the overhead contribution method's logic, 70% (65% + 5%) of the sales price goes toward overhead and profit while 30% (100% − 70%) is reserved to cover the cost of the food. The food cost percentage for entrées in this scenario would be 30%. However, the menu planner can then decide that appetizers should contribute a profit of 15% of their sales price. The combination of overhead and profit represents 80% (65% + 15%) of the sales price, which leaves only 20% (100% − 80%) to cover the food cost. Food cost percentage for appetizers is 20%. The TRA method encourages menu planners or other managers to select a different percentage for profit for each menu category. Slow-moving items within a category may also merit a higher percentage profit than their counterparts to account for the proportionately larger share of inventory space and employee attention per sale that they require. Thus, items that slow down the production line and require a greater share of labor cost are assigned a higher profit percentage in the formula to justify the added cost and hassle of maintaining those items on the menu.

As with the overhead-contribution method, the TRA method is a tool to determine the food cost percentage that a menu planner should use to calculate a sales price from an item's cost per portion. Both methods ultimately conclude with the same sales price = food cost ÷ food cost % formula.

Example 7.4: A restaurant uses the TRA method to price its menu items. If the overhead expenses for a business represent 71% of sales, and the management dictates that desserts should return 12% of their sales price as profit, how much should the menu planner charge for a dessert with a cost per portion of $0.73?

1. Overhead + Profit = 71% + 12% = 83%
2. Food Cost % = 100% − (overhead + profit) = 100% − 83% = 17% or 0.17
3. Sales Price = Food Cost ÷ Food Cost % = $0.73 ÷ 0.17 = $4.29

7.1.2 Prime Cost Pricing Methods

Food cost percentage methods assume that all items on the menu require roughly the same amount of labor to prepare. This is not always true. Imagine a restaurant that offers two dishes. Both cost the same ingredient-wise, but while one can be made in three minutes, the other requires twenty minutes of an employee's labor per portion. Should the customer pay the same for each dish? Should the additional labor cost be factored into the more time-consuming dish's price?

Prime cost is the combined total of food or beverage cost and labor cost. From a per portion perspective, labor is the direct labor cost required to prepare a single serving of the dish (or drink) and does not factor in the cost of other labor overhead (dishwashers, servers, managers, etc.). The direct labor cost does not come from a budget but rather from the observation of the cooks preparing the food and knowledge of each cook's hourly wage. The direct labor cost for any task can be calculated by multiplying the cook's hourly wage by the number of hours (or fraction thereof) spent on that task. For example, if a cook earns $12/hour and spends 45 minutes (or ¾ of an hour) preparing 20 portions of a stir-fry entrée, then the direct labor cost for the 20 portions is $12/hour × 0.75 hours = $9. The direct labor cost per portion is $9 ÷ 20 portions = $0.45. Because cooks often multitask during their day, determining an accurate number of minutes that a cook spends on a given dish or recipe can be challenging. This method is best utilized when cooks are only responsible for one or two recipes or tasks each, as might be seen in a large-production, high-volume operation.

With a direct labor cost per portion for each dish, a manager can calculate the prime cost for each dish by adding the direct labor cost and the food cost per portion. The *prime cost method* generates a preliminary menu price by multiplying each item's prime cost by a price factor. The price factor often starts off as an arbitrary figure, but with the accumulation of historical data, a menu planner can revise the price factor to make the menu more profitable. Mathematically,

1. Prime Cost = Direct Labor Cost + Food Cost
2. Sales Price = Prime Cost × Price Factor

Example 7.5: A restaurant uses the prime cost method and a price factor of 2.35. If a certain entrée has a food cost per portion of $2.73 and a direct labor cost of $0.36, how much should the restaurant charge for this dish?

1. Prime Cost = Direct Labor Cost + Food Cost = $2.73 + $0.36 = $3.09
2. Sales Price = Prime Cost × Price Factor = $3.09 × 2.35 = $7.26

The prime cost method more accurately accounts for direct labor cost, but customers may not perceive the value in the extra labor. Typically, guests are more aware of differences in ingredient costs than they are in labor costs. For example, a fairly complex chicken dish may require so much in labor cost that its prime cost approaches that of a low-labor/high-food cost steak. Still, many guests will question why their chicken costs as much as the steak; they simply will not connect the higher labor cost with the higher menu price.

The *actual pricing method* bases sales prices on each item's prime cost, but it generates a price divisor from the business's budget to generate the ultimate sales price. Similar to the TRA method, the actual pricing method begins by determining the percentage of sales that go toward overhead and profit. Traditionally, the actual pricing method uses the terms *variable cost percentage, fixed cost percentage*, and *profit percentage*. Broadly speaking, variable costs (such as hourly worker wages or food costs) are those that fluctuate with sales, while fixed costs (such as rent or salaries) do not. In the case of the actual pricing method, the variable cost percentage does not include food and beverage costs or direct labor costs, as these are lumped under the heading of prime cost instead. Since 100% of sales goes to cover prime costs, variable costs, fixed costs, and profit, the percentage of sales available to cover prime cost can be thought of as 100% − (variable cost % + fixed cost % + profit %). This figure provides the price divisor used to calculate a sales price from a prime cost. Mathematically, the procedure is as follows:

1. Price Divisor = 100% − (Variable Cost % + Fixed Cost % + Profit %)

2. Sales Price = $\dfrac{\text{Prime Cost}}{\text{Price Divisor}}$

Remember that Prime Cost = Food Cost + Direct Labor Cost.

Example 7.6: A restaurant uses the actual pricing method to determine its menu prices. The budget shows a variable cost percentage of 21%, a fixed cost percentage of 33%, and a profit percentage of 5%. What should the restaurant charge for a dish with a food cost of $3.18 and a direct labor cost of $0.83?

1. Price Divisor = 100% − (VC% + FC% + Profit %)
        = 100% − (21% + 33% + 5%) = 41% or 0.41

2. Sales Price = Prime Cost ÷ Price Divisor
        = ($3.18 + $0.83) ÷ 0.41 = $4.01 ÷ 0.41 = $9.78

The prime cost method uses a price factor while the actual pricing method uses a price divisor, but both rely on a menu item's prime cost as the basis for calculating its sales price.

7.1.3 Gross Profit Pricing Method

Pricing methods based on food cost or prime cost assume that a single factor or divisor will generate menu prices that are both within a narrow range and high enough to support the business's overhead expenses and profit goals. But what if that is not possible for a given foodservice concept? Consider the classic coffee shop. Customers willingly pay over $2 for a cup of coffee and even more for espresso drinks, knowing that the beverage cost is probably less than $0.25. Why don't customers accuse the operation of price gouging? Simply put, the overhead and labor expense percentages for a coffee shop are much higher than they are for a traditional restaurant. The majority of sales are beverage sales, so the food will not cover much of the overhead costs. Consequently, the beverage cost percentage is extremely low.

While a low beverage or food cost percentage can generate prices high enough to cover a business's overhead and profit, such low percentages tend to magnify and exaggerate small differences in food and beverage cost. A drink that only costs an extra $0.05 may translate to a sales price of an extra $0.50 to $1.00. Such wide price variations for similar products are far more frustrating to customers than the low cost percentages. In such a situation, most customers would simply gravitate toward the cheapest option on the menu.

The better approach to menu pricing in this type of operation is the *gross profit method*. Gross profit is the money remaining from sales after food and beverage costs are deducted. This money must cover all labor and other overhead. The manager knows roughly how many customers the business gets in a month and the total monthly overhead and labor expenses. Thus, the manager can figure out how much gross profit he needs to make from each customer to cover his monthly labor, overhead, and profit. As long as each customer pays at least this amount above and beyond the cost of the drink, the business will meet its profit goals. Mathematically, gross profit per customer is:

1. Gross Profit = Total Sales (in a given period) − Total Food and Beverage Cost (for the same period)

2. Gross Profit per Customer = Gross Profit ÷ Total Customers (over the same period)

In a business, the budget may estimate the number of customers per month and the labor, overhead, and profit per month. Assuming the budget is accurate, the sum of the non-food and beverage expenses and the profit is the same as the gross profit, which must cover those costs. Thus, the gross profit per customer can be calculated from a budget, even for a new business with no historical data, as long as the budget is on target. From a budget gross profit per customer is calculated this way:

$$\text{Gross Profit per Customer} = \frac{\text{Total Overhead and Labor Expenses} + \text{Profit (in a period)}}{\text{Total Customers (in the same period)}}$$

In this formula, the total overhead and labor expenses are simply the sum of all non-food and beverage expenses from the budget. This generates not a realized gross profit per customer but rather a necessarily minimum gross profit per customer to use for calculating menu prices in order to stay on budget.

Unlike the aforementioned pricing methods, the gross profit method *adds* a number to the food (or beverage) cost per portion. There is no multiplying or dividing involved. The formula to calculate a menu price using the gross profit method is:

$$\text{Sales Price} = \text{Food (or Beverage) Cost per Portion} + \text{Gross Profit per Customer}$$

Example 7.7: A coffee house uses the gross profit method to calculate its prices. From the operation's budget, the business expects to average 17,500 customers per month with average monthly expenses (excluding food and beverage costs) of $29,500 and a target monthly profit of $2,000. If a certain coffee drink costs $0.27 per portion, what should the menu planner charge for this beverage?

$$\text{Gross Profit per Customer} = \frac{\text{Total Overhead and Labor Expenses} + \text{Profit}}{\text{Total Customers}}$$

$$= \frac{\$29,500 + \$2,000}{17,500} = \$1.80$$

Sales Price = Beverage Cost per Portion + Gross Profit per Customer
= $0.27 + $1.80 = $2.07

Since the gross profit method adds rather than multiplies or divides the gross profit per customer to the food or beverage cost per portion, small differences in portion costs are not exaggerated. A customer, seeing that the prices fall within a narrow range, can ignore the prices and choose whichever beverage he prefers, while the manager knows that the customer will contribute the same amount of money toward the business's gross profit no matter what drink he ultimately purchases. The gross profit method is not ideal for all business models, but it is an excellent approach when food and beverage cost percentages are extremely low. Besides coffee shops, street food carts and certain types of bakeries might do well with this approach to pricing.

7.1.4 Base Price Pricing Method

Sometimes, a menu planner prefers to start not with the cost per portion for a dish but rather with the desired sales price and then to work backwards. This pricing approach usually emanates from a marketing perspective to menu planning. In price-sensitive markets, menu planners recognize that customers will flock to a business at certain price points. The classic example is the "dollar menu" or "$0.99 menu" common in several fast-food operations. Those businesses did not magically discover that certain products work out to a suggested selling price of $0.99. Rather, they began with the desired selling price and a target food cost percentage. Then, using the sales price = food cost ÷ food cost % formula, they calculated the maximum food cost per portion that an item on that menu could have. This approach is termed the *base price method*.

For the base price method, the food cost percentage formula is reworked to read:

$$\text{Food Cost} = \text{Sales Price} \times \text{Food Cost \%}$$

Example 7.8: If a cafeteria chef must sell his entrées at a cost of $4.50 and hit a maximum food cost percentage of 32%, what is the maximum cost per portion for an entrée that he sells?

Food Cost = Sales Price × Food Cost % = $4.50 × 0.32 = $1.44

Any operation could use this approach, and noncommercial foodservice businesses, such as corporate or school cafeterias, often do. They know that their customers or clients require a certain price point. In the case of federally reimbursed school meals, the foodservice provider will be reimbursed only a certain amount of money no matter what the cost of the food they serve. Thus, the menu planners must develop recipes that fall below the maximum per portion food cost determined from the set sales price and the target food cost percentage.

Creating a recipe that hits a target food cost per portion is not as difficult as it might seem. Costs can be modified significantly through portion size adjustment. A meatloaf might switch from 5 to 4 ounces per serving. A turkey sandwich might drop from 3 ounces to 2.5 ounces of turkey per portion. Additionally, certain ingredients can be modified, removed, or added to the recipe. For example, the cost of a salad might drop significantly if the ¼ cup of oil-cured olives is reduced to three olives or removed entirely. Perhaps the chef will opt to switch to a cheaper variety of olive. If a recipe cannot be modified to fall below the food cost target without ruining the dish's quality and appeal, that recipe may be removed from the menu entirely.

7.1.5 Matching Competitors' Prices

One very legitimate approach to price determination is simply to match the prices of competitors. A company with a product nearly identical to its competitor businesses may fail to draw significant market share if it does not compete on price. Price-sensitive customers may not even consider patronizing a restaurant that does not meet or beat the prices of similar establishments in the area.

This pricing method works well from the revenue growth perspective but is extremely risky from the cost control and profit generation perspective. The menu planner or manager in one business rarely knows the cost structure of its competitors. One business may keep its costs artificially low by employing family members who donate their time. A large chain may get a better deal on purveyor prices than an independent restaurant can. Some businesses prefer to keep prices high but use a coupon or discount system to attract customers; a business that matches the prices but not the coupon approach will fail to draw customers away from the competition. Finally, to maintain a monopoly in the area, a business might attempt to temporarily reduce its prices below sustainable levels when a competing company opens nearby. They know they cannot do this for very long, but if a competitor attempts to match its prices, presumably that competitor will go out of business quickly from lack of profits. Then, the original business can return its prices to their original levels.

Generally speaking, matching competitors' prices works best only when paired with a second pricing strategy—typically the base price method. First, the menu planner matches a competitor's price for a given product. Then, he employs the base price method to determine a maximum food cost per portion for that dish. If the business cannot match the competitor's quality, quantity, and price at the same time, he may wish to distinguish his product from the competition in ways other than price.

7.1.6 Choosing the Right Pricing Method

There is no one best method to use for determining menu prices. Each strategy works well in different environments. Food cost methods are easy to use and very popular, but the overhead-contribution and TRA methods require some historical data from the existing business—or at least an accurate budget—to be utilized effectively. Still, the basic food cost percentage method is an excellent starting point for a restaurant with a range of dishes that have similar costs per portion and direct labor costs within the same menu category and a food cost percentage that is not much lower than 20%. Prime cost methods work well when the labor cost for different dishes varies significantly.

The gross profit method is an excellent choice for businesses with exceedingly low food cost percentages, and the base price method works well for noncommercial and fast-food operations. Matching competitors' prices is always a choice but should be utilized in conjunction with another method to ensure that such an approach is viable and profitable.

There is no rule that says that a menu planner must use the same pricing approach for the entire menu. It is perfectly acceptable for a single restaurant to use a prime cost method for appetizers, a food cost percentage method for entrées, a gross profit method for beverages, and a base price method for desserts. Whatever strategy is employed, the menu planner should make sure that the end result will both appeal to customers and keep the business profitable.

7.2 FACTORS THAT AFFECT MENU PRICES

While a menu pricing strategy generates preliminary sales prices for the items on a menu, those prices should not be placed on the menu without some modification first. The formulas provide target prices, but these prices could be viewed as minimum prices. Highly popular or unique items might merit a much higher sales price. Alternatively, the calculated prices may be approximations that the menu planner rounds to the nearest whole dollar. How a menu planner modifies the initial sales price calculations depends heavily on several factors.

Competition   Generally speaking, the more direct competition a restaurant has, the less flexibility the menu planner has to raise the sales price beyond the initial calculation. Direct competition differs from indirect competition though. Indirect competition comes from all other foodservice businesses. Direct competition only comes from similar foodservice concepts—like two pizza parlors or multiple Chinese take-out restaurants. When food, service, and atmosphere are similar in two nearby restaurants, then customers may perceive price as the only distinguishing factor. In such situations, the menu planner must keep prices as low as possible to attract business. However, since foodservice businesses sell more than just food—they sell service and atmosphere, too—a significant difference in only one of these factors may justify higher sales prices.

The less direct competition that a business has, the higher the menu planner may raise his prices above the preliminary sales price calculation. However, when prices become too steep for the product delivered, customers may opt for indirect competitors more regularly; for these customers, the kind of food and service provided is less important than affordability. In those rare instances where there is neither direct nor indirect competition, a foodservice business has a monopoly and can charge much higher prices than it otherwise would. People see this often in small turnpike rest areas and certain airports. There is no competition readily available, so a single business selling food and drink can gouge those few customers hungering for a drink or a bite to eat.

Price Sensitivity   When sales of a particular product change significantly when the sales price changes only slightly, that product is said to be price sensitive. The more price sensitive a product is, the less ability the menu planner has to increase the initial sales price calculation. In fact, he may even reduce the preliminary sales price slightly to drive up business dramatically. Price sensitivity depends heavily on competition and on how much people value a particular product over alternatives. For example, if people in a given city view lobster as a special occasion splurge that is not available at most restaurants, they are less likely to shun lobster because of a $2 price increase. However, if the lobster in a seaside town is present on every restaurant menu for the same low price as other entrées, guests in an establishment selling lobster for a much higher price may opt for one of the less expensive entrée choices.

Perceived Value   When customers believe that something has inherently higher value, they are willing to pay more for it than the sales price calculation might otherwise suggest. This value may be inherent to the product, such as a 100-year-old bottle of rare wine, or it may be subliminally implied through the menu description. A seared scallop, hand-harvested by divers in a faraway bay, is worth more than something advertised as a "scallop plate," isn't it? The difference in sales price can be reflected in the customer's perceived value, even if the per portion cost for both scallop dishes is the same.

Some restaurants increase perceived value by naming the sources or provenance of their ingredients while others do so through larger portion sizes. To some customers' eyes, a plate with 20% more food may be worth 50% more than what a competing restaurant charges for a similar but smaller dish. An ingredient's quality grade, such as prime versus choice beef, impacts perceived value and sales price when the grade is listed on the menu. However the operation chooses to direct the guests' attention to the value of its food, guests will gladly pay more for a dish they view as having a greater value than similar dishes with the same cost per portion.

Product Differentiation   A business that sells an identical product (food, service, and ambiance) as its competition is stuck fighting for customers based on price alone. However, a restaurant that sells a product unavailable anywhere else can almost charge whatever it wants for this unique experience. The more a business differentiates its products from the competition, the more flexibility the menu planner has in raising prices. Service and atmosphere can skew the acceptable selling price for a dish significantly. A menu can charge significantly more for a Caesar salad prepared tableside in a restaurant's rose garden than the average bar can charge for the same salad prepared in the kitchen. Similarly, three New York–style pizza places will battle each other by lowering prices, but a New York–style pizza, a wood-grilled boutique pizza, and a Chicago-style deep dish pizza are all very different products that just happen to share the name "pizza." If each of these pizzas were found only in one of three nearby restaurants, the businesses could charge very different prices. Their products are highly differentiated.

In short, a menu planner can charge more for well-differentiated products with a high perceived value, low price sensitivity, and little competition than he can for similar menu items in a community where they are not significantly different from the many competitors' products and the local market does not find them of high value.

THE RESTAURANT AT PATOWMACK FARM

WELCOMES YOU

May 27, 2012

APPETIZERS

Patowmack Farm Spring Blend 12
a variety of our own garden's greens, leaves, lettuces, and herbs simply dressed with extra virgin olive oil and noble tonic verjus

Carolina Gold Rice Middlins 14
smoked bacon, braised cabbage, sea island red peas
Strawberry Salad 12
obergood feta, arugula, green tea froth, aged balsamico

Tortilla Espanola 16
a traditional spanish omelet of potatoes and onions, sautéed garlic scapes, mushroom mélange

Chesapeake Bay Wild Blue Catfish Fry 15
she crab soup, sherry crema, smoked paprika

ENTREES

Ham and Cheese Waffle 18
surryano ham, pecorino cheese, poached egg, langdon wood maple syrup

Chesapeake Bay Soft Shell Crab 26
anson mills white flint corn grits, pickled mustard seed, malt vinegar, delmarva crab spice

---

Figure 7–1
This is a menu for a restaurant in a glass-enclosed structure set on a hilltop overlooking a river. This highly differentiated luxury experience is reinforced appropriately with whole dollar pricing. Printed with the permission of The Restaurant at Patowmack Farm and Executive Chef Christopher Edwards.

Figure 7–1
(continued)

Quinault River Wild King Salmon 32
escabeche vegetables, pea shoots, fried bread

Fields of Athenry Lamb Hash 30
hoppin' john, fried onions, mustard bbq sauce

Spring Harvest Medley 22
the best of our own spring harvest vegetables, greens and fruits

DESSERT

Cinnamon Sugar Donuts 12
bavarian cream, rhubarb jam, crispy caramel

Mulberry Pie 12
panna cotta, mulberry mash, port wine reduction, chocolate ganache

Strawberry Torte 12
tapioca pudding, strawberry coulis, oatmeal sorbet, white chocolate sauce

Cheese 16
chef's selection daily with accompaniments

Executive Chef, Christopher Edwards

*Consuming raw or undercooked food may increase your risk of foodborne illness
20% gratuity on parties of 6 or more
Owner: Beverly Morton Billand

The Restaurant at Patowmack Farm | 540 822-9017 | www.patowmackfarm.com

7.2.1 Pricing Psychology

The exact price that is written on a menu can make a guest more or less comfortable paying that amount based simply on how the number looks. There are certain prices that Americans are used to paying, so they tend to gloss over these numbers and ignore their true value. In general, prices that end in $0.00, $0.25, $0.45, $0.49, $0.50, $0.75, $0.95, and $0.99 are more common and thus make menu readers more comfortable. If a menu were to list an item as $14.93 instead of $14.95, guests would likely notice the price and fixate on it more than they would the $14.95 price. Since the last thing a menu planner wants the guest to focus on is price, it is best to stick with the traditionally "comfortable" price endings.

That said, all menu prices communicate a subliminal message to the clientele. Prices ending in "9" suggest that the menu item is a bargain. While the difference between $4.99 and $5.00 is hardly significant, most people think of the two very differently. Many would say that $4.99 is cheap; it is not even a full five dollars. The $5.00 price tag, on the other hand, does not provide change from a five-dollar bill. Businesses that want their customers to think that they are a bargain tend to end their prices in nines. Fast-food $0.99 menus are classic examples.

Upscale establishments, on the other hand, want to communicate luxury and indulgence. They want their customers to feel that they are getting a top-dollar experience, which costs whole dollars, not pennies. Thus, high-end restaurants tend to use whole dollars for their prices. Mid-level restaurants often use prices that end in "0" or "5." These numbers suggest that the food is a value but not cheap.

Whether a menu planner rounds preliminary sales price calculations to numbers ending in "0," "5," or "9" depends heavily on the business's concept and the subliminal message the menu planner wishes to communicate about the establishment. For example, a preliminary price of $12.73 might be rounded to $12.75, $12.99, or $13.00 depending on the restaurant. It is important to note that most menu planners will round their sales prices up unless the price reduction is relatively small and delivers a big psychological boost. For instance, a calculated preliminary price of $1.01 might be rounded down to $0.99 to attract a bargain-hunting customer, but dropping a price of $1.33 down to $0.99 would be too severe a reduction. Such a drop would result in a very high food cost percentage for that one item, and since most foodservice businesses operate on low profit margins, rounding sales prices down significantly can easily lead to the complete evaporation of profits. Unlike supermarkets, which may advertise loss leaders (products that sell at very low prices to attract customers) to generate business elsewhere in the store, most restaurants can only sell a small amount of food per customer—the amount that the guest can eat in that one sitting. A loss leader often crowds out profitable purchases that the customer would have otherwise made.

That said, it is a common approach in certain styles of restaurants to "bundle" food into value deals that encourage most people to spend more money than they otherwise would. Such bundling need not give customers a huge bargain; a small price break is normally sufficient to boost sales substantially. For example, if a fast-food operation sells a burger for $2.00, fries for $1.50, and a soda for $1.00, each customer would have to spend $4.50 to purchase all three separately. Some customers might decide that they don't need the fries. However, by offering a package deal that allows customers to purchase the entire meal for a price of $4.35, the business might increase overall sales enough to make more profit over a month than it does without the price break. Small bundling discounts often go a long way to increasing sales of food overall.

Value pricing can also increase profit when an operation offers multiple sizes of a given offering. For example, in those operations offering small, medium, and large sizes of beverages, the largest size is always a better deal per ounce than the smaller size. This persuades the customer to spend a little more money for the larger size. While this arrangement might seem to cut into profits, the only additional cost on a larger size beverage is the beverage (and cup) cost; the increase in labor and overhead is insignificant. Thus, if the operation can add $0.25 to the sales price of the drink while adding only $0.05 to the beverage cost, the business makes an additional $0.20 profit by selling the larger size. (It should be noted that this approach to upselling is becoming controversial in certain parts of the country as Americans battle with obesity. Obscenely large portion sizes that cause the customer to overpurchase and overconsume may be regulated by local governments—research Mayor Bloomberg's limit on soda portion sizes in New York City, for example—which would make it difficult for a menu planner to utilize this approach to increasing sales through value pricing for larger portions. How broader swaths of the country will address this issue remains to be seen.)

Finally, when trying to determine the exact selling price for a dish or drink, menu planners should keep in mind that for many customers there is a psychological price ceiling for a product. Above that point, sales will drop off dramatically. Thus, menu planners may only be able to set a price so high above a calculated sales price no matter how highly differentiated the product is. For example, a 20-ounce, dry-aged, prime grade porterhouse served in an elegant setting by tuxedoed servers might command a $35, $40,

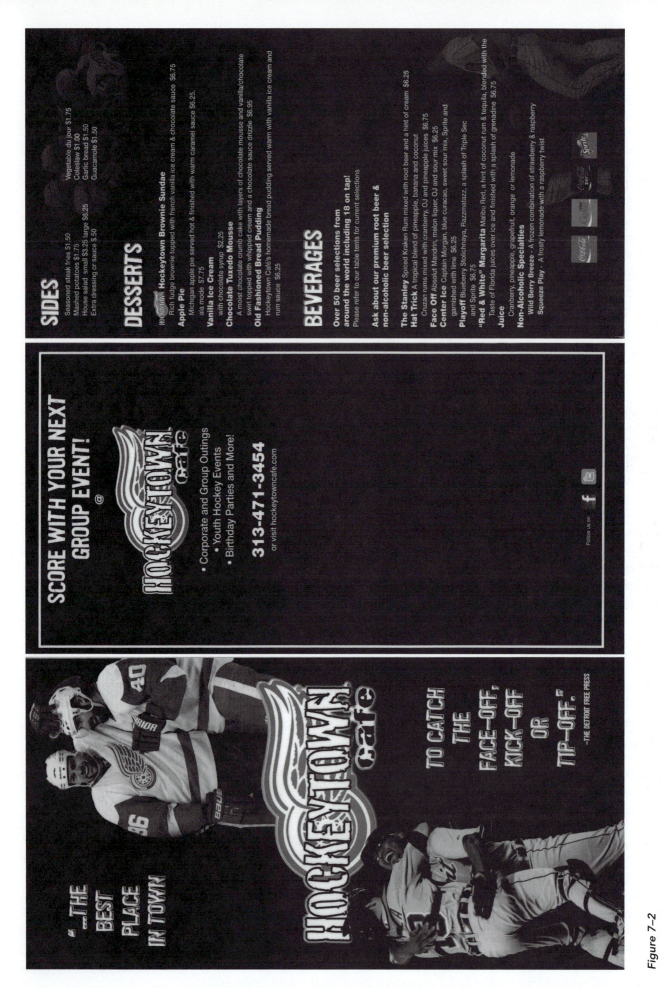

Figure 7–2

A menu with prices ending in "0" or "5" communicates value and a midrange price point.

APPETIZERS
Kick off your meal with one of our great appetizers

Hockeytown Red Wings
Deep fried chicken wings tossed in our buttery Buffalo-style hot sauce. Served with bleu cheese dressing & celery sticks $7.25

Baked Spinach & Artichoke Dip
Creamy mixture of spinach & artichokes baked with mozzarella cheese. Served with tortilla chips $7.95

Loaded Potato Skins
Crispy potato skins with bacon, jack-cheddar cheese & green onions. Served with sour cream $7.95

Chips & Salsa
Crispy tortilla chips served with garden-fresh salsa $4.95

Cheese Quesadillas
Cheese-filled tortilla shells browned in light olive oil served with shredded lettuce, chopped green onions, tomatoes, sour cream & garden-fresh salsa $7.50 Add chicken $3.00

Mozzarella Sticks
Mozzarella cheese sticks served with marinara sauce or ranch dressing $6.75

Nachos Grande
Seasoned ground beef & tortilla chips piled high with green onions, tomatoes, shredded lettuce, black olives & shredded jack-cheddar cheese. Served with sour cream & garden-fresh salsa $9.95

Chicken Fingers Basket
Crispy homestyle chicken fingers served with seasoned steak fries, celery sticks & your choice of BBQ sauce, honey mustard or ranch dressing $9.95

Cajun Beef Tips
Cajun seasoned sirloin tips tossed with caramelized onions & peppers served with bleu cheese coleslaw and garlic bread $10.95

Deep Fried Pepper Rings
Zesty fried banana pepper rings served with a BBQ-bacon ranch dipping sauce $6.25

Corned Beef Sliders
Corned beef topped with sauerkraut, Swiss cheese and Russian dressing served on a brioche with a side of bleu cheese coleslaw $7.95

FRESH SALADS
All salads are prepared to order

Hockeytown BBQ Chicken Salad*
Slices of grilled chicken breast tossed in BBQ sauce and served on a bed of iceberg lettuce with diced red onions, bacon, tomatoes, shredded jack-cheddar cheese & smokey ranch dressing $9.75

Fatoush Salad
Romaine, fresh mint, parsley, cucumbers, tomatoes and bell peppers served with a lemon-mint vinaigrette and toasted pita chips $7.95

Classic Caesar Salad*
With croutons, parmesan cheese & Caesar dressing $6.95, Add chicken $3.00 Add beef $4.00

Southwest Chicken Salad*
Chicken breast served on a bed of iceberg lettuce topped with black bean corn salsa, diced red onions, shredded jack-cheddar cheese, crispy tortilla strips & Mexican ranch dressing $8.95

Taco Salad
Fried tortilla shell filled with shredded lettuce & seasoned ground beef garnished with jack-cheddar cheese, diced tomatoes, green onions, black olives, sour cream & garden-fresh salsa $8.25

Michigan Salad
Mixed greens topped with Boursin cheese, Traverse City dried cherries, diced cucumbers, tomatoes, red onions & chopped walnuts served with a raspberry vinaigrette $9.95 Add chicken $3.00

Cobb Salad
With iceberg lettuce, chicken, bacon, cucumbers, tomatoes, red onions, hard boiled eggs & Gorgonzola Cheese and your choice of dressing $9.95

*Cooked to order, consuming raw or undercooked meat, poultry, seafood, shellfish or eggs may increase your risk of foodborne illness.

PIZZA

Hockeytown Deep Dish Pizza

Large Cheese Pizza $13.95   Small Cheese Pizza $9.95
Additional Toppings: Large Pizza $1.75   Small Pizza $1.00

Available toppings:
pepperoni, ham, Italian sausage, bacon, onions, green peppers, mushrooms, black olives, banana peppers, tomatoes, pineapple, extra cheese

Thin-Crust Pizza

BBQ Chicken Pizza
Topped with grilled chicken, red onions, bacon and sweet BBQ sauce $13.95

Buffalo Chicken Pizza
Topped with grilled chicken, Gorgonzola cheese, Buffalo sauce and crisp celery $13.95

Calzones

Meat Lovers
Bacon, ham, pepperoni, sausage & Boursin cheese $9.95

California Calzone
Fresh spinach, artichokes, parmesan cheese and grilled chicken $9.95

SANDWICHES

Hockeytown Buffalo Chicken
Fried chicken breast tossed in Buffalo sauce & served with lettuce, tomato & bleu cheese dressing on a sesame seed bun $9.50

Smoked Turkey with Guoda Cheese on Flatbread
Served with bacon, lettuce & tomatoes and a pesto mayo $9.95

Chicken Caesar Lawash*
Grilled sliced chicken breast wrapped in a flour lawash with Romaine lettuce, Caesar dressing & parmesan cheese $9.50

Hot Turkey Reuben
Shaved turkey breast stacked with homemade coleslaw, Swiss cheese & Russian dressing on grilled marble rye bread $8.95

Philly Cheese Steak or Chicken*
Juicy sirloin or chicken sautéed with onions & peppers. Served on a hoagie bun with Swiss cheese $8.95 Add sautéed mushrooms $.99

Bar-B-Q Pulled Pork
Boneless pork tossed in BBQ sauce & topped with homemade coleslaw served on grilled Texas toast $8.25

Corned Beef Reuben
Corned beef piled high & topped with Swiss cheese, sauerkraut & Russian dressing on grilled marble rye bread $9.25

Bar-B-Q Chicken Sandwich*
Grilled boneless chicken breast topped with BBQ sauce, cheddar cheese & bacon served on a sesame seed bun $9.25

Mesquite Grilled Chicken Salad
Mesquite rubbed chicken breast diced and tossed with sundried tomatoes, carrots, red onions and celery in a Southwest mayonnaise and served on grilled flatbread with lettuce and tomatoes $8.50

Italian Panini
Italian deli meat stacked with banana pepper rings, tomatoes, red onions & Provolone cheese $8.95

BURGERS
All burgers are prepared from seasoned fresh ground round (80/20), served on a sesame seed bun with seasoned steak fries & a pickle

Hockeytown Hockeytown Burger* - OUR HOUSE SPECIALTY:
1/2 pound of seasoned fresh ground beef served with lettuce, tomato, red onions & your choice of cheese - American, cheddar, pepper jack, Swiss or Provolone $9.95
add your own toppings: bacon $1.00; bleu cheese $.75; sautéed mushrooms $.50; sautéed onion $.50

BBQ Smoke House Burger*
With apple-smoked Bacon, caramelized onions, BBQ sauce & smoked cheddar cheese $11.95

San Fran Melt*
1/2 pound burger melt with pepper jack cheese, sautéed red onions & a Dijon mayonnaise sauce served on grilled Texas toast $9.95

Double-Stacked Black Bean Burger
Two black bean patties each topped with pepper jack cheese served on a sesame seed bun with lettuce, tomato & red onions $9.95

Michigan Cherry Burger*
Our famous 1/2 pound burger topped with Traverse City cherries & Boursin cheese and served with lettuce, tomato and red onions $10.95

Quesadillas Burger*
1/2 pound burger served in a tortilla shell, smothered with roasted Pablano peppers and a Mexican blend of cheeses served with tomatoes, scallions, sour cream and salsa $10.95

ENTREES
All steaks, pastas & salmon are served with garlic bread

Hockeytown Sizzler Steak*
Grilled 8 oz sizzler served with whipped potatoes, seasonal mixed vegetables $15.95
Additional toppings: sautéed onions $.99 sautéed mushrooms $.99
bleu cheese crumbles $.99

Fettuccine Alfredo*
Fettuccine pasta tossed in a fresh Alfredo sauce $10.95 Add chicken $3.00

Pan-Seared Salmon*
Pan-seared Atlantic salmon served with a medley of vegetables, mashed potatoes & a lemon-dill cream sauce $16.95

Rustic Penne Pasta
Penne pasta tossed with sautéed sweet Italian sausage, zucchini, yellow squash, peppers and onions in a pesto sauce $11.95

BBQ Baby Back Ribs*
Slow-cooked baby back ribs brushed with our house-made BBQ sauce served with coleslaw & seasoned steak fries Half Slab $10.95 Full Slab $16.95

Grilled Chicken Breast*
Grilled chicken breast topped with Provolone cheese and smothered with sautéed green peppers, onions and mushrooms served with mashed potatoes $10.95

HOMEMADE SOUPS

Hockeytown Chili   French Onion Soup   Soup Du Jour
$3.35 Cup $4.95 Bowl $2.95 Cup $3.95 Bowl
Add to chili
cheddar cheese $.50;
onions $.50; sour cream $.50

18% gratuity added to parties of 12 or more

*Cooked to order, consuming raw or undercooked meat, poultry, seafood, shellfish or eggs may increase your risk of foodborne illness.

Figure 7-2
(continued)

147

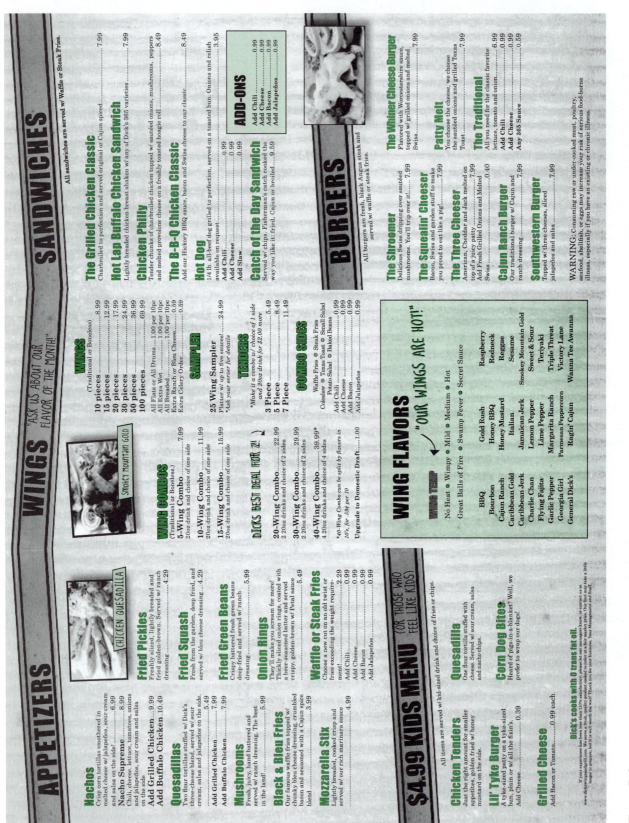

APPETIZERS

Nachos
Crisp corn tortillas smothered in melted cheese w/ jalapeños, sour cream and salsa on the side! 6.99

Nacho Supreme 8.99
Chili, cheese, lettuce, tomatoes, onions and jalapeños, sour cream and salsa on the side

Add Grilled Chicken ...9.99
Add Buffalo Chicken ..10.49

Quesadillas
Two flour tortillas stuffed w/ Dick's three-cheese blend, served w/ sour cream, salsa and jalapeños on the side. 4.29

Add Grilled Chicken 5.49
Add Buffalo Chicken 7.99

Mushrooms
Fresh, juicy, hand battered and served w/ ranch dressing. The best in the land! 5.99

Black & Bleu Fries
Our famous waffle fries topped w/ chunky bleu cheese dressing, crumbled bacon and seasoned with a Cajun spice blend 3.99

Mozzarella Stix
Lightly breaded, cooked crisp and served w/ our rich marinara sauce 4.99

CHICKEN QUESADILLA

Fried Pickles
Freshly sliced, lightly breaded and fried golden-brown. Served w/ ranch dressing 4.29

Fried Squash
Fresh from the garden, deep fried, and served w/ bleu cheese dressing....4.29

Fried Green Beans
Crispy battered fresh green beans deep-fried and served w/ ranch dressing.................5.99

Onion Rings
They'll make you scream for more! Thickly sliced onion rings, coated with a beer-seasoned batter and served crispy, golden-brown w/ Petal sauce 5.49

Waffle or Steak Fries
Choose a new cut on an old twist or fries exceeding the weight require-ment! 2.29
Add Chili 0.99
Add Cheese.................0.99
Add Bacon 0.99
Add Jalapeños 0.99

$4.99 KIDS MENU (OR THOSE WHO FEEL LIKE KIDS)

All items are served w/ kid-sized drink and choice of fries or chips.

Chicken Tenders
Just the right amount for smaller appetite, golden fried w/ honey mustard on the side.

Lil' Tyke Burger
A tyke-sized patty on a tyke-sized bun, plain or w/ all the fixin's.
Add Cheese.................0.39

Grilled Cheese
Add Bacon or Tomato.................0.99 each

Quesadilla
One flour tortilla stuffed w/ cheese. Served w/ sour cream, salsa and nacho chips.

Corn Dog Bites
Heard of pigs-in-a-blanket? Well, we prefer to wrap our dogs!

Dick's cooks with 0 trans fat oil.

If your experience has been less than 110% satisfactory, please let our managers know, or contact us at www.dickswingsandgrill.com. We serve a fresh, quality product cooked to order at a fair market price. Our food may take a little longer to prepare, but it is well worth the wait! Thank you for your business. Your Management and Staff

---

WINGS "ASK US ABOUT OUR FLAVOR OF THE MONTH!"

SMOKEY MOUNTAIN GOLD

WINGS
(Traditional or Boneless)
10 pieces 8.99
15 pieces 12.99
20 pieces 17.99
30 pieces 24.99
50 pieces 36.99
100 pieces 69.99
All Flats or All Drums ...1.00 per 10pc
All Extra Wet.................1.00 per 10pc
All Breaded ....1.00 per 10pc
Extra Ranch or Bleu Cheese....0.59
Extra Celery Order.................0.59

SAMPLER
25 Wing Sampler 24.99
Platter w/ up to five sauces!
*Ask your server for details

TENDERS
*Make it a combo w/ choice of 1 side and 20oz drink for $2.00 more
3 Piece 5.49
5 Piece 8.49
7 Piece 11.49

COMBO SIDES
Waffle Fries ● Steak Fries
Coleslaw ● Texas Toast ● Small Salad
Potato Salad ● Baked Beans 0.99
Add Chili 0.99
Add Cheese.................0.99
Add Bacon 0.99
Add Jalapeños 0.99

WING COMBOS
(Traditional or Boneless)
5-Wing Combo 7.99
20oz drink and choice of one side

10-Wing Combo 11.99
20oz drink and choice of one side

15-Wing Combo 15.99
20oz drink and choice of one side

DICK'S BEST DEAL FOR 2!

20-Wing Combo 22.99
2 20oz drinks and choice of 2 sides

30-Wing Combo 29.99
2 20oz drinks and choice of 2 sides

40-Wing Combo 39.99*
4 20oz drinks and choice of 4 sides

*40-Wing Combo can be split by flavors in 10's, for .59¢ per 10

Upgrade to Domestic Draft 1.00

WING FLAVORS

WING TEMP
No Heat ● Wimpy ● Mild ● Medium ● Hot
Great Balls of Fire ● Swamp Fever ● Secret Sauce

"OUR WINGS ARE HOT!"

BBQ
Bourbon
Cajun Ranch
Caribbean Gold
Caribbean Jerk
Charlie Chan
Flying Fajita
Garlic Pepper
Georgia Girl
General Dick's

Gold Rush
Honey BBQ
Honey Mustard
Italian
Jamaican Jerk
Lemon Pepper
Lime Pepper
Margarita Ranch
Parmesan Peppercorn
Ragin' Cajun

Raspberry
Redneck
Reggae
Sesame
Smokey Mountain Gold
Sweet & Sour
Teriyaki
Triple Threat
Victory Lane
Wanna Tee Awanna

SANDWICHES

All sandwiches are served w/ **Waffle** or **Steak Fries**.

The Grilled Chicken Classic
Charbroiled to perfection and served original or Cajun spiced. 7.99

Hot Lap Buffalo Chicken Sandwich
Lightly breaded chicken breast shaken w/ any of Dick's 365 varieties. 7.99

Chicken Philly
Tender chunks of charbroiled chicken topped w/ sautéed onions, mushrooms, peppers and melted provolone cheese on a freshly toasted hoagie roll. 8.49

The B-B-Q Chicken Classic
Add our hickory BBQ sauce, bacon and Swiss cheese to our classic. 8.49

Hot Dog
1/4 lb. all-beef dog grilled to perfection, served on a toasted bun. Onions and relish available on request. 3.95
Add Chili 0.99
Add Cheese.................0.99
Add Slaw.................0.99

Catch of the Day Sandwich
Served w/ chips. Fisherman's catch cooked the way you like it: fried, Cajun or broiled...9.59

ADD-ONS
Add Chili 0.99
Add Cheese.................0.99
Add Bacon 0.99
Add Jalapeños 0.99

BURGERS

All burgers are fresh, black Angus steak and served w/ waffle or steak fries.

The Shroomer
Delicious Swiss dripping over sautéed mushrooms. You'll trip over it! 7.99

The Squealin' Cheeser
Bacon, Swiss and garden stuff to make you proud to eat like a pig! 7.99

The Three Cheeser
American, Cheddar and Jack melted on top of a juicy patty 7.99
Add Fresh Grilled Onions and Melted Swiss 0.40

Cajun Ranch Burger
Our traditional burger w/ Cajun and ranch dressing 7.99

Southwestern Burger
Topped w/ three cheeses, sliced jalapeños and salsa 7.99

The Whiner Cheese Burger
Flavored w/ Worcestershire sauce, topped w/ grilled onions and melted Swiss 7.99

Patty Melt
You choose the cheese, we choose the sautéed onions and grilled Texas Toast 7.99

The Traditional
All you need for the classic favorite: lettuce, tomato and onion. 6.99
Add Chili 0.99
Add Cheese.................0.99
Any 365 Sauce 0.59

WARNING: Consuming raw or under-cooked meat, poultry, seafood, shellfish, or eggs may increase your risk of serious food-borne illness, especially if you have an existing or chronic illness.

Figure 7-3
Prices ending in "9" communicate that the operation is a bargain, as does the bundling of the wing combos. Dick's Wings & Grill.

DICK'S WINGS & GRILL®

$3.99 DESSERTS

Fried Oreos
Hand-battered Oreo cookies deep-fried and dusted w/ powdered sugar. This one is to die for.

Brownie Bites
Chunks of extra moist brownie w/ chocolate bits covered in a rich semi-sweet chocolate batter, dusted w/ powdered sugar and served w/ a side of chocolate dipping sauce.

WRAPS

All wraps served w/ potato salad

Buffalo Wrap
Chicken tenders shaken in your favorite Dick's sauce, then rolled w/ cucumbers, lettuce, tomatoes and our three-cheese mix 7.29

Grilled Chicken Wrap
Marinated, grilled chicken, cucumbers, onions, tomatoes and lettuce together w/ our three-cheese mix and Dick's Famous Cajun Ranch sauce 6.99

SALADS

All salads served w/ choice of French, Ranch, Lite Ranch, Bleu Cheese, Honey Mustard, Thousand Island, Italian or Lite Italian dressing.

Buffalo Tender Salad
Lightly breaded tenders cut into bite size pieces w/ your choice of Dick's 365 varieties 8.99

Grilled Chicken Salad
Fresh, marinated chicken, grilled, and served on equally fresh greens 8.49

Dick's House Salad
Fresh crisp lettuce, tomato, cucumber, onion and cheese topped off w/ our delicious homemade croutons and your favorite dressing on the side 3.29

LUNCH SPECIALS

Lunch Specials M-F, 11-4 p.m.
*Only combos are served w/ choice of side and 20oz drink.

Lunch Combos
5-Wing Combo 5.99
Lunch Tender Combo 4.99

Lunch Portion Salads & Quesadillas
Buffalo Chicken Quesadilla 5.49
Grilled Chicken Quesadilla 4.99
Buffalo Chicken Salad 6.49
Grilled Chicken Salad 5.99

SIDES
Baked Beans ● Coleslaw

Potato Salad

Waffle or Steak Fries
*substitute for $1 sub charge

Small Salad
*substitute for $1.50 sub charge

*Lunch specials cannot be combined w/ any other offers.

HOW IT ALL STARTED...

As any 16-year-old, I was in love with speed and the girl that didn't know I existed. Figuring I had no shot at the girl, I worked hard to get enough money together to buy my first muscle car. My friend, Gearhead Cooper and I spent every Friday and Saturday night getting that car ready for "Race Day Sunday" at Onondaga Speedway. We spent every Sunday for two years racing that car. And everyday in between trying to figure out how to make Mary Jo Peterson aware that we were alive.

After high school, Cooper went to the Air Force to be a jet jock and me... well I went to the nearest speedway to follow my "need for speed". After a few years of not getting the ride I thought I deserved and completely broke. I decided it was time to get a "real job." Not wanting to stray too far from racing, I started looking around the track. I was looking for an angle, a need that needed to be filled. FOOD. So, I asked around to see what people wanted. What would they like to get their hands on...the conclusion, WINGS.

So I headed out to find the perfect wing. I started where all the great

wings began, Buffalo. While the wings were good, I felt I needed something more to make my wings stand out. I knew I wanted a racing theme but I also wanted the very best tasting wings in the whole country, the kind you would drive miles for.

On my travels, I was thinking about my old friend Gearhead Cooper and the great times we had at Onondaga Speedway. It was about that time that I started to think about what to call my yet famous "wings." One day after a long drive, I pulled over to a roadside eatery. While pondering my namesake, who should walk in, but good old Gearhead Cooper. After a few beers, we talked about my dilemma and he said in his very straight-forward way, "why not just call it Dick's?"

Gearhead Cooper always had the perfect solution for every situation (except for Mary Jo, of course) and he came through once again. That's when Dick's Wings and Grill was born, and we've been burning up the track ever since!

Dick

Dick's proudly serves:

Offers may vary by location. Drink purchase required with all wing specials. All beer specials are non-premium domestic draft. Selected items may be subject to a take-away charge.

Dick's Wings & Grill Menu © 2011 Dick's Wings & Grill®, Inc. Version A.

For Franchising information call (866) 340-9467

FLORIDA

N. JACKSONVILLE
12400 Yellow Bluff Rd.
Jacksonville, FL
(904) 619.9828

ARLINGTON
9A and Merrill Rd.
Jacksonville, FL
(904) 745.9301

THE BEACHES
3rd St. and 3rd Ave.
N. Jacksonville Beach, FL
(904) 853.5004

CALLAHAN
450077 State Rd. 200
Callahan, FL
(904) 879.0993

FERNANDINA
474313 E. State Rd. 200
Fernandina Beach, FL
(904) 310.6945

GREEN COVE SPRINGS
3540 Hwy 17 South
Green Cove Springs, FL
(904) 284-7777

LAKE ASBURY
2853 Henley Rd.
Lake Asbury, FL
(904) 214.9444

LAKEWOOD
1610 University Blvd. W.
Jacksonville, FL
(904) 448.2110

MANDARIN
10391 Old St. Augustine Rd.
Jacksonville, FL
(904) 880.7087

MAYPORT
2434 Mayport Rd.
Atlantic Beach, FL
(904) 372.0298

ORANGE PARK
1540 Wells Rd.
Orange Park, FL
(904) 269.2122

ST. JOHNS BLUFF
10750 Atlantic Blvd.
Jacksonville, FL
(904) 619.0954

ST. AUGUSTINE
525 State Rd. 16
St. Augustine, FL
(904) 825.4540

SAN PABLO
14286 Beach Blvd.
Jacksonville, FL
(904) 223.0115

STARKE
1252 S. Walnut St.
Starke, FL
(904) 368.8158

WESTSIDE
5872 San Juan Ave.
Jacksonville, FL
(904) 693.9258

GEORGIA

WAYCROSS
2470 Memorial Dr.
Waycross, GA
(912) 287.9930

Through our doors walk the most important people in the world ... you, our customers.

www.dickswingsandgrill.com

Figure 7-3
(continued)

149

or even $45 sales price. However, at some point, guests will no longer tolerate a price increase. At $60, they will probably choose another entrée or go somewhere else to eat.

When the price ceiling for an item falls below the sales price calculated by the operation's standard pricing method, the menu planner has a particularly interesting challenge. Should the item be removed from the menu entirely? Not necessarily. A menu planner can leave the main item intact but reduce the food cost by substituting less expensive accompaniments; this approach works well, too, when a dish would otherwise fall well outside the price range for the menu's other dishes. Alternatively, if a specific menu item is the main draw for a large audience, the menu planner could leave that item's sales price artificially low (though still profitable) and increase the price for common add-ons (beverages, appetizers, sides, etc.) to make up the profit difference through sales of those items. In short, there are few absolutes when it comes to setting a menu price, but the menu planner must always find a way to make the business profitable overall.

7.3 SPECIAL MENU PRICING SITUATIONS

While the earlier sections of this chapter have provided pricing strategies for the typical a la carte and semi a la carte menu, other types of menus exist that may require a different approach. The adjustment is often minimal, but without at least a little tweaking, the menu planner may find that his menu prices do not cover all of the business's costs.

Prix Fixe   A prix fixe menu includes all of the courses on the menu for a single price. Typically, the customer has a limited selection for each menu category, but rarely do all of those options cost exactly the same per portion. When calculating an appropriate sales price for a prix fixe menu, the menu planner must first calculate the cost per portion for each of the menu choices. As with a Q factor calculation, the menu planner next determines the total cost to serve the entire menu if the guest orders the most expensive option for each course. For a new business, this sum becomes the food cost basis from which the sales price is derived. In an existing restaurant that is merely adjusting its menu prices, the menu planner may prefer to base the sales price on the average cost per person instead. The average cost per portion calculation is performed by totaling the food costs for a month and then dividing by the number of guests that month. As long as the same number of customers continues to order each menu choice in the same proportions, the average cost per guest will remain the same. Using the average rather than the maximum cost has both pros and cons. The average allows the restaurant to offer lower prices and thus to attract a larger audience. However, if the menu mix (percentage of each item sold) fluctuates and more people start ordering the most expensive options, the restaurant will lose money.

Example 7.9: A prix fixe menu restaurant serves 1,230 guests in one month; the kitchen's food cost for that month is $26,000. If the menu planner uses a 27% food cost percentage and the standard food cost percentage pricing method, how much should the restaurant charge per person for the prix fixe menu?

Average food cost per guest = Total Cost ÷ Number of Guests
= $26,000 ÷ 1,230 guests = $21.14

Sales Price = Food Cost ÷ Food Cost %
= $21.14 ÷ 0.27 = $78.30

Table d'Hôte   On a table d'hôte menu, the approach is similar to prix fixe pricing except that the menu planner can list different prices for each entrée choice. In this situation, the total cost per portion should be calculated using a Q factor in which the value of the Q factor is the sum of all the food costs per portion for all of the non-entrée courses. Thus, the Q factor might be the total cost per portion for the most expensive appetizer, soup, salad, bread, and dessert choices. This Q factor is then added to the cost per portion for each entrée choice. The sales price listed next to each entrée is calculated from the Q factor adjusted cost per portion for each entrée. Which sales price determination method to use still depends upon the menu planner's preference and the business concept.

Noncommercial Menus   A noncommercial operation, such as a corporate or school cafeteria, almost always uses the base price method of sales price determination. These businesses calculate a maximum food cost for their dishes and then adjust the recipes to fit this constraint. Often, the price that a noncommercial operation may charge for its food is set by the parent company (or by the government in the case of public schools). If the parent company subsidizes the foodservice business, that will also impact the food cost percentage that the menu planner can use, typically allowing for a much higher food cost percentage than normal. In some instances, the cost of entrées in a corporate cafeteria are set by the parent company, but all other dishes, like dessert, are priced by the foodservice company. When this happens, the menu planner may use two different methods of pricing—a nonprofit, base price approach for the entrées and a high-profit, food cost percentage approach for the desserts.

Catering   In most restaurants, the sales prices on the menu must generate sufficient revenue to cover the food and beverage costs, labor, and overhead to run the business. Catering works differently. In most catering operations, the client pays separately for on-site staff. Rental equipment may be listed as an additional charge. In short, a catering menu typically works with a somewhat higher food cost percentage than a restaurant. The caterer effectively runs two revenue centers—one to cover the food cost, labor, and overhead of the office and commissary kitchen that preps the food, and another to cover the cost of the front-of-the-house expenses, such as service staff, furniture, and linens. While the menu planner for a caterer may use a food cost percentage or prime cost approach to calculating sales prices, their percentages or factors are different than those typically used in a restaurant. Rarely would a caterer use a gross profit pricing strategy, as the number of customers served by a caterer will fluctuate significantly and unpredictably from week to week.

Buffets   Pricing a buffet is perhaps the most difficult challenge in all menu price planning. While most businesses derive their food cost per portion from a portion-controlled, standard recipe, buffets have no portion control at all. In an all-you-can-eat buffet, guests may continue to consume food until they can stuff no more into their mouths. Even a single-trip buffet cannot control how high the guest piles food onto the plate. And how is a menu planner to account for the fact that one customer may fill up on rice while another may choose to mound his plate with piles of lobster and crab? In a new establishment with no sales history, the menu planner must make a best guess based on how much of each dish he thinks the average customer will consume. He may need to factor in some loss from guests taking extra food that is left on their plates and additional food that never leaves the steam table but cannot be reused the following meal. The guess may be way off, but after a few days, the menu planner will have the historical data he needs to make an accurate sales price determination. With some history, the menu planner can calculate the total cost of food used each day or week, including any food that must be thrown out after the buffet is over. With this total food cost and the total customer count, the menu planner can calculate an average food cost per guest. The Average Food Cost per Guest = Total Food Cost ÷ Number of Customers over the same period of time (just as with the prix fixe menu approach). This average food cost per guest should be the food cost basis from which the menu planner derives an appropriate sales price using one of the aforementioned pricing methods.

SUMMARY

The purpose of employing a menu pricing technique is to generate sales prices within a price range that appeals to the target market while maintaining the business's profitability. The overhead-contribution and Texas Restaurant Association (TRA) methods are examples of food cost percentage pricing strategies. The prime cost and actual pricing methods factor the direct labor cost to produce a given dish into that dish's sales price. The gross profit method adds the same amount to each item's food cost to ensure that each guest contributes equally toward overhead expenses. Of course, a menu planner can always start with the menu price first, using the base price method, and work backwards to create food cost parameters for each dish. While matching competitors' prices is a legitimate approach to menu pricing, it can carry additional risk unless paired with another pricing strategy. The preliminary menu prices generated from a menu pricing approach may be further modified to account for competition, price sensitivity, perceived value, and product differentiation for the menu item and the business concept. Menu prices are next adjusted to make them psychologically comfortable for the guest. The ending digits in the price reflect the brand and image that the restaurant wishes to communicate to the guest. Package bundling and price ceilings may be taken into account as well. Alternate approaches to pricing may be required for prix fixe, table d'hôte, noncommercial, catering, and buffet menus to ensure that they are based on the proper food cost per portion.

COMPREHENSION QUESTIONS

1. Using the food cost percentage pricing method and a food cost percentage of 32%, what is the preliminary sales price for a dish with a cost per portion of $1.36?

2. A restaurant's annual budget calls for $972,500 in overhead expenses, $1,634,000 in sales, and $88,000 in profit. Using the overhead-contribution method, calculate the preliminary menu price for a dish with a cost per portion of $3.62.

3. A restaurant uses the TRA pricing method. Overhead expenses represent 62% of total sales. If management decides that appetizers should return a 15% profit, what is the preliminary sales price for an appetizer with a cost per portion of $1.14?

4. Define the term "prime cost."

5. A café uses the prime cost pricing method and a price factor of 3.25. What is the preliminary menu price for a dish in this café with a food cost per portion of $1.68 and a direct labor cost of $0.22?

6. In a restaurant that uses the actual pricing method, variable costs (excluding direct labor cost) represent 24% of sales. Fixed costs are 37% of sales, and profit is targeted to be 5% of sales. What is the preliminary selling price for a dessert with a food cost of $1.10 and a direct labor cost of $0.67?

7. A coffee shop sees an average of 430 customers daily and budgets for an average of $650 in labor and overhead expenses daily. Using the gross profit pricing method, what is the preliminary menu price for a cappuccino with a cost per portion of $0.37?

8. Using the base price method and a food cost percentage of 35%, what is the maximum food cost that a chef may run for a dish with a sales price of $5.00?

9. Why is matching competitors' prices considered a risky pricing strategy?

10. List four factors that impact how much flexibility a menu planner has in adjusting preliminary menu prices.

11. A menu planner calculates a preliminary menu price of $9.94. What psychologically comfortable price should he list on the menu for a bargain-brand concept? What price should he list for a luxury establishment?

12. A roadside restaurant offers an all-you-can-eat buffet. Each month, the business averages 3,500 customers and runs a monthly food cost of $7,350. If the menu planner uses the food cost percentage pricing method and a food cost percentage of 36%, how much should the restaurant charge per person to eat from the buffet (preliminary menu price)? What price might the menu planner write on the menu if he wants to communicate "value" without seeming "cheap"?

DISCUSSION QUESTIONS

1. The chapter states that to avoid a wide range of menu prices, the menu planner may go back to adjust recipes so that their preliminary sales prices fall within a narrower range. Why wouldn't a menu planner simply leave the recipes alone and just raise the lowest sales prices and drop the highest sales prices to narrow the final price range?

2. Describe the foodservice business concept you would open tomorrow, if you could. What pricing strategy listed in the chapter would you use? Why?

3. Typically, the base price method is used in fast-food and noncommercial operations. When might a midlevel or upscale restaurant use a base price approach?

4. Matching competitors' prices can be risky, but there is a benefit to factoring competitor pricing into one's own pricing structure. What is the risk of ignoring competitor pricing entirely when calculating menu prices?

5. Imagine that you wish to open a café on a strip that already has several restaurants offering relatively inexpensive café menus. What might you do to allow your operation to charge more and still attract customers? Provide at least four specific examples.

6. The chapter suggests that menu prices should end in 0, 5, or 9. Can you think of an example of a foodservice operation you have visited that does not follow this approach? What is your perception of the business and its pricing structure?

7. The chapter discussed value bundling of foods by referencing a typical fast-food model. Describe a situation (experienced or theoretical) where bundling could be applied to a midlevel or even upscale restaurant.

8

Product Descriptions

By the end of this chapter, you will be able to:

- Describe how a business's concept impacts the length of its menu descriptions
- Write a menu item description that accurately communicates key information to a customer
- List the truth-in-menu representation categories and write a menu description that adheres to the truth-in-menu standards
- Write a menu item description that sells that dish persuasively
- List several uses for text on a menu beyond describing menu items

When customers arrive at a foodservice establishment, they do not necessarily know what they want to eat and drink. What they crave, consciously or subconsciously, is direction from the operation. For most restaurants, this requires an informative and persuasive menu.

Menus are the primary communication vehicle for almost every restaurant. They must address the questions that most customers will have about the establishment. These questions go beyond "What is there to eat?" Guests inevitably wish to know how a dish is prepared, what the accompaniments are to an entrée, whether the food contains potential allergens, and many other bits of information. The simplest way to ensure that a customer has a positive experience at a restaurant is to provide her with the information she requires to order the food that will best meet her needs.

However, menus must serve the needs of the business as well. A well-written menu operates as a marketing tool. It encourages sales of certain dishes and persuades customers to order more than just a single inexpensive entrée. Menu descriptions are the most direct way that a foodservice business communicates information while influencing customer decisions. As with menu item selection and pricing, menu descriptions should appeal to the target market and underscore the operation's brand. As the typically brief menu descriptions for beverages were described in Chapter 5, this chapter will focus on menu descriptions for food items.

8.1 PRODUCT DESCRIPTIONS THAT COMMUNICATE INFORMATION

When writing a menu description for a given menu item, the menu planner must first consider the restaurant's concept and brand as well as the target market. The writing style must be appropriate for both. If the business is a quick-service operation in which customers can have lunch in less than thirty minutes, then the menu text must be streamlined and easy to read. On the other hand, an upscale restaurant where diners expect to spend over two hours eating can provide lengthier menu descriptions.

Tone is as important as length to generate menu and audience alignment. A straightforward, no-nonsense operation that serves "serious" food to knowledgeable foodies may prefer menu descriptions that list ingredients and cooking techniques with little embellishment. A casual establishment that stresses theme over food may push to have that theme come across in menu descriptions. For example, a sports bar may use sports terminology in the menu descriptions. A barbecue shack may incorporate country phrases or terminology. There is no one correct way to describe a dish, but the description should match the style of the restaurant.

Example 8.1 illustrates how the same dish can be described in several ways to fit a restaurant's theme. Note that a menu description may

NORTHERN SPY

Snacks
FLAT BREAD caramelized red onion		2
PICKLED EGGS aioli		4
PORK STICKY ROLLS parsnip glaze		7
SMOKED BLUEFISH RILLETTES garlic toast		7
CHICKEN LIVER MOUSSE roasted onions, crostini		6
FARMSTEAD CHEESE BOARD fruit compote, baguette		6 ea

Starters
CHILLED WATERCRESS SOUP cucumbers, lovage, chive blossoms		8
KALE SALAD cheddar, carrots, almonds, pecorino		12
ASPARAGUS SALAD portobello, pine nuts, egg yolk		13
MARINATED BEETS goats yogurt, arugula, escarole hearts		13
FARRO & EGG Landaf cheese, peas, bacon		12
CRISPY POTATO GNOCCHI brussels sprouts, sage, brown butter		14

Mains
ROASTED CARROTS wheat berries, nettles, almonds		18
RUBY RED SHRIMP mussels, fennel, fngerling potatoes		23
FLUKE spring onions, favas, mint, green garlic		25
ROASTED CHICKEN freekeh, swiss chard, golden raisins		20
BATTENKILL RIVER VALLEY PORK black eyed peas, mustard greens, natural jus		21
ELYSIAN FIELDS LAMB savory vadouvan granola, yogurt, collard greens		26

Sides
DUCK FAT FRIES malted spiced yogurt		6
WILD RICE carrots, pickled raisins		6
COLLARD GREENS bacon		5

Northern Spy sources ingredients produced by regional farmers, purveyors, and artisans whenever possible.

Figure 8–1
This restaurant uses ingredient-only descriptions to communicate a serious focus on creative ingredients and innovative flavor combinations. Printed with the permission of Chris Ronis and Northern Spy Food Co.

be written with the dish's name above the description, to the left of the description, or embedded within the description. Separate titles for a dish can make ordering easier, especially if there are multiple dishes with the same main ingredients—two chicken entrées, for example—but brief titles may cause the guest to skip over a more thorough and appealing description of the dish.

Example 8.1: For a single dish, write three menu descriptions for three different types of operations.

Concept 1: Upscale modern American restaurant with a straightforward approach to menu descriptions.

> *Hickory smoked **baby back ribs** with brown sugar–Maker's Mark glaze, maple-bacon baked navy beans, and garlic-Tabasco braised collards*

Concept 2: A casual barbecue establishment that strives to make city folk feel like they're dining outdoors in the country.

> ***Cookie's Baby Back Pork Ribs***
>
> *Slow smoked over real hickory and served with our brown sugar-bourbon barbecue sauce, these are the best dang baby backs this side of the Mississippi. Served with our chuck wagon baked beans and spicy stewed greens, these ribs are sure to make you stand up and shout Yee-haw!*

Concept 3: A sports bar that incorporates sports into everything it does.

> *End Zone Ribs -Score seven ribs with this half rack of tender, smoked baby backs topped with our sweet and tangy end zone barbecue sauce. Don't pass up the sides of slow-cooked baked beans and collards. No penalty for excessive celebration.*

It is important that the menu description only use words that the majority of the target market is likely to know and to appreciate. For example, an upscale French restaurant serving the culinary cognoscenti can incorporate French terms in its menu descriptions in ways that a simple French café serving the local lunch crowd cannot. In the upscale restaurant, the menu planner may assume that most guests will understand and appreciate French culinary terms that describe a classic dish. In the café example, the locals could likely care less about the terminology; they merely want to know what's in the dish they're ordering. (Notice in Example 8.1 that the collard greens are described as "braised" in the first concept but "stewed" in the second. "Braised" is a less well-known term, so the menu planner uses the more common word "stewed" for the more casual operation.) Less familiar culinary jargon is more common in ethnic or upscale restaurants than it is in other types of foodservice operations.

Finally, while the wording used in a menu description can elicit an expectation of a certain level of quality, a spelling or other typographical error can instantly deflate those expectations. Top-notch restaurants do not communicate "flawless execution" when they cannot even spell properly. Headings that are italicized or bold-faced should be consistently so. All grammar, syntax, and punctuation should be reviewed by multiple people to ensure that everything is written correctly before the menus are printed and distributed to the public. Sometimes, a spelling or grammatical error is included intentionally to go with a certain theme, but then the "poor writing" theme should be used consistently throughout the menu and be obviously deliberate to the reader. In most cases, writing errors can make a guest feel like she is overpaying for the dining experience. After all, which sounds like it should command a higher price: "Shrimp and Salmon in a Lemongrass-Shiitake Broth" or "Shrimps and Slamon in a Lemongrass*Shitake Broth"?

NOW WARMING UP
Soups & Chili

Long Wharf Chowdah ......cup $5.00 ......bowl $6.50
There's chowder and then there's chowdah! Just like mom made it.

Candlestick Special ......cup $6.00 ......bowl $7.00
It's chilly and it might get windy. Homestyle vegetarian (meatless) chili, served with cheese, onions, sour cream and salsa.

Chomp d'Elysse – French Onion Soup Gratinée ......bowl $7.00
Soup you chew with croutons and melted Swiss cheese.

The Bill Campbell ......cup $5.00 ......bowl $6.00
The soup man brings you a daily favorite.

Barry Bonds Super Star – Black Bean Soup.cup $6.00 ......bowl $7.00
What do you think of when you hear "B.B."? Round here it's a black bean soup. Now available daily by popular demand. A delicious black bean soup with andouille sausage – served with a shot of the cream, cheese, onions and salsa.

FIELD OF GREENS
Salads

Caesar Salad
Full size – no meat $9.00
Small(er) – no meat $7.00
Full size – with seared chicken breast $13.00
Small(er) – with seared chicken breast $11.00

The Joe Foy – Chinese Chicken Salad
Full size $12.50
Small(er) $10.00
Chicken marinated in sesame oil and rice vinegar on a bed of rice noodles with romaine lettuce, bell peppers, almonds, with a sesame oil dressing. A traditional People's Republic League meal.

The Ty Cobb Salad – Cobb Salad
Full size $12.50
Small(er) $10.00
Mixed greens with sliced chicken breast, avocado, bacon bleu cheese, tomatoes, hard-boiled egg, and spiked (no cleats please) with vinaigrette dressing.

Pollo Vallarta – Chicken Taco Salad $11.00
Almost as exciting as a trip to Mexico, and a lot easier on your Visa (card). Grilled marinated chicken, letuce, black beans, cheese, sour cream, fresh guacamole and salsa served in a crispy taco bowl.

Summer of 2011 – Green Monster Spinach Salad $11.00
Full size
Small(er) $9.00
Fresh spinach with mushrooms, hard boiled egg, and bacon (crumbled like the 2011 Sox), finished with our delicious honey mustard dressing.

STARTERS

The KC Jones $7.00
A big flour tortilla stuffed with peppers, onions, jack, and cheddar cheese (Add $2.00 for chicken).

OJ's Buffalo Wings $9.00
Spicy chicken wings with blue cheese dressing. (Part of the proceeds will go to help O.J. find the real killers).

Irving Fryar's Fingers $9.00
Blackened Cajun-style chicken fingers served with blue cheese dressing.

Roger's Revenge ......half $6.50 ....full $8.50
Our famous Yankee nachos – vegetarian and steroid free (Add $2.00 for chicken).

The Tony Lazzari $9.00
Deep-fried garlic chicken nuggets – served with a spicy mustard sauce.

The John Calipari $11.00
Fried calamari with choice of Cajun tartar sauce or cocktail sauce.

Garlic Bread $4.50
Onion Rings $4.00

POMMES FRITZ

large $8.00
large plate $7.00
A very generous portion of our signature Yankee Fries.

Make the large plate even better by adding these items
Garlic $1.00
Cheese $1.00
Chili $2.00
All Three $3.50

MEAT OF THE ORDER

The New Jim Bouton – Fowl Play $16.50
Large panko-crusted deep-fried chicken breast served with mashed potatoes and gravy.

Lasagne Harding $16.50
"Can't beat it with a stick!" Classic lasagne with sausage and ground beef. Not for vegetarians or Olympic medalists.

The Will Clark – Cajun Gumbo $16.50
Inspired by the ole ragin' Cajun himself. A heaping bowl of authentic "Nawlins" style gumbo (prawns, chicken, andouille sausage) served over rice.

The Marvin Lee Aday $16.50
Cajun meatloaf with plenty of spices, onions, tomatoes and garlic. It's like paradise by the dashboard lights.

Sgt. Pepper's Beef $19.50
Angus N.Y. strip with cracked black pepper, flambee'd in brandy with a green peppercorn sauce. Choice of onion rings or baked potato.

I Love N.Y. $19.50
Why couldn't they call it San Francisco Sirloin? Oh yeah, I forgot, we're more famous for our "Tenderloin." A juicy Angus N.Y. sirloin served with sauteed mushrooms. Choice of onion rings or baked potato.

Á LA (BULLPEN) CARTE
Choice of Yankee Fries, Cole Slaw or Potato Salad.
Add $2.50 to substitute for Green Salad or Cup of Soup

The Wade Boggs $10.50
Wade saw the recipe on Geraldo's show, then we got it from Margo. Grilled Chicken breast, topped with fresh basil, sliced tomato and jack cheese.

The Rico Petrocelli – Garlic Steak $13.00
The Flavor of Boston's North End! A 5 oz. Angus N.Y. Strip grilled to order, served on an old third base bag (actually, a french roll) with a white wine butter and garlic sauce.

The Dr. J $11.50
"Jam one of these down!" "Classic" Philly cheesesteak with peppers and onions on a torpedo roll.

The Larry Bierdger $10.50
The finest grassfed beef (or turkey if you like) with choice of jack, swiss, or cheddar. Served with grilled onions. A perennial all-star (add $1.50 for bacon).

Quiche & Tell $9.50
Don't tell us, we'll tell you. Check the board. Includes choice of soup (not onion, sorry!) or mixed green salad.

The Rooney Burger – Vegetarian Burger $9.50
Sarunas picked up the recipe along with the T-shirts! An Alternative burger made from all non-carnivorous foods (we'll spare you the details) served with a special garlic sauce on a traditional bun with all the usual stuff. Try it – you'll be pleasantly surprised!

The Mike Stivic $11.50
Edith your heart out! Meatballs, jack cheese, and parmesan on a torpedo roll.

The Pee-Wee Herman $10.50
Carolina pulled pork sandwich with home made bar-b-que sauce and slaw. Illegal in most states!

SIDES

Bleu Cheese $1.00
Bacon $1.50
Mushrooms $1.00
Grilled Onions $1.00
Avocado $1.50
Chips and Guacamole $4.50
Chips & Salsa $3.50
Cole Slaw $3.50
Potato Salad $3.50
Mixed Green Salad $5.50
Yankee Fries $3.50

THE RUBEN RIVERA
In a pickle? This house specialty of fried pickle chips is sure to do the trick. At least we can say they're better than his base running.
$5.00

Figure 8–2
This menu communicates playfulness and fun in its menu descriptions. Printed with the permission of Fritz Frisbie and Connecticut Yankee.

157

8.1.1 Communicating the Facts

While the writing style and word choice for a menu description communicate the theme or brand of a restaurant, all menu descriptions must express certain factual data about the dishes they describe. Guests inevitably have certain questions they wish to have answered in order to make an informed choice from a menu. If the menu planner omits that key information from a dish's description, a customer is less likely to select that option from the menu.

Perhaps the most important data to include in a menu description are the key ingredients for the dish. Beyond the main ingredient (steak, chicken, etc.), menu planners should list ingredients that significantly impact the flavor. Guests with a distaste for certain flavors do not wish to be surprised by that flavor dominating a dish. Similarly, menu planners should consider listing common allergens or dietary red flags that are otherwise hidden in dish. For example, a customer with a dairy allergy will likely know that pasta Alfredo includes dairy, but if a bean soup is finished with some sour cream, the customer would not assume that the dish contains dairy unless it is stated on the menu. Ingredients such as anchovies or shrimp paste in an otherwise vegetarian dish should be noted in the menu description so as not to mislead a vegetarian. If a chef uses a particularly rare or expensive ingredient, she will usually highlight that in the menu description as well to help sell the dish.

In addition to main ingredients, a guest will typically want to know other facts about a menu choice, including accompaniments, portion size, and cooking technique. If the dish offers something special in terms of product quality, origin, nutritional value, or presentation, that should be noted in the description as well. In short, guests do not want to be confused or misled by menu descriptions. Menu descriptions tend to elicit images and expectations in a guest's mind. When the actual dish clashes with that expectation, the guest is often likely to be dissatisfied. For example, a customer trying to watch her weight might choose a dish described as "lemon-scented salmon with cauliflower and rice" with the assumption that the dish will be low-fat and healthy. Her expectation will be shattered if the salmon arrives swimming in a lemon-honey glaze with a side of cauliflower tempura and fried rice. While the dish might taste delicious, it does not meet this guest's needs. A little more clarity in the menu description in terms of cooking technique would address this problem.

8.1.2 Truth in Menus

While a poorly written menu description may omit certain key information that confuses the guest, such an action is not illegal. However, lying on a menu is. Many localities have laws against false advertising, and some specifically address misleading language on menus. The National Restaurant Association outlines eleven areas for which menu planners should be extremely accurate so as not to engage in false advertising. These eleven categories are collectively referred to as the truth-in-menu or accuracy-in-menu representations, and menu planners should avoid violating these guidelines at all costs. When a violation is discovered by the public or the government, the result can be as minimal as a fine or as severe as customer loss of faith in the business's honesty and ethics. Lost confidence usually translates to lost revenue—and in some cases, to the business closing. The truth-in-menu categories are as follows:

Quantity   When a menu states or implies a certain size or portion of food, the food provided to the guest must match that size. Thus, if a dish advertises "6 colossal shrimp," there should be six shrimp, all of a size that qualifies as colossal. "Extra large" portions should be larger than the standard portion size for a menu item. The biggest challenge for meeting the quantity requirement has to do with the weight of cooked foods. While it is easy to measure a sandwich with 4 ounces of sliced turkey breast, many entrées advertise a precooked weight for their meats and poultry. Unfortunately, a raw 12-ounce steak does not weigh 12 ounces after it is cooked to medium rare, and a well-done steak will weigh even less. The best way to accurately represent portion size on a menu for steaks, chops, and similar cuts is with a sentence somewhere on the menu stating that the measurements listed are for precooked weight. Those dishes for which this note is relevant can have an asterisk directing the customer to the clarifying statement.

Quality   While a menu planner can describe a dish as "outstanding" or "excellent," she must take care that industry terms with specific definitions are only used when they accurately describe the food being served. For example, beef can earn a grade of USDA prime, choice, or select (among others). If a menu calls its steak "prime," it cannot use another grade of beef. (Note that prime rib refers to the cut, not to the quality grade.) Similarly, eggs advertised as grade AA eggs cannot be grade A when served. Terms that are not defined legally or by the industry are safer to use when a menu planner wishes to suggest that the food is of high quality but knows that the chef uses ingredients of varying or lower quality.

Price   The price listed on a menu is the price that the restaurant must charge. Any additional charges must be advertised to the customer. Common examples are "blue cheese dressing – $0.25 extra" or "add $0.50 for each additional pizza topping." Clubs or lounges must list cover charges or drink minimums if they are going to charge them to customers. Additionally, automatic service charges must be stated, such as "18% gratuity will be added to the bill of parties of 5 or more." In short, there can be no hidden fees that just appear on the bill.

Brand Names   Major food companies have an interest in promoting and supporting their brand. Some invest millions of dollars in creating their brand, and they do not want it undermined by a sloppily run restaurant. Thus, if a menu or server suggests that one brand is being served, another brand cannot be substituted. Examples of violations include filling bottles labeled Heinz with generic ketchup or listing Absolut in a drink description but using another brand instead. This is the reason that a customer may ask for a Coke and hear the server reply, "Is Pepsi OK?" Were the server to simply nod and bring a glass of Pepsi, she would effectively imply that Coke is available for sale, when it is not. The two colas are not interchangeable. These two soft drink powerhouses thrive by promoting brand loyalty and emphasizing the differences between the two brands. Offering a product that is substandard (and each believes the other's is substandard) under a different brand name undermines the brand. Brand-name food companies know this, and they do pursue legal action when they find a violation. When a brand name is listed on a menu or stated by a server (or customer), then that exact brand must be used.

Product Identification   When an ingredient is listed on a menu, that same ingredient must be used in the execution of the dish. This might seem obvious, but some restaurants regularly make substitutions without notifying customers. Substitutions may be necessary due to delivery shortages or price fluctuations, but customers have a right to know about the change. Often, an unethical chef believes that the customers will not notice the difference. After all, what is the difference between a flounder and a Dover sole fillet? About $30. If these two fish were fried and covered with a spicy remoulade, most guests might not be able to tell the difference. But then they should not be charged for the higher-priced Dover sole if flounder is what was served. A switch from canola oil to peanut oil can cause an allergic reaction in guests who read a menu description as peanut-free. When substitutions are required, guests should be notified, so they can decide if the change is acceptable to them.

Point of Origin   It is quite trendy in today's restaurants to list the source of a dish's ingredients. In fact, some guests willingly pay a premium to support local farms through restaurant purchases. If a menu states that an ingredient comes from a specific place, then it must come from that source. An ingredient's source is easy to verify on case labels, packing slips, or invoices (both by a chef and by a lawsuit-happy customer). If the point of origin for a dish is likely to vary, the menu planner should consider alternatives to listing the source on the menu. Servers, chalkboards, and paper menu inserts all allow for daily information changes in ways that a printed menu may not. Of course, menu planners must also be able to distinguish between a point of origin and a place name that is simply the name of that food. For example, Maine oysters must come from Maine, but Manhattan clam chowder does not need to be made in Manhattan (or using Manhattan clams). The chowder is simply the name of a preparation style, just as French fries need not come from France. A menu planner must know the difference in order to ensure that she does not inadvertently list a point of origin for an ingredient that comes from somewhere else.

Merchandising Terms   Menu planners sometimes use terms to make their food seem better. Some are obviously exaggerations or opinions, such as "The Best Crab Cakes in Town." Obvious exaggerations and opinions need not be 100% accurate; a "mile-high" cake should be tall but not literally one mile high. Other terms are easy to verify and should be accurate. "Made fresh daily" or "baked in house" are merchandising phrases that help to sell products, but they must describe the product accurately. Bread that is "baked in house" cannot be brought in fully baked from another source. "Made fresh daily" suggests that leftovers from the day before are not sold. The easiest way to determine whether a merchandising term must be accurate is to ask various people what a given term means to them. If they believe it is meant literally, then it must accurately describe the food being served.

Preservation   When an ingredient is listed in a menu description as having undergone (or not undergone) a method of preservation, then the ingredient used must match that description. For example, if pancakes come with "fresh strawberries," then canned strawberries are not an acceptable substitute. A chef cannot serve a wet-aged steak for one advertised on the menu as "dry aged." Terms such as fresh, frozen, canned, dehydrated, jarred, or bottled must accurately represent the foods being served.

Food Preparation   The words used to describe most cooking techniques have specific definitions. Steaming and boiling are not the same, so they should not be treated as interchangeable. If a menu describes broccoli as steamed, then boiled broccoli is not an acceptable substitute. Grilling and broiling are often similarly misstated on menus. A broiled steak should not be listed as a grilled steak simply because grilling is trendier and sounds better. In short, the cooking technique used in the kitchen must match the technique described on the menu.

Verbal and Visual Presentation   This category simply extends all of the aforementioned truth-in-menu guidelines to pictures and spoken words used in a restaurant. Just because a picture illustrating an eight-piece shrimp cocktail does not use the words "8 shrimp" does not exonerate the restaurant from serving only five shrimp. If a menu or menu board uses illustrations, those pictures must match the visual appearance of that dish when it comes out of the kitchen. Small variations, such as a slightly askew plate presentation, are acceptable, but obvious changes, such as the omission of a pickle or a different type of bread on a sandwich, are not. Words spoken by a server carry equal weight to the printed word or visual illustrations on a menu. Thus, if a server calls it butter, then butter must be served. When a guest asks if a dish contains peanuts, the server's answer is effectively the restaurant's official answer. If the server does not know, she should find out before responding. A guest with a peanut allergy will likely sue a restaurant for passing off a dish as peanut free when it contains peanuts. That the server made an error in describing the dish does not automatically excuse the business owners from liability in the lawsuit.

Dietary and Nutritional Claims   Dietary and nutritional claims are probably the least-used representations on menus because they present many potential pitfalls. While some chefs may think of terms such as "higher in fiber," "low fat," or "low sodium" as relative concepts based on one's sense of how food is typically prepared, these are actually highly technical and well-defined terms that have legal definitions. "Low fat," for example, is defined by the U.S. Food and Drug Administration as "3 g or less per 100 g and not more than 30% of calories from fat."[1] Current definitions for FDA-regulated dietary and nutritional claims are available on the FDA's Food Labeling Guide web page at http://www.fda.gov/Food/GuidanceComplianceRegulatoryInformation/GuidanceDocuments/FoodLabelingNutrition/FoodLabelingGuide/default.htm. The other challenge with a dietary claim is measuring the accuracy of the claim in comparison to the food being prepared. For example, while a chain of restaurants may use strict standards to measure each ingredient in a recipe, single-unit operations may be somewhat more flexible. Allowing the line cooks to determine exactly how much butter or oil to use to sauté each dish can throw off an otherwise carefully calculated claim that the dish is low fat. When nutritional claims are made on a menu for a specific dish, that dish must be executed exactly as described in the standard recipe. If someone were to send a random dish to a laboratory for analysis, the results must confirm that the dish meets the advertised nutritional requirements. Finally, restaurants in certain jurisdictions have been required to post certain nutritional information on their menus. These laws usually apply to chain restaurants and often focus on fat and calorie content. However, as the push for greater consumer information expands, more localities may begin instituting these laws. Every claim listed on the menu must be justifiable and provable if the restaurant is to avoid legal repercussions.

The best approach to use for making a nutritional claim is to define the term on the menu. Some menus do this with little logos, such as hearts next to dishes that are heart healthy, and define the logo just once at the bottom of the menu. Others write the numerical nutritional information for each dish below the menu description. This approach tends to work better than using legally defined terminology, as most guests could not define those terms anyway. Symbols may also be used to highlight an endorsement rather than a specific dietary claim. For example, if a restaurant partners with the local diabetes association, it could highlight those dishes that have been approved by the association as "diabetic friendly." Such an approach allows the association (not the restaurant) to provide the dietary expertise while freeing customers from translating nutritional jargon on the menu.

Other legally defined terms may also be used on restaurant menus. The most recent terminology debate revolves around the word "organic." Organic is a legally defined term, and menu planners should not use it unless they can prove that a dish meets the legal standard. Consequently, many restaurants shy away from this word and prefer terms such as "natural," which does not have a legal definition. For those operations that want to highlight the provenance of their ingredients the better approach is simply to list the farms from which the ingredients come. If the farms are organic, customers for whom that is important will likely recognize the names of the farms. Other customers may simply assume that the farms produce high-quality ingredients—otherwise, why list them by name, right? Using legally defined terms can help a restaurant attract a certain customer base, but unless the menu planner can document compliance with the legal standards, those terms are best avoided.

8.2 SELLING THE PRODUCT

The purpose of menu descriptions is twofold. First, the descriptions must communicate information to the customer accurately about what to expect from a dish. Equally important is the menu description's role in selling the dish to the guest. Some operations prefer to have their servers handle the sales pitch on menu items, but doing so leaves significant opportunity for error and loss of managerial control. An overwhelmed server may not take the time to push appetizers, desserts, or specialty beverages. While most customers will still order an entrée, the loss of sales from beverages

Entrées

Filet Mignon served atop our horseradish crème fraiche sauce with roasted potatoes and slices of seared organic tomatoes 33

Canadian Lobster Tail oven roasted with an herb butter and white wine combination. Served atop a spicy mango sauce, sautéed asparagus and fresh mango risotto 36

Lamb Shank 100% grass fed Australian lamb shank coated with warm Moroccan spices, braised all day then served atop pearl cous cous 24

*Chilean Sea Bass encrusted with Arizona grown pistachios and served over a chilled sea bean salad with crab and a touch of curry. Garnished with a coconut sauce and toasted coconut 34

Roasted Salmon atop a horseradish yogurt sauce and served with roasted beets and a chilled cucumber, jicama and carrot salad tossed in a sesame vinaigrette 28

Marinated Chicken with herbs and fresh lemon zest ~ served with Yukon Gold mashed potatoes and seasonal vegetables and topped with fresh pesto 24

Linguini tossed with asparagus, spinach and organic tomatoes in a light lemon thyme sauce and topped with fresh Parmesan 18 with boneless chicken breast add 6

Pellegrino sparkling water (1 Liter)   4Panna Still water (1 liter) 4
Minted Iced Tea 3 House Lemonade 3 Soft Drinks Coke, Diet Coke or Sprite 3
Corking Fees 750ML bottle 10 1.5L (Magnum) 15
If you wish to open your wine or champagne, a corking fee will be charged. However, we are not permitted to open or serve your wine for you. Hard alcohol strictly prohibited. A $3.50 spilt charge for all entrees. A 20% gratuity added to parties of 6 or more. * The State of Arizona requires us to inform you the consumption of raw or undercooked meat or seafood may increase your risk of foodborne illness.

Figure 8–3

This menu provides excellent descriptions to help sell its products. Coup Des Tartes.

To Start

Brie Brulee Our house favorite! A wedge of warm Brie topped with caramelized apples and bruleed to perfection. Served with toast points & seasonal fruit 12

Chevre / Tomate Baked Vermont goat cheese on toast points served with locally grown oven-roasted tomatoes & mixed greens 9

Pate de Campagne A lovely country style terrine served with Dijon mustard, cornichos & baguette toasts points 9

Three Onion Tarte Our delicate sweet crust filled with savory combination of caramelized shallots, leeks, onions, fresh herbs, a bit of bacon & Gruyere. Served on mixed greens 12

Interesting Cheeses Ask your server about tonight's special cheeses 18

Coup Escargot sautéed lightly with garlic, white wine, and butter, finished with a hint of spice 10

Soup Du Jour freshly made, organic, soup Mmmm... 7

Salads

Fresh Arugula fresh arugula with roasted artichoke hearts, diced tomatoes and pine nuts tossed in a light lemon vinaigrette and topped with shaved Parmesan cheese 12

Mixte Organic Mixed greens tossed in our classic Dijon/shallot vinaigrette 6

Roquefort Our divine combination of mixed organic greens, roasted apples, warm toasted hazelnuts, dried figs & Premier Cru Roquefort. Our signature salad 12

Taleggio Organic greens tossed with fresh raspberries, apples, red onion, sugared pecans in our homemade prickly pear vinaigrette 11

Mozzarella & Tomato McClendon Farm's grown tomatoes served with creamy fresh imported mozzarella then drizzled with aged balsamic vinegar & our homemade basil pesto 10

Figure 8–3
(continued)

and second or third courses can severely impact a company's revenue. It is best to use the power of the menu as a marketing tool and to allow servers to simply reinforce that message.

The biggest challenge to writing menu descriptions is to suggestively sell a dish without overdoing the sales pitch. Subtle suggestion works better than over-the-top descriptions. If a restaurant combines quality ingredients and creative flavor combinations, the menu description may need little more than a listing of the ingredients. Such menu copy may include ingredient sources or portion sizes, but extra embellishment is unnecessary. If a restaurant only serves standard fare that can be found elsewhere easily, then the sales pitch from the menu writer is critical to driving revenue. The text must make the food sound irresistible and encourage the guest to order a dish she might not otherwise order.

To avoid overdoing the sales pitch, the menu planner must keep in mind that a restaurant that is the best at everything does not need to crow about it; the public will find that out through online customer comments and restaurant reviews. These types of restaurants do very little in the way of selling a dish via menu copy. For all of the other restaurants in the world, customers will want to know what the restaurant does best. Not every dish can be "the best you've ever tasted." If this were the case, the restaurant's reputation would precede it in the media. One or two signature dishes can be touted as "our specialty" or "the best in the city," but more than that just comes across as unbelievable. The remaining dishes on the menu should be described deliciously using seemingly objective language. Words that describe texture, flavor, size, and color come across as objective, but subjective words and phrases such as "awesome," "spectacular," "the best," and even "delicious" should be used sparingly. Table 8–1 provides examples of menu descriptions with an appropriate level of sales pitch alongside descriptions that seem so over the top as to be unrealistic.

TABLE 8–1
MENU DESCRIPTIONS AND OVERKILL

Menu Descriptions That Sell Appropriately	Examples of Overkill (unless this is the only item on the menu described in this style)
8 oz of meltingly tender choice filet with house-made béarnaise, local asparagus, and silken mashed Yukon gold potatoes	The most tender, flavorful filet mignon ever! This huge cut from USDA choice grade beef tenderloin is seared and roasted to your liking and paired with a super buttery, tarragon-kissed béarnaise sauce. We then serve it with a whopping pile of pencil-thin, steamed and seasoned local asparagus, and the most creamy, lump-free mashed potatoes you've ever tasted—made from boutique, farm-raised Yukon gold potatoes.
These crab cakes are packed with 6 oz of Chesapeake Bay jumbo lump crab meat, seasoned with our own blend of spices, and coated in coarse brioche bread crumbs. That's it . . . no other filler necessary! Fried in butter and served with a side of piquant remoulade, these delicacies are the classic way to kick off your dinner in Baltimore.	Hon, you can't leave Baltimore without tasting our crab cakes. Made from local, jumbo lump crab, these twin crab cakes are the sweetest, creamiest, most delicious appetizers on the bay. We coat them in brioche bread crumbs to provide that extra rich, golden brown coating you love in a crab cake, and fry them in butter to make them even more indulgent. Our chef's recipe cayenne-lemon-mayonnaise remoulade will wake up your taste buds so you can appreciate the sweet crab inside these must-have cakes. We swear you'll never find a better crab cake in your life.
Chocolate Orange Soufflé – Valrhona Guanaja 70% chocolate, Trickling Springs cream, orange blossom honey, and Gran Marnier. Blood orange garnish.	This lighter-than-air chocolate soufflé will send your mouth soaring to heaven with delight. We use only the best ingredients to infuse the dark, rich chocolate with the tangy sweetness of orange, so you can experience this awesome flavor combination. If this doesn't satisfy your chocolate craving, nothing will.

8.2.1 Non-restaurant Menus

When a menu planner creates a non-restaurant menu, such as a catering, banquet, or tasting menu, the rules on menu description differ. The item descriptions must still communicate key ingredients, but selling the product may be less of a concern. When a catering menu is provided to a client through a salesperson, the menu description should be limited, if only for space reasons. The salesperson can provide personal descriptions of the menu items and guide the client through the extensive menu options based on the client's needs. For upscale catered events the caterer often provides a tasting experience, so the client can see exactly what each dish is like. Casual catering menus, like those provided by sandwich shops, may incorporate slightly more salesmanship, but usually the clients only pursue an establishment for catering if they are already familiar with the product.

Banquet menus can skip the salesmanship if only because the guests typically have no choice in courses. The purpose of the menu description on a banquet menu is to highlight potential problems for guests with allergies or dietary restrictions and to preempt some questions that the guests might ask the servers. The menu should sound delicious, but the guests receive the same set courses regardless, unless they express a dietary challenge. If the guests are required to select their entrées in advance, the menu description at the table is effectively moot.

Tasting menus and afternoon tea menus follow the same logic. If everything on the menu is included, then the menu needs only to describe, not to sell, the food. For this reason, afternoon tea menus tend to have more description lines devoted to the tea (which the customer must select) than to the food (which is usually all inclusive).

Noncommercial and take-out menus are often brief, too, but for a different reason. These types of menus are usually present in operations for which speed is an issue. Guests in a business's cafeteria want to order their food quickly, eat, and return to work. Customers that walk into a restaurant to place a take-out order do not want to wait any longer than necessary. In both cases, speed is essential. The longer the menu description, the longer it takes for the guest to get through the menu to place an order. The menu descriptions should still communicate the essential information, but they should do so in as few words as possible.

Children's menus follow a set of rules all to themselves. Because of the younger audience, the menu descriptions should be written in easy-to-understand language. Sentences should be short and the main ingredients should be the focus. Most children will not know cooking technique terms other than "fried" and "grilled," so the description should emphasize the ingredients and possibly the presentation. For example, a pancake that looks like a face made from berries, bacon, and whipped cream is a huge draw for the under-ten crowd; the presentation should be stated explicitly in the menu description. That the dish is made from buttermilk pancakes, apple wood–smoked bacon, and local strawberries is irrelevant to a child; she only wants to know that it will arrive looking like a face. When a children's menu lists three or more components for each dish—think meat, starch, vegetable, and dipping sauce—the menu planner may wish to name each dish for a zoo animal or cartoon character. It makes ordering by name easier for the child. Additionally, when a child does not normally want to stop coloring to select from the menu, choosing between "Batman" and "Dora the Explorer" can hold the kid's interest just long enough for her to make that choice expeditiously.

New Lunch Special

Monday – Friday: 11:00 am – 2:30 pm
Free Steamed Rice orFried Rice, on Request.
Free Veg. Spring Roll

L1	Kung Pao Chicken	6.75
L2	Sweet and Sour Pork	6.75
L3	Hunan Beef	6.75
L4	Szechuan Beef	6.75
L5	Vegetable Combination	6.75
L6	String Bean Szechuan Style	6.75
L7	Beef w. Green Pepper	6.75
L8	Chicken Chow Mein	6.75
L9	Shrimp Chow Mein	6.75
L12	Moo Goo Gai Pan	6.75
L13	Sweet & Sour Chicken	6.75
L14	Roast Pork w. Snow Peas	6.75
L15	Chicken w. Snow Peas	6.75
L16	Chicken w.Black Bean Sauce	6.75
L17	Beef with Broccoli	6.75
L18	Chicken with Broccoli	6.75
L19	Szechuan Beef	6.75
L20	Szechuan Chicken	6.75
L21	Chicken w. Cashew Nuts	6.75
L22	Roast Pork w. Vegetables	6.75
L23	Hunan Chicken	6.75
L24	Chicken w. Garlic Sauce	6.75
L25	Beef w. Garlic Sauce	6.75
L26	Triple Delight	6.75
L27	General Tso's Chicken	6.75
L28	Orange Chicken	6.75
L29	Shrimp w. Broccoli	6.75
L30	Shrimp w. Vegetable	6.75
L32	Shrimp w. Cashew Nuts	6.75
L33	Scallops w. Vegetable	6.75

Bean Curd 豆腐類

Bean curd is a kind of vegetarian food, which contains mostly protein. The Human body can easily absorb this protein. Consuming bean curd regularly could lower your cholesterol and help to prevent high blood pressure and diabetes.

Hunan Bean Curd (with pork extra $0.60)	6.50	7.95
Bean Curd Szechuan Style (with pork extra $0.60)	6.50	7.95
Kung Pao Bean Curd	6.50	7.95
Bean Curd Mandarin Style	6.50	7.95
Bean Curd with Mushrooms	6.50	7.95
Bean Curd with Mixed Vegetables	6.50	7.95
Bean Curd with Spinach	6.50	7.95

Noodles & Fried Rice 麵飯類

Fried Rice (choice of: chicken, beef, pork or vegetable)	6.95
Shrimp or Combination Fried Rice	7.25
Lo Mein (choice of: chicken, beef, pork, or vegetable)	6.95
Shrimp or Combination Lo Mein	7.25
Vegetables Pan Fried Noodle	9.95
Combination Pan Fried Noodle	11.95
Stick Rice Noodle Singapore Style (curry flavor)	10.95
Stick Rice Noodle Taiwan Style	10.95
Healthy Brown Fried Rice	8.95
(Choice of shrimp, chicken, beef, pork or vegetable)	

Thai Food

new Pad Thai(choice of chicken, beef, shrimp, veggie & combo)	9.95
new Red Curry(Choice of chicken, pork, shrimp and beef)	9.95

Chow Fun 炒河粉

Chicken Chow Fun	8.95
Beef Chow Fun	9.95
Shrimp Chow Fun	10.95
Combination Chow Fun	10.95

Hunan Dynasty
皇朝飯店

World Famous Szchuan & Hunan Cuisine
Best Sushi on Capitol Hill

Serving Capitol Hill over Twenty Years
Private Banquet Rooms Available for
Parties & Conferences, Seating 200
Members of the House & Senate
Frequently Dine here

Tel: **(202)546-6161, 546-6262**

Fax:(202)546-4136

Free Delivery
Minimum order $12.00(Tax not included)

CHINESE FOOD & JAPANESE SUSHI

MasterCard   AMERICAN EXPRESS   VISA

Open Hours:
Monday-Thursday   11:00am - 10:30pm
Friday   11:00am-11:00pm
Saturday   11:30am-11:00pm
Sunday   11:30am-10:30pm

Price subject to change without prior notice

215 PENNSYLVANIA AVENUE, S.E.
WASHINGTON, D.C. 20003

Figure 8–4
This take-out menu avoids menu descriptions entirely, which speeds reading through a lot of options.
Hunan Dynasty.

Appetizers 頭盤

Crispy Spring Roll (2)	2.50
Vegetable Spring Roll (2)	2.50
Fried Wonton (6)	4.50
❦ Sweet & Sour Cabbage (cold)	4.95
Pan Fried or Steamed Vegetable Dumpling (5)	4.95
Pan Fried or Steamed Meat Dumpling (6)	4.95
Fried Cheese Dumpling (6)	5.95
Sweet & Sour Spare Ribs	5.95
Bar-B-Q Ribs (4)	5.95
Shrimp Tempura (4)	5.95
Shrimp Toast (5)	5.95
Beef on Stick (4)	5.95
Pu Pu Tray (for 2)	9.95

(Bar-B-Q Ribs, Cheese Dumpling, Beef Chocho, Spring Roll, Shrimp Toast)

Noodle with Sesame Sauce (cold) 5.50

Soup 湯類

Egg Drop Soup	1.75	3.50
Wonton Soup	1.75	3.50
❦ Hot & Sour Soup	1.75	3.50
Minced Chicken & Corn Soup (for 2)		5.95
Fresh Spinach with Bean Curd Soup (for 2)		5.95
Vegetable Bean Curd Soup (for 2)		5.95
Minced Beef & Egg Flower Soup (for 2)		5.95
Crabmeat & Chicken Soup (for 2)		5.95
Asparagus Crabmeat Soup (for 2)		5.95
❦ Hot & Sour Seafood Soup (for 2)		5.95

Duck 鴨類

❦ House Duck Special	12.95
Yu Ling Duck	12.95
Roast Duck	12.95
Crispy Duck	12.95
❦ Shredded Duck in Garlic Sauce	12.95
Peking Duck	(half)12.95 (whole) 24.95

Chicken, Beef, Pork & Lamb

All Chicken & Pork Entree are Small $6.95, Large $8.95
All Beef & Lamb Entree are Small $7.95, Large $9.95

- ❦ Hunan Chicken/Pork/Beef/Lamb
- Sha Cha Chicken/Pork/Beef/Lamb
- ❦ Kung Pao Chicken/Beef/Lamb
- ❦ Chicken/Pork/Beef in Garlic Sauce
- ❦ Szechuan Chicken/Beef
- Moo Goo Gai Pan
- Chicken/Pork with Almonds
- Chicken with Cashew Nuts
- Sweet & Sour Chicken/ Pork
- Chicken/Pork/Beef with Snow Peas
- Chicken/Pork with Bean Sprouts
- Moo Shi Chicken/Pork /Beef (Sm.2 pancakes, Lg. 4 pancakes)
- Chicken/Pork/Beef/Lamb with Broccoli
- Chicken/Pork/Beef with Black Bean Sauce
- Green Pepper Chicken/Pork/Beef/Lamb
- Chicken/Pork/Beef with Mixed Vegetables
- Chicken/Pork with Pineapple
- Mongolian Chicken/Pork/Beef/Lamb
- Beef with Vegetables
- Beef with Oyster Sauce
- Chicken Chow Mein
- Double Winter Beef
- Pepper Steak

Special Health Diet Dish

~ By plain steamed with original flavor no M.S.G., salt and oil used ~
~ You have to choose with seasoning sauce (white or brown sauce) on the side~

減肥素什錦	D1	Diet Combination Vegetable	.6.50 . 7.95
減肥素菜雞	D2	Diet Chicken with Vegetable	.6.95 . 8.95
素什錦干貝	D3	Diet Mix Veg. Scallop	8.50 10.95
減肥油爆蝦	D4	Diet Imperial Shrimp	8.50 10.95
減肥素菜豆腐	D5	Diet Vegetarian Bean Curd	.6.50 . 7.95

Chef's Special

❦ General Tso's Bean Curd	8.95
❦ General Tso's Chicken	10.95
❦ Orange Chicken	10.95
Sesame Chicken	10.95
Lemon Chicken	11.95
❦ Wonderful Flavors Chicken	11.95
Triple Delight	10.95
Sweet & Sour Delight	10.95
Sauteed Fresh Spinach w/Black Mushroom	10.95
❦ Crunchy Crispy Chicken	11.95
❦ Crunchy Crispy Beef	13.95
❦ Orange Beef	13.95
Jumbo Shrimp w/ Sesame in Lemon Sauce	14.95
Crispy Prawn with Walnuts	14.95
Happy Family	15.95
❦ House Salt and Pepper Shrimp	14.95
❦ House Salt and Pepper Chicken	10.95
❦ House Salt and Pepper Ribs	10.95

Seafood/Fish

❦ Szechuan Shrimp	8.50	10.95
❦ Hunan Shrimp	8.50	10.95
❦ Kung Pao Shrimp	8.50	10.95
❦ Jumbo Shrimp in Garlic Sauce	8.50	10.95
Shrimp with Black Bean Sauce	8.50	10.95
Imperial Shrimp	8.50	10.95
Sauteed Shrimp with Cashew	8.50	10.95
Shrimp with Vegetable	8.50	10.95
Shrimp with Lobster Sauce	8.50	10.95
Sweet & Sour Shrimp	8.50	10.95
Shrimp with Snow Peas	8.50	10.95
Shrimp with Broccoli	8.50	10.95
❦ Kung Pao Scallop	8.50	10.95
❦ Szechuan Scallop	8.50	10.95
Scallop with Black Bean Sauce	8.50	10.95
Scallop with Vegetable	8.50	10.95
Scallop with Snow Peas	8.50	10.95
❦ Scallop in Garlic Sauce	8.50	10.95
Seafood Combination		15.95
Fish Filet with Mixed Vegetable		12.95
Fish Filet with Black Bean Sauce		12.95
Steamed Fish with Ginger & Scallion (Choice of: Sea Bass or Rock Fish)		22.95
❦ Hunan Crispy Whole Fish (Choice of: Sea Bass or Rock Fish)		22.95
Sweet & Sour Crispy Whole Fish (Choice of: Sea Bass or Rock Fish)		22.95

Curry

❦ Curry Chicken with Potato	8.95
❦ Curry Beef with Potato	9.95
❦ Curry Shrimp with Potato	10.95
❦ Curry Triple with Potato	10.95

Vegetables

❦ Vegetables Combination in Hot Garlic Sauce	6.50	7.95
❦ String Beans Szechuan Style	6.50	7.95
❦ Eggplant in Hot Garlic Sauce	6.50	7.95
❦ Eggplant Hunan Style	6.50	7.95
❦ Broccoli in Garlic Sauce	6.50	7.95
Vegetables Combination	6.50	7.95
Broccoli with Oyster Sauce	6.50	7.95
Snow Peas & Water Chestnuts	6.50	7.95
❦ General Tso's Eggplant		7.95
❦ Orange Eggplant		7.95
Sauteed Spinach		7.95

Figure 8–4
(continued)

8.3 HISTORY AND OTHER INFORMATION

Menu listings and descriptions typically comprise the majority of the text on a menu, but rarely are they the only words written on a menu. The menu is an opportunity to direct and enhance the guest's dining experience. Sometimes, the most exciting and unique part of a restaurant is its history; a description of that history on the menu expands the guest's experience beyond the food and service. If a famous person dined in the establishment, worked there, or currently owns it, that may be worth noting on the menu, especially if it is a draw to the clientele.

If a restaurant's concept needs explanation, a description of the concept on the menu may be appropriate. For example, if an Ethiopian restaurant opens in an area unfamiliar with the cuisine, the menu might describe how Ethiopians traditionally eat using their hands and pieces of injera (a flat, spongy bread) to pick up the food. A small how-to guide for using injera would put many customers at ease who might otherwise express concern at the lack of silverware on the table. Expounding on the culture of a cuisine can encourage sales, too. If a traditional Tuscan restaurant explains that in Tuscany guests usually order an antipasto, pasta, main course, and dessert, the customers are less likely to only order pasta for dinner. If the restaurant concept is instead based on the provenance of the ingredients, that should be stated on the menu. Customers may appreciate the food (and the price they pay for it) more if they know that the chef's goal is to support local farmers and to use only local ingredients.

Long vignettes about a restaurant can enhance the dining experience, but they also slow the speed at which customers can get through the menu. Thus, historical anecdotes or cultural information should only be included if they add to the guest's experience. If there is excess space on a menu and the menu planner wishes to fill it with something, unless the written text will make the guests more excited to dine there, the void should be filled with appealing and brand-appropriate photographs or illustrations. Alternatively, the menu layout could be adjusted to break up the extra space.

While historical information is not a necessary component of a menu, pricing and food safety disclaimers are. The menu planner should always make space to provide the common "undercooked food" disclaimer on the menu. Not to warn people of potentially hazardous foods invites lawsuits from guests who get sick after ordering rare seafood or eggs over easy. Automatic price inclusions, such as the addition of an 18% gratuity for large parties, must also be written on the menu to maintain fidelity with truth-in-menu guidelines.

Finally, as the menu is a marketing tool, the menu planner should consider promoting its other services on the restaurant menu. For example, if a restaurant offers catering or plans an upcoming special Valentine's Day dinner, that information may be stated on the menu. If the menus are laminated and not printed regularly, short-term announcements may be advertised through table tents or menu inserts instead. Other examples of promotion might be onsite cooking classes taught by the chef, wine or beer dinners, upcoming special events or deals, or commercial products available for sale at the restaurant, such as jarred pickles or the chef's cookbook.

For casual and mid-level restaurants, it may also be appropriate and wise to advertise the business hours, address, phone, and web address for the restaurant. This type of information is essential for take-out menus but may also make sense for disposable dine-in menus that guests often take with them as mementos. Customers may store restaurant menus in their desks at work as a reminder to return to a certain establishment. Sometimes, they share these menus with friends and coworkers. The more data the restaurant lists on its menu about its hours, location, and contact information, the easier it is for a customer to decide to patronize that establishment.

ENTREES SERVED WITH...

Fort Breads -A selection of pumpkin walnut muffins and dinner rolls.

Fort Dinner Salad - Seven crisp greens topped with pickled ginger, diced jicama and toasted pepitas. Add shrimp or smoked duck for $4

Dressing Choices: Chunky Maytag Blue Cheese, Herbal Damiana* House Vinaigrette, Buttermilk Ranch, Chipotle Honey or Balsamic Vinegar & Fine Extra Virgin Olive Oil
Reputed aphrodisiac herb

FROM THE PRAIRIE AND FOREST

William Bent's Buffalo Tenderloin Filet Mignon

The most tender of all, an 8-ounce buffalo filet with Chef's vegetables and Fort potatoes.
MARKET PRICE

Smoke House Buffalo Ribs

Smoked buffalo ribs, slowly braised and smothered in our tangy Jack Daniels barbecue sauce. Served with a fresh jicama slaw and campfire beans. 1/2 rack (4) $30 full rack (8) $48

Elk Chops St. Vrain

Two 4-ounce bone-in elk chops, grilled to perfection with wild Montana huckleberries. Served with Chef's vegetables and Fort potatoes. $49

The Fort's Game Plate

Our most popular dish! South Texas Antelope medallions, Buffalo sirloin medallion, and a grilled teriyaki Quail. Served with Chef's vegetables, Fort potatoes and wild Montana huckleberries. $49

The Frontier Platter- a sampler of adventurous game meat cuts.

A Buffalo sirloin medallion, Wild Boar chops, and a grilled teriyaki Quail. Served with Chef's vegetables, Fort potatoes and cherry demi-glace. $49

All of The Fort's buffalo (bison) are from selected ranches in the Rocky Mountain Region

Consuming raw or undercooked meats, poultry, seafood, or eggs may increase your risk of foodborne illness.

Sissy Bear's paw print denotes a heritage recipe featured on The Fort's menu in the 1960s

**20% service charge will be added to parties of 8 or more

Figure 8–5
In addition to well-written menu item descriptions, this menu includes a paragraph describing the operation's commitment to local beef. The Fort Restaurant.

Figure 8–5
(continued)

PRODUCT DESCRIPTIONS | CHAPTER EIGHT 171

OTHER FORT FAVORITES

General Armijo's Lamb T-bones - In 1845, he was known to sell your sheep back to you!
Two spiced, 5oz. Colorado Lamb t-bones served with leek and garlic mashed potatoes and sautéed chayote squash, drizzeled with fig demi-glace. $34

Atlantic Salmon
Dusted in cornmeal and red chile, pan fried. Served with mole verde, quinoa wild rice pilaf and calabacitas. $32

Mary Schlosser's Taos Trout - Given to Saml' in 1948, recipe from The Taos Pueblo
Oven roasted trout, topped with crawfish salsa, stuffed with fresh mint and wrapped in applewood smoked bacon. Served with quinoa and wild rice pilaf and sautéed chayote squash. $29

Quinoa Vegetarian Tower - The ancient grain of the Incas is a highlight of this recipe. Quinoa is a complete protein, ... A vegetarians delight!
Sautéed squash, anasazi beans, roasted red peppers, corn, green chile, and garlic sit atop a quinoa cake spread with huitlacocha, (also known as the truffles of Mexico), avocado relish, with chile aioli and cilantro oil. $20

FROM THE YARD

Guinea Hen Leg Quarters
Marinated with jalepenos then roasted, Served with leek and garlic mashed potatoes, calibacitas and wild Montana huckleberries. $32

William Bent's Grilled Quail
Teriyaki marinated quail served with wild Montana huckleberry preserves, Chef's vegetables, and Fort potatoes. Two - $28 or Three - $36

Crispy Half Duck
Rubbed with Ancho chile and coffee then roasted to perfection. Served with quinoa and wild rice pilaf, chayote squash and fig demi-glace. $34

Consuming raw or undercooked meats, poultry, seafood,
or eggs may increase your risk of foodborne illness.

**20% service charge will be added to parties of 8 or more

Figure 8–5
(continued)

AVAILABLE EXTRAS

Forest Mushrooms..$8

Toasted Garlic Chips...$2.50

Campfire Beans..$4

Fresh Chef's Vegetables...$4

Jicama Slaw..$4

Sautéed Spinach...$4

Chayote Squash..$4

Quinoa and Wild Rice Pilaf...$4

Garlic & Leek Mashed Potatoes...$4

Our Famous Sauces..$4

Choose from: Hot or Mild Gonzales Green Chile
Huckleberry Gravy
Dixon Red Chile
Jack Daniels Barbecue

OUR STEAK GUIDELINE FOR DEGREE OF DONENESS

Rare - Warm/Cool center, bright red color throughout. (Juicy)

Medium Rare - Warm/Hot center, bright red center with pink outsides. (Very Juicy)

Medium - Hot center, bright pink throughout. (Juicy/Slightly Dry)

Medium Well - Hot center, light pink center. (Sometimes dry)

Well Done - Very hot center. (Dry)

Consuming raw or undercooked meats, poultry, seafood,
or eggs may increase your risk of foodborne illness.

**20% service charge will be added to parties of 8 or more

Figure 8–5
(continued)

SUMMARY

The writing style for a menu description must match the restaurant concept and theme as well as appeal to the target market. Spelling and grammatical errors should be avoided unless that is part of the business's theme. Fundamentally, menu descriptions communicate information about a dish—its ingredients, portion size, cooking technique, nutritional value, presentation, accompaniments, and so on. The description should be clear and honest. Guests end up disappointed if they cannot understand the description or if the description of the dish does not match what arrives from the kitchen. The National Restaurant Association lists eleven truth-in-menu categories to which menu planners should pay careful attention so as to avoid misrepresenting or falsely advertising the product being sold. The truth-in-menu categories are quantity, quality, price, brand names, product identification, point of origin, merchandising terms, preservation, food preparation, verbal and visual presentation, and dietary and nutritional claims. Menu planners should ensure that they use legally defined terms, such as "organic," accurately as well. A well-written menu description not only informs the customer but also encourages her to buy the product. Selling the dish should be done according to the business's style and avoid hyperbole and exaggeration. Catering, banquet, tasting, and afternoon tea menus generally require less "salesmanship" in the menu descriptions than other types of menus. Noncommercial and take-out menus often use brief descriptions to speed service, while children's menus require simple wording that children can understand. In addition to describing menu items, menu text may describe historical or interesting data about the establishment or instructional information about the cuisine. Undercooked food disclaimers and automatic price additions must be stated somewhere on the menu as well. When space is available, the menu planner should consider promoting the restaurant's other services and noting its standard contact information. Properly done, menus become both a communication and a marketing tool for the business.

COMPREHENSION QUESTIONS

1. Should menu descriptions be longer on a quick-service menu or on a fine-dining menu? Why?
2. List the eleven truth-in-menu categories.
3. Go online to the FDA's Food Labeling Guide. Select one legally defined nutritional term. What is its legal definition?
4. List three things that a menu planner might write into a menu other than menu item descriptions.
5. A menu description states, "12 oz of grilled Montana prime strip steak served with Tabasco parsley butter and house-cured, fat-free cucumber pickles – $22.50." What truth-in-menu categories are applicable to this menu description? For each category you list, note how an unethical chef might violate this menu description's accuracy.
6. Briefly describe two different restaurant concepts. Create a dish that could be served in either place. Write two menu descriptions for the dish—each appropriate to its corresponding concept—that both inform and appropriately sell the dish. Be sure to note which description pairs with which restaurant concept.
7. Write a menu description for an item on a children's menu.

DISCUSSION QUESTIONS

1. Think of a restaurant you have visited recently. How detailed were the menu descriptions? Did they fit the restaurant's theme? What drew you to the food you ultimately ordered?
2. Have you ever heard of or personally observed a restaurant violating a truth-in-menu representation? Describe the violation.
3. Have you ever felt misled by a menu description (even if the description was technically accurate)? Describe your expectations and the item that was actually served. What is your current perception of this establishment?
4. Think of a restaurant in your area (or in a nearby city) that could enhance the dining experience by providing a paragraph or two about the restaurant's history or about the traditions surrounding the cuisine. Write a paragraph or two that you feel would be appropriate for printing in that menu.
5. Imagine that you are a restaurant owner and that you want to write one over-the-top menu description to highlight a dish as the best thing you serve. Which dish would you describe that way—the best seller, the slowest mover, your personal favorite, the chef's personal favorite, the most profitable, the least profitable, etc.? Explain your rationale.

ENDNOTES

1. http://www.fda.gov/Food/GuidanceCompliance RegulatoryInformation/GuidanceDocuments/Food LabelingNutrition/FoodLabelingGuide/ucm064911.htm. Accessed 2/9/12. Appendix A: Definitions of Nutrient Content Claims. U.S. Food and Drug Administration Food Labeling Guide, revised Oct. 2009.

9
Unwritten Menus

By the end of this chapter, you will be able to:

- Describe how to market food visually on a buffet
- State the difference between an all-you-can-eat buffet and a cafeteria-style buffet
- Describe several possible layouts for buffet and cafeteria lines
- Organize food on a buffet to promote sales or to control costs
- List three ways caterers can charge based on a customer count guarantee
- Describe the role that servers play in communicating unwritten menu components

Restaurant menu descriptions play a vital role in both informing and marketing to the guest. But what about those instances when a printed menu is not utilized? In most restaurants, servers communicate daily specials orally. Buffets and cafeterias may not provide a printed menu to their customers at all; in these instances, the food must sell itself. Food that looks attractive on a buffet is likely to sell well while unattractive dishes will typically be passed over by guests.

The visual appearance of the food on the buffet, the decorations added to the buffet, and the cleanliness of the buffet all contribute to a guest's perception of the buffet's appeal. An attractive and clean buffet will draw lots of customers and perhaps persuade them to purchase larger quantities of food. A visually unappealing buffet represents excessive food cost as the food is unlikely to go anywhere but the trash can. Knowing how to set up and arrange a buffet is essential for a menu planner. The buffet presentation plays the same role that menu descriptions do. They underscore the brand and the theme of the business (or event), and they help to sell the product. Simply because a menu is unwritten does not absolve a menu planner from achieving the communication and marketing goals that are normally performed using the written word.

9.1 SELLING AND INFORMING WITHOUT A MENU

As buffet operations do not always provide the customer with a printed menu, these businesses must inform customers about the food and encourage sales through other means. Informing is typically achieved either through printed placards or through service staff. At a casual buffet or in a cafeteria line, large signs or small cards may be used to label each dish. Extremely casual operations typically employ larger signs with more information, so the servers are not called upon regularly to address customer questions. The amount of information to list on the signs depends on the needs of the target market. For example, a college cafeteria may list only the name and key ingredients of a dish while a hospital cafeteria may include detailed nutritional information; both would likely list prices unless the buffet is all-you-can-eat. As guests can see and smell the food in front of them, the signs should inform customers about the dish but not waste space selling the dish with flowery language. These signs may be laminated index cards or printed 8½" × 11" pieces of paper inserted into clear plastic holders. Unless the buffet options never change, the signs are rarely permanent or high cost.

Fancier operations often employ much smaller placards on their buffets, if they use signage at all. These labels simply provide the name of each dish and focus on the main items. Upscale businesses do not have less of a need to communicate with guests; rather, they tend to provide that service through human interaction. These types of buffets often have service staff available behind the buffet tables to greet guests and to answer any questions they may have about the food. Buffet staff use words to inform customers, but their actions help to sell the food. A buffet server must maintain the cleanliness of the buffet and replace platters that run low on food or that lose their attractive appearance. No matter how deliciously a sign or server describes a dish, it is difficult to overcome customers' negative perceptions of a dirty or unattractive display.

So how does a business sell food on a buffet or cafeteria without the use of a persuasive menu description? In a word—visually. Any food placed on a buffet or cafeteria line must look colorful, fresh, and visually attractive. Wilted, damaged, or monochromatic food on a buffet simply does not sell well. Just as with an a la carte menu, buffet planners must pay attention to variety of color, shape, and texture both within each dish and across the entire buffet. Since customers can see all of the items on the buffet at the same time, not every dish can follow the same color scheme. If one dish uses orange and red julienne vegetables with a white fish, the platter next to it should provide a different set of colors and shapes, such as dark green spinach and golden brown meat. The only constraint to variety on a buffet that does not apply to an a la carte menu is that not all foods and cooking techniques are appropriate for buffet service. For example, fried food, which offers a crisp texture not easily achieved via other cooking techniques, loses its crisp quality rather quickly sitting in a chafing dish on a buffet. Thus, certain dishes and cooking techniques may not be appropriate for a buffet, even if they would otherwise increase the variety of the display.

Once a menu planner has determined what to include on a buffet to yield a stunning visual effect, the cooks and service staff must maintain the visual appeal of the buffet through the entire service. A dish that looks inviting when first placed on the buffet can become an eyesore just a few minutes and a few customers into a meal period. To keep a buffet looking appetizing, cooks should only send out small batches of food at a time and replace them regularly. Thus, rather than sending out enough food to serve the entire restaurant, the chef should only prepare enough to last fifteen to thirty minutes and then replace each dish regularly throughout the service period.

When replenishing a buffet, servers should not dump new food on top of old food. Not only will such an act turn off customers who see it, but the process is unsafe from a food sanitation perspective. The food at the bottom of the platter may end up sitting in the danger zone for hours and cross-contaminate the new food that regularly arrives on top of it. Instead, old platters, bowls, or chafing inserts should be removed from the buffet and replaced with new dishes that have been set up in the kitchen. Once a buffet dish has returned to the kitchen, the chef can determine whether it is appropriate to place any food remaining on the dish onto the next outgoing platter, to reserve it for employee meals, or simply to toss it in the trash. Frequently replenishing the buffet keeps the food looking fresh and the service platters clean. Additionally, hot food should be held hot and cold food held cold on the buffet. Chafing dishes (for fancy buffets) and steam tables (for casual cafeterias) maintain the heat and quality of the food they contain. Permanent buffet spaces often possess tables with the capacity to hold ice or to refrigerate hotel pan inserts, so cold food placed in them is held at a cold temperature. Off-premise caterers who must rely on portable equipment may not be able to place every cold dish over ice, but certain highly perishable ones (think shrimp cocktail or cold lobster tails) should still be presented on ice. When a caterer or other food service provider does not have the ability to maintain food at the proper temperature on a buffet, it is that much more important that the food be rotated from the kitchen to the buffet every fifteen minutes or so.

Figure 9–1
This ice carving not only makes a beautiful centerpiece but also serves to keep the shrimp at the right temperature. Printed with the permission of USAICE.

Figure 9–2
This buffet exhibits variety in height, color, and serving platters as well as creative centerpieces supporting a fall theme to yield a visually interesting and appetizing buffet. Molly M. Peterson Photography for Occasions Caterers at RdV Vineyards.

In addition to the food placed on a buffet, service staff must also pay attention to the appearance and cleanliness of the buffet as a whole. As customers tend to spill food and disturb platter arrangements in the process of serving themselves, the staff must continually clean the buffet to maintain its quality appearance. Garnishes also help to distract attention from customer-disrupted platter arrangements. Garnishes on a platter should be colorful and arranged to one side of the platter (or bowl or chafing dish), so they are less likely to be disturbed by customers taking food. Ideally, they should relate in some way to the food they garnish, such as a bunch of oregano and colorful chiles for a bowl of black beans flavored with chiles and oregano. As long as the garnish remains visually appealing, guests are less likely to notice that the platter is no longer as perfectly arranged as it was when first placed on the buffet table. However, any garnish placed on a platter must be edible. Most guests will not attempt to eat a garnish, but occasionally a customer does. Eating the edible pansies from a platter's garnish, a customer may ruin the display, but he suffers no physical harm. Were he to consume poisonous daffodil flowers, however, the restaurant would have a lawsuit on its hands.

Inedible garnishes should only be utilized on the buffet table, not on the serving dishes. These table garnishes not only provide visual appeal, they should communicate the theme of the buffet. Thus, if the buffet is a BBQ theme, the table might be garnished with (clean) cowboy hats, boots, horseshoes, and lassos. Ice, tallow, or salt dough sculptures are dramatic table adornments that can be crafted to suit a theme, but even businesses without the staff and budget to create these sculptures can greatly enhance a buffet with a few simple, inexpensive purchases, such as beads and plastic masks for a Mardi Gras party. General buffets without a particular theme might opt simply for flowers or other generic decorations.

Many buffet planners use the serving pieces themselves to enhance the visual appeal of a buffet. Extremely upscale operations may utilize only silver to communicate elegance to the guests. Other buffet planners may choose mirrors or decorative platters and bowls to lend visual interest to the buffet. Linens also add to a buffet's appeal. Various colorful cloths suggest whimsy and fun while a solid black or white display communicates formality and refinement. Height is an additional variable that aids in selling a buffet. Platters may be placed at an angle or at various heights by using risers (blocks or small dishes, often covered by cloths) to lift them off the table surface. Buffet businesses may stock tiered stands to allow for the presentation of several plates one above the other.

The shape of the tables offers yet another opportunity to vary a buffet. While a single straight line of rectangular tables can be decorated to enhance its beauty, a combination of rectangular, round, and serpentine tables adds another dimension of visual variety. Table shapes cannot be varied randomly as guest flow must be considered, but carefully arranged tables support both the aesthetic and practical needs of the guests.

Finally, buffets can offer one more level of variety to excite the guest—multiple styles of service. While most people think of a buffet as self-service from communal platters, a buffet can include some dishes that are portioned or prepared a la minute by an employee. For example, a carver may slice portions off a large roast at the buffet and present them to each guest. An omelet cook may prepare omelets to order for breakfast buffet customers. College cafeterias may have a cook, using portable burners at the buffet line, who prepares stir-fries to order. This additional level of service helps to sell customers on a buffet purchase, especially when a restaurant wants to push much of its business to the buffet rather than to any a la carte options that may be available.

In summary, buffets offer an opportunity to appeal to guests' visual senses. Variety in color, shape, texture, height, garnish, decoration, linen, table shape, and service style all help to make a buffet a visually stunning dining experience. Small signs or service staff may be required to inform customers about certain dishes and their ingredients, but when done right, the visual impact of a buffet sells the food as well as or better than the item descriptions included in a written menu. On a buffet, the menu and its functions still exist in unwritten form through the display of the many food choices presented for visual inspection by the customer.

9.2 BUFFET LAYOUT

By definition, a buffet is a display of food from which the customer serves himself. Within this simple definition are multiple variations, including the aforementioned buffet at which service personnel may portion or prepare to order some of the dishes on the buffet table. The two most common types of buffets are the all-you-can-eat buffet and the cafeteria. In the all-you-can-eat version, the business charges a single fee per person, and each customer may visit the buffet as many times as he wishes. Portion sizes on this type of buffet are nearly impossible to control, so an all-you-can-eat buffet is priced to account for the average amount and cost of food consumed. A cafeteria, on the other hand, charges each guest based on the type and quantity of food he selects. Cafeteria portions are either controlled by having each plate portioned—in advance or to order—by cafeteria workers or by weighing the food at the cash register and charging the customer per ounce of food (as is commonly done for cafeteria salad bar purchases).

Whether a buffet is all-you-can-eat or cafeteria style, there are some common challenges. One of the greatest is speed of service. All-you-can-eat buffets are often utilized at large catered events, such as weddings, where all of the guests hope to eat at the same time. If the guests are too slow in serving themselves, the first diner might be finished eating long before the last customer begins to pass through the buffet. Slow service leads to hungry, dissatisfied customers. Cafeterias run into a similar challenge. In an office or school cafeteria, many of the customers may arrive simultaneously with a limited amount of time to eat. The longer they stand in line, the less time they have for the actual consumption of food. Customers who have a long wait are likely to purchase less food as they won't have time to eat it. Smaller purchases lead to less revenue and lower profits. Thus, cafeterias must also speed service as much as possible.

Because buffet guests serve themselves some or all of their food, the best way to speed service on a buffet is through the buffet's layout. A guest in a restaurant with table service would be horribly inconvenienced if he had to wait for every prior customer to read through the menu and order before he is given the menu to read. Yet that is exactly the effect of a buffet with a single line. To make buffet service as efficient as possible for large parties, more than one guest ought to be able to take food at the same time. This means multiple buffet lines, so guests are not all funneled into a single line.

A single buffet line can generally serve fifty people efficiently within a short period of time. An event with more than fifty attendees requires a separate buffet for every fifty guests. There are two approaches to creating multiple buffets. The menu planner can set up identical buffet lines for every fifty people, or he can divide the menu choices among several buffets so that guests will find different options at each buffet table. There are pros and cons to each approach.

Multiple, identical buffets allow guests to get the same items no matter which buffet they approach. For a relatively small buffet selection, this is a great way to go. Customers will not waste time checking every buffet line to see if there are better options at a different table. Additionally, even though such buffet lines may be all-you-can-eat, most guests will likely only need one pass through the buffet to taste all of the foods being served.

Menu planners must consider anticipated guest traffic flow to help determine the best location for multiple buffet lines. For 50–100 guests, a double-sided buffet line, starting at one end of the table and moving to the opposite end, may be the best approach. For 150–200 guests, the menu planner may consider having guests approach the middle of a line of tables to pick up their plates and then head off in opposite directions. Figure 9–3 illustrates three possible guest traffic patterns at a straight-line buffet.

The type of buffet layout chosen also depends upon how easily the kitchen and the guests can access the buffet. For example, a four-line buffet placed in the middle of a 200-person room may make sense if the kitchen staff can easily get to those tables through the crowd. However, if the kitchen can only access the buffet tables when they are located around the perimeter of the room, then the menu planner may choose to lay out multiple double buffets lines along the sides of the room. If the buffet will have servers behind the tables to portion food for guests, then guests may only pass along one side of the buffet tables. To ensure that a buffet serves all guests as quickly as possible, the menu planner should locate the buffets for convenient access by both guests and kitchen staff and with enough lines that each line services only fifty people.

While multiple identical buffet lines work well for a moderate number of food selections, they are unwieldy options when there is an extensive buffet menu from which guests may choose. For example, an international gathering of five hundred people may dine on a buffet highlighting foods from ten different countries. If each country were represented by only three dishes, that is still a thirty-item buffet. No guest could eat from thirty different dishes on a buffet, so the service line is naturally

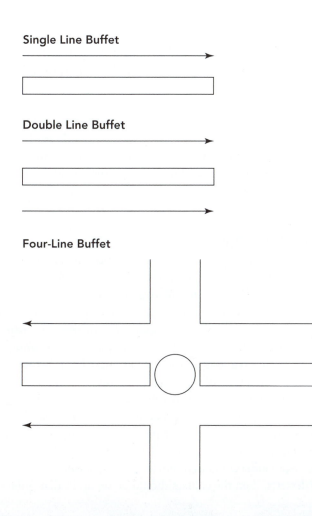

Single Line Buffet

Double Line Buffet

Four-Line Buffet

Figure 9–3
Sample buffet traffic patterns.

slowed as guests try to decide which dishes they'll choose and which they'll pass over. A better approach is to make each cuisine (or two) a different buffet line and to locate the various buffet tables in different parts of the room. Guests might be notified in advance that where they sit will determine from which buffet tables they dine, or, with enough signage, guests could choose to search out the food they desire. Unless the quality of the food at each buffet differs significantly, the guests will naturally disperse throughout the room. Those who do not care which cuisine they eat will gravitate toward the shortest lines.

While offering separate areas with different buffet options might seem an unusual approach, it is quite common in large office cafeterias. The cafeteria might locate the salad bar in one location, hot entrées in another, pizzas at yet another buffet line, and cold sandwiches in their own separate buffet line. Just as guests skip through a written menu to find the category of food they want, customers at such a cafeteria can jump directly to the line serving the type of food they crave. Each line may still provide multiple options, but with the vast number of options subdivided across different areas, customers choose from a smaller selection much more quickly. Service through an area layout is much faster for an extensive menu than is service using multiple identical straight-line buffets. But menu planners must keep in mind that some guests will inevitably feel cheated that they did not get to see and taste everything in an area layout. Whether to use the area or the straight-line method depends heavily on the size of the group served, the number of dishes being offered on the buffet, and, of course, the amount of space available to arrange the buffet tables. An area layout requires much more floor space than a four-line buffet does. When space is tight, the menu planner's options may be similarly limited.

One compromise between the area and the straight-line buffet layouts is the bypass line, more common for cafeterias than for all-you-can-eat buffets. In the bypass line, all quick-service or grab-and-go options are placed flush along the straight buffet line. Any dish that would normally slow the speed of the line, such as portioning hot food entrées to order from a steam table or cooking food to order, is located in the bypass—an indented section of the straight line. Thus, customers who prefer to skip the individually portioned foods can bypass that segment of the line, grab their pre-portioned food items, and proceed directly to the cafeteria cash register. Those guests who want to wait for the more time-consuming dishes can step into the bypass indent and wait there without slowing the rest of the line. Figure 9–4 illustrates all three buffet layouts.

9.2.1 Buffet Food Arrangement

While the layout of the buffet line impacts speed of service, the menu planner arranges the food on the buffet line to control costs and to maximize profits. The theory behind food arrangement differs significantly for all-you-can-eat versus cafeteria buffets. An all-you-can-eat operation should be set up to encourage guests to select larger quantities of the less expensive dishes and smaller quantities of the more expensive ones. Since an all-you-can-eat buffet has a set price but no limit on consumption, the only way to control costs is to fill up guests on the cheaper ingredients before they binge on the most costly dishes. If this type of buffet is set up incorrectly, the business's food costs will skyrocket. A cafeteria, on the other hand, charges for each bit of food sold. If the guest takes more food, the cafeteria generates more revenue and profit. Thus, a cafeteria should be set up to encourage multiple purchases and, ideally, purchases of the most profitable items.

If an all-you-can-eat buffet contains dishes that would normally be classified as appetizers, entrées, and desserts, then the courses should be set up in that order—appetizers

Straight Line

Bypass Line

Area Layout

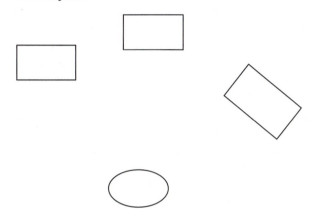

Figure 9–4
Examples of buffet layouts.

first, entrées second, and desserts last. This type of setup often occurs at upscale catering events that utilize buffets. Within each category, however, the food should be arranged so that the least expensive dishes within each category come first in the line and each subsequent dish is more expensive. The pattern repeats for each course. Most guests will take larger portions of the first few items they see in each category and have less room left on the plate by the time they get to the more expensive dishes.

Casual all-you-can-eat buffets, typically found in less expensive restaurants, need not follow the appetizers, then entrées, then desserts pattern, but if the buffet line does have a beginning and an end (i.e., not an area setup), the less expensive dishes should still come first. These operations sometimes put entrées, rather than appetizers, first, as they assume most guests will get the entrées no matter how full they are. Using this logic, the restaurant hopes that a number of guests, having already filled up on entrées, will skip appetizers (and possibly desserts) entirely. Ironically, because guests psychologically do not feel they've had a meal if they do not eat an entrée, they won't skip the entrée choices even if they have filled up on appetizers.

Whether the buffet is upscale or casual, desserts may be located in a separate area for the sake of speed. Many guests will only take dessert after they have eaten the savory offerings. Having them wait in the same line as people making their first pass through the buffet makes the line unnecessarily long. Having desserts on their own table with their own line allows guests who have already eaten their entrées to skip the main buffet and go directly to dessert without standing in line.

Placing less expensive foods first in the buffet line helps to control food costs, but the approach is not foolproof. Thus, only the most upscale all-you-can-eat buffets (which charge exorbitant rates for their food) should include extremely pricy dishes. Typically, any dish that costs more a la carte for a single portion than the entire buffet does should not be included on the buffet. For example, if a restaurant offers a boiled shrimp entrée for $15 and the buffet only costs $12 per person, then boiled shrimp should not be included on the buffet. No matter how far down the buffet line the shrimp are located, guests will quickly recognize this as a bargain opportunity. They will order the buffet and fill their plates, multiple times, with piles of shrimp. This is particularly true if the rest of the dishes on the buffet are far less expensive than the shrimp are. For instance, on a seafood buffet full of lots of expensive dishes no single dish gets "rushed" by the guests, but the price is set to account for the higher food cost. The buffet costs more, but guests will find the buffet worth the price because of the many costly dishes. Were a restaurant to set up a buffet with only one expensive dish but price the buffet under the assumption that guests will flock to that dish, the customers would not view the buffet as a deal. They would, instead, order that one dish (or something else) off the menu. Shrimp, of course, are not the only example of a dish that would get hit hard by customers on a buffet; lobster, crab, lamb chops, and filet mignon would all suffer a similar fate, which is why they are rarely seen on an inexpensive buffet. Large roasts should be portioned only by staff to keep guests from cutting their own thick steaks. In general, while some foods will inevitably be more expensive than others, all of the dishes should fall within a similar price range on an all-you-can-eat buffet.

Unlike an all-you-can-eat buffet operation, cafeterias might love it if guests rushed their most expensive dish. Priced accordingly, a mad rush on shrimp might generate more profits than a surge in spaghetti sales. However, cafeteria guests typically are not looking for a fine dining experience (or they would probably search out a table service restaurant); value-priced dishes are often the best choices for a cafeteria.

When laying out the food on a cafeteria line, menu planners should organize the food in the order in which it would normally be eaten—appetizers first, entrées second, and so on. Beverages should be placed both at the beginning and the end of the cafeteria line to encourage sales of these high-profit items as much as possible. Some cafeterias locate desserts both at the front and the back of the line with the hope that some guests will take dessert before they realize how much food comes with the purchase of an entrée. Finally, all add-ons, such as portable, packaged snacks, should be located by the cash register. The cashiers have an opportunity to encourage the purchase of add-ons at the time of sale. Additionally, customers may decide to grab an extra snack for later while they are standing in line waiting to pay.

An area buffet layout may not follow any of the rules for the arrangement of food that a line layout requires. Guests may float from one table to the next in any order, and in the case of round tables, there may not be an obvious starting point and direction for guest traffic flow at each table. For cafeterias, signage helps to direct guests to each area, but they may skip over certain tables, which limits a cafeteria manager's marketing opportunities. The only places that all of the guests will see are the entrance and the exit by the cash register. Thus, these two areas are prime marketing spots. Cafeteria managers should locate the items (or station) they most want to sell near the cafeteria entrance and place desserts and snacks as close to the cash register as possible. With an all-you-can-eat buffet, an area setup is the most difficult layout for controlling food costs. Consequently, it is absolutely critical that the costs of each dish in an area layout all-you-can-eat buffet are similar to each other.

9.3 GUARANTEED GUEST COUNTS

Chapter 7 covered how to determine a per person price for a buffet. All-you-can-eat operations require calculating the average food cost per person as the basis for determining a sales price per person. Cafeterias, like most other foodservice operations, can determine a food cost per portion for each item and then price each dish accordingly.

Caterers face a significant challenge when it comes to calculating a sales price for their menus. Unlike other foodservice operations, caterers may have to lock in a per person price a year in advance with a client. Thus, menu planners for caterers have to anticipate future price fluctuations for ingredients. Additionally, a client may come in with a defined budget. In such cases, the caterer must provide *inclusive pricing*—that is, a price that includes tax and tip. Even when a client does not state his budget, the caterer should still state in advance whether tax and tip are included in the price or will be added to the final bill.

Caterers have a particularly difficult challenge with buffets, which are almost always an all-you-can-eat format, as they must know how much food to prepare for a given event. Unlike a buffet restaurant, a caterer does not have a sales history for forecasting how many guests to expect on a given day or how much this particular group of diners will consume; estimating an average food cost per person becomes that much more difficult. Additionally, the caterer is beholden to the client to forecast how many guests to expect. Since most caterers cannot use the food from one party elsewhere, they aim to prepare just enough to satisfy all of the guests without running short on food. But what about a client whose prediction is way off? If extra guests arrive, can the client complain that the caterer should have had more food on the buffet? If only half of the anticipated guests show up, is the client permitted to pay only for those who attend, essentially forcing the caterer to eat the cost of the excess food? The best way to protect the interests of the caterer and the client fairly is through the use of a guarantee.

A *guarantee* (or guaranteed guest count) is the customer's prediction of how many guests the caterer should expect to serve; it is also the foundation upon which the caterer's food production and the client's price will be based whether or not the client's prediction is accurate. Caterers use their experience to determine how much of each dish to prepare per person for a catered event. For a plated banquet, the quantities may be embedded in the menu and the contract; for a buffet, the client, not knowing how much each guest will eat, simply expects the caterer to provide enough to satisfy all of the guests, no matter how heartily they eat. Fewer items on a buffet mean partygoers will consume more of each dish than they would with a much larger spread. Caterers are expected to adjust their production appropriately regardless of the menu or forecast guest count.

Because caterers have a brand and reputation to protect, they have an incentive to overproduce for a buffet, so the food does not run out. A client, knowing that a given caterer serves large portions, has an incentive to understate the guest count and pay for fewer guests under the assumption that there will still be plenty of food for the extra attendees. If the caterer does not feed all of the attendees, his brand is tarnished. If he overproduces significantly, his costs become exorbitant. The caterer naturally wants a guarantee that is accurate, but even an honest client cannot predict if a guest will get sick last minute or decide to attend despite not replying to an invitation. Flexibility in a guarantee puts the customer at ease and helps to protect a caterer's brand, but too much flexibility precludes cost controls.

There are three ways that a caterer can treat a guarantee to ensure that he gets paid appropriately and protects the company's reputation while addressing unforeseen guest count fluctuations. While clients have the largest incentive to low-ball a guarantee with a buffet, all three types of guarantees apply equally to catered events no matter what the style of service. The first type of guarantee is a *minimum guarantee*. With a minimum guarantee, the client will pay for the number of guests stated in the contracted guarantee, even if fewer show up. If the guest count exceeds the guarantee, then the client will pay for the exact count up to a point. Typically, the caterer agrees to accommodate only some additional guests, usually 5%–10% above the count. The caterer prepares enough food for the 5%–10% buffer, and the client knows that if he has low-balled the guarantee too much, there will not be enough food for the guests. The caterer knows that he can charge for any additional guests that arrive, but that at a minimum, he will collect a fee based on the guarantee.

The second type of guarantee is the *over/under* or *approximate guarantee*. Using this approach, the caterer allows for some flexibility in the client's guest count by charging as little as 5% below the guarantee and as much as 5% over the guarantee. To protect his reputation, the caterer prepares food for 5% over the guarantee, so the food does not run out. The client will not be penalized financially if the actual attendance falls slightly short of the guarantee. However, there is still a minimum charge below which the event's price cannot fall, and there is a maximum attendance above which the caterer will not accommodate. The client is incentivized to be as accurate as possible in his guarantee.

Finally, the third type of guarantee is the *exact guarantee*. As the name suggests, there is no flexibility in count. The client will be charged for the contracted guarantee, and the caterer will not accommodate any additional guests. This approach allows the caterer to control costs extremely well, but clients may be turned off by the lack of flexibility. This type of guarantee works best for small business meetings to which additional last-minute guests would not be invited and which all invitees are required to attend.

9.4 VERBAL SPECIALS

Cafeterias and buffets are not the only examples of unwritten menus. Many restaurants with printed menus also offer one or more daily specials. Sometimes these specials rotate on a cycle and can be included easily in print on the menu. Other times, they are spontaneous creations based on available product and the chef's inspiration. These spur-of-the-moment inventions may be printed on a daily menu, written on a chalkboard, or placed on a menu insert, but for many restaurants, the easiest way to present them is through the server. As with written menus, oral descriptions by the server must be accurate and sound delicious. In some operations, the kitchen requires the servers to taste the daily special before service, so they can answer questions about its flavor, ingredients, and presentation. Because a lengthy speech about a special will delay a server from other responsibilities, the server should keep his specials presentation brief. If the price of the special does not fall within the range of the regular menu prices, then it should be disclosed. Otherwise, the restaurant may opt not to have servers state the price of the special unless asked by the guest.

Whether a dish is printed on a menu or not, the server has incredible power to influence the sales of certain dishes being offered by the restaurant. Servers can provide personal recommendations and additional details for the dishes printed on the menu. When a menu provides minimalist, ingredient-only descriptions, the server has the opportunity to describe flavors, textures, and visual qualities for a given dish. A server who provides menu description orally at the table operates as an unwritten menu and should complement rather than undermine the printed menu. The server is no less bound by the truth-in-menu rules than is the printed menu.

Whereas a printed menu sells to a general audience, the server is able to direct his selling to the individual guest. If a guest states a preference for a low-fat dish, the server can provide the best recommendation. If a guest wants to taste the specialties of the house, the server can guide the customer through that experience and menu selection. A printed menu offers upper management control of the message being communicated to the guests, but a server offers personalized attention that may increase sales and the quality of the guests' experience.

This personalized persuasion allows the server to upsell products to a guest. *Upselling* is the encouragement of a higher-priced or additional product to a guest who orders a standard one. For example, a guest might order a gin and tonic. The server could reply, "Would you like that made with Tanqueray?" If the guest says yes and the Tanqueray commands a higher sales price than the basic gin and tonic, then that is an example of effective upselling. The guest gets a higher-quality product, but he willingly orders it, which authorizes the higher charge. The restaurant ends up with more revenue, and the server presumably gets a higher tip based on a larger bill. Upselling need not be done solely on alcoholic drinks. In an Italian restaurant, if bread comes with an entrée for free, the server might ask if the guest wants garlic bread instead (which usually comes at a price). Indian restaurants, in which bread is not usually included, do the same thing when they ask a guest if he would like naan with the meal.

Upselling is a form of suggestive selling, which is usually less tailored to an individual guest. Delicious menu descriptions, presented in writing or orally, are an example of suggestive selling. They encourage the guest to order something in particular. Suggestive selling can persuade a customer to choose one dish—perhaps a more profitable dish—over another through a simple server recommendation. A more powerful form of suggestive selling is to encourage the sales of additional courses. When a server greets a table, he might ask the guests if they would like to start with an appetizer or some drinks. He can recommend dessert after clearing the entrée plates. The most effective way to suggestive sell is for the server to assume that the guest wants multiple courses and then to phrase his questions to the table from that perspective. For example, rather than say, "Would you like an appetizer to start?" try, "Would you care to start with an order of our famous chicken wings this evening, or would you prefer one of our other spectacular appetizers?" The customer can always decline anything from that course, but some guests are inevitably persuaded to make the extra purchase through this form of questioning. Consider the difference between a server who hears a guest order a hamburger and states, "I'll put that right in for you," and one who instead replies, "Would you like cheddar or gorgonzola on your burger?" (upselling), followed by, "And would you care to start with a house salad, or are you looking to save room for dessert?" (suggestive selling). The second server may not convince every guest to make an additional purchase, but over the course of a meal, he will greatly outsell the first server. Suggestive selling and upselling by a server are excellent ways to perform the marketing and selling functions of a menu beyond the printed word.

SUMMARY

When a foodservice business does not provide a written menu to the guest, it must sell the product and inform the customer in other ways. All-you-can-eat buffets and cafeteria lines are the most common examples of unwritten menu operations. Small signs or service staff inform the guests, but the food must sell itself visually. To keep food attractive, service staff must keep the buffet clean, replenish products frequently, and maintain food at its proper temperature. The food itself must display variety in color, shape, and texture. Garnishes, table decorations, china, silver, centerpieces, and linen add to the appeal while variety in height and table shape provide further visual spectacle. Buffets may be laid out in a straight line, bypass, or area setup; for large parties, multiple buffets may be identical or distinct to aid traffic flow.

Food should be arranged on a buffet either to control costs or to increase revenue. To control costs, place the less expensive foods near the front of the line or to the front of each "course." Cafeterias wish to increase revenue, so they should locate add-ons and beverages in prime locations where customers are likely to see them. Caterers utilize a guarantee to protect themselves from financial and reputation loss. The three types of guarantees are minimum, over/under, and exact. Servers also operate as unwritten menus when they present specials, suggestive sell, or upsell at the table. Their work further markets the product to guests. There are many obvious differences between written and unwritten menus, but the foodservice business must inform customers and market its product regardless of the form the menu takes.

COMPREHENSION QUESTIONS

1. List five things that a menu planner and/or chef can do to make the food on a buffet visually appealing.
2. List three things that a manager can do to make a buffet attractive beyond the food itself.
3. What is the difference between an all-you-can-eat buffet and a cafeteria?
4. List and describe three ways to lay out tables for a buffet.
5. How should a menu planner arrange the food for an all-you-can-eat buffet? Why?
6. In a cafeteria, which two locations should display add-ons?
7. List and define the three types of customer count guarantees commonly used by caterers.
8. Define suggestive selling and upselling.

DISCUSSION QUESTIONS

1. Imagine that you are a server in a restaurant. Write out a brief introduction that you could present upon greeting a table that would include an example of suggestive selling.
2. List two examples of upselling that you have experienced in a restaurant—one that is done by a server and one that is simply written as an available option on a menu. Which one was more persuasive to you?
3. Imagine that you are catering an event (theme: your choice). Write out a list of twelve dishes that you would include on the buffet, keeping in mind that variety is essential. In what order would you arrange these dishes on an all-you-can-eat buffet with a straight-line layout?
4. If you were catering a buffet party for 1,000 people, how would you lay out the tables in the room? How many buffets would you have? Why?
5. As a caterer with a 1,000-person party, what type of guarantee would you use? How much food would you produce (in number of portions)? What are the pros and cons of using this particular guarantee method?
6. The chapter has referred to a cafeteria as a type of buffet. While a cafeteria sometimes includes a true buffet (like a salad bar sold by weight), not all of the items are completely self-service. Why is that? In your opinion, does it make a difference in how the cafeteria line is set up if the cafeteria is 100% buffet or not buffet at all? Why?

IO
Layout of the Written Menu

With the menu items, headings, prices, and descriptions determined for a menu, the menu planner is finally ready to lay out and print the menu. In an era where people print documents at home all the time, this task might seem quite simple and straightforward. However, care and consideration must go into every detail of the process if the menu is to maximize its effectiveness. From the choice of paper and font to the layout of graphics and text, each decision has the potential to enhance or to undermine the guests' experience and the business's brand.

Menu design and printing can be performed by a professional menu designer and printer or by a menu planner with a little training and access to the right technology. Learning the considerations that go into menu layout and production allows the menu planner to perform the task in-house, if she chooses. Should she outsource the work, a knowledgeable menu planner will be able to communicate more effectively with the designer. Done properly, a printed menu can increase sales and sublimi-nally direct customers toward the most profitable purchases. Poorly cre-ated, a menu can turn off customers, persuade them to purchase less, and even encourage them not to return. As menus can take the form of menu boards, web page displays, and single-use pieces of paper, considerations for the layout of these types of menus are discussed as well.

10.1 MENU SIZE AND LAYOUT

The first decision a menu designer must make is to select the ultimate size of the menu. The typical size of copier or printer paper is 8½" × 11". Some establishments use this standard size inserted into a cover. Others go several inches larger to allow for bigger print, more images, or possibly to squeeze the entire menu onto one or two pages. A dessert menu or table tent menu may be significantly smaller. However, a menu designer should consider the practicality of the menu when selecting the size. A too-small menu may require a large number of pages, which can slow guests in their ordering. An overly large menu may feel clumsy and knock over water glasses on the table. Menus that are comfortable to hold and read should be the goal. Because the 8½" × 11" size is the most common, defaulting to this size may result in cost savings, too.

The size of the paper determines the number of pages required for the menu, which in turn impacts the layout. A menu can be printed as a single sheet, as a two-page folio (possibly with content on the back cover), as a multipage book, or as a trifold in which the left and right sides close over a larger center page. Menus should always support the theme and concept of the restaurant. Thus, a quirky restaurant may have a nonrect-angular menu or one that opens vertically rather than right to left, but

By the end of this chapter, you will be able to:

- Describe the factors menu designers must consider when selecting menu paper and font
- Lay out a menu to locate high-profit items where they are most likely to be sold
- Depict possible formats for menus with one, two, three, or more pages
- List several considerations for selecting a menu cover or page treatment
- State the pros and cons of contracting out the layout and printing of a menu versus doing the work in-house
- Calculate the quantity of menus to print for a restaurant
- Describe special concerns related to menu boards, elec-tronic menus, and single-use menus

a menu designer must keep in mind that nonrectangular menus often cost significantly more to produce than rectangular ones do.

Whatever shape or form the menu takes, the pages should not be cluttered. Empty space at the margins and between listings makes the menu appear clean and orderly. As guests need places to hold the menu without covering up text, and since reading a menu should feel less laborious than reading a book, a good amount of empty or "white" space is essential. Some operations reserve as much as 50% of the menu for white space to maintain this uncluttered look. If too much blank space exists, the menu designer can include photos, drawings, text on the history of the building and owners, or information about the business and other services it offers. The designer must always include room for pricing policies or food safety statements to keep the restaurant in compliance with truth-in-menu and food safety regulations. The business's location, hours of operation, and contact information are optional for a sit-down establishment, but they are a must for a take-out or online menu.

When considering the location of certain menu items, designers should consider the menu's "hot zones." A hot zone is the location where a guest's eyes typically fall first—the location that all guests will see even if they only glance briefly at the menu to make a quick selection. Because Americans read from left to right and top to bottom, their eyes tend to settle on the upper half of a page and gravitate to the right. Thus, on a single-page menu, the hot zone is top center. On a two-page or multipage menu, the upper half of each right page is the hot zone. Finally, on a trifold menu, the hot zone is located on the upper half of the center page. (See Figure 10–1.)

Knowing the location of a menu's hot zone allows the menu designer to locate the items she most wishes to sell in the hot zone. Items there are likely to get additional

One-Page Menu   **Two-Page Menu**

Trifold Menu

Figure 10–1
Menu layouts and their hot zones.

attention from the guest and to garner a larger share of the business over time. Highly profitable items are best located in the hot zones.

Of course, menu items cannot be randomly moved throughout the menu just to put the most profitable ones in the hot zones. Menus are typically organized under headings and subheadings, listed in the order in which the courses are normally eaten. Thus, appetizers come first, soups and salads appear next, entrées follow, and desserts, if they are included on the main menu, come last. When beverages are listed on the food menu, they may be placed at the beginning (common with cocktails) or at the end of the menu (more prevalent for soft drinks). Because the courses must come in a prescribed order, menu designers may experiment with font size and the location of images to get the most profitable items in a category to end up in the hot zone. If a category falls completely outside of a hot zone, the designer at a minimum should place the items she most wishes to sell in the upper half of that menu category.

Another way to grab the customers' attention is through inserts or clip-ons. An insert is a page (usually the same size as the other menu pages) that is placed inside the menu but not bound to it. Because the insert is removable, the guest must hold and handle it separately to keep it from falling. This extra handling draws the guests' focus to the insert and to the menu items listed on it. A clip-on is a small piece of paper that provides a list of specials. It is usually attached or clipped on to the top of one of the menu pages. Because the clip-on does not lie flat on the main menu page, it, too, draws the attention of the guest. Clip-ons should never cover other menu items, as not all guests will lift the clip-on to see the options that lie beneath. Instead, the clip-on should be located over a visual image that contributes to the business's theme but is otherwise unnecessary. That way, if a clip-on is not used, the image, rather than a blank space, is visible to the customer.

Where the menu designer chooses to locate the price of each item greatly impacts sales. One cardinal rule is to keep the customers' focus on the product, not on the price. That is not to say that a menu can avoid listing the price, but the designer should not highlight, bold, or otherwise draw attention to a menu item's price. Similarly, menu items should not be listed in order of price (either highest to lowest or lowest to highest), as this pattern encourages guests to notice price differences in each subsequent menu listing. Some designers choose to list the price at the end of the menu description, so the reader must go through the entire description to get to the price. Others locate a dish's name on the left-hand side of a menu and the price on the right-hand side; the two may be connected with a dotted line. This approach informs the customers of the price but forces them to look away from the food listing if they wish to find out the price of a dish. Some guests may not look over at the prices at all.

Another approach to minimizing the impact of sticker shock on guests is to avoid listing prices in the format that most people associate with money. In most businesses, people see prices written as a dollar sign with a number, such as $9.95. Simply removing the dollar symbol or putting the numbers into words (writing "9.95" or "eighteen," for example) subtly eases the impulse some people have to bargain shop every time they see a dollar symbol.

While some operations choose to emphasize their discount prices (think 99-cent menus), the menu designer should keep in mind that drawing a guest's attention to one price will make them consider all of the prices on the menu. Thus, a fast-food establishment that tries to make every purchase seem like a bargain—99-cent menus, value meals, etc.—can successfully appeal to a price-sensitive market without undermining sales it might otherwise make. Were a table service restaurant to attempt to highlight a few discounted items, it would likely draw business away from other, more profitable sales.

Executive Chef
Matthew Revak

In an effort to showcase this area's local, agricultural treasures and support our community, we try to use local products whenever possible. The Inn at Turkey Hill works closely with Everview Farms, Wild for Salmon, Kli-Vey Farms, Tewksbury-Grace Farm and Inn to the Seasons Farm to ensure the freshest, high quality and best local ingredients available

APPETIZERS

CRAB CAKES
Served with basil pesto aioli, tomato relish, and microgreens
Ten dollars

BLACKENED AHI TUNA
Rare, seaweed salad, pickled ginger, marinated cucumbers,
wasabi paste, sesame soy sauce
Thirteen dollars

CORNMEAL CRUSTED OYSTERS
Avocado, Roma tomato, applewood smoked bacon, mache greens,
green goddess aioli, grilled brioche
Thirteen dollars

SMOKED TROUT
An individual fillet with horseradish-dill sauce
Twelve dollars

BRAISED PORK CHEEKS
Vegetables, tomatoes, herbs, Spanish Rioja, demi-glace, toasted pearl barley pilaf
Nine dollars

BACON AND EGGS
Braised pork belly, sunny side up quail eggs, creamy goat cheese grits
Seven dollars

VEGETABLE RISOTTO CAKE
Golden beet carpaccio, arugula pesto, baby mache greens
Nine dollars

1

Figure 10–2
This upscale country inn writes out its prices in words to keep the focus on the food, not the price.
Printed with the permission of Inn at Turkey Hill and Executive Chef Mathew Revak.

SOUP

BUTTERNUT SQUASH BISQUE
Szechuan style, pickled ginger, mache greens
Six dollars

GOURMET SOUP DU JOUR
Chef's choice, changes daily
Priced Accordingly

SALADS

HOUSE SALAD
Mixed greens, sliced cucumber, grape tomatoes, feta cheese, apple cider vinaigrette
Six dollars

CAESAR SALAD
Crisp romaine lettuce, house made croutons, traditional Caesar dressing
Eight dollars

SPINACH SALAD
Baby spinach, Mandarin oranges, tofu, hard boiled eggs, bacon,
creamy sesame miso dressing
Seven dollars

BABY SWISS CHARD SALAD
Baby Swiss chard, Bulls Blood beets, goat cheese, spiced peanuts,
Meyer lemon vinaigrette
Eight dollars

2

Figure 10–2
(continued)

ENTREES

Entrees may be served without sauce upon request
Please inform your server of any special dietary needs or allergies
Following each entrée is a recommended wine by the glass and by the bottle
All entrées served with potato du jour and fresh, seasonal vegetables

GROUPER
Herb and horseradish crusted, lobster sauce
Thirty-four dollars

~ Pio Pinot Grigio ~
~~ Bin #49 Bollini Pinot Grigio ~~

GRILLED HERB CHICKEN
Marinated, topped with crabmeat
Nineteen dollars

~ Pio Pinot Grigio ~
~~ Bin #56 Sycamore Lane Chardonnay ~~

WILD ALASKAN SOCKEYE SALMON
Yucca crusted, rock shrimp and roasted sweet corn sauce
Twenty-seven dollars

~ Salmon Creek Chardonnay ~
~~ Bin #56 Sycamore Lane Chardonnay ~~

PANKO CHICKEN
Prosciutto, provolone, baby spinach, gorgonzola cream
Twenty-two dollars

~ Pensfold 'Rawsons Retreat' Merlot ~
~~ Bin #13 Willamette Valley Pinot Noir ~~

ROCK SHRIMP - PUMPKIN RAVIOLI
Rock shrimp, pumpkin ravioli, pine nuts, peas, baby spinach, tomatoes, sage cream sauce
Twenty dollars

~ Sycamore Lane Chardonnay ~
~~ Bin #87 Stags Leap Viognier ~~

ROAST DUCK
Served with Cumberland sauce
Twenty-nine dollars

~ Pensfold 'Rawson's Retreat' Merlot ~
~~ Bin #22 Gorrebusto Tempranillo ~~

3

Figure 10–2
(continued)

MONGOLIAN PORK PORTERHOUSE
Garlic-wasabi sauce, pickled ginger
Twenty-four dollars

~ Pensfold 'Rawson's Retreat' Merlot ~
~~ Bin #14 Matua Valley Pinot Noir ~~

KANGAROO
Sage and savory rubbed, brandied sun-dried cherry sauce
Thirty-two dollars

~ Pensfold 'Rawson's Retreat' Merlot ~
~~ Bin #15 Pensfold 'Rawson's Retreat' Merlot ~~

PITTSBURGH FILET MIGNON
Pan blackened, herb butter, sautéed mushrooms
Thirty-seven dollars

~ Sycamore Lane Cabernet Sauvignon ~
~~ Bin #31 Greg Norman 'California Estates' Cabernet Savignon ~~

VENISON OSSO BUCCO
Root vegetables, plum tomatoes, red wine, herbs, demi-glace
Thirty dollars

~Sycamore Lane Cabernet Savignon ~
~~ Bin #12 Montevina 'Terra D'Oro' Sangiovese ~~

RIOJA–BRAISED LAMB SHANK
Rioja wine, leeks, fennel, garlic, lamb jus
Thirty-one dollars

~Sycamore Lane Cabernet Savignon~
~~Bin #32 Kendall Jackson 'Vintner's Reserve' Cabernet ~~

VEAL TENDERLOIN
Applewood smoked bacon, sauce Champignon
Thirty-three dollars

~Juan Benegas Malbec~
~~Bin #33 Bodega Benegas 'Juan Benegas' Malbec~~

GOAT CHEESE PIEROGIE
Sautéed with Vidalia onions, artichokes, tomatoes, mushrooms, and basil
Fourteen dollars

~Sycamore Lane Chardonnay~
~Bin #53 Pine Ridge Chenin Blanc-Viognier ~

4

Figure 10–2
(continued)

10.2 MENU CONSTRUCTION

With the layout determined, the menu designer next selects the type of paper and print best suited for the foodservice operation. Each business is different, and the menu should reflect the theme and feel of the establishment. A casual restaurant might use brightly colored paper with lots of photos on its menu, but to communicate a more serious food environment, an expensive restaurant would probably do better with fewer splashes of color and photos. The type of paper, kinds of images, and even the size and style of font project a certain experience to the consumer. That experience should always support the business's brand and concept.

In addition to choosing a paper's size, the menu designer can select the paper's color, weight, and texture. A designer can choose any color paper and font, but because of the contrast, the easiest to read is black lettering on a white background. A restaurant with a specific color theme might go with a similarly colored menu, but the paper should still be light and the writing dark. For example, a special Valentine's Day menu might be printed on a light pink paper with black lettering, but a deep red paper would not provide sufficient contrast for ease of reading, especially in a dimly lit restaurant. While black paper and white lettering do provide contrast, they are far more difficult to read than pages in which the light color is reserved for the background.

A paper's weight and texture impact the guests' perception of the menu. A heavy-weight paper, which often correlates to a thicker paper, communicates seriousness, while a thin paper feels flimsy in the hands. Of course, the weight may be irrelevant if the menu is slipped into a larger cover or laminated, as the guest will be unable to tell the weight of the paper under such circumstances. A paper's texture can range from coarse and bumpy to smooth and glossy. The rougher paper feels like antique parchment, which feels more substantial in the hands; it also holds type well. A glossy paper, on the other hand, works well for photos. The coarse option is often better when the guest holds the paper directly without any covering, but again, the feel of the menu must support the restaurant's concept.

The font that a menu designer chooses should be easy to read but also suggestive of the business's brand. Roman fonts, which use straight lines and simple curves with few embellishments, are the easiest to read, but they can come across as plain. Scripts and other nontraditional fonts are creative but difficult to read. It is best to reserve the suggestive but difficult-to-read fonts for menu headings while utilizing the simpler fonts for menu listings and descriptions. The business name, which customers already know when they sit down, is the best opportunity to communicate a brand through a font. As suggested earlier, the color of the type should be dark and highly contrasted with a light background.

The size of a font is as important as its style for ease of reading. Many restaurants are dimly lit to create an intimate setting for the guests. While low lighting can make conversation and dining fun, it can make reading a menu quite a challenge. Font size is measured in "points." The 11- or 12-point font of a computer word processor is easy to read in a brightly lit office but rather difficult to read in a restaurant setting. A slightly larger 12- to 14-point font is much easier for restaurant guests to read; menu headings should be even larger than that. Leading (pronounced LEHD–ing) refers to the space between lines of text. While many types of printed work can be easily read with no additional space between the lines, the low-level light of a restaurant setting calls for some additional space to aid reading.

The font size and style need not stay consistent for every word on the menu, but they should be the same for words serving the same purpose. For example, menu headings ("Appetizers," "Entrées," etc.) are often larger and of a different font than menu listings and descriptions, but all menu headings should use the same font. Menu descriptions should similarly match each other's fonts. The use of bold

Proper Use of Font Guides the Guest's Eye	Improper Use of Font Creates a Cluttered Mess
MEATS	**MEATS**
Dry-aged 14 oz **porterhouse** grilled over hickory wood and served with twice-baked potato and green beans	Dry-aged 14 oz **PORTERHOUSE** grilled over hickory wood and served with *twice*-baked potato and green beans
Seared twin **pork chops** stuffed with spinach and gruyere, topped with port wine-fig demiglace, and served with mashed sweet potato and braised cabbage	Seared twin *PORK CHOPS* *stuffed* with spinach and gruyere, topped with port wine-fig demiglace, and served with *mashed sweet potato* and braised cabbage

Figure 10–3
Proper and improper variations in typeface.

and italic typeface should be limited, so it catches the customer's eye when it does appear. Other than its use in category headings, bold or italics is often used to highlight a dish's name (for ease of ordering) when the name is embedded within the menu description or to offset a policy or notice at the bottom of the menu. Otherwise, these font adjustments should not be used. Overuse of bold, italics, and font variations creates a cluttered, disorganized menu that does not direct the gaze of the viewer effectively.

An effective way to highlight certain dishes rather than resorting to font changes is through colors, symbols, or boxes. Sometimes, a restaurant wishes to highlight its specialty. The menu designer can emphasize a particular dish simply by enclosing it in a box, so it is differentiated from the other dishes on the menu. The box may have a colored background, which makes a menu listing stand out even more. Symbols are popular tools to point out dishes that conform to certain nutritional guidelines, that are particularly spicy, or that are specialties of the house. For example, a menu designer might place a heart symbol next to the low-fat, low-sodium options or a chile pepper next to the spicy ones. Alternatively, she might place a star or other symbol next to those dishes for which the restaurant is famous. When symbols are used, they should be defined at the bottom of the menu, but the use of boxes or shading designed to highlight a dish the restaurant wishes to sell needs no further explanation. It is important to note that highlights, boxes, and symbols can be overused. If everything on the menu is a specialty, then nothing is special. Menu designers get the best results when they only highlight a couple of dishes on each menu page.

Some menu designers use images to convey the business's brand or to sell certain products. Photographs of certain dishes help the customer to understand what a dish will look like upon arrival, but menu planners must recognize that the food served must appear significantly similar to the depicted dish to avoid truth-in-menu violations. Menu photographs may portray things other than food, too. An ethnic restaurant might include a photo of the cuisine's country. An organic operation might show photos of the farms from which the ingredients are sourced. Some menu designers prefer black-and-white sketches or drawings, which are cheaper to print than color photos are, to elicit emotional responses that support the business concept. For example, a drawing of a cactus, a sombrero, and a map of Mexico might provide a sense of place in a Tex–Mex restaurant. A sketch of a school of fish or an oyster with a pearl might effectively reinforce the theme of a seafood restaurant. Whatever images are selected, the menu designer must ensure that they appear clearly on the printed menu. Blurred or difficult-to-interpret images add little to a menu and can frustrate or disorient a customer who cannot make out the image clearly.

STEPHAN PYLES

Appetizers

Ceviches:

Aji Tuna with jicama and grilled orange 10   *Bronzini* with fennel and vanilla 12

Laughing Bird Shrimp with passion fruit and coconut 10   *Lenguado* with smoked corn and sweet potato 12

Sea Scallops with creamy garlic, aji amarillo and cucumber 12   *Mixto* with spicy tomato, celery and tarragon 10

Ceviche de Hongos with black bean and lemon 10   *Merluza* with saffron pil pil and garlic croutons 10

Salmon Veracruzano with capers, green olives and jalapeños 11   *Lobster* with guayaba and avocado 22

Tasting of any Three 28

Tasting of any Six 55

Tasting of all Eight 75

Tasting of all Ten 95

($ 6 Supplement for Lobster)

Tiraditos:

Loch Duart Salmon with dill lemonette and mustard-coriander oil 10

Halibut Cheeks with spicy orange and ginger 10

Sustainable Blue Fin Tuna with lime and toasted coconut 14

Tasting of any Two 19

Tasting of all Three 28

◆

Today's Selection of Oysters   *market price*
½ dozen
1 dozen

Today's Selection of Assorted Chilled Shellfish   *market price*

★ Tamale Tart with Roast Garlic Custard, Peekytoe Crab and Smoked Tomato Sauce 16

Seared Hudson Valley Foie Gras Tacu Tacu with Bruléed Banana 19

Sea Scallops Migas with English Pea Emulsion, Spanish Chorizo and Parmesan "Snow" 16

Pressed Pork Shoulder with Grilled Pineapple Empanada and Caramelized Texas 1015s 14

Shad Roe with Scamorza-Risotta Croquette, House Bacon and Sorrel 14

Figure 10–4
This menu uses simple, tasteful stars to highlight the chef's signature dishes. Chef-Owner Stephan Pyles Concepts.

Soups and Salads

★ Stephan's Original Southwestern Caesar Salad with Jalapeño-Polenta Croutons
and Parmigiano Reggiano "Chicharron" 10

Tassiano, Barking Cat & Motley Herb Farms Salad with Asian Pear, Paula's' Scamorza Cheese
and Texas San Saba Pecan Vinaigrette 14

Garden Greens with Really Good Olive Oil, Balsamic and Spanish Sherry Vinegars

and Fleur de Sel 8

Champagne Compressed Pears with Motley Herb Farm Beets with a Hazelnut Vinaigrette, Monte Enebro Cheese,

and Tassiano Freckles Lettuce 14

Sunchoke Soup with Sunflower Truffle Oil, Bay Scallop Ceviche, and Fennel Serrano Chile Foam 14

Main Courses

Butter Poached Lobster and Short Rib Napoleon, Apple Fennel Slaw, Smoked Plum Sauce,
and Parsnip Yucca Polenta 42

Sable Cod with Black Olive on a White Bean Stew, Chorizo Foam, Grain Mustard and Rosemary
Sauce and Clams 39

Baramundi, Rutabaga Piquillo Gratin, Garlic Pure, Olive Oil Emulsion and Caper Fluid Gel with Brussel Sprout Petals and Bacon 38

Pan Seared Arctic Char, Tempura Frisée, Cauliflowers in Escabeche, Chipotle Caramel, Celery Root Purée 36

★USDA Prime Bone-In Cowboy Ribeye with Red Chile Onion Rings and Pinto-Wild Mushroom Ragout 49

USDA Prime Beef Tenderloin with Sweet Potato Purée with Mole Coloradito and Anaheim Relleno 39

Coriander-Cured Rack of Lamb with Ecuadorian Potato Cake, Haricot Verts and Cranberry Mojo 38

Herbed Ricotta Stuffed Roast Juha Ranch Chicken with Oaxacan Mashed Potatoes, and Caramelized
Onion-Chipotle Broth 28

★ *Stephan's Signature Dishes*

20% Gratuity added to parties 8 or more   *$7.00 Charge for all split Main Courses*

Figure 10–4
(continued)

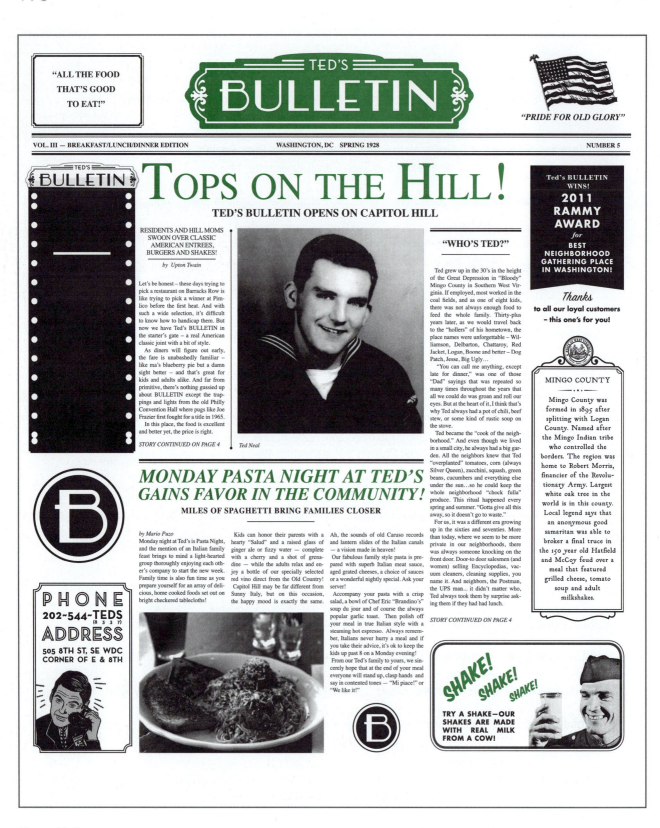

Figure 10–5

This menu uses images very effectively to support its 1930s–1950s theme, to market certain menu items, and to promote other restaurants owned by the same parent company. In the restaurant, the menu is printed and folded to resemble a newspaper or "bulletin." Property of Matchbox Food Group.

BREAKFAST
~ ANYTIME ~

THE BIG MARK BREAKFAST
~ $12.79 ~
3 eggs, 2 bacon, 2 sausages, hash browns,
toast and homemade pop tart

MARK ON AN OFF DAY
~ $8.79 ~
2 eggs, choice of meat, hash browns and toast

THE WALK OF SHAME BREAKFAST BURRITO
~ $11.79 ~
Marinated skirt steak, scrambled eggs, cheddar,
green chile sauce (yes, it's all in there)
~ served w/ hash browns

**T.U.B.S.
(TED'S ULTIMATE BREAKFAST SAMMY)**
~ $9.49 ~
Texas toast, fried egg, scrambled egg,
sausage, bacon, cheddar
~ served w/ hash browns

**NANA'S BEER BISCUITS AND
SAUSAGE GRAVY**
~ $10.29 ~
~ Served w/ 2 eggs and hash browns

JON'S OMELET
~ $11.79 ~
Mushroom, spinach and Swiss
~ served w/ hash browns and choice of meat

**PANCAKE STACK OR
THICK-CUT FRENCH TOAST**
~ $8.89 ~
~ Served w/ 2 eggs and hash browns

HOME MADE CORNED BEEF HASH
~ $10.49 ~
~ Served w/ 2 eggs your style and toast

~ A LA CARTE ~

**SUBSTITUTE TOAST WITH A POP TART,
BAGEL, MUFFIN OR CROISSANT** ~ $1.59

SERIOUS SAUSAGE PATTIES ~ $3.99

TURKEY SAUSAGE LINKS ~ $3.99

**APPLEWOOD SMOKED
BACON (3 SLICES)** ~ $2.99

GRILLED SPAM ~ $3.29

COUNTRY SMOKED HAM ~ $2.29

HASH BROWNS OR CHEDDAR GRITS ~ $2.29

CORN BREAD OR TOAST ~ $1.79

2 EGGS COOKED YOUR WAY ~ $2.79

1 BISCUIT AND CUP OF SAUSAGE GRAVY ~ $4.49

BAGEL AND CREAM CHEESE ~ $2.99

PREMIUM MIXED BERRIES ~ $4.29

HOME MADE CORNED BEEF HASH ~ $3.79

Healthy Options: Yes, we can do egg whites ~ 75¢

LUNCHTIME
~ 11AM ~
○ SOUPS ○

Everybody needs soup! Made fresh from scratch daily – cup or bowl

TED'S FAVORITE TOMATO SOUP
~ $3.29/$5.49 ~

WHITE BEAN CHICKEN CHILI
~ $4.29/$6.29 ~
~ Served with cornbread and dollop of sour cream

WORLD'S BEST CHICKEN NOODLE
~ $3.29/$5.49 ~

SOUP O' DAY
~ MARKET ~

○ SALADS ○

*Salad Dressings: 1000 Island, Blue Cheese, Green Goddess, Red Wine Vinaigrette,
Creamy Vidalia Bacon Ranch, Caesar, Orange Poppy Seed*

GREEN GREEN SALAD OF HOME
~ $6.29 ~
Egg, cucumbers, tomatoes, onions,
Kalamata olives, croutons
~ tossed lovingly with Green Goddess dressing

OLD SCHOOL CAESAR SALAD
~ $9.79 ~
Add chicken or shrimp $4.00
Romaine, house-made croutons
~ tossed w/ our anchovy Caesar dressing
(with or without anchovies on top!)

THE WEDGE
~ $6.29/$9.79 ~
Baby iceberg, egg, tomatoes, onions, bacon,
Maytag blue cheese, Gorgonzola blue dressing

PARTHENON GREEK SALAD
~ $9.79 ~
Romaine, pepperoncini, Kalamata olives,
cucumbers, feta cheese w/ grilled pita bread
~ tossed with red wine vinaigrette

CITRUS SALAD
~ $9.79 ~
Mesclun greens, orange supremes,
strawberrries, sliced almonds, goat cheese
~tossed with orange poppy seed dressing

TY COBB
~ $13.79 ~
Fried chicken, diced tomatoes,
egg, bacon, Maytag blue, pickled onions, avocados
~ choice of dressing on the side

○ SANDWICHES ○

THE SLOPPIEST JOE
~ $12.29 ~
Sesame seed bun, angus beef, cole slaw
~ served with hand-cut fries and pickle

E.B.'S BRISKET SAMMY
~ $14.29 ~
Grilled onion bun, Applewood smoked,
cider BBQ sauce
~ side of cole slaw, hand-cut fries and pickle

**TED'S FAMOUS GRILLED CHEESE
& TOMATO SOUP**
~ $9.79 ~
*See "Who's Ted" article, page 1

**CHICKEN SALAD OR
TUNA SALAD SANDWICH**
~ $9.79 ~
~ Your choice of bread with hand-cut fries and pickle.

THE REUBEN
~ $12.29 ~
Grilled marbled rye, corned beef, sauerkraut,
Swiss cheese, 1000 Island
~ served with hand-cut fries and pickle

THE BIPARTISAN COMBO
~ $9.79 ~
~On Texas toast
½ Chicken, ½ Cali Club or ½ Tuna Sandwich
with cup of soup or
½ Chicken, ½ Cali Club or ½ Tuna Sandwich
with Green Green Salad
or
Green Green Salad and a cup of soup

THE RACHEL
~ $12.29 ~
Grilled marbled rye, turkey, cole slaw, 1000 Island,
Swiss cheese
~ served with hand-cut fries and pickle

CALI CLUB
~ $12.79 ~
Toasted wheat, turkey, Applewood smoked bacon,
avocado, alfalfa sprouts, sun-dried tomato spread
~ served with hand-cut fries and pickle

Healthy Options: Make it a wrap! Ask your server.

○ BURGERS: BEEF, CHICKEN, TURKEY OR VEGGIE ○

Choose beef, chicken breast, turkey or veggie burger for all below. Served with hand-cut fries and pickle

CREATE YOUR OWN
~ $10.29 ~
Ted's Certified Angus Beef, chicken breast,
turkey or veggie burger
add cheese .50, Maytag $1.50,
add bacon $1.00, a topping or two .50 each

BLT BURGER
~ $12.29 ~
Sesame seed bun, Applewood smoked bacon,
fried green tomato, tomato mayo

THE TED'S 'BURGH
~ $12.29 ~
Toasted white bread, fried egg, fries, cole slaw,
American cheese... smash with palm

DREW'S PEANUT BUTTER BACON BURGER
~ $12.29 ~
Sesame seed bun, sweet and spicy Roma tomato
~ jam on the side

BLACK AND BLUE
~ $12.29 ~
Sesame seed bun, Maytag blue, bacon,
whole grain mustard

SOUTHWEST (WEST VIRGINIA) BURGER
~ $12.29 ~
Sesame seed bun, avocado, roasted red peppers,
green chile sauce, white cheddar

TZATZIKI GREEK
~ $13.29 ~
Grilled pita, lamb burger, feta cheese,
pepperoncini, tzatziki sauce

BREAKFAST BURGER
~ $12.29 ~
English muffin, country ham,
hash browns, fried egg,
chipotle ketchup

THE BACKYARDER
~ $12.29 ~
Sesame seed bun, bacon, potato salad,
BBQ sauce, cheddar cheese
~ this one served with Bowling Alley
Onion Rings!

HAWAII FIVE-O
~ $12.29 ~
Sesame seed bun,
grilled pineapple,
grilled SPAM,
teriyaki glaze

ALL PARTIES OF 7 OR MORE, 18% GRATUITY WILL BE ADDED.

Figure 10–5
(continued)

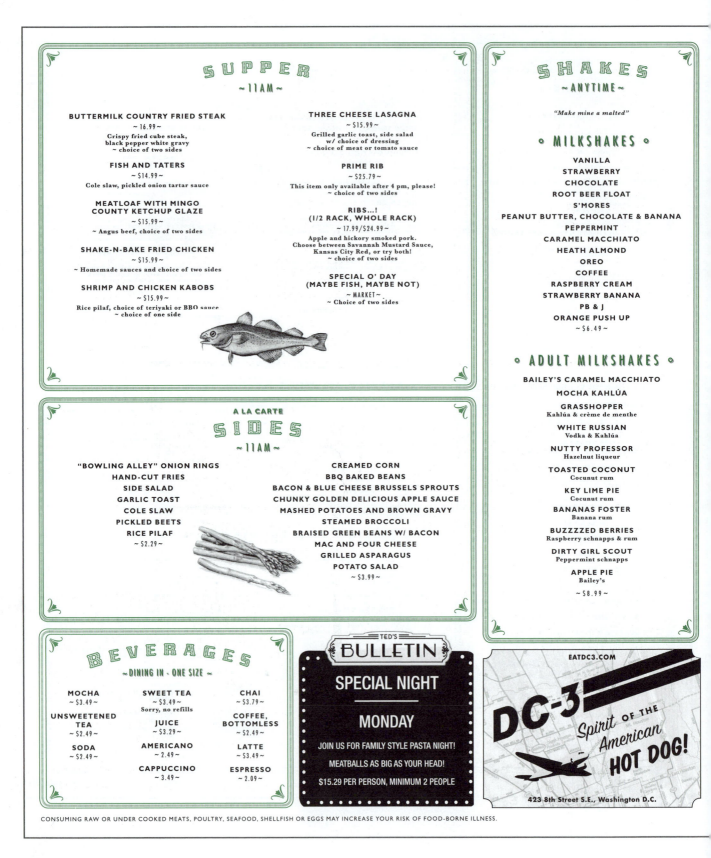

SUPPER
~ 11 AM ~

BUTTERMILK COUNTRY FRIED STEAK
~ 16.99 ~
Crispy fried cube steak,
black pepper white gravy
~ choice of two sides ~

FISH AND TATERS
~ $14.99 ~
Cole slaw, pickled onion tartar sauce

MEATLOAF WITH MINGO COUNTY KETCHUP GLAZE
~ $15.99 ~
~ Angus beef, choice of two sides ~

SHAKE-N-BAKE FRIED CHICKEN
~ $15.99 ~
~ Homemade sauces and choice of two sides ~

SHRIMP AND CHICKEN KABOBS
~ $15.99 ~
Rice pilaf, choice of teriyaki or BBQ sauce
~ choice of one side ~

THREE CHEESE LASAGNA
~ $15.99 ~
Grilled garlic toast, side salad
w/ choice of dressing
~ choice of meat or tomato sauce ~

PRIME RIB
~ $25.79 ~
This item only available after 4 pm, please!
~ choice of two sides ~

RIBS...!
(1/2 RACK, WHOLE RACK)
~ 17.99 / 24.99 ~
Apple and hickory smoked pork.
Choose between Savannah Mustard Sauce,
Kansas City Red, or try both!
~ choice of two sides ~

SPECIAL O' DAY
(MAYBE FISH, MAYBE NOT)
~ MARKET ~
~ Choice of two sides ~

A LA CARTE
SIDES
~ 11 AM ~

"BOWLING ALLEY" ONION RINGS
HAND-CUT FRIES
SIDE SALAD
GARLIC TOAST
COLE SLAW
PICKLED BEETS
RICE PILAF
~ $2.29 ~

CREAMED CORN
BBQ BAKED BEANS
BACON & BLUE CHEESE BRUSSELS SPROUTS
CHUNKY GOLDEN DELICIOUS APPLE SAUCE
MASHED POTATOES AND BROWN GRAVY
STEAMED BROCCOLI
BRAISED GREEN BEANS W/ BACON
MAC AND FOUR CHEESE
GRILLED ASPARAGUS
POTATO SALAD
~ $3.99 ~

SHAKES
~ ANYTIME ~

"Make mine a malted"

• MILKSHAKES •

VANILLA
STRAWBERRY
CHOCOLATE
ROOT BEER FLOAT
S'MORES
PEANUT BUTTER, CHOCOLATE & BANANA
PEPPERMINT
CARAMEL MACCHIATO
HEATH ALMOND
OREO
COFFEE
RASPBERRY CREAM
STRAWBERRY BANANA
PB & J
ORANGE PUSH UP
~ $6.49 ~

• ADULT MILKSHAKES •

BAILEY'S CARAMEL MACCHIATO

MOCHA KAHLÚA

GRASSHOPPER
Kahlúa & crème de menthe

WHITE RUSSIAN
Vodka & Kahlúa

NUTTY PROFESSOR
Hazelnut liqueur

TOASTED COCONUT
Cocunut rum

KEY LIME PIE
Cocunut rum

BANANAS FOSTER
Banana rum

BUZZZZED BERRIES
Raspberry schnapps & rum

DIRTY GIRL SCOUT
Peppermint schnapps

APPLE PIE
Bailey's

~ $8.99 ~

BEVERAGES
~ DINING IN · ONE SIZE ~

MOCHA
~ $3.49 ~

UNSWEETENED TEA
~ $2.49 ~

SODA
~ $2.49 ~

SWEET TEA
~ $3.49 ~
Sorry, no refills

JUICE
~ $3.29 ~

AMERICANO
~ 2.49 ~

CAPPUCCINO
~ 3.49 ~

CHAI
~ $3.79 ~

COFFEE, BOTTOMLESS
~ $2.49 ~

LATTE
~ $3.49 ~

ESPRESSO
~ 2.09 ~

TED'S
BULLETIN
SPECIAL NIGHT
MONDAY
JOIN US FOR FAMILY STYLE PASTA NIGHT!
MEATBALLS AS BIG AS YOUR HEAD!
$15.29 PER PERSON, MINIMUM 2 PEOPLE

EATDC3.COM
DC-3
Spirit of the American **HOT DOG!**
423 8th Street S.E., Washington D.C.

CONSUMING RAW OR UNDER COOKED MEATS, POULTRY, SEAFOOD, SHELLFISH OR EGGS MAY INCREASE YOUR RISK OF FOOD-BORNE ILLNESS.

Figure 10–5
(continued)

TED'S ON THE HILL

STORY CONTINUED FROM PAGE 1

Ted's corporate Art Deco features were salvaged from the Philadelphia Civic Center, circa 1928

It's a joint for Hillys of all ages and for the money, you can't get a better burger in town; No jokes here – just a good, old made in the US of A ground chuck cooked the way you like it.

Where else can you strap on the old feedbag and get Chef Eric Brannon's snappy take on a grilled cheese made for kids of all ages, bubbling hot between two slabs of the real deal – Texas Toast! Dunk it in a bowl of his homemade tomato soup and it's a runaway winner. Sure to round out as a top favorite with the fans will be hits such as the classic Cobb salad with Green Goddess dressing, meat loaf and real un-canned peas and hot cornbread on the side; With all of this on the menu, it'll be just like hitting the trifecta!

For the drop in diner and neighborhood early birds, sweets for the honeys include homemade toaster pastries, shakes, cookies and peanut butter pie. Coffee and Italian-style frothy espresso drinks won't set you back either. Venture in or rap on the takeout window for Pastry Chef Jack Revelle's homemade twinkies, ho ho's and a moon pie or two.

Finally, a real winner is the projector that grinds out flickers for the edification of elbow-benders who might be present. The movie menu includes such stalwarts as The Marx Brothers and Jimmy Stewart – and miracle of miracles – there's no cover or minimum.

You'd have to go far to do better than Ted's Bulletin; and relax – this place doesn't do trick dogs, talking dolls or assorted feats of magic. It's just a mecca for the hungry and it's damn pleasant any time of day!

BULLETIN opens daily at 7am, 7 days a week. TedsBulletin.com

TED REMEMBERED

STORY CONTINUED FROM PAGE 1

He fed them all. Simple **grilled cheese and tomato soup** was a staple, and as always – that pot was on the stove.

As kids, we were always embarrassed by this gesture, but looking back, he knew that food was a great equalizer, it was his way of keepin' it real…he firmly believed, and told us often, that he thought that making a meal, dining together, was one of the most civilized things we could do with our fellow man.

Ted would "hold court," in the kitchen or on the front porch, often with Miller Lite in hand "pontificating" with all who would join in. He was the perfect host and would've been a natural at the restaurant business. Though he never did own his own place, we have long talked about opening a place in his honor…so here we are in Washington, DC – light years from those early days. We know he would have had fun here at Ted's BULLETIN. Enjoy!

Ted was partner Mark and Ty Neal's father.

FRED HERRMANN
CAPITOL HILL
RENAISSANCE MAN

Special thanks to Director of Operations and pal, Freddie Herrmann, for sharing his entire music collection for our restaurant soundtrack. It has been speculated that Fred may have been born in the wrong musical era, favoring the sounds of the 30s and 40s to today's modern "junk" as Fred puts it.

Not so coincidentally, his name works for that era as well, somehow we can see "Freddie Herrmann and the Fred Herrmann All-Stars" on the bandstand. No small stretch, Fred was a proud member of the Washington Redskins Band for a fine ten year stint from 1987-1997, in what Fred calls "The glory days of R.F.K.!"

Just as interesting is Fred's longtime Capitol Hill association. Just across the street at the current "Frame of Mine" storefront at 522 8th Street, is the site of the former Fred Herrmann Restaurant which was in operation over 100 years ago from 1895-1905. That great building was built specifically to house the restaurant. Upon Fred's great great grandfather's passing, the letters MRS. were added to the signage, when the misses took over.

A serious piece of Capitol Hill history, with Fred keeping up the family tradition in restaurants and residence!

Figure 10–5
(continued)

10.2.1 Covers and Treatments

With the interior of the menu constructed, the menu designer must decide what cover or treatment, if any, the menu will require. Some businesses purchase permanent covers that allow for menu pages to be held inside and changed as desired. Others create menus in which the cover and content are affixed together; any change to the menu requires that the cover be reprinted as well. Still other establishments dispense entirely with covers and simply hand guests a single-page menu. Which approach the menu designer chooses depends on the company's brand and the relative permanence of the menu.

Menu covers come in a wide range of materials. Some are made of padded or synthetic leather while others are composed of hard plastic, wood, metal, or some other durable material. As with everything else related to menus, the cover should reflect the concept of the business. Leather is traditional for old-fashioned, high-end restaurants while metal may be used for a hip, modern, urban place. The front cover typically includes the business's name and logo. Sometimes the business's address, phone number, and URL are included, though these may be located on the back cover instead. When permanent covers allow for multiple iterations of the menu to be rotated within, little else should grace the cover. This provides the restaurant flexibility in changing its operation without having to purchase new covers. For example, if business hours are printed on the cover, then the restaurant cannot change its hours without paying to produce new covers. Since non-paper covers are more expensive to produce than the rest of the menu, the less frequently they are replaced, the better. Permanent menu covers should be durable, stain-resistant, and easy to clean. Even if the content on a menu cover is accurate, it must still be replaced once damaged or stained. A dirty or torn menu reflects poorly on a restaurant, and it can turn off customers who might otherwise enjoy the establishment.

There are significant benefits to using a permanent menu cover that allows for printed pages to be placed inside. With a permanent cover, a soiled menu page can be easily replaced without having to purchase an entirely new menu. Similarly, the menu planner can inexpensively print a new menu in-house every day should the chef wish to adjust the menu. This helps to keep a business compliant with truth-in-menu regulations even when an ingredient is shorted on a delivery. In short, a permanent menu cover with inserts allows for flexibility without significant expense. Menu pages may be held in place at the corners or simply slid into a transparent cover, but changing the pages does not require changing the menu cover.

When a restaurant knows that its menu will not change for months at a time, the designer has the option of printing a menu of which the cover is a permanent part. In these cases, the cover and the first page inside the cover may share a single sheet of paper. Alternatively, the menu listings may begin on the cover itself. Typically, under these circumstances, the menu designer has the menu laminated. Lamination is a clear, plastic coating sealed around each page of the menu. It usually contains two back-to-back papers to generate a single double-sided menu page. Because lamination is highly durable and easy to wipe clean, laminated menus are popular in family restaurants where the menu does not change often but spills on the menu are common. The expense of lamination, however, does not make this type of menu cost-effective in operations that change their menus daily or weekly.

Another approach to menu printing is to dispense with a cover entirely. Foodservice operations that can fit their menus on a single page may opt to print their menus without a cover. These menus may be laminated or not. They may be single- or double-sided. Without a cover to worry about, menu designers sometimes include the restaurant's name at the top of the first page, but other contact information may be

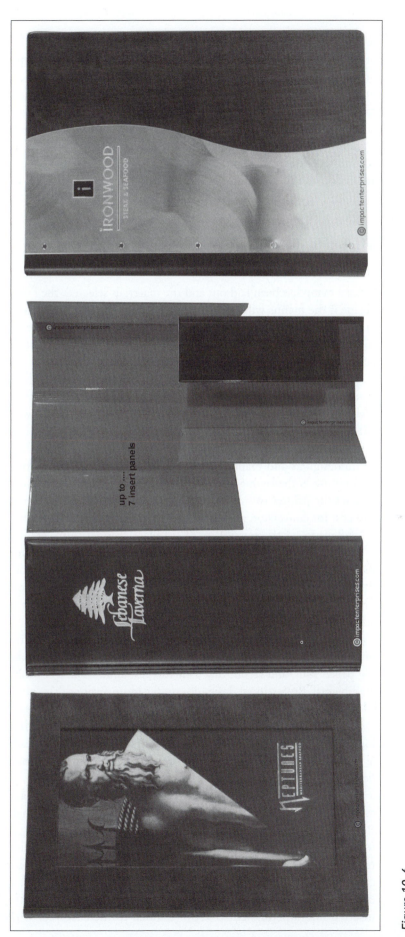

Figure 10–6

Permanent menu covers come in a wide range of materials, including these paper, faux leather, and aluminum–mahogany combination versions. Courtesy of Impact Enterprises, Inc., Warwick, NY.

omitted for space reasons. High-end operations with limited listings that change daily often prefer this style of menu. Using heavy-weight, quality paper, the menu can be printed daily and handed to the customer without a cover. The menu designer may include the date at the top and permit guests to take the menu home with them as a memento and marketing tool. Should the restaurant wish to modify the menu for certain guests—to personalize a greeting at the top for a birthday party or to include only certain items for guests with dietary restrictions, for example—the task is as easy as adjusting the menu file on the in-house computer and hitting print. Such personalized attention can vault a restaurant from an above-average operation to a must-visit special occasion destination.

10.3 PRINTING IN-HOUSE VERSUS PROFESSIONALLY

Once a menu has been laid out and the materials selected, the business's manager must decide if the menus will be printed in-house or by a professional printer. Professional printers use high-caliber machinery that can produce crystal clear images in a range of colors. They are able to die cut menus into a range of shapes, if desired, and they can laminate menus as part of the service. Of course, professional printing costs money.

The greatest challenge to using a professional printer is that printers usually use specialized software for their machines. Thus, a menu planner might design a complex menu using Microsoft Publisher only to discover that the software is not compatible with the printer's software, or that converting the document to the printer's software adjusts the layout and requires additional paid time from the printer. Professional menu designers and graphic designers usually use the same software that professional printers use. If the layout is to be done in-house, the menu planner and designer should contact the printer to find out both what software the printer uses and how much it will cost for conversion adjustments from the menu planner's software.

Because of the possibility of software compatibility error, the menu designer must confirm the accuracy of the printer's menu proof before authorizing the printer to print multiple copies. With the enormous opportunity for communication errors, the designer cannot simply assume that sending corrections to the first proof will result in a perfect menu. The designer must continue reviewing proofs until a correct one is achieved.

Professional menu designers are a valuable resource for restaurant employees unskilled in menu design. An experienced designer can make recommendations regarding paper, font, and layout that a chef or restaurant manager probably has not considered before. Professional designers are far more aware of the range of paper and font choices that exist. They are able to efficiently lay menus out electronically, whereas a restaurant professional may be more skilled with food than with a computer publishing program. Most can also design the company's logo, letterhead, and business cards as well as the menu. For many foodservice operations, the cost of a professional menu designer is well worth the investment.

That said, a menu with a fairly straightforward design can be produced quite easily in-house. When a restaurant contracts with a professional printer, the cost is significant enough that the menus should last for several months. If a restaurant wishes to change its menu daily or weekly, it should print them in-house. In-house printing requires a high-quality laser or inkjet printer to ensure that images and words read clearly. Menus printed in-house are typically done in black-and-white rather than in color, and they usually contain few, if any, images. These menus are almost always inserted into a permanent cover or handed to the customer without a cover; rarely would a restaurant laminate in-house. In-house printing still has costs in ink and paper, but these are far less expensive than asking a professional printer to reprint a menu daily to accommodate content changes. As long as a business is comfortable with a simple, straightforward menu with few images on a standard 8½" × 11" page, in-house printing is a highly cost-effective option.

10.3.1 Print Quantities

Calculating the number of menus to print depends heavily on the number of seats in the restaurant and on how long the menu is intended to last. Menus tear and stain over time, which requires that they be removed from circulation. Some guests take menus with them at the end of the meal. Employees may need a few copies to address questions of price or as training tools for new servers. While a restaurant that prints its menus daily may be fine with only enough menus to cover 25% of its seats, a restaurant that expects its menus to last for three to six months will need a much larger supply.

Typically, when a foodservice business has its menus printed professionally, it should plan on printing double or triple the number of seats in the dining room. As menus are damaged or stolen over time, the staff can pull from a backup supply to get through the future months. If a menu is only designed to last for a month, fewer copies are needed. However, if a menu is intended to last for over a year, it is still wise to stick with only enough to get through a six-month period—two to three times the number of seats. Menus must change periodically to account for market shifts and price fluctuations. A year's supply of menus may force the manager to choose between sticking with a menu that isn't generating sufficient profit after six months and throwing out clean, unused menus that are no longer effective cost control tools.

After estimating how many menus to print, the menu designer should inquire with the professional printer about price breaks for certain production quantities. Printing is usually priced per unit or per page with per page discounts over certain quantities. Thus, a printer might charge $0.06 per page for 1–499 copies but $0.05 per page for 500 or more copies. In this example, if a restaurant calculates that it needs 480 copies, it will make more financial sense to order 500. Why? 480 copies × $0.06 = $28.80 while 500 copies × $0.05 = $25.00. It is cheaper to order the larger quantity even if the extras are simply thrown away. However, if the price break occurs at a much higher quantity than the business needs, the per unit savings will not result in overall savings. For example, if a restaurant must order an extra 1,000 menus to save $0.02 per menu, the business will end up paying far more money for the printing only to end up with an abundance of out-of-date menus in less than a year.

To reduce the number of copies lost to theft, business owners should consider printing inexpensive copies of menus for customers to take with them, especially if the regular menus are costly to produce. Operations with significant take-out business, such as pizza parlors or Chinese restaurants, should have a large supply of take-out menus that are less expensive to print than the menus used for sit-down customers. Because these take-out menus are a marketing necessity to generate take-out business, these restaurants should print several thousand and encourage people to take them rather than hoarding a few to save on printing costs.

10.4 OTHER TYPES OF MENUS

Not all menus follow the same rules as those for menus handed to customers when they sit down in a restaurant. Take-out menus, for example, should be produced more cheaply, using less expensive paper than the identical menu for the same business's sit-down operation. Take-out menus may be done in color or in black-and-white, but the cost of printing should be balanced against the recognition that, for the most part, each copy of a take-out menu will be viewed by only one customer, and some will be tossed aside and never read by anyone. The best take-out menus are eye-catching and appealing, but inexpensive enough that a restaurant can afford to give out hundreds per day.

When a company transmits its menu by fax machine, the menu must be designed so that it is easy to read even after the fax transmission. A fax machine often blurs lettering, making it difficult to read. A catering company or take-out operation that sends out its menu by fax machine must ensure that the lettering on the menu is of a larger and clearer font than might be necessary otherwise. That way, even after being sent by fax, the words will still be legible, and customers will be able to place an order. If orders are also received by fax, the fax number and instructions for placing orders should be clear and obvious on the menu. Confusing instructions will result in incorrect orders and dissatisfied customers. Should those customers resort to phoning in orders instead, the process of order taking may be slowed significantly. To address the challenges with fax machines, some operations have moved to taking orders online rather than by fax machine.

Not all menus are designed to be printed and handed out to customers. A menu board is a large menu display, usually located behind an order taker in a restaurant with counter service. Menu boards can be professionally produced and printed like small billboards on hard plastic, or they can be blank slates on which restaurant managers affix plastic letters. A large chalkboard in a coffee shop is an example of a menu board, as are the translucent panels in fast-food restaurants that are rotated in and out in front of a light source to show the menu offerings for a given meal period.

The moveable type and chalkboard versions allow for easy changes at no expense. A single small change alerts all customers to a new product or price, and since there are no other printed menus to change, there is no printing cost to make the change. Professionally produced boards do not have such flexibility, but they have a more professional appearance. They can include logos, photos, and a range of colors in clearly written type. Interchangeable panels, illuminated from behind, strike a balance between professional appearance and ease of modification. Because each panel only represents a small portion of the menu, one menu change requires the production of only one new panel, not the entire board. The panels may include logos, photos, and other information that is difficult to replicate on a chalkboard. Additionally, because the panels are easy to remove or rotate, breakfast menus can shift to lunch menus in a matter of seconds. With rotating menu boards, guests know exactly what is available to order based on what is displayed on the menu board behind the cashier.

One final variation of the menu board is the electronic display. Electronic displays can be simple, single-color text lines on a larger board (as one might see at a train station or airport) or complex images on screens, like those sometimes found at movie theater concession stands. Electronic displays combine a professional appearance with incredible flexibility. To change an electronic display, the menu planner need only make an adjustment to the computer program running the display. The screen modifies the display accordingly.

Menu boards of all forms are more commonly utilized by operations in which quick service is part of the brand. Thus, menu boards are typically laid out to make ordering as quick and efficient as possible. Menu boards rarely include much in terms of menu item descriptions. In fast-food operations, they also tend to offer bundled meals that can be ordered by number. Thus, a guest who can order "meal number 3" does not slow down the service line by ordering each separate meal item a la carte. These bundled options tend to be the most prominent and heavily marketed items on the menu to encourage higher revenue and faster service speed. Regardless of the type of operation, menu boards should be easy for customers to read while standing in line to place an order. When customers can read the menu board and decide on their orders before reaching the cash register, they do not inordinately slow down the service line for those behind them.

Children's menus require another completely different approach to menu production because they are typically designed to be written upon. These menus should be prepared inexpensively, as they are single-use items. Once a child colors all over one, it cannot be used again. While colorful children's menus are attractive, black-and-white photocopies which the child colors herself are equally, if not more, effective. In these cases, the design work for creating games and activities takes some doing, but once created, they can be photocopied cheaply. The print savings are diverted instead to the cost of purchasing crayons.

Children's menus are not the only form of menu upon which guests write, however. Sushi restaurants often provide lists upon which customers write their order by marking order quantities next to each dish they wish to purchase. Room service menus work similarly, with places for guests to check off the dishes they want before hanging their order on their room's door handle. These menus can be printed as single-use copies, or they may be laminated for repeated use. Special wax pencils can be used to mark the laminated page; then, the page can be wiped clean after the order is served. (Note, because of the need for special pencils, the laminated versions are more appropriate for the sit-down sushi restaurant example than they are for room service menus.) While the laminated versions cost more to produce, fewer copies are needed. Single-use menus usually cost more over time.

Placemats in casual restaurants sometimes double as a menu. Because these are single-use items, they might call for inexpensive production. However, because the guest is staring at the placemat for quite a while at the table, most restaurants that use them put a little extra cost into the production of the placemat. To offset this cost, most sell advertising around the perimeter of the placemat and reserve the menu for the center. (Some places fill the placemat with advertising and use traditional menus for ordering.) The placemat as menu as advertising medium illustrates how creative restaurateurs cover the cost of menu printing when the opportunity makes sense with the brand.

High-end restaurants cannot avoid printing menus by selling advertising on placemats, but thanks to modern technology, a few can now combine the menu and order placement process in a single piece of electronic equipment. Small-screen, portable computers can be provided to the customer to read the menu and to place her order through a touch screen. The upfront investment in the technology can be steep, especially as a single menu theft would be quite costly, but integrated into the restaurant's point of sales system, such an approach to menu production speeds service while allowing for extreme versatility. Should a menu planner wish to modify the menu daily or even hourly, the change would require just a few keystrokes into the main computer system—no additional printing cost required. While not all customers will feel comfortable ordering through a screen, as more Americans gain comfort with handheld technology, computerized menus may become more popular.

10.4.1 Web Menus

Today, thanks to the bounty of restaurant web pages, many diners can review a restaurant's menu before they even arrive. For some operations, the menu listed on the company's web page is an exact copy of the print menu, usually in the form of a PDF file. For other businesses, the menu printed on the web page is designed solely for the web (though the content should not contradict the printed menu's text). There are pros and cons to each approach. A PDF version requires a download, which can be slow, but it is easy to store on one's own computer, to email to a friend, or to print out.

The specially designed web page menu allows for a wider range of features. In addition to faster access to the menu, web links may allow guests to jump to the menu section of their choice. If a customer wants to review dessert options, she may not have to scroll through the rest of the menu. The web menu can include things that the corresponding printed menu does not, including nutritional information and a photo for each dish. Menu planners can easily adjust a web-based menu to list daily specials, too. However, knowing that, customers expect an online menu to be constantly updated and perpetually current and accurate.

Consumers who email their friends the web address of a restaurant's online menu drive traffic to the company's web page. This peer-to-peer referral helps with the company's promotion and may expose customers to marketing on the web site beyond the menu itself. The growth of social media (and its use by businesses of all sorts) has dramatically increased the number of customers whose first encounter with a restaurant is its web site, which they find after clicking through links located on a blog or social media page. This trend means that more and more foodservice operations need to invest in professional-looking web sites to survive. Web pages work best when a customer does not have to scroll way down the page to read the entire page. To fit compactly on a screen, web menus often require the customer to click on at least one link to get to the section of the menu they want to see. This approach to menu layout results in a professional, user-friendly web page menu, but also one that works better on a screen than it does in print. The cost to develop a web-based menu page is typically more expensive than the PDF download version, but it is becoming an increasing necessity in today's plugged-in society. For those operations that want to cater both to the tech-savvy crowd and to those who prefer a printed menu, the best compromise is to offer a web-based menu and the option for downloading a printer-friendly version.

When a restaurant permits "off-site" ordering, the menu designer should consider allowing the process to occur through the business's web site. Not that long ago, fax and phone orders were the only options for ordering off-site. Today, restaurant patrons can order through a company's web page or smart phone application. These online systems should be simple, intuitive, and easy to use. If an online ordering page is too difficult to navigate, customers will not use the system; the high-tech crowd may even choose another restaurant just for the convenience of ordering online. In most cases, restaurants hire professional web designers to ensure that their online ordering system operates properly and becomes a convenience rather than a hassle for customers. As with a foodservice business's web page, a frustrating, difficult-to-navigate online service can turn a theoretically positive benefit for the public into negative PR for the company.

This chapter has included images of the print menus from Stephan Pyles Restaurant and Ted's Bulletin. Both of these operations have highly effective web sites, too. To see how they approach web menus, visit www.stephanpyles.com and www.tedsbulletin.com.

SUMMARY

Once the menu planner has all of the menu content in hand, laying out the menu is the next task. To do so, the menu planner or a menu designer selects the size and shape of the paper to yield the desired number of pages without making the menu too small or too cumbersome to hold. The items the business most desires to sell should be located in the menu's hot zones, the areas to which the eye is naturally drawn on a menu. Clip-ons and inserts also attract the guests' attention. Prices should be written and located to keep customers from focusing on pricing in their purchases. The menu's and font's color should provide high contrast for easy reading with a light background and dark text. Font size and style should be easy to read in dim lighting while supporting the business's concept. Judicious use of bold or italics can draw guests' attention to a few items on the menu; boxes and symbols work similarly. Images, such as photographs or drawings, can further support the company brand while enhancing the guest experience.

Menu covers may be constructed from a range of materials and allow for new internal menu pages to be inserted as the menu changes. Some operations prefer to laminate menus to keep them clean and reusable for months. A menu designer can opt to dispense with covers entirely. Menus may be printed in-house or professionally. Professional printing costs more, but for complex designs with images, professional printing typically results in a higher-quality product. In-house printing is better when the menu changes often. How many menus to print depends on how long the menus are intended to last before they change and on the number of seats in the dining room. Ideal print quantities may vary from a portion of the dining room capacity to two or three times the number of dining room seats. Single-use menus, such as those for children, take-out, room service breakfast, or sushi, require greater print quantities, but the extra cost may be justified by cheaper printing quality or by using these menus as direct marketing pieces.

A menu board is far more expensive than a printed menu is, but only one menu is required to service all customers. Electronic menus, which allow for menu flexibility and speed customer service, may become more popular in the near future. Web-based menus are extremely popular and excellent marketing opportunities, but they often require a different format than do print menus in order to appear user-friendly on the screen. If a company accepts orders electronically through its web site, that ordering process should be easy to use as well. All menus should be designed to appeal to the target market and to support the company's image, but within those limitations, the creative possibilities for menu design are endless.

COMPREHENSION QUESTIONS

1. Draw three examples of possible printed menu layouts and mark the hot zones on each menu.
2. List four ways to draw a guest's attention to certain menu items that are not located in a hot zone.
3. How can a menu designer write prices to keep the customers from focusing on price first?
4. Some printed documents are perfectly readable at 11-point font with no leading. Why would this arrangement not work for a printed menu?
5. List an example of a type of font that is easy to read. What kind of font is often difficult to read?
6. What qualities should a menu designer look for in a permanent menu cover intended to last for years? List three materials that would be appropriate for a permanent menu cover.
7. List one benefit to creating a laminated menu. When should a restaurant not laminate its menus?
8. List two reasons to use a professional menu designer and printer. What kind of restaurant would definitely want to print its menus in-house?
9. If a restaurant can accommodate one hundred guests in its dining room and it intends for its menu to last for six months, roughly how many menus should it have printed by a professional printer? (You may provide a range.)
10. Describe three styles of menu boards that a counter-service restaurant might use.
11. List three examples of single-use menus.
12. How does a web page menu typically differ from a printed menu?

DISCUSSION QUESTIONS

1. Imagine that you are designing a permanent menu cover. What would you include on the front of the cover (if anything)? What would you include on the back of the cover (if anything)? Explain your answer and note two pieces of information you would not include on the cover.

2. A New Orleans–themed restaurant is decorated in purple, green, and gold—Mardi Gras colors. The menu planner wishes to have a creative menu that reflects their concept. How would you recommend incorporating these colors and this concept into the menu? State one example of a bad approach to incorporating the colors into the menu.

3. A seafood restaurant has a large menu and a diverse market of customers. Among the menu options are three dishes that the owner wishes to highlight, as each appeals to a different segment of the market. The crab cakes are their most famous dish, and they have been highlighted in every restaurant review of the place. The heart-healthy poached scallops are intended to satisfy the older clientele. The broiled lobster is the most profitable dish on the menu. As the menu designer, you can use symbols, boxes, and hot zones on the menu. Which of these three techniques would you use for each dish? Why? (Recommend a different technique for each dish.)

4. You are a menu designer for a Mexican restaurant. You are trying to decide between laminated menus and menus with exposed paper inserts attached at the corners of a permanent cover. What information would you want to know to help you make an informed decision?

5. This chapter describes the possibility of menus displayed on a handheld screen and provided to customers to make their own selections—not particularly different from what many people do on a smart phone. What potential problems would you envision with such an approach to menus? (List three.) What steps or procedures could a manager take to address those problems?

6. Think of a restaurant you enjoy. Visit its web page and look at its menu. How user-friendly is the site? How does the web menu differ in format (if at all) from the printed menu at the restaurant? What changes, if any, would you recommend this operation make to its online menu or to its web site in general?

11

Evaluation: Menu Analysis and Adjustment

Once a menu has gone to print and is ready for distribution to customers, menu planners consider the menu finished. But a menu is never a permanent fixture for a business. It is designed for a specific period of time. Like the food it offers, a menu has a shelf life, and once it has outlived its value, it must be created anew. A revised menu may be necessary to adapt to changing tastes or to update prices. Some restaurants change their menus seasonally while others may not adjust their menus for two or three years. The frequency with which a business modifies its menu depends in part on the business concept and in part on the stability of the customer market and ingredient prices. Over time, every foodservice business must change its menu to remain profitable.

Of all the information that a menu planner should consider when updating a menu, the menu's profitability is perhaps the most important. Some items inevitably bring in more profit than others. However, removing less profitable items and adding high-margin ones is a simplistic and often unsuccessful approach to menu modification. Customers come to a foodservice operation in part because they like certain menu offerings. Removing low-profit, popular items from a menu may result in a menu that makes more money per customer but brings in fewer customers; the result may be a less profitable business overall. Both popularity and profitability of menu items must be considered in tandem to maximize a foodservice business's profit.

After a menu planner evaluates a menu's performance, he can adjust the menu in many ways. Sometimes the best approach is to add and remove dishes entirely, but often a menu can be made more profitable through subtle changes to menu descriptions, sales prices, and menu layout. The process of analyzing a menu is fairly straightforward, but how to address each identified problem is completely up to the menu planner's professional judgment and experience. A good menu planner can generate a profitable menu for a business's opening day. A great menu planner knows that even the best menu's profitability will wane over time and that the best way to maintain company profits is to evaluate and update a menu as it approaches the end of its useful life. Learning how to analyze a menu for popularity and profitability as well as how to use that information to modify a menu is a key requirement for any future menu planner.

By the end of this chapter, you will be able to:

- Perform a menu analysis to calculate each menu item's popularity and profitability
- Adjust a menu to increase the overall profitability of a foodservice business
- Describe the value of a point-of-sales system in conducting a menu analysis

11.1 MENU ANALYSIS

Periodically, every menu should be reviewed by a menu planner or by a business's manager. Some menu items that seem like a good idea when the menu is first created may lose their luster over time. There is simply not enough space on a menu for some menu items not to pull their own weight toward keeping the business profitable. Technically, the sale of a menu item does not generate profit; instead, it yields a contribution margin. The contribution margin of an item is its sales price minus its food (or beverage) cost. Mathematically,

Contribution Margin = Sales Price – Food (or Beverage) Cost

Every foodservice business has fixed costs and variable costs. The variable costs are those that increase with each sale. Food cost is an example of a variable cost since the business's food cost goes up as more food is sold. Fixed costs do not change with the amount of sales. Rent, salaries, and insurance are examples of fixed costs, as they must be paid in the same amount each month whether the company serves one customer or one million customers. The contribution margin generated from the sale of each item goes first toward covering fixed expenses for the month, then toward building profit.

Depending on the size of a menu item's contribution margin, a dish may help a business pay off its fixed costs and generate profits quickly or slowly. For example, imagine a restaurant with two menu items—the first with a contribution margin of $1 and the second with a contribution margin of $10. It takes ten sales of the first menu item to cover as much fixed cost expense as the business earns from just one sale of the second menu item. Thus, foodservice managers refer to items with higher contribution margins as being more profitable than items with lower contribution margins.

Even if all menu items have the exact same food cost percentage, items with different food costs in dollars will have different contribution margins.

Example 11.1: What are the contribution margins for a hamburger with a food cost of $1.25 and a steak with a food cost of $3.18 if both have sales prices based on a food cost of 30%?

First, calculate the sales price for each item using the formula

Sales Price = Food Cost ÷ Food Cost%

Sales Price (hamburger) = $1.25 ÷ 0.30 = $4.17

Sales Price (steak) = $3.18 ÷ 0.30 = $10.60

Next, calculate the contribution margin.

Contribution Margin (CM) = Sales Price – Food Cost

CM (hamburger) = $4.17 – $1.25 = $2.92

CM (steak) = $10.60 – $3.18 = $7.42

In Example 11.1, even though the two items both have a 30% food cost percentage, the steak generates a contribution margin of $7.42 to cover fixed costs and profit while the hamburger only generates $2.92—a difference of $4.50. This business would make far more money in profit selling only steaks than if it sold only hamburgers.

However, rarely can a restaurant survive selling just a single product. Most sell a mix of items. The *menu mix* is a statement of the number of each menu item sold over a period of time. Menu mix is often stated in percentages, so each item is expressed as a percentage of total items sold.

A balanced menu mix in which menu items sell in equal quantities provides some benefits to a business. No single station is overly taxed with orders, and all of the ingredients in inventory move quickly with none languishing unused for a long period of time. However, a perfectly balanced menu mix is not necessarily highly profitable. Because each menu item generates a different contribution margin, increasing sales of those items with the highest contribution margins will increase the menu's overall profitability.

Menu analysis is a system for analyzing each menu item's profitability and popularity against the average of all of the menu items. Each item is scored as high or low profitability and high or low popularity. Once a menu planner knows how each item rates, he is better able to tweak a menu to make it more profitable.

The data used to conduct a menu analysis is easily compiled from sales records and recipe costing sheets. As a single unusual sales day can skew the data, it is best to use sales and costing data over a period of several months, not days or weeks, to minimize the impact of any anomalies.

The process to conduct a menu analysis can be complex, so the computations for calculating an item's popularity and profitability are described separately below.

11.1.1 Popularity

The first step in conducting a menu analysis is to determine the relative popularity of each menu item. While it is possible to compare any item to any other menu item, the best comparison is between items from the same menu category. For example, almost everyone who patronizes a restaurant orders an entrée. If a menu planner were trying to decide which dishes to remove or to modify, is it helpful to know that each entrée sells better than the best-selling appetizer? No. A menu planner would be foolish to constantly replace appetizers and leave the entrée selections alone in order to increase sales. Guests looking to eat a full meal will not stop ordering entrées to purchase appetizers instead, no matter how good the appetizers sound. A more valuable analysis would compare entrées to other entrées and appetizers to other appetizers.

To calculate whether a menu item is an above-average or below-average seller within its category, a menu planner must first determine the average number of each item sold within that category. To do so, the menu planner begins with a chart listing each of the menu items and how many of each are sold over a period of time—usually one or more months. Each menu category is considered separately. The average number sold is calculated by totaling the number of items sold in a category and dividing by the number of menu listings in the category. Table 11–1 illustrates this process for a set of entrées.

Table 11–1A shows that there are seven entrées available for sale. Over the examined period, 6,025 entrées are sold. Calculating 6,025 (the total number of entrées sold) ÷ 7 (the number of entrée choices on the menu) = 860.7 (the average number of each entrée sold).

Now a menu planner can easily see if a given menu item is an above-average or below-average seller for its category. However, a strict above- or below-average delineation is somewhat unfair for a measurement of popularity. For example, consider a menu in which the average number of each item sold is 400. Should a menu item that sells 401 units be considered popular while one that sells 399 units is considered

TABLE 11–1A
MENU ANALYSIS—NUMBER OF EACH ITEM SOLD

Menu Item	Number Sold
Chicken	1,380
Beef	1,092
Pork	881
Lamb	600
Salmon	905
Crab	746
Vegetarian	421
Total	6,025

Average Number of Each Item Sold 6,025 ÷ 7 = 860.7
(total ÷ number of offerings)

unpopular? Mathematically, not every item can have above-average sales. A menu planner would make a serious error to change certain menu offerings with relatively equal sales quantities simply because some fall a couple of units below average and others fall a couple of units above average.

To change the focus from theoretical math to something statistically significant, the industry labels "popular" any item selling at a rate of at least 70% of the average number of each item sold. Thus, it is possible to have a menu in which all items are considered highly popular. Only those items with sales below 70% of the average number are considered to have low popularity.

Calculating the 70% industry standard is simple. To do so, multiply the average number of each item sold by 70% or 0.7. The resulting figure is referred to as the *popularity benchmark*. Any item with unit sales above the popularity benchmark is considered popular (high popularity) and any item with unit sales below it is labeled unpopular (low popularity). Table 11–1B shows the popularity benchmark for the menu presented in Table 11–1A and labels each entrée as high (H) or low (L) popularity.

In Table 11–1B, the popularity benchmark is the average number of each item sold 860.7 × 0.7 = 602.5. Any item that sells more than 602.5 units is labeled high popularity. Every item with sales below 602.5 is labeled low popularity. In this example, the lamb and the vegetarian entrées are the only two items considered to have low popularity.

11.1.2 Profitability

Identifying the popular and unpopular dishes is only half of the equation. Menu planners must also know if a dish has an above-average or below-average contribution margin. A popular dish that is not particularly profitable is just as much of a problem as a highly profitable but unpopular dish. To calculate a menu item's

TABLE 11–1B
MENU ANALYSIS—CALCULATING POPULARITY

Menu Item	Number Sold	Popularity (H/L) (based on number sold above or below 602.5, the popularity benchmark)
Chicken	1,380	H
Beef	1,092	H
Pork	881	H
Lamb	600	L
Salmon	905	H
Crab	746	H
Vegetarian	421	L
Total	6,025	
Average Number of Each Item Sold (total ÷ number of offerings)	860.7	
Popularity Benchmark (Average × 0.7)	860.7 × 0.7 = 602.5	

relative profitability, the menu planner must first calculate each item's contribution margin. Recall,

Contribution Margin = Item Sales Price − Item Food (or Beverage) Cost

Table 11–1c provides the sales price and food cost for each entrée from the Table 11–1 series. This information comes from recipe costing sheets and menu sales prices. The final column calculates each item's contribution margin. (The popularity column has been removed for ease of instruction and will be returned to the table later in the process.)

With the item contribution margin calculated for each item, the menu planner must next calculate each item's menu contribution margin, which factors in the number of units sold.

Menu Contribution Margin = Item Contribution Margin
× Number Sold (for that item)

The menu contribution margins can be summed to determine the total menu contribution margin earned from the sales of these menu items over the period measured. This total menu contribution margin is the amount of money from the entire menu category (entrées, for the Table 11–1 series) that went to cover fixed expenses and profit during the period in question.

Table 11–1d illustrates the process of computing each item's menu contribution margin and the total menu contribution margin for these entrées.

There are a couple of things to notice from the menu contribution margin calculations in Table 11–1d. First, every single item contributes some money to cover fixed costs and profit for this operation. Thus, the purpose of menu analysis is not to determine which items are not profitable, as all of them are profitable to some degree,

TABLE 11–1c
MENU ANALYSIS—ITEM CONTRIBUTION MARGINS

Menu Item	Number Sold	Item Sales Price	Item Food Cost	Item Contribution Margin (item sales price − item food cost)
Chicken	1,380	$11.95	$3.47	$8.48
Beef	1,092	$19.00	$5.22	$13.78
Pork	881	$14.50	$4.51	$9.99
Lamb	600	$21.00	$6.29	$14.71
Salmon	905	$16.25	$4.88	$11.37
Crab	746	$19.00	$5.26	$13.74
Vegetarian	421	$9.95	$2.30	$7.65
Total	6,025			
Average Number of Each Item Sold (total ÷ number of offerings)	860.7			
Popularity Benchmark (Average × 0.7)	602.5			

TABLE 11–1D
MENU ANALYSIS—MENU CONTRIBUTION MARGINS

Menu Item	Number Sold	Item Sales Price	Item Food Cost	Item Contribution Margin	Menu Contribution Margin (number sold × item contribution margin)
Chicken	1,380	$11.95	$3.47	$8.48	$11,702.40
Beef	1,092	$19.00	$5.22	$13.78	$15,047.76
Pork	881	$14.50	$4.51	$9.99	$8,801.19
Lamb	600	$21.00	$6.29	$14.71	$8,826.00
Salmon	905	$16.25	$4.88	$11.37	$10,289.85
Crab	746	$19.00	$5.26	$13.74	$10,250.04
Vegetarian	421	$9.95	$2.30	$7.65	$3,220.65
Total	6,025				$68,137.89 (total menu contribution margin)
Average Number of Each Item Sold	860.7				
Popularity Benchmark	602.5				

but rather to see if there is a way to generate more profit from the menu as a whole. Second, there is not a direct correlation between the most popular items and their menu contribution margins, nor is there a direct correlation between the most profitable items and their menu contribution margins. This restaurant sells far fewer lamb than pork entrées, yet the lamb has a greater menu contribution margin. Additionally, the lamb has a much higher item contribution margin than the chicken does, but the more popular chicken generates a higher menu contribution margin than the lamb does. In short, to determine just how profitable a menu item truly is, a menu planner must consider both a menu item's popularity and its relative profitability.

To determine each menu item's relative profitability, the menu planner must first calculate the average weighted menu contribution as follows:

Average Weighted Menu Contribution = Total Menu Contribution Margin ÷ Total Number of Items Sold

Using the information in Table 11–1D, the average weighted menu contribution is $68,137.89 (total menu contribution) ÷ 6,025 (total number of items sold) = $11.31.

Finally, each menu item's contribution margin is measured against the average weighted menu contribution to determine its relative profitability. For example, from Table 11–1D, the item contribution margin for chicken is $8.48, below the average weighted menu contribution of $11.31. Thus, the chicken is labeled as having a low profitability. The item contribution margin for beef, on the other hand, is $13.78, well above $11.31, so beef is rated as highly profitable. Table 11–1E compares each item contribution margin to the average weighted menu contribution margin to categorize each dish as high or low profitability. The popularity column has been returned to the table to create a single summary menu analysis chart.

TABLE 11–1E
MENU ANALYSIS—COMPLETE

Menu Item	Number Sold	Item Sales Price	Item Food Cost	Item Contribution Margin	Menu Contribution Margin	Popularity (H/L)	Profitability (H/L)
Chicken	1,380	$11.95	$3.47	$8.48	$11,702.40	H	L
Beef	1,092	$19.00	$5.22	$13.78	$15,047.76	H	H
Pork	881	$14.50	$4.51	$9.99	$8,801.19	H	L
Lamb	600	$21.00	$6.29	$14.71	$8,826.00	L	H
Salmon	905	$16.25	$4.88	$11.37	$10,289.85	H	H
Crab	746	$19.00	$5.26	$13.74	$10,250.04	H	H
Vegetarian	421	$9.95	$2.30	$7.65	$3,220.65	L	L
Total	6,025				$68,137.89		
Average Number of Each Item Sold	860.7						
Popularity Benchmark	602.5						
Average Weighted CM (total menu CM ÷ number of items sold)	$11.31						

As the process for conducting a menu analysis can be quite unwieldy for the novice menu planner, below is a summary of the steps to conduct a menu analysis.

Step 1: Using sales data, total the number of items sold in a given menu category. Then calculate the average number of each item sold utilizing the formula (separately for each menu category):

Average Number of Each Item Sold = Total Items Sold
÷ Number of Choices on the Menu

Step 2: Multiply the Average Number of Each Item Sold by 70% or 0.7 to yield the popularity benchmark.

Step 3: Label each menu item as high or low popularity based on whether its number of units sold is higher or lower than the popularity benchmark.

Step 4: From recipe costing sheet and menu sales price information, calculate each menu item's contribution margin using the formula:

Item Contribution Margin = Item Sales Price − Item Food (or Beverage) Cost

Step 5: Calculate each item's menu contribution margin using the formula:

Menu Contribution Margin = Number Sold (for an item)
× Item Contribution Margin (for that item)

Step 6: Total all of the menu contribution margins for the category. Then, calculate the average weighted menu contribution using the formula:

$$\text{Average Weighted Menu Contribution} = \text{Total Menu Contribution Margin} \div \text{Total Number of Items Sold}$$

Step 7: Label each item as high or low profitability based on whether its item contribution margin is higher or lower than the average weighted menu contribution.

11.2 MENU ANALYSIS CATEGORIES

Determining a menu item's relative popularity and profitability is no mere theoretical exercise. The menu planner should use this information to determine what, if any, changes to make to a menu to make it more profitable overall. The goal is to increase profit without reducing revenue or losing customers—no small feat when a menu undergoes a major overhaul. Subtle changes can direct sales to more profitable items or make the less profitable ones more profitable. Low profit and popularity dishes may need serious reworking, but their role on the menu should not necessarily be abandoned.

Before deciding what to do about each individual menu item, the menu planner should first divide the menu items into categories based on their menu analysis scores. With only two variables (popularity and profitability) and two possible results (high and low) for each, menu analysis classifies all menu items as one of four types. Rather than constantly referencing a dish's popularity and profitability, the industry uses more colorful terms to denote each of the four menu analysis categories.

Star A star is a dish that possesses both high popularity and high profitability. From the menu planner's perspective, this dish is doing everything right. It sells well and generates a lot of profit for the business. In general, these dishes should be left alone (though adjustments to other menu items will inevitably impact the sale of stars). In Table 11–1E, the beef, salmon, and crab entrées are all stars.

Plowhorse A plowhorse is a dish with high popularity but low profitability. This creates a conundrum for the menu planner that often requires further research. The goal is to make the plowhorses more profitable without reducing the number sold, but low profitability may be the exact reason that a plowhorse is popular. If a plowhorse attracts lots of customers to the business because they recognize the plowhorse as a value, it may be best to modify the dish only slightly or to leave it alone entirely. These customers may end up purchasing highly profitable beverages or other courses while dining. However, if the plowhorse is popular because of suggestive selling by servers or because of its location on the menu, it may allow for greater flexibility in price and portion size. To make a plowhorse more profitable, the menu planner can increase its sales price or reduce its portion size slightly. Too great a change may turn off customers, but small changes may be accepted readily.

If a plowhorse is located in the menu's hot zone or highlighted with a box or icon, the menu planner should consider a possible change. By highlighting or relocating more profitable items that are not selling as well, a menu planner could squeeze higher profits out of the same menu offerings. Still, the menu planner must be careful not to reduce overall business in the process. If a restaurant is known for one of its plowhorses—i.e., a signature dish—emphasizing that dish may be a necessity to attract and retain a growing customer base. In Table 11–1E, the chicken and the pork are plowhorses.

Puzzle A puzzle has low popularity but high profitability. The challenge for the menu planner in this situation is to increase sales of the puzzles without decreasing their profitability. Because these dishes are already less popular, there is less risk of losing large numbers of customers by changing a puzzle. Increasing the portion size or decreasing the selling price of a puzzle eats away at its profitability, so this approach should be used only if the food cost or sales price of the puzzle is way out of line compared to the other dishes on the menu. A better approach is to sell and market puzzles heavily. Menu planners may consider relocating a puzzle to the menu's hot zone or rewriting the menu description to make the dish sound more appealing. The menu planner might put a box or other highlight around the puzzle to attract the attention of customers. Suggestive sales pitches by the servers also help to drive sales of puzzles.

Depending on the style of service, perhaps a change in presentation or sample portions would help to drive sales of puzzles. For example, a dish with a lackluster presentation could draw the interest of other guests in the dining room just from a rearrangement of the dish's components. The same is true for items presented on a cafeteria line. If a chef believes that customers would order the puzzle repeatedly if they just tried it once, he might consider providing free samples to regular customers, especially those ordering less profitable dishes. Similarly, the company could try to build a loyal fan base for a puzzle by offering it at a reduced price as a special or through a coupon promotion. If customers love the dish, they may return to buy it another day at full price. In Table 11–1E, the lamb is a puzzle.

Dog A dog is low in both popularity and profitability. It is the biggest drag on a menu's ability to increase total profits. Its ingredients take up space in inventory, and cooks spend time preparing a dish that does not sell particularly well. Worse, the dog takes up menu space that could be devoted to a more profitable dish. The first step in dealing with a dog is to determine the role that the dog plays on the menu. Is it a random dish that does not belong on the menu, or is it there to appeal to a specific segment of the market that might not otherwise patronize the establishment? For example, a chicken dish at a seafood restaurant allows larges parties to dine there when a single guest with a seafood allergy might otherwise require the entire group to eat elsewhere. A vegan dish on a menu that includes animal products in all of its other dishes serves the same purpose.

Whether the dog serves a specific purpose or is simply inappropriate on the menu, the menu planner should first figure out how to increase the dish's contribution margin, so the dog becomes a puzzle. The dog might be modified to reduce its food cost, or increase its sales price, or both. Alternatively, the dog could be replaced entirely by another dish as long as the market segment the dog serves continues to have viable options on the menu. Once the dog has been converted into a puzzle, the selling and marketing approaches appropriate for puzzles may be implemented. What a menu planner should not do is attempt to increase sales of a dog without first addressing its low profitability. To do so might pull sales from more profitable stars and puzzles, which in turn reduces the menu's overall profitability. In Table 11–1E, the vegetarian entrée is a dog.

Within each category there are further subtle differences to consider. For example, two plowhorses may be ranked as low profitability, but one is likely to be more profitable than the other. If a menu planner cannot make either plowhorse more profitable, he might consider directing sales from the less profitable to the more profitable plowhorse. Such a change will improve the menu's profitability overall. Similar adjustments can be made within each menu analysis category through the relocation of items on the menu; the reassignment of icons, boxes, and other highlights; and the redirection of suggestive selling programs. For example, dogs are typically thought of as more problematic than plowhorses; however, a dog could have a higher contribution margin

DAILY SPECIALS

MONDAY
Meatloaf

_____

TUESDAY
Paris Bistro

_____

WEDNESDAY
Little Italy

_____

THURSDAY
Rack of Lamb

_____

FRIDAY
Fish on Friday

_____

SATURDAY
Date Night

_____

SUNDAY
Chicken Dinner

_____

Figure 11–1
This restaurant menu from 2011 was due for a menu analysis and possible updating. Figure 11–2 shows how the menu changed in 2012. Chef Ris Lacoste.

APPETIZERS

Asparagus and Gingered Grapefruit Salad
with sesame, scallion and miso vinaigrette   10

Scallop Margarita
lime marinated scallops with chiles, orange, avocado and tequila ice   16

Grilled Octopus Salad
feta and cucumber, cured lemon, spinach and yogurt   12

Spicy Shrimp Tempura
on napa cabbage slaw with yuzu and pea shoots   15

Gnudi
fresh ricotta dumplings on tomato and eggplant fondue
with spinach and crisp prosciutto   12

Bowl of Mussels
with tomato, chorizo, garlic, herbs and grilled bread   13

Caesar
escarole and romaine with lemon anchovy vinaigrette
and Parmesean aioli   9

Greens
crisp greens and herbs with Champagne Dijon vinaigrette
and shaved Parmesean   9

Spinach Salad
fresh goat cheese, sherried beets, candied walnuts and sunflower seeds
honey mustard and sherry vinaigrette   9

small PLATES
Charcuterie, Sausage, Cheese & Crudos

Figure 11–1
(continued)

Chef's Selection

ENTRÉES

Grilled Veal Chop
on artichoke cream with white beans, escarole,
grilled red onion and tomato vinaigrette   38

Pan Roasted Alaska Halibut
with warm potato salad, olives, pickled onions,
cured lemon, Parmesan cream and pine nuts   28

Sesame Crusted Salmon
with gingered beets, bok choi, soba noodles
and red curry coconut broth   25

Grilled Brace of Quail
on creamy polenta with a fava bean and spring mushroom ragout,
bourbon cherry sauce   26

Grilled Whole Lemon Salted Branzino
with fennel salad and salsa verde,
caper-olive oil potato with chopped egg   28

Glazed Beef Short Ribs and Barley
with grilled spring vegetables, piquillo pepper sauce
goat cheese and citrus herb butter   28

Spinach, Caramelized Onion and Gruyère Quiche
with your choice of side salad or frites   16

Cheeseburger
daily ground beef with cheese of your liking,
special sauce and onion jam   10
with your choice of side   16

Figure 11–1
(*continued*)

Maltagliati Pasta
with garden Swiss chard, pine nuts, lemon, roasted tomato,
and goat cheese   19

Braised Lamb Shank
on chick peas, with yogurt, pita, pomegranate, mint and
pine nuts   26

 SIDES
6

French Fries
Garlic Spinach
Side Salad
Escarole
Chick Peas
Gingered Beets and Bok Choi
Caper Olive Oil Potatoes
Swiss Chard
Lemon Barley
Asparagus
Creamy Polenta

Figure 11–1
(continued)

❧ small PLATES ❧

CHARCUTERIE
8

chilled spring lamb sausage with raita, cured lemon and pomegranate

pork rillettes classically with cornichons and Dijon mustard

duck prosciutto and duck pastrami
with oranges, balsamic glaze and market salad

chicken liver parfait with cherry mostarda and grilled brioche

FISH
8

pickled herring with beet vinaigrette, dill crème fraîche potatoes,
brown bread and apple horseradish cream

smoked trout panna cotta with citrus crème fraîche
and smoked steelhead trout caviar

miso salmon tartare with chile dressing, cucumber yuzu slaw
and shrimp crisps

CHEESE
5

served with honey comb, house made jams, crackers and toast
Chef's Daily Selections

SIDES
6

French Fries	Garlic Spinach
Side Salad	Asparagus
Calasparra Rice	Chick Peas
Mushrooms	Swiss Chard
Almond Wild Rice	Spring Vegetable Medley

Figure 11–2
This is the 2012 version of the restaurant menu referenced in Figure 11–1. Notice that certain dishes have been retained (though sometimes moved) on the menu. Other dishes have gotten modified menu descriptions or prices, and still others have been replaced entirely.
Chef Ris Lacoste.

Before 6:30pm & After 10:00pm

Chef's Soup of the Day

Swiss Chard and Leek Ravioli
with walnut-wheatberry pesto, red peppers and goat cheese

Greens
crisp greens and herbs with Champagne Dijon vinaigrette
and shaved Parmesan

Mustard Crusted Salmon
on a spring vegetable ragoût of asparagus, English peas, mushrooms
and fava beans on artichoke cream
with savory roasted potatoes and mustard seed vinaigrette

Maltagliati Pasta
with spinach, eggplant, tomato, pine nuts and raisins,
fresh ricotta and olive grilled bread

Portuguese Grilled Skirt Steak
served classically with rice, fries, garlic chips, pickled peppers,
blackened onions and an over easy egg

House-Made Ice Cream & Sorbet
with cookies

Butterscotch Pudding
with chocolate sorbet and cocoa crisps

$35

Figure 11–2
(continued)

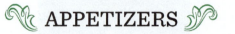

APPETIZERS

Asparagus and Gingered Grapefruit Salad
with sesame and miso vinaigrette 12

Grilled Octopus Salad
feta and cucumber, cured lemon, spinach and yogurt 14

Spicy Shrimp Tempura
on napa cabbage slaw with yuzu dressing 15

Swiss Chard and Leek Ravioli
with walnut-wheatberry pesto, red peppers and goat cheese 14

Bowl of Mussels
with tomato, chorizo, garlic, herbs and grilled bread 14

Scallop Margarita
lime marinated scallops with chilies, orange, avocado and tequila ice 16

Crispy Soft Shell Crab
with braised rhubarb and spring onion salad,
red curry yogurt, lime salted cashews 14

Spinach Salad
with apricots, almonds, cherries, sherry vinaigrette,
blue cheese and pancetta cream 12

Caesar
hearts of romaine and escarole with lemon anchovy vinaigrette,
Parmesan cream and garlic toast 9

Greens
crisp greens and herbs with Champagne Dijon vinaigrette
and shaved Parmesan 9

Figure 11–2
(continued)

ENTRÉES

Portuguese Grilled Skirt Steak
served classically with rice, fries, garlic chips, pickled peppers,
blackened onions and an over easy egg 28

Mustard Crusted Salmon
on a spring vegetable ragoût of asparagus, English peas, mushrooms
and fava beans on artichoke cream
with savory roasted potatoes and mustard seed vinaigrette 28

Jumbo Lump Crab Cakes
on roasted corn, jalapeño and bacon ragout,
with chile pasilla sauce 30

Maltagliati Pasta
with spinach, eggplant, tomato, pine nuts and raisins,
fresh ricotta and olive grilled bread 21

Breast of Muscovy Duck
with smoked Spanish paprika, almond wild rice,
sweet and sour cherry orange sauce and pan braised endive 32

Cheeseburger
daily ground beef with cheese of your liking,
special sauce and onion jam 12
with your choice of side 18

Pan Seared Sea Scallops
with toasted farro, glazed radish, celery and carrot cream 27

Braised Lamb Shank
on chickpeas, with yogurt, pita, pomegranate, mint and pine nuts 27

Figure 11–2
(*continued*)

than a plowhorse, even though both possess a below-average contribution margin. Were the menu planner to direct sales from the plowhorse to the dog, the menu would increase its profit generation.

Such menu changes are subtle. When a foodservice operation chooses to overhaul its entire menu, it should consider retaining at least a few stars from the original menu to ensure a stable market of customers willing to buy highly profitable dishes. Even menus that adjust with the seasons often maintain elements of their most popular dishes to keep the food recognizable and appealing for their most loyal customers.

Finally, it should be stressed that increasing profits is a process that goes beyond strict menu analysis computations. On paper, it might seem that the way to maximize a menu's profitability is to reduce the menu to one choice in each category—the items with the highest contribution margins. While such an approach would maximize the amount of profit made per customer, it would sacrifice long-term profits for a short-sighted view. Too limited a menu will drive away customers who might otherwise patronize the establishment. While those guests might not order the most profitable dishes, every dish on the menu generates some contribution margin. Unless a dish is priced below its variable cost or a restaurant has more customers than it can accommodate, it is always better to have more customers ordering anything from the menu than it is to lose customers in an attempt to drive them toward more profitable dishes.

Incidentally, a menu should never offer a dish with a sales price that does not cover its food cost plus the additional direct customer expenses, such as server wages, linens, and water, associated with every customer. Such a dish causes the business to lose more money every time a customer orders it.

A foodservice company that cannot accommodate all of its customers because of an overabundance of business can usually afford to make more drastic changes to its menu. As long as it still retains enough customers to fill to capacity, such a business could easily increase the prices of its plowhorses and dogs to make them more profitable. Losing a dog from the menu and its small following of customers might merely allow other customers to dine and spend money on more profitable items.

11.3 POINT-OF-SALES SYSTEMS AND ONGOING CHANGES

Any foodservice operation ought to maintain sufficient sales records and recipe costing data to make the process of menu analysis simple to execute. With the use of a computerized spreadsheet program such as Excel, a menu planner could simply enter the sales and pricing information into a worksheet with a few formulas and rather quickly have the menu items categorized by profitability and popularity. However, the process is time-consuming enough that a menu analysis is not typically performed in such a way every day of the week. When menu planners make adjustments to a menu, they typically wait days or weeks to see if their recommendations have made a difference in the menu's profitability.

Point-of-sales, or POS, systems streamline the process to make menu analysis computation an almost effortless activity for any given period of time. A POS system is the computerized system most foodservice operations employ today to place customer orders, generate customer checks, and process customer payments. POS systems come in a range of price points, so not every system has the same functionality. However, some have the ability to perform a menu analysis for a manager upon request. The ease of such a system allows a manager or menu planner to see day by day whether certain process changes and menu adjustments are succeeding.

A POS system can present sales numbers for each menu item at the end of each meal period or day. The menu planner can review this information to see how the menu mix has changed. (Recall that the *menu mix* is the number of each item sold in relation to the other items; it typically describes the sale of each item as a percentage of the total number of items sold.) If a menu planner had hoped to increase the sales of certain dishes relative to others, he can find out instantly if those shifts in buying patterns have occurred. Similarly, the menu planner can see if overall sales have dropped as a result of certain changes.

While a menu planner would not normally change a menu daily or even weekly to tweak menu analysis results, he can recommend other interventions based on daily data. For example, the printed menu might stay the same, but the menu planner might encourage additional suggestive selling for certain dishes. Alternatively, he could recommend an advertising or promotional program to direct sales in other ways. The POS system allows for immediate feedback on the success of a menu change. Menu planners must keep in mind that a single day's data is not sufficient to make major menu decisions, but small changes addressed quickly can help to direct the potential impact of a menu adjustment until a broader trend—positive or negative—takes hold. Operations without POS systems can do the same, but their reaction time is often slower due to the time required to compile sales data from each day.

Whether a menu planner tracks the results of menu changes by hand or by computer, the more important point is that menu evaluation and modification never ends. A new menu may replace an old ineffective one, but from the moment the new one takes effect, managers begin monitoring the results. Sales and profit data collected over days, weeks, and months can tell a menu planner if a menu is generating sufficient profit as is, if it needs minor changes, or if an immediate overhaul is required. Menu analysis and adjustment is a cyclical process rather than a destination. From a broader perspective, the process of menu creation described over the many chapters of this text is circular rather than linear. From market analysis to sales price calculations, from menu content development to layout considerations, the creation of a menu begins anew from the moment a business's prior menu is implemented.

SUMMARY

The amount of money that an item's sales price contributes to the coverage of fixed costs and profit is called the contribution margin. Items with higher contribution margins are considered more profitable than those with lower contribution margins. To modify a menu to make it as profitable as possible, a menu planner should first conduct a menu analysis, which considers both a menu's profitability and its popularity. The popularity benchmark is set at 70% of the average number of each item sold. An item's popularity is determined by comparing the number of units sold to the popularity benchmark. An item's profitability is determined by comparing its contribution margin to the average weighted contribution margin. Using the variables of profitability and popularity, all menu items are labeled as stars, plowhorses, puzzles, or dogs. Each requires a different intervention to increase the menu's profitability, but all adjustments to the menu must be done in ways that shift buying patterns without driving away customers. The menu modifications can be evaluated by conducting a menu analysis after the changes to the menu have been implemented. A POS system can provide instantaneous feedback on how the sales and menu mix have changed, if at all. A completed menu is monitored and evaluated soon after it has been put into operation. Should modifications be required, the menu planner begins the cycle of menu creation all over again but this time with even more information and knowledge about the market and its buying habits.

COMPREHENSION QUESTIONS

1. Using the following chart of a menu's appetizer selection and its sales and cost data, conduct a menu analysis to determine the level—high or low—for the popularity and profitability of each item.

Menu Item	Number Sold	Item Sales Price	Item Food Cost	Item Contribution Margin	Menu Contribution Margin	Popularity (H/L)	Profitability (H/L)
Beef Skewers	151	$6.25	$2.88				
Potato Skins	209	$5.45	$1.44				
Calamari	439	$6.95	$1.89				
Soup	303	$3.00	$0.48				
Salad	518	$3.75	$1.44				
Total		X	X	X		X	X
Average Number of Each Item Sold							
Popularity Benchmark							
Average Weighted CM							

2. Label each appetizer in question 1 as a star, plowhorse, puzzle, or dog.
3. For each of the appetizers described in question 1, state one thing you would do to that appetizer to increase the menu's overall profitability.
4. Over how long a period of time should the data used for a menu analysis be collected—a day, a week, or a month?
5. What is the value of a POS system as it relates to menu analysis?

DISCUSSION QUESTIONS

1. Imagine that you are a restaurant manager in the process of revising a menu. You have conducted a menu analysis already. What additional information would you want to know about the menu (beyond what you have learned from the menu analysis) before proposing any menu changes? Where might you get this information?
2. This chapter focused on menus for restaurants, but a menu analysis would operate the same way for any menu from which people select items with varying sales prices and food costs. Having conducted a menu analysis for a cafeteria, what changes might a menu planner make to the cafeteria to make the operation more profitable? Remember that a cafeteria sells items of varying sales prices and food costs but does not provide a written menu.
3. Consider an all-you-can-eat buffet. Would a menu analysis be applicable here? Why or why not?
4. Consider a dessert menu for which all of the desserts have the same selling price even though they all have different food costs. Is a menu analysis applicable here? Why or why not?
5. After going two years without changing the menu, a restaurant manager has finally decided to perform a major overhaul to the menu. The manager uses his POS system to carefully track each item and the new menu's overall profitability. Less than a week into the new menu, the manager notices that the new menu is not as profitable as the old one, so he releases yet another new menu just a few days later. This pattern repeats for four straight weeks with four new menus; though each menu differs in overall profitability, none is as profitable as the original. What could the manager have done before releasing the first menu to improve the potential profitability of that menu? Given the situation he is currently in four menus later, what should the manager do at this point to stabilize the situation and return to the desired level of profitability?

12

How the Menu Directs Business

This text has approached menu planning from the perspective that many parameters exist that inherently delimit a menu. The target market has certain desires and needs, including nutritional ones. The staff and equipment are only capable of executing dishes of a certain caliber and style. The price point potential customers are willing to pay impacts the food that can be prepared and sold at a profit. The importance of a menu's fealty to a brand and business concept has been stressed repeatedly as well. In other words, all these factors and more direct the ultimate content and form of the menu.

But can the opposite also be true? Can the menu actually direct and define the other variables? Yes, sometimes it can. An entrepreneur, foodservice business owner, or manager can create the menu first and then make all other decisions to support the menu. The menu epitomizes the vision and defines the brand. Such an approach is risky for a business and not always appropriate, but it can work under certain circumstances. This chapter addresses this approach to menu planning and the potential benefits and pitfalls associated with putting the menu first.

By the end of this chapter, you will be able to:

- Describe how a menu can create a market and drive revenue
- Describe how a menu can guide certain business decisions
- State the pros and cons of creating a menu first in the menu planning process and allowing all other business decisions to follow from there

12.1 THE MENU'S MARKETING FUNCTION

One of the key functions of a menu is to market the food and drink that the business sells. Often, this task is relegated to the first few minutes after the guest enters the foodservice establishment. Normally, it is the brand, not the menu, that brings customers in the door in the first place. Perhaps they have heard about the business from someone else, or perhaps they have seen an ad describing the place in generic terms. They may like the setting or the reputation for service. They may know the cuisine or type of food, but not necessarily the specific dishes on the menu. However, if the menu is the driving force behind a restaurant, the menu should be placed front and center for all marketing strategies. In this case, customers come because they know the menu, even if they know little else about the place.

A foodservice marketer can post menus in the window of a restaurant that receives a lot of foot traffic. She can provide copies of the menu to local offices, hotels, gyms, and other places where people might use a menu to make a decision about where to dine. Print ads sometimes have sufficient space to include a menu or a portion of one. A business's web page can and should include its menu, too. Any foodservice business, no matter its approach to menu planning, can and should utilize these marketing techniques to drive revenue. However, when a foodservice operation begins with a menu to direct its business decisions, the menu's role in marketing is slightly different and absolutely critical. Such a menu must communicate the feel of the establishment—its atmosphere, style of service, and quality of food and drink. The menu descriptions must be evocative, the layout and images suggestive of the ambiance. Because the menu precedes the business in this situation, the owners and managers design everything about the company to support the menu's vision, not the other way around. If the menu is vague in what it communicates about the operation, both managers and customers will be unsure of what to expect from the business.

STARTERS

BLUE CRAB "HOT N COLD"* $15
Yuzu Chilled Crab Salad, Grapefruit, Watercress, Fried Cake, Pancetta Water Chesnut Vinaigrette

ARTICHOKE & ASIAGO TART $13
Baby Carrots, Radishes, Sun Dried Tomato & Fennel Emulsion

SPRING LAMB FRICASSE* $15
Fava Beans, Baby Potatoes, Citrus Yogurt, Spiced Naan Bread, Merguez Cream

TUNA TWICE* $16
Nori Crusted Tatake, Crispy Rice Noodles, Creamy Tar Tar, Avocado & Ponzu

FOIE GRAS $17
Watercress, Toasted Milk Bread, Apricot Ginger Coulis

LOBSTER "SOUP N SALAD" $24
Lobster Bisque, Pernod Roasted Cauliflower & Fennel, Mizuna Greens, Garlic & Herb Poached Lobster Tail

SPECK WRAPPED PRAWNS* $15
Marinated Tomato "Cocktail Style", Exotic Fruit Chutney, Hot Mustard

SOUPS

CREAM OF ASPARAGUS $10
Manchego Cheese, Beets, Truffled Potato Croquettes

SPRING CHOWDER* $14
Tender Clams, Purple Potatoes, Sea Bass, Herb Tomatoes

FRENCH ONION $10
Brandy, Fine Herbs, Comte Gruyere

ROASTED CAULIFLOWER $10
Chopped Egg, Pancetta, Fried Onions

HEIRLOOM BEANS $10
Pickled Pearl Onions, Bacon, Confit Garlic, Cherry Tomato, Yellow or Green Beans

WHIPPED POTATO $9

BEEF MENU

All Steaks Include Choice of One Opportunity and Sauce
Steaks Available "Au Poivre" Upon Request

ANGUS

28OZ TOMAHAWK RIBEYE CHOP* $65
24OZ PORTERHOUSE* $56
12OZ FILET MIGNON* $49
8OZ FILET MIGNON* $39

DRY AGED

NEW YORK STRIP* $36 / $44
10oz / 14oz

WAGYU

10OZ FLAT IRON* $58

STEAK TEMPS
Blue– Very Red, Cold Center
Rare– Red, Cool Center
Medium Rare– Red, Warm Center
Medium– Reddish Pink, Hot Center
Medium Well– Mild Pink, Hot Center
Well Done– No Pink, Hot Center

SAUCES

BÉARNAISE   CABERNET

HORSERADISH   BRANDY
CREAM   PEPPERCORN

CHIMICHURRI

SUPPLEMENTS

FOIE GRAS* $12   CRAB GRATIN* $16

POACHED EGG* $4   LOBSTER TAIL* $19

BORDELAISE* $4   MAYTAG BLUE CHEESE
                        CRUST $4

TRUFFLE PORCINI DEMI $4

OPPORTUNITIES
{Big Enough For Two}

SPINACH $9
Sauteed or Creamed

BRAISED FINGERLING POTATOES $10
Duck Confit, Comte Cheese, Chives

SALADS

ICEBERG "COBB" $12
Baby Lettuce, Bacon Wrapped Bermuda Onion, Oven Dried Tomato, Point Reyes Blue Cheese Dressing

GRILLED ASPARAGUS $12
Young Cress, Manchego Cheesecake, Raspberry Black Pepper Vinaigrette

BABY ROMAINE $12
Crispy Fried Poached Egg, Shaved Aged Cheddar, Breakfast Radish, Asiago Anchovy Dressing

ENTRÉES

CHILEAN SEA BASS* $36
Tapanade Crusted, Young Spinach, Artichokes, Roasted Rock Shrimp, Saffron Pernod Cream

GRILLED ATLANTIC HALIBUT* $36
Roasted Spring Onion, Macadamia Nut Pesto, English Peas, Cippolini Bacon Jus

SPRING CHICKEN* $29
Roasted Beets, Goat Cheese, Fried Thigh "Nuggets", Apricot Curry Sauce

COLORADO LAMB RACK* $44
Herb Crusted, Sweet Pepper Ratatouille, Lamb Shank Tortelloni, Aged Balsamic

VEAL PORTERHOUSE* $45
Aged Cheddar Polenta, Pickled Ramps, Morels, Mesquite Tomato Reduction

WILD CHANTERELLE PEROGIES $28
Black Mission Fig, Peppered Arugula, Local Feta, Caramelized Shallot

ASPARAGUS $9
Citrus Gremolata, Peppered Hollandaise

SALT BAKED POTATO $9
Russet Potato, Sea Salt

MAC N CHEESE $9
5 Cheeses, Applewood Bacon

CHEF DE CUISINE EARL MORSE
Consuming raw or undercooked meats, poultry, seafood or eggs may increase your risk of food-borne illness 4.12

SAMPLE MENU   SUBJECT TO CHANGE

Figure 12–1

A well-done menu reflects the brand of the business it represents, whether the menu or the business is conceived first. This figure, as well as the others in this chapter, shows the menu from one of the restaurants at Nemacolin Woodlands Resort alongside a photograph of that restaurant. Notice how the menu always reflects the concept depicted in the photo.
Nemacolin Woodlands Resort.

Figure 12–1
(continued)

While most company leaders choose to create the concept vision first and then a core menu to support it, it is somewhat common for business owners to sprout ancillary services and products from nothing more than the main menu. For example, a restaurant may advertise its catering services through its restaurant menu. In reality, no plan for catering may exist yet, but customers may trust the restaurant and assume that the catering operation would be similar in style and quality. The chef or owner may only begin the logistical planning for the business's catering side once a customer expresses interest. A special catering menu can be developed, and in time, the catering division of the restaurant takes off on its own.

Restaurants can market temporary or periodic events on their menus as well. For example, a restaurant might promote a special food and wine dinner, a beer tasting, a weekly pasta night, or a special holiday menu. Often in these situations, the menu is created first to promote the event, and the logistics are planned afterward. In reality, the menu planners already know their staff and equipment, but they might make small changes for a special event.

Hotels commonly promote one of their foodservice operations through another of their foodservice outlets. For example, the room service menu might invite guests down to the lounge for a drink. The lounge menu might suggest breakfast in the hotel restaurant. Because all of the money ultimately flows to the parent hotel, the food and drink outlets all benefit when they direct customers to each other. Hotel guests can tire of eating in the same place every day, but encouraging them to rotate locations within the hotel allows the hotel to keep more of the customers' business. When a parent restaurant company owns multiple concepts, similar cross-promotion usually occurs. Like a hotel, the parent restaurant group would prefer to keep their customers within the family of businesses, so they promote each other on their menus and in their advertising. While the menu providing the promotion in this situation is not the menu of the business being promoted, the customer base typically assumes the same level of quality will be present in all of the outlets.

Normally, a menu planner surveys the market to ensure that a customer base for the intended product exists. However, an entrepreneur, passionate about her product, might prefer to create the menu and the concept and then build the market for the product. If such an approach is to succeed, there cannot be too wide a disconnect between the concept and the market. For instance, a low-income community will not be able to afford a five-course, high-end gastronomic tasting menu no matter how much they might want to enjoy it. However, if a survey of a small

Figure 12–2
A menu and a photo of the operation it represents. Nemacolin Woodlands Resort.

Figure 12–2
(continued)

town shows that the residents enjoy Chinese food, a restaurateur might successfully gamble that they will patronize a Thai restaurant, even if there is no suggestion in the psychographic survey that they crave such a restaurant. A persuasive menu could convince locals to sample and ultimately return regularly to the Thai place. The risk comes in that the entrepreneur may guess wrong, and the market may never materialize. Creating the menu out of known market needs is a much safer approach.

12.2 THE MENU AS A CONTROL TOOL

In addition to driving revenue, the menu has the ability to direct certain management decisions. Again, most operations take stock of their facility and employee constraints before writing the menu, but a brand-new business or one undergoing a complete overhaul has the opportunity to build the business concept around the menu. The food and beverage offered on the menu determine the specific equipment needed to execute those products. Any equipment needed to prepare those dishes and drinks is purchased; all other potential equipment purchases are passed over. For a complete renovation or new construction, the layout of the kitchen and dining room may be designed to facilitate the menu efficiently. The potential pitfall, of course, is that future menus are tied to the new equipment, too, so the initial construction must be flexible enough to accommodate future menu changes.

Staffing levels and employee skill sets can be determined by the menu as well. While an existing foodservice operation may write a new menu that falls within the abilities of its current staff, a new business may write job descriptions to attract and hire only those employees capable of executing the menu. Labor costs may be controlled to some degree by not hiring overqualified workers either. Advertisements for employees, job specification standards, and interview questions may all be adapted to support the new menu. Staffing levels can be similarly set through an analysis of what is needed to properly prepare and serve the menu's offerings. The business ends up employing the exact number of workers it needs.

Storeroom needs are always determined by the menu, no matter when in a business's evolution the menu is created. There is no point in purchasing ingredients that the operation does not need. The product specifications must support the menu or the menu cannot be executed profitably. However, the size, layout, and equipment needs of the storeroom may change when the menu drives managerial decisions.

THE TAVERN
Lunch

Subject to Change

Sample Menu

Snacks

Pittsburgh Fries » Garlic Fries, Pepper Jack Cheese Sauce, Cheddar Cheese, Scallions, Bacon

$9

Southern Fries » Sweet Potato Fries, Bacon, Bleu Cheese, Jalapenos, Pepper Jack Cheese Sauce

$10

*Famous Candied Bacon » Five Strips of Chipotle-Sugar Coated Applewood Smoked Bacon, Whiskey Glazed Apple Butter, Toasted Sourdough

$7

Hummus Duo » Traditional Hummus & Hummus du Jour, Fried Flatbread Chips

$8

Chili Cheese Nachos » Tri-Colored Tortilla Chips, Housemade Chili, Our Special Pepper Jack & Mac & Cheese Sauces, Sour Cream, Scallions, Fire Roasted Salsa & Shredded Cheddar Cheese

$12

Additions
Pulled Chicken $4 » Grilled Shrimp $5
Have all Three for $19!

Appetizers

Tavern Chicken Wings » Eight Seasoned & Floured Fried Wings, Blue Cheese Dressing, Celery & Carrot Sticks

Choice of Mild, Hot, General Tso's, Yuengling Black & Tan Honey-Dijon BBQ

$10

Fat Bird Pierogies » Five Fried Pierogies, Pulled Chicken, Sweet & Spicy Onion Jam, Pepper Jack Cheese Sauce

$11

*Reuben Fritters » Seven Fried Corn Beef, Sauerkraut, & Swiss Cheese Fritters & 1000 Island Remoulade Sauce

$9

*Shrimp Cocktail » Three Large Old Bay Poached Shrimp, Tequila-Lime Cocktail Sauce, Lime Salt

$8

Jalapeno Mac & Cheese Corn Bread »Penne Pasta, Jalapeno Cheese Sauce, Sweet Corn Bread Bottom

$8

Soups & Salads

*Bacon Corn Chowder » Blue Crab Gremolata

*Tavern Chili » Shredded Cheddar Cheese & Scallions

Cucumber-Watermelon Gazpacho » Grape Relish

Cup $8 » Bowl $10

Strawberry-Spinach » Spinach, Strawberries, Goat Cheese, Candied Walnuts, Pickled Onions, Strawberry-Walnut Vinaigrette

$11

*Sesame Salmon » Seared Salmon, Chilled Lo-Mein Noodles with Shiitake Mushrooms, Carrots, Snap Peas, Red Peppers, Red "Akai" Chili Vinaigrette

$16

Baby Wedge » Baby Iceberg, Grape Tomatoes, Bleu Cheese Crumbles, Bacon, Pickled Onions, Cucumbers, Choice of Dressing

$8

Tavern Caesar » Romaine, Asiago Cheese, Garlic-Herb Croutons, Tomatoes, Black Olives

$9

Black & Bleu » Spring Mix, Grape Tomatoes, Cucumbers, Carrots, Pickled Onions, Garlic French Fries, Bleu Cheese Crumbles, Sweet Bleu Cheese Dressing

$10

Jerk Chicken $14 » Seared Steak $16

Salad Additions
Grilled Chicken Breast $8 » Seared Steak $11
Seared Salmon $10 » Grilled Shrimp $11
Roasted Vegetables $7

Tavern Cup & A Half
$11
Ask about Today's Special Half Sandwich with a Cup of One of Our Soups!

Chef de Cuisine William J. Price III

*Consuming raw or undercooked meat, poultry, seafood, shellfish, or eggs may increase your risk of food borne illness 4.12

Figure 12–3

A menu and a photo of the operation it represents. Nemacolin Woodlands Resort.

Figure 12–3
(continued)

A menu with few frozen desserts or ingredients may need only a reach-in freezer while another menu based on large quantities of prefabricated products may require a walk-in freezer. An operation with a streamlined menu that utilizes the same ingredients across multiple dishes may get by with less shelf space than can one with an extensive menu that does not repeat ingredients.

Typically, a menu planner would not include an ingredient on a menu if she were not certain that she could source that product from her purveyors. A menu-first approach might require the chef to partner with farmers to produce those ingredients specifically for the establishment. Similarly, if a chef wants to create a restaurant based on a menu that highlights exotic ingredients, she can reach out to specialty purveyors and ask them to source and carry it in their product line. If they cannot, she might consider contacting producers overseas and asking them to ship directly to her.

12.3 THE CHICKEN AND THE EGG PARADOX

All of this discussion about the menu driving the business or being a reflection and supporter of the business is a chicken and the egg conundrum. Can a menu be created without first considering at least some of the other variables for a potential business? Is any business ever truly built and staffed before the menu is developed? Most of the time, both menu and business evolve together. Just as a menu should be revised after it loses its effectiveness, a menu-driven operation may make adjustments to the menu during the construction and hiring phase of the business. Only a fool would hold firm to a menu concept in the face of insurmountable obstacles that threaten the proper execution of the menu. Adjusting to the current circumstances is much wiser. Conversely, a menu planner looking to make minor updates to a current menu can still add one dish that stretches the market's comfort level in order to try to expand the market. The revision might require the hiring of a new employee or the purchase of a single piece of equipment, but such a change is less risky than basing an entire menu on a nonexistent market.

There are some benefits to working with a menu-first approach. Creating menu content and layout is much easier than designing a comprehensive business plan. For operations in which the brand is essentially the chef (think eponymous restaurant), the concept will work better to let the chef illustrate her strengths on the menu and then to have everything else fall in line behind that menu. It is also much easier to make business decisions to support a concrete menu—even one that has not been laid out yet—than it is to determine staffing, equipment, and purveyor needs for an abstract menu that has yet to be written.

Of course, there are potential pitfalls to the menu-first approach, too. Without conducting market research first, it is easy to misread what the market wants and to end up with no customers for the business. It may be more difficult or more expensive than expected to find staff, equipment, and ingredients when the menu defines the required caliber and quantity of these resources. Finally, some businesses are simply not designed for a menu-first approach. For example, a room service menu planner must know something about the hotel's brand, its guests, and its other dining options before writing a menu. A banquet planner would turn off many potential clients by writing a set-in-stone menu before interviewing the clients to find out what they want in a banquet.

The two approaches to menu planning—working from existing parameters to create a menu and using a menu to define the parameters—come with benefits and pitfalls. Some challenges are easily overcome; some require costly interventions to address or correct. Fortunately, the dance between the menu and the business it represents (or directs) is always in motion. Menus get created, implemented, revised, and rolled out anew regularly. No menu is ever permanent, just as foodservice businesses—their staff, budgets, customers, and products—are perpetually in flux. The goal of the menu planner is not to strive for the perfect menu, but rather to create the best menu possible for the business at that time and then to evaluate and improve it for the continued success of the company it represents and supports.

SUMMARY

Menus can be prepared by designing them to accommodate a range of existing parameters or by creating the menu first and manipulating the variables to support the menu. Menus help to market the business and drive revenue. In a menu-first approach, the menu must be the main focus of initial marketing strategies. Menus can also define the caliber, quantity, and type of staffing, equipment, and ingredients needed. A menu-first approach works well when the chef is the brand for the business; it also helps to make management decisions somewhat easier to have a concrete menu as a guide. The risk to this approach is that the customers and required resources to execute the menu may never materialize.

COMPREHENSION QUESTIONS

1. List three ways that a menu can be used to market a restaurant.
2. Other than the food available for sale at the current meal, what other products or services can a menu promote? (List three.)
3. What three variables can a menu define when the menu is written before anything else in the business creation process?
4. List two benefits that come from a menu-first approach to menu planning.
5. List two potential pitfalls that come from a menu-first approach to menu planning.

DISCUSSION QUESTIONS

1. If you were to create a restaurant from scratch, would you begin by writing the menu or by defining the brand in other ways first? Why?

2. The menu does not have to be created first or last when creating a foodservice business. The menu and the rest of the business are often developed simultaneously. What benefits might come from that approach?

3. Besides those mentioned in the chapter, what other management decisions might be directed by the menu in a menu-first approach?

4. Can a foodservice business use a menu-first approach each and every time it revises its menu? Why or why not?

5. Can a menu-first approach be conducted without the menu laid out, finalized, and printed before any other management decisions are made? What parts of the menu planning process must be performed early in the business development process and which can be left until closer to opening day?

6. In your opinion, what restaurant management functions should always be directed by the menu (rather than having them delimit or define the menu)? Why?